Reflections of An American Political Prisoner

★

Reflections of An American Political Prisoner

★

THE REPRESSION AND PROMISE OF THE LAROUCHE MOVEMENT

AS SEEN BY
MICHAEL O. BILLINGTON

EIR News Service
Washington, D.C.

Billington, Michael O. Reflections of an American Political Prisoner: The Repression and Promise of the LaRouche Movement, as seen by Michael O. Billington.

First printing: November 2000.

Library of Congress Catalog Number: 00-110168
ISBN 0-943235-17-0

Please direct all inquiries to the publisher:
EIR News Service, Inc.
P.O. Box 17390
Washington, D.C. 20041-0390

Cover and text design: Rosemary Moak, World Composition Services, Inc.
Cover photo: Mike Billington works on EIR's Chinese Newsletter during "temporary liberty," August 1992. (EIRNS/Philip Ulanowsky.)

Printed in the United States of America

EIRBK 2000-1

CONTENTS

Preface: July 1996 *ix*

Foreword *xv*

1 A Student in the 'Sixties *1*

2 I Become a Political Organizer *19*

3 Local Control: The Tavistock Grin *32*

4 The American System *49*

5 Campaigning *66*

6 The Morality of Science *79*

7 Airport Organizing and LaRouche's SDI *93*

8 Abscam, Music, and Freedom *110*

9 Breakout—And the 'Get LaRouche Task Force' Counterattacks *126*

10 Toe to Toe with the Oligarchy *151*

11 Targetted *168*

12 Arrest and Jail *185*

13 The Crash of '87 *208*

14 Trials *223*

15 Treachery *244*

16 Three Prosecutors *264*

17 Prison Labor/Labor of Love *278*

18 Temporary Liberty *293*

19 Discovery *308*

20 'By Michael and Gail Billington' *318*

21 Virginia Prison Life *332*

AFTERWORD The Assault on the Asian Tigers *342*

Appendix I Toward the Ecumenical Unity of East and West: The Renaissances of Confucian China and Christian Europe (abridged) *349*

Appendix II Britain's Cold War Against FDR's Grand Design: The East Asian Theater 1943–63 (excerpts) *393*

Sponsors *425*

Illustrations follow pages 96, 200, and 328.

A Note from the Publisher

Just prior to publication of this volume, Michael Billington was granted his petition for parole by the Virginia Parole Commission. After serving more than ten years in state and Federal prisons, he was released on parole on October 19, 2000.

The Injustice to Mike Billington

You sullen judges of the robe and hood,
  You think you've stared poor justice to its end;
  Condemned this prisoner for he would not bend,
Denounced him for the straightness that he stood
Before you, so attent upon the Good,
  That he would bring the Good to judge the laws.
But you, keen judges of the sticks and straws;
His heart beat much too strongly for your blood.
And who is stronger for this rage of yours?
  His jailers? or the swift spirit that expands
His friends, and swells, and stirs them to new wars?
  St. Peter's prison broke in the angel's hands.
    Go, rage, that to your power he must plea!
    You bound by sin, and he by virtue free!

—Paul Gallagher

PREFACE

July 1996

On the wall above the make-shift desk in my prison cell is a postcard-sized print of Rembrandt's "Paul im Gefängnis" ("Paul in Captivity"). Sitting on the cot in his prison cell, St. Paul holds on his lap an open manuscript and a letter-in-progress. There is a broadsword by his side, and a quill pen in his hand—but mightier than both is the power in his eyes, as he gazes, deep in thought, beyond the stone and flesh of his captivity, into the infinite, pondering the mission which lay before him. I have retained this print, sent to me by a friend in Germany, through several years and many prison cells, as evidenced by the ragged edges and coffee stains—but, perhaps more than ever before, on that particular night, Rembrandt and St. Paul speak to me, and I decide to write these reflections on my life.

Earlier that day I had received the decision written by Judge Richard Williams of the U.S. Fourth Circuit Court of Appeals in Richmond, denying my *habeas corpus* motion in Federal court (which decision inspired the poem quoted above, by my incarcerated co-defendant Paul Gallagher). My lawyers and I had presented voluminous documentation, in writing and in two days of testimony in a hearing held before Judge Williams, on the blatant denial of my fundamental constitutional rights in the course of being railroaded into a 77-year sentence in a 1989 trial, held in state court in Roanoke, Virginia. Although I had long since come to expect the "LaRouche exception," whereby the mere facts, and the laws governing those facts, are regularly ignored in regard to the multiple state and Federal prosecutions brought against Lyndon LaRouche and his associates, I nonetheless shared a guarded optimism with my family and my associates that *this* case, being arguably the most outrageous of the many "LaRouche" cases, would mark an exception, and perhaps a turning-point in the effort to find justice in the U.S. judicial system.

Instead, Judge Williams ruled that, in the United States, in 1996, if one is a supporter and collaborator of Lyndon LaRouche, then that fact alone is an adequate basis for the intentional and systematic denial of one's constitutional rights. I had explained to the court my desire to demonstrate to the jury that my political organization was extensively involved in various international affairs, and was rapidly expanding in influence, thus refuting the government charge that our politics were simply a "ruse" to gain people's financial support, while also showing that I had every reason to be optimistic about our ability to meet our financial obligations. Judge Williams ruled that this showed I was a "zealot." It was thus both proper and fitting, said Judge Williams, that my lawyer should attempt to have me declared mentally incompetent, solely for exercising my constitutional right to a jury trial, and that the lawyer was also justified *and correct,* in *refusing* to prepare me to testify in my own defense, even though the right to testify is another fundamental constitutional right.

The judge pulled together a series of "justifications" for this finding, either provided to him by unidentified enemies of LaRouche, or constructed entirely from the mish-mash of popular opinion and preconceptions about me and my political organization in his own mind, without a trace of evidence from the record. He claimed, for instance, that I had not been interested in winning an acquittal, but only in having a show-trial; that my purpose in wishing to present the truth about my actions and intentions was merely to extol the virtues of my organization and of Lyndon LaRouche for some unseen audience outside the courtroom. Even the Commonwealth of Virginia's Attorney General did not make such wild accusations against me, and all the evidence proved quite the opposite—that my only concern was the truth and acquittal, and that I was not the least bit concerned with what the jury thought about our ideas or our policies, but only that they understood that we actually did precisely what we said we did, and that I believed, and had good reason to believe, that we could meet our obligations.

The judge's contrived and false "justifications" demonstrate the disastrous tendency in the United States judiciary to disregard one of the most crucial tenets formulated by the Founding Fathers in constructing the Constitution—that "popular opinion" must never be the standard for the application of justice. Just as Supreme Court Justice Antonin Scalia has ruled that the judicial murder of teenagers was "legal," since (in his view) current popular opinion in America accepted it, so also Judge Williams effectively ruled that "popular opinion" had determined that Lyndon LaRouche led a fraudulent movement, and that any effort to demonstrate otherwise was a sign of zealotry and outright madness. The fact that the judges in these two cases took upon themselves to determine what was to be deemed "popular opinion" at the time, is *not* the important point, but rather, that truth and justice have been reduced to a question of commonly accepted opinion, rather than universal principle.

When notions of universal truth are replaced by popular opinion, as manipulated and defined by a ruling oligarchy, we have departed the realm of the constitutional republic, and are heading in the direction of a fascist society. In such an environment, even procedure rises above truth in the application of justice, as demonstrated by recent Supreme Court decisions allowing executions of those admitted to be most likely innocent, but whose right to appeal has passed a procedural time limit. Similarly, the fact that I, and my associates, remain condemned as felons—despite the overwhelming evidence on the record that those who brought these various prosecutions against us knew, from the beginning, that we were innocent of all charges—constitutes an indictment of the criminal justice system itself. Thus am I a political prisoner, a prisoner of conscience in America.

★ ★ ★

Prison is certainly not a place conducive to serious work, and the vast majority of the lost lives that fill these institutions pass their time in meaningless, mindless boredom. The average prisoner is terrified of silence, afraid to be alone with his thoughts, and will often create noise for the sake of the noise itself. Men instinctively turn the volume up on the cell-block television to full blast, whether or not they are watching it, and the others willingly raise their voices to a shout to compensate.

Nonetheless, my years in captivity have provided me an unusual opportunity. I entered prison in 1989 after 17 years of political activity in the National Caucus of Labor Committees (NCLC), the philosophical association founded by Lyndon LaRouche, which is the core of what is now popularly known as the "LaRouche movement." I had over these years developed not only a passionate love for philosophical inquiry, but also a practice of strenuous work and strict personal discipline, shaped by the intense pressure under which we built the organization against the overwhelming power of our opponents. From the beginning of my incarceration, I thought of myself in the light of the monks of old who, while not removing themselves from the concerns of society, would occasionally retreat to a monastery for a period of intensive theoretical work, meditation, and reflection. To the extent that I could circumvent the usually horrendous conditions of life in prison—the constant noise and chaos, in particular—I knew I could utilize the time to address the issues which *should* have been the subject of my early education. In prison, it appeared that the lack of time would no longer stand as an impediment, as it had while I was active on a daily basis in political activities. I could now read in depth the classics of philosophy, theology, and science, which I had begun to study over the years of my participation in the Labor Committees.

At the same time, I agreed to take responsibility for aspects of the organization's China work. I had been involved at various times in political-intelligence functions in regard to Asia, partially as a result of my Peace Corps experience in Thailand. I therefore welcomed the request from the editor of EIR magazine's Asia desk to follow current developments in China, while also exploring the vast cultural and scientific history of the Middle Kingdom.

This process rapidly transformed my life. LaRouche had revived a tradition of Platonic method in science, including economics and politics, which had virtually disappeared in the 20th Century, a tradition which extends from Plato to the geniuses of the Renaissance: Leonardo da Vinci, Nicholas of Cusa, Johannes Kepler, and Gottfried Wilhelm Leibniz; and then to the mathematicians Karl Friedrich Gauss, Bernard Riemann, and Georg Cantor in the 19th Century. In studying China's history, I quickly recognized that the battle in the West between the Renaissance scientific method and its enemy, the Aristotelian tradition of empiricism and its oligarchical sponsors, was paralleled in China in the historical conflict between Confucianism and its Daoist and Legalist enemies. Further, the Confucian philosophical worldview had been obscured in China, just as the Platonist one had been in the West, despite the fact that some of the greatest minds of history, such as Leibniz and Sun Yat-sen, had devoted much of their lives to examining the truths derived from this method, and to building international collaboration on the basis of such an understanding.

I thus became aware that I had an extremely exciting, and historically necessary task ahead of me—a task which, ironically, proved that I lived under no less pressure from the passing of time than I had "on the street." My life was passing just as rapidly, and the great tasks to be achieved were just as urgent, regardless of the 77-year sentence imposed on me.

This work became my passion. Understanding another great culture, such as that of China, demands the constant re-evaluation of our own Western culture, including the necessity of critical evaluation of existing Western scholarship towards China and the East. LaRouche has often emphasized that only by reliving the intellectual experience of the great discoveries of history—rather than merely learning the results of those discoveries in textbooks—can one develop his or her own creative powers. This, I have learned, is also the source of true joy.

The fact that my wife Gail has shared both my tribulations and my creative work over these difficult years, has been an immeasurable source of strength to me. It is also true that the international notoriety of my case, both because it is part of the LaRouche witch-hunt, and because of the barbaric sentence imposed upon me, has created a certain symbiotic relationship between myself and the hundreds of thousands of people who have followed my situation. While there is a natural curiosity about the work product of a person unjustly subjected to such conditions, there is also an enhanced sense of responsibility and urgency imposed upon me, precisely because of that international interest.

Why, then, would I entertain the idea of investing a great deal of valuable time writing an autobiographical study? The primary reason is twofold. First, I am certain that the process of writing about the development of my own creative powers, of forging an intelligible explication of my own thinking, will serve to enhance those powers. This, you might say, is my *selfish* reason. At the same time, however, those who find reason to read this, will have the opportunity to share in my process of discovery, and perhaps learn thereby.

I have lived through the social and economic breakdown crisis which began in the late 1960's, a crisis which has now reached critical mass. If we are to survive this systemic breakdown, it will only be by coming to terms with the moral decay of the population which tolerated flight into a fantasy-ridden, "virtual" reality, while the world descended into economic dissolution and escalating strategic instability. The fact that the American population accepted the illegal prosecution of LaRouche and his associates, just as it had earlier accepted the coverup of the assassinations of President John F. Kennedy and Dr. Martin Luther King, is a crucial expression of that moral decay. It is my hope that this book, by addressing the flawed assumptions of the post-World War II generations which have brought us to this dangerous moment of history, will contribute to the revolutionary transformation needed to avert the onrushing cataclysm, and to the building of the new world economic and social order necessary for the progress of mankind as a whole. To see the fate of every newborn child on earth as a personal responsiblity—this is the passion which has guided the life of Lyndon LaRouche, and my own. Especially at a time of historical transformation such as ours, this passion must not be seen as *zealotry*, but as man's normal, human response to the plight of his brothers and sisters, and to the well-being of his posterity.

FOREWORD

When I undertook the task of writing this book, I assumed that completion would come many years later during the course of my 77-year prison sentence. I expected that work on the book would have to be squeezed in between more immediate research and writing responsibilities.

As often happens in life, fate had a different course in store for me. On August 7, 1996, just a few days after the loss of my *habeas corpus* appeal, and my decision to write this book, three inmates at Nottoway Correctional Center took a guard and two nurses hostage at knife-point in an attempt to escape. After an eight-hour standoff, SWAT teams rushed and disarmed the inmates and released the hostages, without any serious injuries.

I knew one of the three men who attempted the desperate and dangerous escape. He was not atypical of many young, black men who had already spent years in prison, and could look forward to most, if not all, of the rest of their lives in the same circumstances. But this man was particularly angry at the world. He seemed to me to live in a time warp, as if it were still the 1960's, and he were a member of a Maoist revolutionary organization, reading Marx and the "Little Red Book." He repeated phrases without any real meaning, jargon about liberation, exploitation, the people, and even the "falling rate of profit." When I first met him, and told him I was on the Asian desk of *Executive Intelligence Review* (EIR, the weekly news magazine founded by LaRouche), he did a doubletake, exclaiming, "Oh, you're Billington! I read your garbage in EIR about the British and Mao. That really made me mad!"

I was stunned, if only because EIR magazine does not circulate as widely as the LaRouche movement's newspaper, *The New Federalist*. But he clearly knew the article—in fact, he quoted back to me several of my arguments, even though he had read it two years earlier. The article exposed the British role in fostering the creation and development of Maoism, through the direct work of Bertrand Russell in shaping the ideas of Mao and his circle, while the British colonial office and intelligence services were sabotaging the republican movement led by Dr. Sun Yat-sen. My article intrigued, but infuriated this young man. We spoke often over the years, but he was too far gone to modify his rage, and he never got beyond striking a revolutionary pose during our political discussions. Finally, he lost control—the escape attempt sealed his fate as a life-long prisoner.

As a result of the hostage incident, the "Gingrich conservative" Governor George Allen and his fire-breathing prison director, Ron Angelone, decided to make an example of our prison. The institution was locked down on a high-security status—24-hour confinement to cells, no visits, no phone calls, and, for two weeks, not even any showers. After six weeks, prisoners were finally allowed out once a day for either a shower or a phone call; after ten weeks, some visits were permitted. The lock-down continued for five months.

The administration used the opportunity to impose a new, more restrictive policy on inmates' personal property. Among other things, all typewriters were confiscated (or, technically, "sent home," which is the equivalent of confiscation for a long-term inmate). I also lost my treasured electronic keyboard—a 50th birthday gift from my mother and siblings, which had provided me an hour or so each day with Mozart and Beethoven, a welcome respite in an environment of prison ugliness.

I now faced total isolation 24 hours a day. I continued my research, of course, along with my political intelligence work, and my Chinese language studies. I maintained contact with my wife Gail and my other associates by mail. But I also found myself devoting several days each week to this book, and after five months in lock-down, it was more than half done. I told no one about the project for the first four months, not even my wife, with the exception of my close friend in prison, Evans (Hop) Hopkins, a former Black Panther Party member serving a life sentence for robbery, who became my editor and critic. Hop, who had established himself as a contributor to the *Washington Post* on prison and other social and political issues, had come to share many of the organization's ideas over the years of our association, reading all of our publications—even the "Morning Briefing" summary of political-intelligence news and analysis which was mailed to me daily. I worked closely with him on a few of his articles for the *Post,* and I was editing chapters of the book he was writing on the American prison crisis. His contributions and suggestions were much appreciated, but even more important to me was his encouragement.

I have often thought of my incarceration as an opportunity to contribute to greater justice in the world—to achieve through my work enough good to cause George Bush and his underling Ollie North to regret their decision to impose this injustice upon me—a story that will unfold in some detail in the following pages. Perhaps that barbaric, interminable lock-down, also served a higher purpose, providing me an opportunity, without which this book would still be, at best, a "work in progress."

The philosopher-scientist Gottfried Wilhelm Leibniz, who, in a very real sense has been my closest companion over the years, convinced me that this is, indeed, the best of all possible worlds, even if we must, at some time in our lives, taste of a bitter cup. By following Christ's example at Gethsemane, we are led to find in ourselves that which is more important than life itself—that which is an endless source of joy, and which liberates us even from the strongest bonds of tyranny. It is my hope that this book will contribute in some way to illuminating that path to freedom for others.

Department of Corrections, Virginia
April 9, 1999

Editing a book for a man in prison would be an onerous task for anyone. In this case, one individual, Ken Kronberg, the editor of *Fidelio* magazine, did the entire job himself, including the selection of material from a humungous manuscript, and considerable conceptual advice. The fact that Ken is also a leading member of the NCLC and an old friend, made his work, for me, invaluable, and our collaboration a delight, for which I am most grateful.

Lawrenceville Correctional Center, Virginia
September 20, 2000

Reflections of An American Political Prisoner

★

[1]

A Student in the 'Sixties

A child of post-World War II surburban America, I was approaching manhood in the 1960's, just as the nation lurched into the madness that has characterized the past thirty-plus years. I glimpsed that coming madness through the peripheral vision of my mind, such that the process of choosing a career seemed somehow a bit absurd. I knew that my life was not likely to follow the prescribed path for the average graduate of an elite New England college.

★ ★ ★

Sometime during the year preceding my graduation in 1967 from Trinity College in Hartford, Connecticut, the government adopted a lottery system for the draft, dropping nearly all of the deferments which had provided various "outs" for those not anxious to fight in the war raging in Vietnam. I drew number 13, which was equivalent to receiving a draft notice. I was not a pacifist—my father had served in World War II, and I had always considered military service as a necessary and honorable duty in a time of war. Nor was I violently opposed to the war in Vietnam. There was not a significant anti-war ferment on the Trinity campus in the winter of 1966-67, and I considered those few who had begun to protest the war to be rather lacking in reasoned argument. My knowledge of communism in Asia at that time was limited to the "popular opinion" in America that China under communist rule was a hideous dictatorship, demanding total conformity of thought and action by the impoverished people. I had heard a few stories of the then-emerging Great Proletarian Cultural Revolution, in which mobs of youth waving Mao's "Little Red Book" were torturing all "class enemies." (Although I later learned how distorted my views of China had been, I also learned that the Cultural Revolution was far worse than I had imagined.) I could not imagine that anyone would want to allow a country like Vietnam to be transformed along such lines.

I was anything but certain, however, that the U.S. was going about things in the right way in Vietnam, nor that I wanted to be part of it. Two things played in my mind. One was the growing sense of a breakdown in the "American Dream" of the 1950's white suburban environment in which I had grown up in East Cleveland, Ohio. The Kennedy assassination, a few months after I entered college in 1963, was associated in my mind with the 1965 riots in Watts—events which shattered any dwindling sense that America had discovered "built-in stabilizers" against social disasters, like the "built-in stabilizers" which many (including my economics professors at Trinity) claimed had been discovered for the economy. The failure of the country to address the obviously just cause of the civil rights movement carried the same general message. My mother had been very active in the civil rights movement, both in Cleveland and in one of Dr. Martin Luther King's marches on Washington. I rather naively thought there would be immediate, sweeping changes in the South. By 1967, however, things seemed to be going in the opposite direction from the American Dream. If things were so chaotic at home, could the foreign policy, and the direction of the Vietnam War, be any better?

The second consideration in pondering my future, was my fascination with foreign cultures. In the summer of 1965, I had travelled to Japan for two months, paid for by the Experiment in International Living of Putney, Vermont. I stayed with a wealthy family in Nishinomia, near Kobe. Although, in retrospect, it was a rather superficial (if thoroughly enjoyable) summer, it fired my curiosity about Asia and Asian culture. When I returned for my junior year at Trinity, I considered applying to President Kennedy's Peace Corps after graduation, and began reading about various Asian nations, settling my mind on Thailand as a preferred assignment.

Of course, there was also the option of accepting one of the numerous offers from the business world. With a major in mathematics and a minor in philosophy, I was being offered positions with IBM and several other corporate giants, with salaries that seemed astonishing to me at the time. Although I went through the motions of meeting the recruiters, my "American Dream" was not that of getting rich as a corporate executive.

There was yet another possibility, which was graduate school. I received an offer for a fellowship as an International Scholar in an interdepartmental program at the School for International Affairs, at Columbia University in New York. The offer surprised me, given my rather modest academic performance at Trinity. I decided that I could not pass up such an opportunity, and abandoned my Peace Corps plans, looking forward to an academic situation which would almost certainly take me overseas as part of the course of study.

Graduate school, before the new lottery-draft policy came into effect, had served as a safe haven from the long arm of Uncle Sam and the Vietnam War. When that changed, and I drew number 13, I quickly opted back to the Peace Corps, which still carried a deferment from the draft. However, the offer from the Peace Corps was not Thailand, as I had requested, but a country I had never even heard of: Guyana, on the northern coast of South America, a former British colony, recently granted independence (and a new name, from the previous "British Guiana"). This small, poverty-striken, diverse land of many races, was to have a deep and lasting effect on my view of Pax Americana, while providing my first whiff of the putrid stench created by the British wherever they have imposed their imperial power.

Guyana had won its independence from the British only the year before I arrived in 1967. The population was about one-third black, descendants of African slaves, and one-half Indian, brought over as indentured servants from the Crown Colony of India in the 19th Century, when the British realized that colonial subjects were even cheaper than chattel slavery. I learned that, previously, all the communities in Guyana had been racially mixed and relatively peaceful. Like *every* British colony granted its independence, the British first arranged the break up of any nationalist tendency in the country which could potentially challenge the Commonwealth (the new name for the British Empire). Just as India had been ripped apart by carefully nurtured and manipulated riots between Hindus and Muslims, so Guyana was turned into an inferno of racial hatred between blacks and Indians. Riots in the early 1960's left the country divided into black towns and Indian towns, with festering rage everywhere.

I taught school in the most undeveloped part of the country—the Essequibo Coast—an area which had been least affected by the racial turmoil. My school was the first secondary school in that region, having opened just the year before. The students, racially mixed, were poor, mostly children of rice farmers, but bright and extremely enthusiastic. In retrospect, years later, after teaching in inner-city schools in Ohio and California, I realized how much more inquisitive and better motivated were these children of the Third World, who came from such humble conditions, but who were so full of hope. I developed very close friendships with some of my fellow teachers, one of whom later came to the U.S. with his bride, sponsored by my parents, and went on to become a lawyer, and then a judge in Florida.

Much later, in the 1970's, I became a close friend and collaborator of the Guyanese statesman and scholar Frederick Wills, the nation's former Justice and Foreign Minister, with whom I occasionally shared war stories about life and death in British colonial enclaves, while we fought together with LaRouche to end the imperial system once and for all.

I have often reflected on the irony inherent in my aborted plans to begin Columbia Graduate School in the fall of 1967. It was in April 1968, that Columbia exploded into the strike led by the Students for a Democratic Society (SDS), which became a spark for the anti-war movement and the emergence of the "New Left." The Columbia strike also saw the birth of Lyndon LaRouche's political movement. One faction of the strikers was led by a group of students who were studying with LaRouche in a one-semester course which focussed on the emerging depression crisis he had forecast, and which demanded that the war be superseded by national and international development policies. This faction adopted the name "SDS Labor Committees," later to become the National Caucus of Labor Committees (NCLC), the philosophical association at the center of the movement founded by LaRouche.

However, I was not to hear of LaRouche until 1972, in Berkeley, California. I can only wonder whether I would have been on the ramparts at Columbia's Low Library in 1968, if events had unfolded slightly differently.

★ ★ ★

The next major choice in my life came four years later, at the age of 26 (and thus, beyond draft age), at the completion of four years of Peace Corps service. I had succeeded in getting to Thailand after all, when a special position as a mathematics supervisor of secondary education at the Thai Ministry of Education was made available for an experienced Peace Corps volunteer, just as I was completing my two-year service in Guyana. I eagerly accepted this position. The following two years in Thailand, while delightful in terms of the work experience and relations with my Thai counterparts, at the same time convinced me that American foreign policy had descended into the maelstrom. On my frequent trips up-country, where I taught in seminars for mathematics teachers in the government secondary schools, I often visited the U.S. airbases. I would sometimes sit on the runways, watching the Phantom jets taking off, continuously, returning within minutes, having deposited their loads of deadly ballistics on peasant fields and villages not much different from those surrounding the bases. I was once invited to play bridge with the officers at the airbase in Korat, in Northeast Thailand. Occasionally, one of the players, all of whom were dressed in their flight suits, would ask someone to sit in for a few minutes while they flew a scheduled mission. I recall still today, the sense of horror provoked by that "brief diversion" from our bridge game—not only because of the carnage which was the certain result, but also because of the casual nature of the process.

By the end of my two-year contract in Thailand, I had become a fierce opponent of the war. Accompanied by several other Peace Corps volunteers, I visited the U.S. Ambassador to Thailand, demanding a halt to the U.S. invasion of Cambodia and an end to the war. We made public our letter of protest, causing a bit of a ruckus at the Embassy over whether or not we were U.S. government employees, and thus forbidden to publicly protest. They decided to let that pass, as it would certainly have been worse publicity for them if we had been thrown out of the Peace Corps.

The Embassy already had a file on me, for a totally different reason. In the few weeks between leaving Guyana and proceeding to Thailand, I had stopped by at the U.S. State Department in Washington, asking about non-military positions in Vietnam. I explained to several officials, who quite enthusiastically responded to my unannounced visit, that I was generally opposed to the war, while at the same time, I felt compelled, out of a sense of patriotic responsibility, to do something constructive to improve U.S. policy in Vietnam. I had presumed that this would result in an immediate request to leave their hallowed halls, but, to my surprise, they were anxious to have people like me to be "Liaison Officers" in the villages. They told me that I would have been hired immediately, except for a hiring freeze that President Nixon had imposed a few weeks earlier, but that if I would wait a few weeks, they expected that the freeze would be lifted.

The position I had been offered in Thailand, however, was scheduled to begin the next week, and I decided to proceed, rather than wait for an uncertain offer from the State Department. As it turned out, about a month later, they notified me that the position was now available. Having settled into my Thailand situation, I decided to stay put.

It was only years later that I learned what I would have been doing in Vietnam. The "Liaison Officers" were the administrators of the Strategic Hamlets, forcing peasants into confined camps, designating all areas outside the hamlet as free-fire zones, to be carpet-bombed and napalmed indiscriminately, while Operation Phoenix, the covert assassination operation, rooted out targets within the hamlets who were suspected of Vietcong sympathies. Thank God for that timely hiring freeze!

At the completion of my Thailand assignment in 1971, and with my concern over the draft behind me, I was ready to return to the U.S. to join in the anti-war movement, which I had thus far only watched from a great distance. One personal hurdle remained, however. While the movement was far away, the counterculture, which had exploded into existence in the U.S., rapidly found its way to Bangkok. The group of Peace Corps volunteers who trained with me in 1967, for the Guyana assignment, had been a very serious and straight-laced crew. They were committed to performing a service to the world, and generally believed that, despite the serious problems in America, these problems could and would be solved by an enlightened citizenry. It was the last of the pre-baby boomer generation—everyone in the group was born in 1945 (as I was) or earlier, before the end of World War II. These were the Kennedy youth, who believed with JFK that, while one had a duty to the country, the country must take on the *real* cause of insurgency and communism in the underdeveloped portions of the world—poverty, economic backwardness, and the lack of education. Many of the countries where Kennedy and Sargent Shriver deployed the early Peace Corps brigades, were those which the remaining McCarthyites in the Congress would have preferred to bomb, as "communists," rather than to develop as potential allies. My fellow volunteers understood the "peace" in Peace Corps in the manner of Pope Paul VI's 1967 declaration that "development is the new name for peace."

When I arrived in Thailand just two years later, however, I was stunned by the character and appearance of the volunteers. Although there were certainly many who fit the description of my associates in Guyana, a large portion looked and acted like something I had only seen in *Time* magazine coverage of the "love-ins" and anti-war demonstrations. The transformation of many of my slightly younger contemporaries, in the brief two-year span since my 1967 departure from the U.S., into various forms of counterculture freaks and pot-heads, was an enormous culture shock for me. (My first encounter with the counterculture had occurred while I was travelling to Thailand, when I stopped for a few days in California to visit my older brother Joe, who had settled comfortably into the Berkeley culture of the 1960's. A summer day on Berkeley's Sproul Plaza in 1969 was a psychedelic carnival ride!)

Still, I was surprised to find "flower children" in the Peace Corps. I moved into a house with three other volunteers, all of whom were much like my associates in Guyana. However, I learned that the room was available because another volunteer had cooked a batch of marijuana brownies, and fed them to the others, without their knowledge, causing total chaos, and a quick trip home for the perpetrator. I learned that drugs were pervasive, and generally, but not officially, tolerated by the Peace Corps staff. I soon found myself playing folk songs on my guitar in a nightclub with a fellow volunteer, and living an evening and weekend existence not far different from the stateside counterculture world I had previously avoided.

I began to consider the possibility of not even returning to the U.S., of becoming one of the many expatriates who settled in to enjoy the loose lifestyle in Thailand. I was offered a position as a mathematics professor at the University of Chiang Mai, the idyllic city nestled in the northern mountains, one of the corners of the "Golden Triangle," the world's primary source of opium and heroin. The university is, in fact, a center of serious research with high academic standards, and I had fallen in love with Chiang Mai during my several trips there to give seminars for the government secondary school teachers. But I realized that my motivation was not academic, nor altruistic—but rather, a romantic dream of "dropping out," which, ultimately, I could not do.

There was clearly something very wrong in America, beyond the issue of the war. While I had come to detest the public justifications for the hideous conduct of the war put out by the various government agencies, I was also very uncomfortable with the dogmatism of the anti-war movement, including the radical reporters and others who were regularly passing through Bangkok. There was a clear bias in the movement which demanded that the U.S. totally disengage, not only from the war, but from the Third World, arguing that somehow the poverty and backwardness would be alleviated by the disappearance of any U.S. presence whatsoever. I also found that many of these anti-war radicals were simultaneously espousing a set of political policies which were totally new to me, but that I would later identify as "New Left" or "New Age": opposition to industrial development, especially nuclear energy; population control; and a fixation on the environment. Such a prejudice against progress, rather than concern for the development needs of the world's population, seemed both selfish and ridiculous to me even then.

All of these things appeared to me to be either totally wrong, or at least exaggerated. I had absolutely no doubt that should the U.S. back away from the kind of global development policies which were identified with JFK, it would be both morally reprehensible for the U.S., and disastrous for the Third World. Kennedy had sponsored a Green Revolution, which had visibly expanded global food production; he had continued Eisenhower's Atoms for Peace program, which gave the promise of nuclear power to solve the problem of scarce energy resources in developing nations; and, of course, he created the Peace Corps, which, despite its limitations, provided a boost for the idea of universal education worldwide. These were the things I saw as the positive side of a badly flawed U.S. policy, and yet, they were all under attack by many in the peace movement, including the sympathetic media.

Although the reason was not entirely clear to me at the time, I drew a connection between my rejection of popular opinion on these issues of science and development, on the one hand, and, on the other, my most important discovery as a college student, that of the existence of the "transfinite" in mathematics. Later, to my great delight, I learned that the concept of the transfinite had also played a crucial role in the early development of Lyndon LaRouche's ideas, and in his commitment to reestablishing science on a higher, more truthful epistemological basis.

Gödel and Beethoven

During my sophomore year at Trinity in 1964, I had decided to major in mathematics. I was fascinated by a course in abstract algebra and by my first encounter with topology, but I was, in fact, far more intrigued by a logic class, given in the philosophy department. The professor, Dr. Howard DeLong, devoted the second semester of the course to a review of various opposing philosophies of mathematics, counterposing Georg Cantor's transfinite number theory to Bertrand Russell's *Principia Mathematica*. Cantor's demonstration that there were different orders of infinite sets, some "larger" than others, captured my imagination. Dr. DeLong included in the course, a study of Kurt Gödel's famous proof of 1932, in which Gödel extended Cantor's work by demonstrating that any axiomatic system, if it was not inconsistent, would be inherently incomplete—in the sense that a legitimate and intelligible theorem can be shown to exist which is incapable of being either proven, or disproven, by the methods of proof within the axiomatic system. This meant that, even at the level of simple arithmetic, there is a higher source of truth, than could ever be programmed into a computer (since any machine is ultimately nothing but an axiomatic system, no matter how complex). Man is not himself the higher source of this truth, but man is capable of *discovering* the truth of the "undecidable" theorem, through the exercise of his cognitive powers. This proved to me that, at the least, all the popular clatter about man being a machine, about artificial intelligence, was demonstrably bunk. Not only was human intelligence beyond the scope of any axiomatic system (i.e., of any machine), but even mathematics itself was incapable of "reduction" to an axiomatic base. This also made me reconsider the question of the existence of God, a question which I had, in my youth, decided was meaningless and unanswerable.

I proceeded to arrange, with two classmates, a senior seminar with Dr. DeLong, to study the original document by Gödel (rather than the textbook-style treatment which we had read in the logic course), and other original documents on the debate over so-called Turing machines—the issue of finding the conditions necessary for the establishment of a complete axiomatic system—which led to Gödel's definitive demonstration that such conditions *do not exist*.

Dr. DeLong took great delight in showing that Gödel's work had relegated the monstrous creation of Bertrand Russell and Alfred North Whitehead, the *Principia Mathematica*, to the shredder. The *Principia* was an attempt by Russell (the man I would later come to recognize as the most dangerous fraud of modern times) and the philosopher Whitehead, to create a system reducing all conceivable mathematics to a basic unifying set of axioms. According to Dr. DeLong, when Gödel's results were published in 1932, proving that the premise of the *Principia* was itself fatally flawed, Whitehead, unlike Russell, had the decency to destroy his manuscripts.

Cantor's work, fifty years earlier, had already demonstrated the fatal flaw in Russell's thinking—even though Russell nonetheless continued to present himself as an expert on Cantor. First showing the existence of different "sizes," or *cardinalities* of infinite sets, Cantor then proved that the measure of such sets, the ordering of infinites, is only possible outside the sets themselves, in the metamathematical realm, in the human mind. Cantor's "transfinite" number system already demonstrated that Russell's efforts to reduce mathematics—let alone the human mind—to a mechanical process, were pure folly. Gödel simply made the case more general, in regard to all axiomatic systems.

This struck me as the death blow for dogmatism, for any attempt to stick blindly to a fixed set of ideas. I also recognized that a fool could take this to be a justification for anarchy, as a proof that there *are* no rules. Such an argument, however, would be ignoring the second half of Gödel's proof—that the "undecidable" statement in question was in fact true, as determined by reason. What Gödel *actually* proved was that anyone who thinks and acts according to a fixed set of beliefs is both a fool, and is not even looking in the right place for those things which are most interesting in life—those concepts which correspond to theorems which are undemonstrable according to currently accepted belief, but which are nonetheless true, and which therefore demand the construction of new axioms.

I was on guard against the potential of anarchistic interpretations. Although I had not yet become involved in politics, I had taken another seminar, with the same Dr. DeLong, on Friedrich Nietzsche. I couldn't make much sense out of Nietzsche at the time, and it is rather embarrassing to remember that my sophomoric seminar paper for the course argued that the Nazi theoreticians, who used Nietzsche to justify their cause, had misrepresented his thought. I later came to understand that the Nazis understood Nietzsche all too well. Nonetheless, it was through that process that I first confronted the popularity, amongst my peers in the academic world, of nihilism, hedonism and "intellectual" anarchy, which argued that all the rules of conduct should be thrown out. Nietzsche's *Beyond Good and Evil* did not even attempt to justify existential man as a "greater good," but simply denied the existence of any measure of goodness acceptable to the Nietzschean Superman. Besides finding that idea to be ridiculous, I made the connection in my mind to Gödel's proof and to Cantor's work, that it was *indeed* revolutionary to reject the dogma of a society's fixed beliefs; but that the *new* order must be rigorously derived from a new and more perfect measure, rather than throwing out *all* measure, as Nietzsche did with his declaration that "God is dead."

Although my various philosophy courses touched on the works of Plato and Leibniz, two men who were to become my teachers and personal allies in later years, they were at that time presented to me only as part of a popularized "Great Books" approach to history. Professors and textbooks alike refrained from making any value judgments about the smorgasbord of philosophers whose selections were compiled chronologically in anthologies. Human knowledge, according to this approach, must be seen as cumulative, in a linear fashion; essentially, every thinker who is considered "great" by the editors, represents an assimilation of all who went before, with a little bit of "value added," which we obedient students were to digest for future regurgitation at exam time. While differences were acknowledged, they were generally intellectual debates within schools of thought which were defined by the *age*. Thus, "Greek thought" included Aristotle and Plato, whose likenesses supposedly far outweighed their differences, while "The Age of Reason" lumped Leibniz with Descartes, Kant, Hegel, and so on. I was not to discover for another ten years, when I reread the philosophers from the perspective of universal history (as Friedrich Schiller termed it), that Western civilization can only be understood as a life-and-death struggle between Platonism and Aristotelianism. Such a view, however, did not conform to the "pluralism" demanded of a "liberal education" in America, whereby we were required to approach history in a value-free, "Beyond Good and Evil" state of mind, which state of mind was praised as being "objective."

This left me cold, but I was not prepared to challenge it head on. So, rather than major in philosophy, I majored in math, but arranged special permission to have some of my philosophy courses (on Gödel and the philosophy of mathematics) counted toward my requirements in the mathematics department. But, my view of mathematics changed dramatically in the process.

The pleasure I found in solving math problems had derived from the fact that one knew ahead of time that a solution existed, and that when a solution was found, there was no question about whether or not it was the *correct* solution. *Mathematics, therefore, was very safe.* Complex algebra or topology problems were difficult, at times, but there were never any moral or intellectual decisions to be made or defended in the process. Eventually, this began to bore me. I also recognized that Gödel's proof demonstrated that such "problem-solving" was impotent, since the only interesting problems, even in mathematics, were those that could *not* be solved by such algebraic methods. It was at that point, that I decided to reject mathematics or engineering as a career, at least in the form that those disciplines had been presented to me. I knew even then that I was not acting out of an anti-scientific impulse, but that there was something fundamentally wrong with the method of presentation of the subject matter. LaRouche, I later discovered, had struggled with precisely these same problems twenty years earlier, a struggle which led to his discoveries in the science of physical economy.

I completed my college studies without resolving this paradox, but satisfied that the philosophy courses, at least, would serve me well in the future.

The other college courses which proved to be of lasting value in my later life were in music. I had learned to play the piano and the cello during my elementary school years, and I spent many Sundays, during sixth grade, travelling by myself to Severence Hall, to hear the Cleveland Orchestra, in which my teacher played second cello. Elvis Presley and the beginnings of the rock era seduced me away from classical music by the time I reached junior high, and classical music became associated in my mind with "background music" at the movies, as "program" music, rather than anything worth listening to on its own merits. Only my singing provided a thread of musical sanity throughout my school years, as I sang in the school chorus and in a community choir, which performed Handel's *Messiah* every year. At Trinity, I took several courses from an eccentric old fellow who was the organist at the campus church, and who loved Bach—and very little else. It rubbed off, and although I continued listening to rock and folk music (and started playing the guitar), I also collected a large number of Bach recordings. My friends laughed at this music, but in my senior year, I had a single room, and found myself listening primarily to Bach. I associated Bach and Gödel in my mind as a single reality, as the basis of a "private" world, separated from the popular culture shared with my fellow students, and even from the general curriculum of the college—a world in which the ideas of universal truth, and of beauty, first became substantial objects of knowledge in my mind.

★ ★ ★

These were the thoughts that determined my decision, four years later, as I pondered whether to return to the chaos of the U.S., or "drop out" and become a university mathematics instructor in Chiang Mai. The idyllic but static prospects of life in Chiang Mai simply did not address that "private" part of my life.

In addition to the sense of responsibility I felt for the political mess in the U.S., music again entered the equation. Two close friends in Bangkok invited me to join a chorus preparing to perform Beethoven's Ninth Symphony for a royal concert. The experience was overwhelming. At the time, I could not even distinguish Beethoven from other classical composers, and did not anticipate the power and glory of his music. By the time we had perfected the piece (relatively speaking), I found that I could barely restrain tears during the rehearsals, and nearly lost control at the performance. This was a kind of joy I had never imagined, a joy that begged for further investigation, which I knew would not take place in the northern hills of Thailand.

Singing Beethoven's Ninth also revived my speculation concerning the existence of God. I had (somewhat formally) decided during my college years that one of the implications of Gödel's proof, was the existence of God. The existence of truths which were beyond the capacity of proof within the structure of any set of axiomatic beliefs, but were recognizable as truths by reason, yet were never the *complete* truth, meant that there must exist some natural law governing change in a manner that was self-perfecting. Was that not God? And was not the music of Bach, and now Beethoven, proof that the divine was capable of expression by man?

My early church experience had done little to nurture a belief in God. My mother was a Protestant, a Sunday School teacher, and a community and civil rights activist. The suburban city of East Cleveland, bordering the black ghetto of the east side of Cleveland proper, was all-white, but, after the years of my schooling, became all-black. All the conflicts of integration in Cleveland focussed on the east side, including the Cleveland riots in 1965. My mother and some of her friends set up a coffee shop, called "The Well," in the border region between the black and white neighborhoods. Her church became involved in the struggle for civil rights, turning the church into a community center for meetings, demonstrations, and so forth, and was later officially turned into a "People's Church." These activities seemed essential to me, and I was glad to see that the church was involved, but I remained aloof, concentrating on my studies.

In Thailand, as I began to think seriously about religion, I looked into the Buddhist culture, which totally dominated the country, but found it to be a depressing mishmash of negation and ethical rules, which few followed, and which were only motivated by the selfish desire for *karma*, to get ahead personally in the cyclical chain of being. Most strange was the notion that the ultimate goal was to stop thinking altogether, and to escape the misery of life. A friend of mine in Malaysia recently observed that nirvana is what goes on in a computer when you turn off the power! Buddhism appeared to ignore the question of moral responsibility for social and political progress.

I had befriended a fellow Peace Corps volunteer, Barbara Thomas, a preacher's daughter from Knoxville (who later joined the NCLC), who had become involved in a religious sect called Subud, based in Indonesia, a spinoff of Islam, but (as I later learned) theosophist in nature. I began attending their Bangkok meetings with Barbara, and we subsequently planned to attend a conference at the group's headquarters outside Jakarta, which happened to fall just after our two-year contracts with the Peace Corps were completed. We treated it seriously while we were in Asia, and spent over a week at the conference in Indonesia, but it was essentially a mystical cult based on physical experience of "the spirit," rather like the "speaking in tongues" of Pentecostals in the U.S. Later, back in the States, we both laughed at the experience as the blind leading the blind. I later thought of it in much the same way as my flirting with Maoism, when I leapt into the cauldron of American radical politics in 1971.

Back Home and Berkeley

Back in Cleveland, my youngest brother, Dan, had become an activist with a group of radicals loosely associated with the Black Panther Party. I came to know one of the Panthers through a number of extended private discussions, and attended a class he gave, in which he used Mao's "Little Red Book." Despite the silly nature of the "Red Book," which I sensed he was using because that was the "party line" rather than because of any personal preference, he was an intensely serious fellow who was anxious to share with me a large range of books he had been studying, mostly of the left-liberal variety, such as I.F. Stone on the Korean War.

I joined my brothers, Joe and Dan, in attending one session of a class series on *Das Kapital* at the local Communist Party bookstore, which reminded me sadly of an esoteric meeting of academics at Trinity, discussing some subject of no interest to anyone in the world who was not in the room.

After about a year of such meandering, I ended up joining brother Joe in Berkeley, California, and I dove headlong into the "swamp" of the Left. I took a job substitute teaching at Berkeley High School, and volunteered as a clerk at a little Maoist bookstore called Yenan, just off the infamous Telegraph Avenue. I never got along very well with the group that ran Yenan, who were associated with the two major radical Maoist groups in the U.S., both centered in the Bay Area. One was Robert Avakian's Revolutionary Union, which subsequently went through various transmogrifications to become the overtly terrorist Revolutionary Communist Party, working out of London's Bertrand Russell House, supporting fanatical genocidalists such as Pol Pot's Khmer Rouge, the Kurdish PKK, and Abimael Guzmán's *Sendero Luminoso* in Peru. The other group was the Venceremos, of the same general pedigree, led by Air Force Intelligence officer H. Bruce Franklin.

The bookstore collective all accepted the Maoist gobbledygook as Biblical truth. Although I was anxious to investigate what was motivating the revolutionaries in Vietnam, and to learn the history of the Left, hoping to figure out whether or not it could provide some alternatives to the mess the world was in, I quickly learned that there was little interest amongst those Maoists in learning anything, and great interest in posturing.

I read some of Trotsky's writings, and was confronted by one of the Yenan group (who, of course, believed fervently in the "one true revolutionary line of Marx, Engels, Lenin, Stalin, and Mao"), who assured me that Trotsky should not be read. He provided me with the definitive book by the master himself, Joseph Stalin, which would provide me with the truth about the "renegade traitor" Trotsky. While I had found Trotsky to be moderately interesting, Stalin was mind-boggling. I was so disgusted with the totally formal, dogmatic idiocy of Stalin's "theoretical" works, that I wrote a refutation, more in the hope that my associate would be provoked to use his brain in response, than in any real interest in defending Trotsky.

In any case, as I was to learn, China was still in the midst of the Cultural Revolution (it was 1972), and the mentality of that madness had been carefully spread internationally amongst the New Left (not by the Chinese so much as by the leading establishment foundations and church institutions in the West), which required that all thinking be suppressed in favor of feeling good about the "power of the people"—although absolutely nobody knew what that meant. I soon parted ways with Yenan.

Brother Joe, meanwhile, had not attempted to associate with any one group, but wandered about, gathering literature and trying a little of everything. He had been through several years of hippydom in California and his girlfriend was the quintessential flower child of the 1960's. He had participated in such "revolutionary" actions as the Yuppie occupation of Tom Sawyer Island at Disneyland, and was once photographed for *Life* magazine picketing a Playboy Club, with a sign calling on the Bunnies to throw off their Bunny outfits to end "sexploitation." But he was now determined to figure out what was real, convinced it lay somewhere within the otherwise rather ridiculous, delusional ideologies of the Berkeley swamp.

Joe could well be considered to be the James Carville of 1970's Berkeley. While he didn't pretend to have all the answers (yet), there was absolutely no doubt in his mind that "we're right, and they're wrong," and he was glad to explain that to one and all. He had another Carville-like trait, insisting regularly that, "It's the economy, stupid!" One memorable day in our shared house in Berkeley, Joe literally came running down the stairs yelling, "Eureka! This is it—this guy Marcus is right on! You guys have to read this! I knew it was the economy!" He had picked up a pamphlet called "Socialism or Fascism," by one Lyn Marcus. "This guy Marcus says that the entire economy is going to blow up, that there's no way to stop it if these idiots keep running things, and that when it blows, if we're there with the right ideas, then *we win!*"

Lyn Marcus was the pen name of Lyndon H. LaRouche, Jr.

[2]

I Become a Political Organizer

Read it we did. Lyndon LaRouche was trying to build something out of the various organizations on the Left, although he was a severe critic of Marx, and an even more severe critic of the New Left. The pamphlet in question had been produced soon after the August 15, 1971 decision by President Nixon to pull the plug on the U.S. dollar, by taking the dollar off the gold reserve standard and implementing Phases 1, 2, and 3 of an economic austerity program. LaRouche (Marcus) had made a name in the anti-war movement, dating back even before the days of his intervention at the 1968 Columbia University strike, as an economist, warning that the myth of the impregnability of the U.S. dollar would soon collapse, and that the fabled "built-in stabilizers" of the Bretton Woods System would soon be destabilized. Nixon's August 15 decision sent a shock wave around the world, but nowhere more powerfully than through the ranks of "the Movement," where LaRouche, the only economist in the world to have forecast this development, suddenly became the most credible voice.

★ ★ ★

Socialism or Fascism" explained the method by which LaRouche had forecast the collapse of the Bretton Woods System, and his proposals for implementing a new monetary system and a massive global development program, utilizing the most advanced technologies available or to be developed. He also forecast that a failure to implement such a program would result in the devolution of the economy into a depression, and the society into fascism, with a full-scale financial collapse by the late 1970's.

"Fascism" was a term tossed about casually by the 1960's radicals, generally describing anything connected to advanced technology or the military-industrial complex. LaRouche, on the other hand, described fascism clinically, as a political form governed by an economic policy, which extracted value from labor not through enhanced technologies and education to increase productivity, but through "recycling" the workforce at ever lower wages and standards of living, down to the concentration camps for the "useless eaters"—a term which captured the bestial conception of man in a fascist economy. This was the direction of Nixon's Phases 1, 2, and 3, and the "post-industrial society" policies of the establishment, aimed at sustaining the mounting financial bubble at the expense of both real industrial development and the standard of living of the workforce.

The nation's credit, LaRouche said, was being diverted from investment in the real economy, used instead to cover bad debt, or for short-term investments looking for a quick profit, while the long-term investments in infrastructure and scientific research and development were being eliminated. Worse, the money thus *not invested* was being called *profit*. Not only were such short-term monetary gains *not* real profit, but they were the result of the looting of the necessary infrastructural investments needed to create real profit in the economy. Real profit could not be measured in monetary terms, but only by considering the physical output of society as a whole, and increases in the productivity of the labor force. If the necessary investment in infrastructure, including both physical infrastructure and "soft" infrastructure, such as education and health care, were sacrificed in favor of paper "profits," then the economy was heading for a collapse, regardless of the euphoria on Wall Street.

LaRouche also identified the emerging counterculture as a virtual replay of the movement built by "that Austrian hippy" Adolf Hitler. The hedonistic glorification of feelings was the makings of a fascist movement, replacing moral judgment and responsibility with unrestrained personal will, and rejecting "the tyranny of reason" in favor of the "freedom" of "felt needs." LaRouche identified the "rock-drug-sex counterculture" as a recruiting ground for fascism.

Reading "Socialism or Fascism" created a transformation in my thinking, which I would later recognize as the equivalent of a "mathematical discontinuity"—a singularity which characterizes a phase-shift from one view of the world to another, leaving nothing in the old unaffected. The material in the pamphlet seemed self-evidently true, and yet it was totally different from any of the economics I had learned in school (like the chapters in Samuelson's Economics 101 textbook explaining the infallibility of the built-in stabilizers), and was equally opposed to the simplistic "anti-profit" dogma of the Left. The events of the day were placed in a context of the long waves of history—what LaRouche would call "current history"—and the reader was called upon to act not only on current issues or local concerns, but on history itself. The predicates of LaRouche's ideas were to change over the years, as he developed his own thinking, but the fundamental method, and the moral vision to uplift the economic and cultural existence of every nation on earth, has been invariant, and was encapsulated for me in that pamphlet.

★ ★ ★

We learned from the "Socialism or Fascism" pamphlet that "Marcus" was associated with an organization called "The National Caucus of Labor Committees" (NCLC). A few days after Joe's discovery, I discovered a weekly newspaper published by the NCLC, called *New Solidarity*, in a Movement bookstore. I picked up several copies, and asked that one be reserved for me each week.

The folks at home were delighted to hear there was a newspaper associated with Lyn Marcus, and we decided to call the local number listed in the newspaper. We learned that there was no organized group on the West Coast, but that a student at Berkeley had a set of audio tapes of a class series given by Marcus in New York. We arranged to listen to them, and thus was born the Bay Area Labor Committee.

In the beginning, Joe's girlfriend and my friend from the Peace Corps, Barbara, did not attend the meetings. They were involved in a women's group—the "feminist" mentality was all the rage in Berkeley. There was an open bias amongst feminists against cognitive thinking, in favor of "emotive" thinking, arguing that women were more in touch with feelings and emotions, while men used their power over society to impose the "uncaring" dominance of rational thought. Politics, economics, etc., was too "male," too "yang," not enough "yin." In any case, the ladies did not attend the Labor Committee meetings at first, either because they considered it a "male thing," or because we men subtly discouraged them from attending, depending on whom you asked. After a month or so, that foolishness was discarded, and we four proceeded together.

We also learned that there existed a theoretical journal published by the NCLC, called *The Campaigner*. A member of the organization visited the Bay Area, and, learning of our interest, visited our house in Berkeley. This was Marianna Staple (later, Wertz), who would become one of my closest friends over the years—close enough that she confided in me her shock at that first meeting. Apparently, when she knocked at the door, whoever answered was buck naked (there were others living in the house besides us, and the story is entirely believable). She almost gave up at that point, assuming that Berkeley was too far gone, but, luckily, she persevered. We, who were all fully dressed, spoke with her at some length. She showed us *The Campaigner*, and we anxiously bought all the back copies she had with her.

The LaRouche (Marcus) tapes and the *Campaigner*'s provided a continuous source of new ideas, as well as a grand sweep of history, which was at once both incredibly rich and deep, and yet presented in a manner which made it intelligible, despite the gaping holes in my own knowledge. LaRouche's economics, and his critique of Marx, addressed fundamental ideas, as he did with every subject, rather than the ridiculous formulas (usually based on false premises) taught in university courses.

For example: What is wealth? Throughout history, oligarchical societies had defined wealth, variously: as an excretion of nature (feudalists and physiocrats); as the profit derived from trade (the British "free trade" school of Adam Smith); or, as the product of man's physical labor (the Marxists). LaRouche used "a worldwide cup of coffee" as a heuristic device to refute these various approaches. Where does your morning cup of coffee come from? Consider the bean, grown in Brazil, its storage in Rio, its transport in ships produced in Japan, with crews from around the world, its packaging in New York with paper from Canada, transported with trucks from Detroit, on tires from Malaysia and oil from Saudi Arabia, the Chinese porcelain of the coffee cup, the Puerto Rican sugar and Florida lemon. Consider also the production of all the machinery used along the way, and the research and development efforts that generated that machinery. Add in the education and health care of all those involved—soon you'll discover that nearly everyone in the world is connected in some way to that morning cup of coffee. How do you measure its cost, its value?

LaRouche insisted that nature has no value in and of itself. Even the most primitive human societies, those early men and women who first domesticated animals and began agriculture, created real wealth only through the creative power of reason, by discovering technologies through which to *transform* nature in a way which allows for the growth of the population at expanding levels of consumption. Thus is man free of the condition of the beasts, such that each generation need no longer live in the same manner as the previous generations. Were man to have remained in a hunting and gathering mode, like the monkeys, he could not have surpassed the total global population of the monkeys—no more than a few millions.

Besides increasing productivity, new technologies also redefine those things in nature which are deemed by mankind to be resources, such that what early man viewed as, at best, a rock, was later seen as ore; what today is viewed as seawater, in a fusion economy will be an inexhaustible source of deuterium fuel. This is real economics, not "supply and demand," nor "the distribution of scarce resources." The science of physical economy is that science which deals with the creative mental process of generating the scientific discoveries necessary to advance to higher levels of technology, and the application of these technologies to the transformation of nature and society. The productivity of labor is not measured in brute-force man-hours, but in increasing qualities of technology which increase mankind's power over nature, and increasing skill levels of the workforce necessary to utilize and improve upon those technologies.

Wealth derives from *reason,* the unique quality which separates man from beast. The taped classes by LaRouche covered broad sweeps of history, political analysis, and philosophical concepts, with biting, often hilarious, polemics against most of the pundits of modern academia and the Left. But what stood out to me was the recurring theme that human existence and human progress rest on the capacity for creative discovery, which takes place only within the mind of an individual, transforming all previous knowlege. Every child is born with the capacity for creativity, and it is on this basis that every child is worthy of mankind's love.

It was here that LaRouche awakened in my consciousness a capacity to identify in my own mind, and to give a name to, that which I had theretofore considered only as my "private world," a hazy structure which I knew to exist but could not precisely identify. It was that which had motivated me to forego the normal "career opportunities," to join the Peace Corps, to explore "the Movement," but which I also knew was associated with Kurt Gödel, and with Beethoven. LaRouche would later emphasize that such a discovery about oneself cannot be learned in a formal manner, but only metaphorically, reliving the process of a profound discovery by someone else, or through the beauty of Classical works of art. In fact, scientific discoveries and Classical art share the qualities of truth and beauty, precisely in that they both are ultimately measured by the capacity to uplift mankind's creative mastery of the universe, and thus glorify God.

The discovery—and I insist that this must be viewed as a valid scientific discovery—that one has the power to act for the benefit of all mankind, is a discovery which itself awakens a hunger to delve into the infinite realm of human knowledge, both known and unknown. It is a joyful discovery, and a continuing source of joy, albeit with enormous and devastating roadblocks along the way. In the tapes, LaRouche told a story (one which he still loves to tell today) about a man being carried to the graveyard, leaning up out of his coffin, looking back, and asking: "What was that all about?" The ephemerals of life soon prove to have little meaning, as we all pass our short, allotted time on this Earth. It is only when we can look at ourselves, and know that our lives have had some meaning, that something of value has been added to future history which would have been missing, but for our existence, and that our having lived has fulfilled some of the aspirations and dreams of those who went before—this is what makes it possible to face the grave with a smile.

I was also delighted to find that LaRouche and his associates addressed those two areas I considered part of my "private world," Gödel and Beethoven. Early in his career, in the 1940's, LaRouche confronted the issues of "artificial intelligence" and cybernetics, questions very similar to those I had battled with in my study of Gödel. He had undertaken, as one of his first political challenges, to refute the work of Norbert Wiener, the author of *Cybernetics*, and his associate John von Neumann, both followers of Bertrand Russell. Just as Russell tried to reduce mathematical knowledge to a mechanical set of rules in a closed axiomatic system, Wiener tried to prove that human thought could be represented by a mechanical process based on statistical analysis, while von Neumann did the same for economics—the source of modern "systems analysis." LaRouche drew on the discoveries of Riemann, Cantor, and Gödel to refute the *premises* of Weiner's and von Neumann's radical positivism. I could see that I had, in my previous studies, only scratched the surface of these issues, but that my earlier endeavors had put me on a productive course. I had formidable enemies, but there was a good fight ahead.

As to Beethoven—LaRouche treated the development of music as perhaps the most crucial scientific discipline of human existence. He insisted that anyone who did not love the Classical tradition in music was incapable of fundamental creative discovery in any discipline. Drawing on my somewhat elementary but impassioned knowledge, I leapt into a delightful new learning process.

LaRouche differentiated between two fundamentally opposed schools of thought in regard to musical development, the Classical and the Romantic.

The Classical, which is exemplified especially by the works of Bach, Haydn, Mozart, Beethoven, Schubert, Schumann, and Brahms, conceived of music as a means of uplifting the mind, appealing to and instructing the aesthetical nature. Percy Shelley, in his *A Defence of Poetry*, saw the poet as the statesman of renaissance and revolution, when "the awakening of a great people" creates conditions such that "there is an accumulation of the power of communicating and receiving intense and impassioned conceptions respecting man and nature." So also, Classical composers viewed their music as an even higher form of poetry.

The Romantics, and especially the movement in the 19th Century led by Liszt and Wagner, rejected such a conception of man, and viewed music as an appeal not to the intellect, but to the senses, and to the emotions associated with the senses, rather than those associated with the mind. The perfect "effect" became the purpose and goal of composition; the overwhelming wall of sound, the use of pulsating repetition and crescendo, the "vertical" impact rather than the "horizontal" development of contrapuntal ideas—this was the Romantic movement that led through the 20th Century to the cult of the ugly in music, as in art generally, known as modernism and post-modernism.

For pedagogical reasons, LaRouche focussed on the late works of Beethoven, as the pinnacle of musical discovery. The late quartets and piano sonatas, especially, were used as examples in the context of his lectures, no matter what subject was under discussion. It was not long before I could no longer stand listening to the rock and folk music that had enthralled me for many years—I even sold my guitar! It was not so much the ugliness of rock that disturbed me at first, as the sense of the loss of those many valuable years of my youth, when I could have been discovering the wealth contained in history's vast collection of beautiful music, rather than "feeling good" to the primitive beat produced by stoned-out freaks. I found it very easy to break with that particular bad habit.

★ ★ ★

The NCLC was engaged in a campaign to stop the emerging "forced-work" programs, the fascist-style labor recycling of the unemployed, targetting in particular the Federal government's Work Incentive Program (WIN). An organization called the National Welfare Rights Organization (NWRO) had been established, with government support, to represent the interests of welfare recipients, mostly single mothers. As the Nixon Phases 1, 2, and 3 austerity policies were implemented, there were efforts to force welfare recipients to "work for welfare," so-called "workfare," under WIN (the trial balloon for today's "welfare reform" policies). Some of the leadership of NWRO wanted to negotiate the best possible deal within this framework, while the NCLC insisted that the program itself was fascist in nature, turning welfare recipients into a scab force of virtual slave labor, forced to work at sub-standard wages, without benefits, pitted against unemployed workers competing for ever more scarce jobs.

I attended a local NWRO meeting in Oakland, where one of the local leaders was vociferously attacking the workfare program as slave labor. I spoke with her afterwards, showing her the *New Solidarity* newspaper articles analyzing the situation and reporting on activities around the country opposing such programs. She was very excited to hear my briefing, and to know of the existence of an organization fighting along these lines. Thus began my career as a political organizer. We began meeting with other active welfare organizers and with trade union leaders, some of whom recognized the urgency of the issue for their own members (and many who didn't). Jeanette Washington, a fiery, experienced organizer from the New York NWRO, who had joined with the NCLC to fight these and other broader issues, visited the Bay area. We set up a series of meetings for her, creating a network of organizers of the employed and the unemployed, capable of deploying in a nationally coordinated fashion against labor recycling.

LaRouche also visited Berkeley. We set up a forum for him on the Berkeley campus on the subject of fusion energy, which drew a very large crowd, perhaps 100 people. It was only then that I realized how widely Lyn was recognized, as a result of the August 15, 1971 decoupling of the dollar from the gold reserve system, confirming his well-known warning. His presentation began with the necessity of the development of fusion power, pushing forward on the cutting edge of mankind's knowledge of the workings of the physical universe, and providing an exponential increase in the availability of energy to the human race. Proceeding then to the economy and the global financial crisis, LaRouche had already eliminated, through the discussion of fusion, the axiomatic assumptions of the various New Left critics who wanted to confront him with either anti-big business or anti-growth ideological arguments.

We held a meeting for the members of the group, in the living room of a Berkeley house where I had taken a room. A totally apolitical girl who lived at the house with her large, shaggy dog, attended the meeting with Lyn, primarily because she didn't understand that it was political and that she wasn't invited. The result was that Lyn spent nearly an hour talking with her about dogs and their similarities and dissimilarities with people, replete with many jokes!

This was to be my first taste of Lyn's character. When I had the opportunity to share living quarters with Lyn, in an Alexandria jail cell block, for six months in 1989, I saw him interact with every inmate, from the kingpin of a major drug and murder ring, to the illiterate street kids caught up in petty crime, with the same gusto, compassion and humor. Perhaps because he did not know the members of our newly formed group in Berkeley, LaRouche used the dog to get at certain issues of human habits as opposed to those of the beasts—showing that often the beasts come out ahead!

At the end of 1972, nearly everyone in the group decided to drive across country to attend the year-end conference of the NCLC, in New York. We stopped in Cleveland on the way, spending a night at my parents' house in Cleveland Heights. Our youngest brother, Dan, was there, and we spent the evening pouring out all the new ideas we'd discovered in the Labor Committee literature, and making fun of the Maoist gobbledygook. Dan, who was 20 at the time, was still heavily involved in the Maoist-leaning, white "support" group to the Black Panther Party. But Dan had an excellent sense of humor, and was not in the least defensive of the "party line." In fact, he referred to the icons of the "Little Red Book" as Marty Tsetung, Larry Piao, and Joe Enlai. Dan was fascinated with our discussions. He agreed to come along to New York for the conference, and subsequently joined the organization.

My only sister, Margaret, who was 21 in 1972, took more time to recruit. Both she and Dan had gone through junior and senior high school in the midst of the cultural dislocation of the late 1960's—drugs, Beatlemania, Woodstock, Vietnam. Intellectual discipline, and the capacity to concentrate, were under attack from the "counterculture," preaching that "if it feels good, do it." Although my parents and the first three children (Joe, myself, and Pete) all graduated from college, Margaret, the fourth sibling, dropped out of Ohio State after one semester, and Dan, the fifth and youngest sibling, decided after high school to skip college altogether. Margaret had the distinction of being the only daughter (my father always teasingly referred to her as "my favorite red-haired daughter") in a heavily male-dominated family. Hollywood images, the jock/cheerleader culture of suburbia, topped off by the drug-rock-sex counterculture, left little room for young people in the 1960's to develop an intellectual identity.

However, Margaret was fortunate to have discovered early on a love for classical music. She studied piano for eight years, becoming an accomplished pianist—a key source of intellectual strength. When her "political" brothers came storming through Cleveland, Marg sat in on the discussions, and began to read *New Solidarity* and *The Campaigner*, but she was terrified at the idea of being an "organizer." Marg and I had always been very close, and I encouraged her to keep reading, but also to renew her piano lessons, which she did. I bought her the recordings of Beethoven's late quartets, which she listened to intently over the next few years. I kept working with her, discussing ideas, music, politics, and the irrational fears which prevent people from acting on the "outside world." During the next few years, she attended a number of NCLC meetings in the Cleveland area, and in 1978, she also joined the organization. When I learned to sing properly in the 1980's, Margaret and I would spend many glorious hours together, praticing and performing classical *Lieder*, including at a number of public concerts in 1988, the year before I went to prison.

When Margaret joined, that brought the number of Billington siblings in the organization to four, which made us the largest clan in the Labor Committee!

New York

I have only one firm memory of the speeches presented at my first NCLC conference, in December 1972. The country was still in a total uproar over the war in Vietnam. Nixon was nonetheless re-elected with a massive majority in the 1972 election, despite the war and despite the emerging scandal of the Watergate break-in. But at the end of December, Watergate was still not that big an issue, and Nixon's popularity seemed at an all-time high, easily able to withstand the rage within the Movement, and in the press, against the war. LaRouche, in his keynote address to the conference, covered the global economic crisis, world history, aesthetics and philosophy, but didn't mention Nixon or the war in Vietnam. One of the first questions after his presentation was from a fire-breathing radical, who wanted to mobilize the masses against the war-monger Nixon and to end the Vietnam War. LaRouche's response was something like: "Forget Nixon. He's finished. 'Watergate' Nixon? He'll be the most hated president in American history within the year. We don't have to lift a finger. He's already done it to himself. Don't worry about the war. It will soon be over. The problem is what to do *in place* of Nixon and *in place* of the war."

This was shocking, since it certainly did not cohere with the appearance of things as presented on the evening news. The point LaRouche was making is that we must, as he does, view the world from the standpoint of being responsible for bringing into being what *ought to be,* not merely criticizing what is. There are many evil things in the world which deserve to be attacked, but to bring about change with limited forces and resources, it is necessary to target those aspects of policy which represent a transformation into a more degenerate form of society, and counterpose a program for real development on the broadest scale.

For example, LaRouche later emphasized the impotence of merely protesting the war in Vietnam, pointing to the incredible irony that the anti-war movement was run by the same people who ran the war itself! McGeorge Bundy, one of the leading architects of both the military and social debacles in Vietnam in the Kennedy and Johnson administrations, had moved over to direct the Ford Foundation, where he designed and financed the anti-war campaign. The underlying policy of *both* the financiers of the war *and* the anti-war movement, was the "post-industrial society," bailing out the financial institutions by diverting the world's credit away from long-term development projects, into short-term boondoggles and looting schemes. The war was useful—a surrogate war between the superpowers in a small corner of Asia—in order to keep the world poised in a bi-polar confrontational mode, preventing any potential for global collaboration towards the development of the Third World, of the sort that President Roosevelt had envisioned, or that President Kennedy had proposed for Africa, Ibero-America, and Asia. The Cold War, said LaRouche, was not being fought in order to stop communism, but as a means to reestablish colonialism in a new guise. Unless the economic issues driving the world financial system into bankruptcy and colonial looting of the Third World were addressed, nothing fundamental could be changed by ending the Vietnam War.

At the end of the conference, one of the members of the National Executive Committee (NEC) of the NCLC, the leadership body composed of about a dozen people, suggested that I stay in New York to work at the National Center. I was hesitant—I had not considered myself to be a fully committed member of the national organization—but it was an opportunity I could not pass up. I stayed, as did my brother Joe, moving into a crowded apartment on 97th and Broadway with about five other members. I had become a New Yorker.

[3]

Local Control: The Tavistock Grin

New York provided a rapid-fire education as a political organizer. Being in the national headquarters of the NCLC, I took part in the production of our newspaper, while also leaping into the rough-and-tumble world of New York local politics. The message we carried into that situation was that local politics, to become effective, had to be governed by national (and international) realities. This did not always make us the most welcome voice, but always the most thought-provoking.

★ ★ ★

There was no "field organization" in those days of the NCLC. The operation was divided into different "files," as determined primarily by the intelligence needed for the publication of the newspaper, *New Solidarity*. I joined the "Asia file," which was directed by Dan Sneider, the son of a senior State Department official with intelligence connections. I worked closely with Dan for the next year, out of our apartments, and in various libraries. Our work in Asia was primarily focussed on gathering a database on the economies of the Asian nations, and examining the manner in which the International Monetary Fund (IMF) policies were oriented toward preventing the development of strong, industrialized economies. This was not hard to demonstrate.

Everyone who lived in New York was part of both the Regional and the National Office staff, and everyone worked in a "file," while also participating in literature distribution, interventions at political meetings, demonstrations, and so forth. Generally, the NCLC team would set up a literature table outside a meeting, or nearby a rally or demonstration, and engage the people coming and going in polemical discussions. When appropriate, we would intervene in meetings to direct the discussion away from local, parochial issues, onto the global economic crisis and the emerging "workfare" and related fascist-type programs which we were trying to stop. When necessary, we disrupted presentations by various charlatans, or spokesmen for the financial establishment, exposing or denouncing them. Picking a public fight would ferret out the true face of the enemy, while also provoking potential thinkers and leaders to step forward and join us.

One of my first assignments to attend a political meeting produced a confrontation which taught me a great deal about the infantile posturing of the various groups on the Left. Two of us attended the meeting (some sort of trade union conference), intending to ask questions and talk with union leaders about our proposal for a debt moratorium as necessary to stop the collapse of the city. On the way in, several different Marxist groups were distributing their newspapers. Amongst them were the Progressive Labor Party (PLP), the Spartacist League, and a similar assortment of Trotskyists, Maoists, and other "ists." I talked with one fellow from the Spartacists for a few minutes. He laid out his "line," and I responded, mentioning that, in regard to the looting of the city's services and infrastructure, what was happening to New York was similar to the "primitive accumulation" carried out by Hjalmar Schacht, the Nazi Finance Minister. This was a bit of history I had picked up in our classes. The "Spart" (as their members were known by the in-crowd on the Left) suddenly stood erect, with a blank look on his face.

"NCLC," he said, coldly, sounding almost frightened.

"What?" I responded.

"Marcus, you're with Marcus of the NCLC," he said, with a tone that told me the conversation was over. Indeed, the mere use of the term "primitive accumulation," a very commonly discussed concept among Marxists and non-Marxists alike, tipped off this doctrinaire automaton that I must be connected to the NCLC!

I was quite startled. "You mean, that anyone who even talks about economics must be with Marcus?"

But it was too late. He began babbling about the "correct line" and the glories of Trotsky. Thus did I learn of the impotent posturing of the Left in America.

One of the greatest dangers in the effort to build a political movement based on *ideas*, is the temptation to appeal to the simple prejudices and opinions of the population. This danger is most evident, and most insidious, when that prejudice or opinion happens to be in *favor* of the position held by the organization in regard to some particular issues. Capitulation to such mindless appeal to mere opinion leaves an organization wide open to infiltration and sabotage. But far more dangerous is the fact that those who join on the basis of "opinion," have in no way changed their thinking, or overturned past prejudices, in the process of joining the battle. Such support will soon evaporate, when the "issue of the moment" passes.

In contrast, the civil rights movement, under Martin Luther King, succeeded because it challenged *everyone*, supporter or enemy, black or white, to *change*, to root out the sources of prejudice and hatred, to *love one's enemy*, while accepting nothing less than true equality and justice. With Dr. King's assassination, no one of that moral stature was able to sustain that objective, and the movement was all too easily destroyed.

★ ★ ★

The NCLC had cut its teeth in New York City during the late 1960's, when it took the lead in the defense of Albert Shanker's American Federation of Teachers (AFT), which had come under attack from the advocates of "community control of the schools." The AFT, which had a large percentage of white, and especially Jewish members, was denounced as "racist" and corrupt. A heavy dose of anti-Semitism was evident in many of the anti-teacher tirades. The movement for local control of the school boards received massive funding from the Ford Foundation, the Rockefeller Foundation, and similar would-be "gods of Mt. Olympus" (or gods of Wall Street, in this case). Their purpose was to divide the population, while diverting attention from the fact that the funding for education was collapsing, along with the rest of the city's infastructure. While McGeorge Bundy's Ford Foundation turned the population's anger against the teachers, LaRouche and the NCLC carried out intelligence warfare against an oligarchy which was increasingly running economic and social policy from their Wall Street boardrooms.

This "local control" movement expanded through the 1970's, stoking the fires of racism, hatred, and rage between various sectors of the population, while the economy collapsed and the cities decayed. By 1973, there were well-funded local-control movements, including the emerging "black nationalists" such as Leroy Jones (a.k.a. Imamu Baraka), with financial backing from the Wall Street foundations, and from Federally funded programs, such as the Law Enforcement Assistance Administration (LEAA). These "black nationalists" militantly demanded that they be given control of the slums: ("They may be hell-holes full of rats, but they are *our* hell-holes, and *our* rats!")

Against such divisive idiocy, the NCLC fought to build a national alliance of the employed and the unemployed, to rebuild our cities. In New York City, we launched our first electoral campaign. Anton Chaitkin, who would later publish ground-breaking material on the historical battle between British Free Trade and the American System of political economy, ran for Mayor, while Leif Johnson (who had convinced me to stay in New York) ran for Comptroller, and Jeanette Washington, the welfare rights organizer, for City Council President. The Chaitkin-Johnson-Washington campaign was our first effort at "soap box" organizing. I attended our first street-corner rally. All three candidates, and a few others, set up a table with a bullhorn in Spanish Harlem, gathering signatures to put the candidates on the ballot, and signing people up as subscribers and contacts.

We held torchlight parades at night in the Bedford Stuyvesant area of Brooklyn, the South Bronx, and even in Newark, New Jersey. With drums, banners, torches and bullhorns, we marched through the streets of the ghettos, into the projects. Our slogans called for the unity of the employed and the unemployed, and an end to the counterinsurgency operations of the Wall Street foundations who financed the local-control scam. To make the point, we published a poster of Imamu Baraka, superimposed on a swastika, with a burning slum in the background, and the words "Imamu Baraka, Fascism in Newark." On midnight deployments, we plastered the ghetto areas of New York and Newark with posters, followed up by daytime street rallies, and evening torchlight marches, to mobilize support. Baraka's gangs attempted to stop us by physical threats and actual assaults, but we generally met with an enthusiastic response, with the parades swelling to hundreds of community people by the time we reached the rally area in the projects.

We wrote up a resolution to the Newark City Council, demanding that the counterinsurgency operations from the LEAA, the Ford Foundation, and so on, be removed from the ghetto before they succeeded in provoking race riots. We also proposed a moratorium on the debt as a basis for funding reconstruction of the city. We arranged to address the next meeting of the City Council to present the resolution, and organized a march through Newark preceding the meeting. I was asked to pick up a lawyer friend of ours in New York, who had agreed to be a witness to the meeting, a precaution we took after certain Newark officials had attempted to ban the march.

Before I arrived, the march had already reached the government building, where a short rally was held on the steps. As Dennis Speed, a young black intellectual who headed our New Jersey organization, began addressing the crowd on a bullhorn, a group of Newark police came up and *arrested* him, dragging him away, over some incident from several weeks earlier having to do with (if my memory serves me) a citation for a rally without a permit, or something equally innocuous. It was Dennis who was scheduled to present the resolution to the City Council. Undaunted, the marchers took up a chant: "Free Dennis Speed," and proceeded into the council chambers.

I arrived with the lawyer at about that time. We walked in from the back of the hall to find the chambers packed with marchers chanting "Free Dennis Speed." Council members succeeded in quieting the crowd, only to announce that they had nothing to do with police business, and that the meeting would proceed without Dennis Speed. Another roar erupted from the hall, which lasted for only a few minutes, when the doors at the rear and both sides of the chamber suddenly burst open, and dozens of police in riot gear plunged into the rows and aisles of the crowded room, wildly swinging their billy clubs. A few of our members lost control and began to fight back, taking punches and struggling with groups of crack riot police—a mistake they would sorely regret. The police picked up steam as the melee proceeded, pushing people down stairways, kicking and clubbing them severely. About a dozen were arrested. The front page of the *New York Daily News* the next morning was a half-page picture of several police carrying a member of our National Executive Committee out of the hall, with the banner headline: "COPS BATTLE LEFTISTS IN NEWARK." While this was not exactly the sort of publicity we had anticipated, or desired, it certainly announced our presence in the New York area.

NUWRO

Our campaign against the forced-work programs grew rapidly. In the spring of 1973, I joined a group of about 25 NCLC members who travelled to Atlantic City to attend the national convention of the National Welfare Rights Organization (NWRO). We had made many friends and allies in the leadership of the local branches of the NWRO, who were trying to persuade their national organization to take our approach. However, the national leadership proved to be primarily "poverty pimps"—administrators who put on a militant front, but ultimately would do what those who held the purse strings in Washington demanded of them, including serving as *gauleiters,* herding welfare recipients into slave labor. The convention, held at a huge convention center on the Atlantic City Boardwalk, was intended to blow off steam among the increasingly angry and militant NWRO members. The officials who had designed and implemented the workfare programs, such as Caspar Weinberger (now "Sir" Caspar), were invited to address the convention, supposedly to show NWRO's willingness to compromise.

Our efforts to have the convention take a stand against workfare were squelched, but we recruited many new collaborators from around the country. Caspar Weinberger's presentation, rather than establishing peace between the membership and the creators of the slave-labor programs, was disrupted by denunciations, and shouts of "Cap the Knife." The serious NWRO members from around the country were ready for a new approach.

It was clear that a new organization was required to unite the employed and the unemployed against workfare, and for real job creation. We called a planning meeting in New York, bringing in our supporters from NWRO, as well as trade unionists and other organizations concerned with the growing unemployment crisis. It was decided to create a new organization, called the National Unemployed and Welfare Rights Organization, or NUWRO. A founding convention was scheduled for Philadelphia, in April 1973.

That founding NUWRO conference, however, became the target of a violent, FBI-orchestrated assault against our organization. The Communist Party (CP) turned up with a picket line, calling the NCLC "racist" and "fascist," in an attempt to provoke a race riot. The conference participants refused to be provoked. They marched through the picket line into the hall, without incident, and the conference successfully launched NUWRO. Over the next year, our organizing exposed the slave-labor programs at every turn, and "workfare" died on the vine. Only in 1996, with the emergence of "Newtzi" Gingrich and his Contract on America did the forced-work programs reappear.

There could be no more transparent proof that the CP was deployed by the same forces within the government who were responsible for the introduction of fascist-like programs such as labor-recycling and local-control. The Communists had facilitated such schemes with their opportunistic pandering after "black nationalism," "Latino nationalism," feminism, parochial worker issues and every other "single-issue" subdivision of the population they could find. With this deployment against NUWRO, to prevent the organization of an alliance of employed and unemployed, black and white, against workfare, the CP went beyond being "useful fools" for the financial oligarchy, and became overt shock troops against the organization of the population in defense of their common and crucial interests.

Further proof of this was obtained several years later, through the Freedom of Information Act (FOIA). Under the heading, "Subject: Lyndon H. LaRouche, Jr.," a memo from the head of the New York FBI field office to the Director of the FBI, dated Nov. 23, 1973, discusses using the Communist Party U.S.A. to "eliminate" LaRouche and the "threat of NCLC operations." The memo reports, "A discussion with the New York [FBI] case agent indicates that it is felt that if the subject was no longer in control of NCLC operations, that the NCLC would fall apart from internal strife and conflict." It goes on to call for LaRouche's "removal" at the ealiest possible date, states that LaRouche's real fear is "assassination," and includes LaRouche's address, and the addresses of his family, "for your assistance in eliminating this threat."

I learned first-hand that the FBI was preoccupied with destroying the NCLC, using every string it could pull. My father, despite his serious reservations about his children's new preoccupation with LaRouche and the NCLC, did not like to cower before threats and intimidation from the powers-that-be. He received a message that an FBI agent had called for him, leaving a number for a return call. He returned the call, but set up a tape recorder to record the discussion. He later played the tape for me. My memory of the call includes the following approximate reconstruction:

FBI: "Did you know, Mr. Billington, that your son Dan is actively involved with a violence-prone revolutionary organization?"

Al: "My son is an adult, and has every right to be active in political organizations. I doubt very much that they are a violent organization. What proof do you have of that?"

FBI: "I'll be glad to send you ample proof. Do you know where your son is?"

Al: "Of course I do—I should think your organization would know where he is—with your capabilities!"

FBI: "Do you know that he travels about, and that their activities may be seriously breaching the laws of the United States?"

Al: "He's an adult, and I doubt if he'd break any laws."

FBI: "We're very concerned, and would be glad to help you with your problem."

Al: "I have no problem, what's yours?"

FBI: "I'll send you some things and call you later."

The FBI never sent anything, nor called back, according to

my father. He was furious, but despite his courage in standing up to such intimidation, he ultimately showed that the fear of being ruined by McCarthy-style witch-hunts still haunted him—he destroyed the tape. The existence of such illegal government COINTELPRO (the code name for the Counterintelligence Program carried out against domestic political and civil rights organizations in the 1960's and 1970's) operations against the NCLC were, for years, denied, then finally admitted following the 1970's reforms of domestic intelligence. These illegal FBI operations are the subject of a lawsuit, *LaRouche v. Freeh,* which is still in litigation as of 1999. The FBI is still trying to circumvent court orders to reveal details of their illegal activities in those early days—a concern which is easily explained by the fact that the FBI *never stopped* its illegal, politically motivated operations against us, up to and including my continued incarceration today.

★ ★ ★

I returned to California for one tumultuous year in 1974. The Bay Area, in particular, was the center of a series of carefully orchestrated "sociological experiments," aimed at creating controlled terrorist capacities and renewed race-war potential. The supposedly "home-grown" West Coast version of FBI-created Black terrorism was called the Symbionese Liberation Army (SLA). The group's first public action was the assassination of the California Superintendent of Schools—a clear tip-off as to their pedigree as controlled provocateurs. In 1974, I became involved in exposing that particular excretion of the CIA/FBI social-control laboratories. When the SLA kidnapped newspaper heiress Patty Hearst, it was immediately revealed that their leader, Donald DeFreeze, and several others in the group, had been together at Vacaville State Prison. A forum was announced at the University of California campus in Berkeley, featuring a counselor of some sort from Vacaville, claiming to know all about the SLA. I attended, alone, intending only to monitor the event. I was unprepared for what I heard.

The spokesman turned out to be a sophisticated intelligence operative with obvious experience in the spook world of covert activity, posing as a "sociologist" with "insights" into the emergence of the SLA. He began describing a series of classes he had set up within the prison, all centered around the same "Ujama" black-nationalist rhetoric I had heard in Newark from Imamu Baraka's outfit. We had investigated the operation in Newark, publishing the results in a pamphlet and in *New Solidarity*. With money and control from the psychological warfare division of the intelligence community, deployed through the Law Enforcement Assistance Administration (LEAA) and other "community" organizations, the "Ujama" ideology used basic animist, pagan terminology borrowed from Swahili, to induce belief in a "black" racial essence. Devoid of any notion of creative mentation, the belief structure emphasized tribal values (family, community, etc.), geared to facilitate both "local control" and black separatist ideology. The "sociologist" from Vacaville had obviously not only *observed* the creation of the SLA—in all likelihood, he was its *creator*.

When he finished his presentation, I rose and, in a polite and restrained tone, told him that I was familiar with his Ujama belief structure from Newark, and briefly described what I knew about the divisive and violent intentions of the operation, as well as its government sponsorship.

"One of the purposes of this brainwashing scheme," I said, "is to induce blacks to accept the actually racist notion that black people don't think cognitively, but through feelings and associations. Such a denial of reason leaves the victims subject to manipulation by their controllers, to carry out acts of terror or violence, as a diversion from serious resistance, or as a justification for police-state counter-measures."

The room was very silent. The speaker finally interrupted with, "What's your question?"

"Could you tell us," I said, "whether you used the same instruction books as were used to create fascism in Newark, and also, what government agencies you work for?"

He was not pleased. He muttered something about "your opinion," and tried to regain his macho persona, but he'd lost control of the audience, and rapidly shut down the meeting. A couple of angry-looking characters came over to me as the meeting broke up, apparently intending to challenge or threaten me, but, at the same time about a dozen reporters and students crowded around with questions, neutralizing the situation.

The SLA charade continued for several months, including the nationally televised bank robberies with the brainwashed Patty Hearst. The SLA orchestrated "free food distributions" in San Francisco and in East Oakland, where the food distributors succeeded in provoking a riot. The ugly episode ended in a fusilade of bullets and fire bombs, which wiped out virtually the entire SLA in their Los Angeles hideout—their "usefulness" having been exhausted.

'Beyond Psychoanalysis'

The brainwashing of individuals—and entire communities—spurred an NCLC exposé of the use of psychological manipulation for social control, published in 1973 under the general title "The Tavistock Grin" (London's Tavistock Institute was the center for such military/intelligence studies), and created a forum for LaRouche's full-scale critique of modern psychoanalytic theory. It was a critique based on Classical scientific method, but aimed also at the question of political organizing—how to transform oneself, and others, into "world historical" personalities.

LaRouche presented a lecture series in New York on the questions of psychology, and published a book-length study in *The Campaigner* called "Beyond Psychoanalysis." He debunked the dominant Freudian ideologies, which define man as a collection of bestial impulses, while defining "normal" as the control or suppression of such bestial impulses (or, in the radical Jungian variation, the acceptance and glorification of such "natural" bestiality). "Normal," said LaRouche, must be viewed instead as the process of utilizing that which *distinguishes* man from beast, the creative intellect. While Freudians attempt to explain creativity as a form of madness (since it's not "normal," perhaps), LaRouche insisted that every child is born with the creative potential for genius. One of the most insightful and provocative issues of our theoretical journal, *The Campaigner*, was entitled "Genius Can Be Taught," a concept which challenged virtually everybody's preconceived notion that genius is a freak act of nature, generally inaccessible to analysis or comprehension by "normal" people.

In "Beyond Psychoanalysis," LaRouche sought to identify the cultural characteristics which enhance or detract from a child's creative development. The first unit of measure is the nation-state, or the language-culture of a sub-region of the world. The ideology identified with such a language-culture will depend on such things as the relative power of the language to express profound ideas, the relative value placed on education (especially in science and the Classical arts), and similar historically specific measures. The shortest unit of action is generational, such as the generation spanning the depression and World War II, followed by the post-war generation known as the "baby boomers." The question to be addressed is, what fixed ideological beliefs are common to a generation, often unbeknownst to those who hold such beliefs as axioms of their thought processes? Which of these beliefs can be shown to be contrary to reality, thereby inhibiting the capacity of individuals in society to make the historically necessary creative discoveries demanded of mankind to assure the development of the species?

The children of the World War II generation, the "baby boomers," had been carefully sheltered from the harsh realities their parents had faced in the Great Depression, the war, and the post-war depression of the late 1940's. Armed with Dr. Spock, mothers told their children to "be themselves," to be free to do whatever comes "naturally" without fear of punishment, and, most important, to be "popular." For the parents, that meant keeping ahead of the Joneses (perhaps sleeping with the Joneses); for the kids, it meant sports, dates, and making it into the "in-crowd" at school. Americans became "other-directed," losing the "inner-directedness" demanded of a creative human being. Long-term goals, which require sustained concentration (such as serious study, or the learning of a Classical musical instrument), were far less important than the instant achievement of popularity through sports, social life, a guitar and a "good personality."

In a 1974 internal discussion document called "Mother's Fears," LaRouche addressed the psychological blocks to individual creative thinking—and to taking personal responsibility for mankind's future—among the members of the organization. In the 1950's, with the new-fangled televisions in the suburban living rooms broadcasting the McCarthy witch-hunts, with even the gods and goddesses of Hollywood being destroyed by the slightest hint that they may be less than "politically correct," the once-proud soldiers and their hard-working wives became terrified, "little" people, while Mother was absolutely dedicated to protecting Johnny from the horrible fate awaiting those who failed to conform. The "freedom" of the Spock babies was, in fact, a cover for the transmission of "mother's fears" to the children, the "freedom" not to question anyone's opinions, and certainly not one's own. "What's good enough for Ozzie and Harriet's kids is good enough for you," and that does not include a serious thought about anything. It was not only the real mother, of course, who conveyed these fears to the baby boomers, but Hollywood and the emerging television culture, which became surrogate parents to the Pepsi generation.

My Parents

When it came to dealing with our real parents, many members of the Labor Committees, only half understanding the ideas presented in "Beyond Psychoanalysis," used them as an excuse to "confront Mom and Dad"—something quite common among the "'60's" generation. My brothers and I were not blameless in that regard, which caused some grief on the home front. My father, Joseph Alford Billington II (called Al), was a bright and very good-natured fellow, with a sharp sense of humor. He joined the Navy when the war broke out in 1941. As a college graduate, he was automatically made an officer, but spent the entire war stateside. (I was born in the Naval Hospital in Jacksonville, Florida, on July 8, 1945, just before VJ day.) After a few years selling insurance, he began his own business as a manufacturer's representative.

Billington Metal Sales, Inc.—which was for the most part just himself and a secretary—represented high-precision forge shops which produced forgings and castings for such things as military aircraft and submarines, including nuclear reactor parts. Although generally a "salesman," he took great pride in the importance and the quality of the material he sold, to customers such as Babcock and Wilcox. He made a point of taking all of his children to see the forge shops, including a full tour of the chemistry labs and the metallurgy shops. My brother Pete (that makes five: Joe, Mike, Pete, Margaret and Dan), the only sibling who *didn't* join the Labor Committee, went to work with my Dad after finishing college, and, when Dad died in 1979, took over the business. Before Dad brought him into the business, however, he arranged for Pete to spend one year in an apprenticeship program that the owners of his primary forge shop, McWilliams Forge in New Jersey, provided for their own children. It entailed a few months training in each division, learning every aspect of the operation, from forging the metal to quality control. It was a solid grounding in the productive process—something few yuppies on Wall Street even know exists.

Al made a decent living—in fact, we probably would have been a fairly "wealthy" family if not for the paint gun. In 1956, Al was persuaded to invest in a paint gun, which had been invented by an acquaintance. Al sunk over $80,000 into it—a fortune by his standards—which was mostly borrowed. I recall watching the 1956 Republican convention on television, waiting for the advertisement they had purchased for the paint gun, and the excitement when it came on—a man in a suit spraying paint on a board. Westinghouse had given its backing, and Dad was dreaming of being rich. The only problem was that the damn thing didn't work. After the gadgets had been distributed to stores around the country, they all began being returned, and the venture collapsed.

That was a bad time for my usually good-humored father, and things were a bit tense at home for a few years. We lived in debt after that, but Dad was able to sustain both the business and a very decent standard of living for the family. He always kept one of the paint guns on a shelf in his office—"to remind me not to try to get rich quick," he told me.

Al was an Eisenhower Republican, and my mother Ruth was a liberal Democrat. He accepted my mother's numerous social activities, such as the coffee shop and various church-connected civil rights activities, but he never participated, and often joked about them. The "Discussion Group" which Mother attended every week was referred to as the "Disgusting Group." He was certainly not opposed to civil rights for all, nor to support for the poor, but he considered ridiculous the "anti-big-business" mentality of many of the liberals. In our pre-Labor Committee days, when Joe and I would occasionally challenge him with some Leftist diatribe about corporate profits looting the workers, he'd respond: "Oh, bullshit. If there's no profit, there's no reason to set up the company. If there's no profit, there's no way to pay the workers more, let alone expand the business. Who the hell do you think pays most of the taxes that pay for all the programs Ruth is fighting for?" Although he invested in the paint gun venture, he was never a speculator in the stock markets, and eventually came to agree with LaRouche about the parasitical nature of the financial oligarchy, as opposed to the industrial, productive sector of the economy.

Ruth, the liberal, was always more understanding of her children's radical politics than was father Al, although she refused to lose faith in liberalism, and defended Left-leaning causes against our criticisms. She had never been personally targetted by the McCarthy witch-hunts, but her sister Jean's husband, Jack Campbell, was. Uncle Jack was a scientist at GE's Nela Park facility in East Cleveland, and was one of the inventors of fluorescent lighting. He had been called to testify against the "patriotism" of several of his associates, and was threatened with contempt charges. Others of Ruth's friends had had their careers ruined by McCarthyism. While I admired her sustained commitment and participation in civil rights issues, I questioned her fixed notions in regard to "liberal" and "conservative" issues.

An anecdote from the 1976 Presidential election is revealing. LaRouche was a candidate for President for the first time. He ran as the U.S. Labor Party candidate, a party he had formed for that purpose. (Later, in 1979, he entered the Democratic Party.) Ruth, who always expressed sympathy for LaRouche's policies, voted without hesitation for Jimmy Carter, although we had demonstrated in great detail that he was a totally owned candidate of the Trilateral Commission apparatus from Wall Street, the same "big money" people Mother ostensibly opposed. Dad, on the other hand, who always prefaced any response to anything LaRouche had to say with, "Oh, bullshit," returned from the polls with a curious look on his face. "What happened, honey?" asked Ruth.

"Well, I got in the booth," Dad answered, "and I looked at the lever for Jimmy Carter, and I looked at the lever for Gerald Ford, and I thought, God, what has this country come to? So, I took hold of the LaRouche lever, closed my eyes, held my breath, and pulled!"

That was funny enough, but the best part was that Ruth became absolutely furious, and remained so for a good while. Not because she disapproved of someone voting for LaRouche, but because she considered it hypocritical for Al to vote for him. Actually, I am certain that Al knew exactly what he was doing, and why. He died before the next election, a victim of liver cancer, at the age of only 63.

I asked my mother recently if she could account for the fact that she and Al produced four children dedicated to effecting revolutionary change in the world (even though brother Dan eventually left the organization). She laughed, and said that I should let her know when I figured that one out.

Perhaps I need to look further back, to my grandparents. My father's father was born in 1869, just after the Civil War. He worked his whole life on the B&O Railroad, raising four children in the small western Pennsylvania town of Albion, and lived to the ripe old age of 99. I knew him as a venerable old soul, always ready with a few words of wisdom for his many grandchildren.

My mother's father, Tom O'Mara, was a hard-drinking, hard-working second-generation Irishman, who worked on the Hoover Dam and other heavy construction sites around the world, including Afghanistan and British Guiana (so, I was actually the *second* of our family to work in that country!). He was a union man all the way, when such a commitment could cost a man his life. He supported the Wobblies, and read Eugene V. Debs, and was proud of it until the day he died. But Grandpa O'Mara left his wife and four children, spending the Depression years trekking from one project to another. When their mother died, the kids were divided up among friends and relatives. Although they all led productive, creative lives, there were many scars.

So, my heritage is a product of America's successful Civil War, and the subsequent development of the continent through the railroads, as well as our global nation-building commitment and the fight for social justice—all tempered by the tribulations of the Great Depression. I believe that my parents, whatever their shortcomings, passed on the best of that extraordinary American heritage, to the extent that we siblings were open to receiving that legacy.

[4]

The American System

The next few years were extremely difficult for me personally, although the intellectual excitement and development continued apace. I had entered into a relationship with Connie Reynolds, a member of the Bay Area Labor Committee since 1972. In the fall of 1974, Connie, her two daughters from a previous marriage, and I packed up and drove from San Francisco to the Big Apple, taking an apartment in Washington Heights, a few blocks from the George Washington Bridge.

The hardship of raising two children, while maintaining almost full-time political activity, exacerbated the trauma of a difficult marriage. We separated in early 1975. I continued to see the girls regularly over the next years, and helped out financially as long as it was necessary.

★ ★ ★

Back in New York City, I took a job driving a cab on weekends, an expedient used by many of the New York Labor Committee members. By putting in two 12- to 14-hour overnight shifts, one could make enough to sustain a bachelor for the week. But, with two kids to take care of, I had to grind out three such shifts, which proved to be extremely taxing, if not quite debilitating, physically and emotionally. I could have become a substitute teacher, which—while no picnic, especially in the New York City schools—would have been a far better choice, but I was worried about the irregularity of the schedule and the paychecks. As it turned out, I spent nearly five years behind the wheel of a yellow cab. This, more than anything else, turned me into a "real New Yorker."

During that period, I happened to read a story by Edgar Allan Poe, called "How to Write a *Blackwoods* Article." It was a hilarious assault on the leading British literary magazine of the day. In the story, Poe ridiculed the *Blackwoods* approach to fiction, which permitted only that which was based on feelings, existential angst, and moral decadence, while rejecting anything which addressed such old-fashioned notions as reason or beauty. A young aspiring writer, submitting her artistic composition to the editors, is told that to make it as a writer, she must go out into the hard, cruel world, get drunk, raped, lose everything, wallow in the gutter—*then* she'd have something to write about!

I realized that I had, as a "benefit" of my job as a New York cabbie, the makings for the perfect *Blackwoods* article! All that was needed was to adopt the self-conception as a "victim," and embrace with abandon the lifestyle of the menagerie which passed through the back seat of my cab, which included every conceivable variety of squalor, perversity, and brutality, separated from me by a bullet-proof plastic screen. A surprising number of people tried to draw me into their lives. I chose instead to bring along a tape recorder, and to spend the long hours engrossed in Beethoven's late quartets and Bach's unaccompanied violin and cello sonatas, with an occasional opera thrown in. Nonetheless, reading Poe's works during those days played a significant role in keeping my head above water and my eyes on a higher goal.

I returned to my earlier position on the Asia intelligence file, and later transferred over to the Middle East file when manpower was needed there. Because my schedule made it difficult to sustain the concentration necessary to do effective daily intelligence work, I eventually switched to the regional organizing team, deploying "in the field" to rallies, meetings, and newspaper distribution sites across New York City.

Regional organizing generally entailed two or more organizers heading out early in the morning with a couple of bundles of *New Solidarity* and other literature, spending most of the day at high-density sites, selling newspapers and getting names and phone numbers of people for future contact. The subways, of course, were as high-density as you could get. I spent many days walking from car to car on the A-train, or the IRT, shouting out a brief polemic based on our leading campaigns at the time, then passing quickly through the car, selling papers to those who reached for their quarters. Weather permitting, we would find intersections in the city where traffic backed up. Hanging signs on posts or around our necks, we would walk down the line of traffic, selling papers and magazines. We would usually sell 100 or so copies of *New Solidarity* per day, and generate about a dozen contacts for follow up. Over time, many people became "regulars" and depended on seeing us to get that week's paper, but this was largely a process of "throwing papers over the wall," for the purpose of creating a general recognition of our ideas in the population. We usually deployed about ten teams, each selling about 100 papers per day in the city, while thousands of people saw our presence and our signs. Income from the deployments, although relatively modest, was adequate to meet the costs of production and the overhead. Virtually everyone had some sort of part-time employment to sustain him- or herself.

Evenings were filled with house meetings, local meetings, and phone calls to recruit contacts to our meetings. We ran electoral slates across the city (and around the country), for both local and Federal elections.

The intellectual climate in the organization was intense. Everyone, with few exceptions, whether in the National Office or in field work, was engaged in some area of historical research. Reports and studies of all sorts floated around the organization, some becoming articles for the publications, but most just serving to expand collaborative thinking on history, philosophy, education, science, and other subjects.

Within the membership, at this time, there was a process of re-discovery of long-obscured aspects of the history of the United States, which was to dramatically shift the conscious self-perception of our historical mission-orientation and our self-identity as patriots. This process emerged, in part, from a study of the works of the Founding Fathers, up to the period leading into the Civil War, and the discovery of what had once been commonly known as "The American System" of political economy.

Unfortunately, the term "American System," or "American Way," has, in the 20th Century, become a cliché for blind patriotism, often in its worst form. With the likes of the racist Anglophile Teddy Roosevelt, and the equally racist and Anglophile Woodrow Wilson, the term "the American Way" became a variation of "the British Way," at best substituting the United States for Britain as the center of an oligarchical and colonial empire. "American capitalism" came to be identified with the pursuit of Adam Smith's free-trade dogma and the power of the Anglo-Saxon race.

The misperception of what America *truly is,* in its historical context, rather that that which the British have (often successfully) manipulated the U.S. to do on behalf of the British Empire, is a crucially important problem today, both within the U.S. and, especially, in developing-sector nations. This misperception serves as the British oligarchy's primary cover for imposing their evil upon the world.

The American System, we discovered, was a different thing altogether from the British system. The United States fought three wars against the British in its first hundred years as a nation: the Revolutionary War, the War of 1812, and the Civil War (which was, in fact, a war against the British, who had sponsored the Confederacy from its inception). Throughout those first hundred years of our republic, the American System represented a specific school of thought, and a specific form of political economy—one directly opposed to the British system. Unlike the British *laissez-faire* free trade, Alexander Hamilton and his followers proposed direct government involvement in providing protection and credit for national development, especially large infrastructure projects, while fostering universal education and scientific research as the means to increase the productive powers of the population. Even the *use* of this term, the American System of political economy, as well as the ideas it represented, have been, in the 20th Century, *totally eliminated* from the history textbooks used in American universities, and from the consciousness of the citizenry.

Perhaps the most astonishing proof of this suppression of America's real history is the fact that one of the greatest thinkers and statesmen of our nation's history, Henry Carey, is virtually unknown in today's America, and, at best, has been accorded but a footnote in contemporary histories. Carey was Abraham Lincoln's economist and political adviser, known internationally as the leading spokesman for the American System of political economy. His books were read throughout the country, and around the world, and his ideas were instrumental in creating modern economies in many nations, including especially Germany, Russia and Japan. He had come from a long line of American System proponents, which included his father Mathew Carey, Alexander Hamilton, George Washington, John Quincy Adams, Friedrich List, and Henry Clay.

Incredibly, I first encountered Henry Carey while reading Karl Marx! I was studying the history of the late 19th Century in the U.S.—the era of Andrew Carnegie and the growth of industrial America, following Lincoln's crash industrialization during the Civil War—while also reading Marx's analysis of various "capitalist" doctrines. Marx mentions in a letter to Engels, that he had indirectly learned of the American economist Henry Carey, who seemed to have some merit, but was, in the end, but another bourgeois apologist, trying to cover over the inherent contradiction in capitalist theory. I poked around among my associates to see if anyone knew about this mysterious, unknown American, and learned that Allen Salisbury, a member of the National Executive Committee, had encountered Carey *from the same source,* and was deeply involved in rooting out the story. Allen would subsequently publish a series of articles on Carey, and a book entitled *The Civil War and the American System, America's Battle With Britain, 1860-1876,* which both revealed these forgotten aspects of our history, and indicted those responsible for its falsification.

Henry Carey's most widely read book, his 1851 *The Harmony of Interests,* was a blistering polemic against Adam Smith and the British system of free trade. Smith, in the service of the expanding British Empire, was actually *contracted,* by Lord Shelburne, to write his 1776 *Wealth of Nations,* precisely to counter the republican forces in the American colonies. Smith was called upon to write a theoretical justification for the "forced backwardness" policy of the British Colonial Office, which would continue as the foundation of British foreign policy through to the present day. Smith concocted the notion that nations must follow the law of "relative advantage" in a free-trade world. This meant that England, as the nation with the most developed industrial infrastructure, should retain that advantage—claiming that it was actually economically disadvantageous for the colonies to attempt to manufacture anything!

To debunk such ideas, Henry Carey pointed to the history of the United States itself as proof that Adam Smith was a fraud. He exposed the genocide in those countries where England had succeeded in imposing its will, such as Ireland, India, and China. In India and Ireland, the history of British rule was one of recurring famines, far more frequent than before the arrival of the British. During the famines, the exportation of foodstocks to London continued, unabated, enforced at the point of a gun, while millions starved to death. According to Smith and the British, to break the "contracts" imposed on the "wogs" would go against the laws of free trade. It would be *immoral*, they argued, and harmful to the laws of economics, to allow any sentimental concessions to the short-term needs of the natives.

In China, British free trade required that the "unenlightened" Chinese, who foolishly tried to prevent the importation of opium from British India, be taught a bloody but necessary lesson in the "natural law" of free trade by British gunboats, resulting in the "Opium Wars."

Against this unmitigated evil, Carey counterposed the American System of protective tariffs, government-financed infrastructure projects, national banking to assure a flow of credit to private industry, and universal education. Carey developed the concept of a "harmony of interests" between agriculture, industry, and government. This became the foundation upon which the North, under Lincoln, created the overwhelming productive power which defeated the British-sponsored Confederacy.

Our research during this period also uncovered the extensive impact of the American System of political economy on other nations. Friedrich List, a German citizen who worked in the United States in collaboration with Mathew Carey and other nationalists, became one of the leading theoreticians for the American System. When List returned to Germany in 1832, he founded the *Zollverein* (Customs Union), which became the basis for the unification of the various German states into a true nation-state. Germany already enjoyed the highest level of Classical education in the world, owing to the reforms of Wilhelm von Humboldt, which produced many of history's greatest artists and scientists. With List's American System economic reforms, including protective tariffs, national investment in infrastructure, and national credit policies for industry, Germany was also transformed into the leading industrial power in Europe.

Germany was not the only country which would prove the efficacy of the American System over the British system. List's and Carey's influence extended into Russia, where the modernization and industrial development under Czar Alexander II was inspired by the ideas of the American System. Likewise, in Japan, where the architects of the Meiji Restoration, and the industrial transformation of that country, drew heavily on the "German school" of List and other American System advocates. The potential for Germany, Russia, and Japan, with the inspiration and leadership of the United States, to create an alliance for global development based on the rapid advancement of scientific and technological progress, became a serious threat to Britain's global empire. We were to learn, through further research over the coming years, the extent to which the world wars of the 20th Century were directly provoked by the British, precisely in order to prevent the emergence of such a grand alliance between European and Asian nations, based on the American System of political economy.

These discoveries were exhilarating for all of us. We had found an entire school of philosophic and scientific thought, developed in America 200 years earlier, which had reached many of the same conclusions as we. It was the discovery of several generations of collaborators, whose ideas could now be brought back to life, after a century of deceit and obfuscation by 20th-Century historians. New historical friends were appearing every day, as we probed through the American System networks which had spread around the world during the 19th Century, awakening hope and optimism in nation-building and cultural renewal. We even discovered that the great "Industrial Revolution" in England, was the result of networks begun by Benjamin Franklin, against the wishes of the British free-traders, who were determined to keep their own country backward! And the one common thread amongst these 19th-Century networks, whether in Europe, Asia,

Ibero-America, or Africa, was the recognition of the evil of British colonialism and British liberal philosophy.

LaRouche wrote a fascinating study on this issue, published in *The Campaigner* under the title "Dr. Karl Marx Refuted," by "A Veteran of the War." Using the device of a manuscript supposedly written in 1870 by a Civil War veteran, but only recently discovered in its previously unpublished form, LaRouche provided a devastating refutation of British economics and its Marxist variation, demonstrating how the Confederacy was an explicit British creation—and how the "free trade" in human bodies was but the most hideous aspect of the British economic model. The Confederate Constitution rejected the concept found in the Declaration of Independence, which declares mankind's inalienable right to life, liberty, and the pursuit of happiness. In its stead, the Confederates added the fundamental right to *property*. This reflected the debate between the followers of John Locke and those of Gottfried Leibniz. Locke, speaking for the British oligarchy, defined "property" as the most fundamental right—even going so far as to equate "natural law" with the right to inheritance, showing that the maintenance of the power of "the families" was foremost on his mind. (Presumably, natural law simply does not apply to a person without property!) To Locke, a nation was no more than a contract among property-holders, for the purpose of assuring the security of that property, and the right to inheritance.

Leibniz, wrote the "Veteran of the War," insisted that Locke was totally wrong—that God did not assure property rights, but He *did* assure the freedom to pursue happiness, through the development of that creative potential which is man's God-given birthright—that quality of mind which distinguishes man from beast. By defining it as "inalienable," it was asserted that this right could not be taken away, even by the most evil tyrant, provided the mind was free (and it most *certainly* did not depend upon membership in land-holding families!). Government was not just a social contract to protect against crime, but an institution constituted to enhance the fundamental rights of its citizens, through education and development, for the general welfare of all. America's successful development, and its victory over Britain in three wars between 1776 and 1865, wrote the "Veteran of the War," was primarily due to the fact that the Founding Fathers had the wisdom to follow Leibniz, rather than Locke. The Confederacy, gratefully, had failed in its effort to reverse that wise choice.

As to Marx, the "Veteran" explained that he was by and large a British creation, controlled by British intelligence official David Urquhart of the British Museum. Marx was trained in the fundamentals of British economics, as developed by Adam Smith and David Ricardo. Although Marx was an improvement on Smith and Ricardo, since he emphasized industrial production and the living conditions of the labor force, he nonetheless never broke from the methods or assumptions of the British school of economics. Ignoring Leibniz, and the American experience, Marx accepted the British assumption that production results from the input of raw materials and labor, with labor considered only for its brute-force power, its relatively mindless physical activity. He recognized the importance of machines, but did not consider the *source* of those machines, nor the source of their change and improvement, in the power of *mind* of individual scientists, and in the power of *mind* of the workforce to master and utilize constantly improving technological principles and their corresponding mechanical application.

Rediscovering the American System finally laid to rest the question of "Right" and "Left." For the past 200 years, all political views have been characterized by one or the other of these supposedly all-inclusive, but mutually exclusive, categories of Left and Right (terms which derive from the seating arrangements in the National Assembly, during the French Revolution). What "Left" and "Right" actually mean varies from person to person, based at best on vague, but popularly accepted definitions. In the context of our discovery of the American System, these categories became suddenly, and self-evidently, ridiculous. I asked myself, was Abraham Lincoln Right or Left? How about Benjamin Franklin? The same problem exists with the terms "liberal" and "conservative." The very *use* of these "paired opposites"—the yin and yang of modern Western "political science"—presupposes two neatly packaged "positions," *which supposedly define all options.*

In the 20th Century, this evolved into the "communism vs. capitalism" dichotomy, or "socialism vs. free enterprise." This nonsense has been particularly intense over the past thirty years, as the Thatcherite, Conservative Revolution ideology replaced any lingering notion of "industrial capitalism," with free trade and unregulated speculation. Russia, after being liberated from communism, was *destroyed* by "shock therapy," while the Western nations and the IMF simply lied, asserting that any government support for industry, or for scientific research and social welfare, was a remnant of "communism," which had to be eliminated. Similar policies are regularly imposed by the IMF on Third World nations, which are told that all state-sector industries are inherently "socialist," and therefore must be "privatized." Failure to obey such demands results in the cut-off of international credit.

The American System defines a scientific approach to political economy which defies such misconceived notions as Left and Right, locating the actual self-interest of everyone (except perhaps the yuppies on Wall Street and other related parasites) in the process of scientific and technological development.

The NCLC, up until that time, had a general self-conception as an institution on the Left. We were fighting for a new world economic system that would end the oppression and economic looting of working people, the poor, and Third World nations. We were determined to identify and destroy the fascist-like institutions and policies which were rapidly emerging as the financial crisis reached a breaking point. To most of us, that seemed "Left." But LaRouche, who had uniquely recognized the inevitability of a financial breakdown under existing economic policies, also insisted that the solution lay in fostering entrepreneurial initiative through national banking, in order to generate huge investments into advanced science and technology, national infrastructure, space programs, and entrepreneurial private industry. This certainly was not "Left." As we developed an understanding that our roots in Leibniz and in the Platonic philosophic tradition also encompassed the Founding Fathers and the architects of the American System, we were able to put aside the labels.

An enormous weight was suddenly lifted from my shoulders—a weight which I barely knew had been there before it disappeared. No longer did I feel that gnawing, nagging pressure, from friends, family, and the media, insisting that I *choose* between two equally bad alternatives. The apparently safe path of taking sides on set issues defined by the social planners was exposed as a deadly trap, cutting off the mind and deadening the spirit. Like the little boy who shouted, "the Emperor has no clothes," simply throwing off the blinders of "Left" and "Right" could go a long way to liberating the sheep-like population from its deadly, media-induced trance. It was just as challenging, and just as much fun, to organize those whose self-perception was as a "liberal," as those who were "conservative," since both were human, with an underlying desire to do good, but who were both caught in a vicious game.

Music

In the fall of 1975, there was virtually no work being done on music in the organization. Lyn talked about music all the time, and those of us with little or no familiarity with classical music began listening to the great works, focussing primarily on Bach, Mozart, and Beethoven. We had, within our ranks, a few talented musicians, including a young pianist, Christine Berl, who presented a class series at Barnard College for members and contacts, performing and discussing Mozart and Beethoven piano sonatas. Although many members had learned to play the piano or some other instrument in their youth, or had sung in school or church choruses, these talents had generally been put aside in the rush of political activity.

John Sigerson, a member of the Germany desk for *New Solidarity,* had studied bass viol at Julliard, and had a beautiful tenor voice. When I learned of this, I approached him to suggest getting some people together to sing. As it turned out, he was looking for a bass to join him and two women members, who were anxious to sing. Thus was born the first nucleus of a chorus, and the first tentative steps towards a process which would eventually imbue our political work with active music-making. Later, in 1983, we had the good fortune of meeting up with a brilliant voice teacher from the National School of Music at the Autonomous University of Mexico, Maestro José Briano, who transformed our knowledge—and our practice—of singing and the human voice. Between 1975 and 1983, however, it was strictly amateurs taking great joy in learning and performing beautiful music.

Although John had received some vocal training, no one in our quartet had a clue as to proper singing method, nor how to solve basic vocal problems. But our sessions were productive nonetheless. We began by working through some of the great Renaissance composers—Josquin des Prés, Orlando di Lasso, Dietrich Buxtehude, and J.S. Bach. Occasionally, we would sing at the opening of our public meetings. Soon, a larger group came together to form the first Labor Committee chorus, which John conducted. Some members picked up their dusty violins, flutes, and oboes, and music flourished throughout the organization. Nonetheless, the chorus and orchestra were generally restricted to those who had either studied an instrument in the past, or who could already sing adequately enough to carry a part. *Listening* to great music, and the role of music in history, were integral parts of the organization's practice, but the concept that every human being could—and should—be provided the necessary training so that he or she could *perform* beautiful music, and perform beautifully, was an idea that would await the arrival of Maestro Briano.

Our chorus performed several major works, including masses by Beethoven, Mozart, and Schubert, Haydn's *Creation,* and (our finest performance) Bach's motet, *Jesu, Meine Freude.* But perhaps the most immediate benefit of the chorus work was psychological. As people struggled to either correct or (more often) cover over their vocal problems, they tended to feel quite naked in front of the other chorus members. The problem of "performance"—with all the sexual implications—were exposed for all to hear and see. Various neurotic self-protection devices gushed forth in chorus rehearsal, which created some hilarious moments, and some very useful insights when treated appropriately.

I had an opportunity to try my hand as conductor (and psychiatric counselor) when John stepped aside temporarily in 1978. He had reached an impasse with the choral work, and I took over temporarily. From that time forward, until I went to prison in 1989, I had the pleasure of conducting many choruses in various cities—I even led a church choir at my first Federal prison, and, after a nine-year hiatus, started a "prisoners chorus" in Virginia!

I also attempted to deal with my own vocal problems. Although I had a strong voice and true pitch, the quality of the instrument was hardly pleasing. I took voice lessons from three different professionals in New York before Maestro Briano arrived, but none was able to do anything with the throaty, flat quality of my voice. At the time, I came to accept the "natural condition" of my voice, resigned to my fate as one who simply wasn't blessed with a beautiful singing voice. Later, I would realize that a more accurate conclusion would have been that the science of voice training was a lost art, even in the artistic capital of the United States.

★ ★ ★

In 1975, LaRouche launched his first campaign for President of the United States, creating a new political party called the U.S. Labor Party. Running against Jimmy Carter and Gerald Ford, his actual target was neither candidate, but the "Eastern Establishment" which controlled the political process. In particular, the primary British-spawned institution in the U.S., the New York Council on Foreign Relations (CFR), had, in the early 1970's, created a spin-off called the Trilateral Commission. Nelson Rockefeller, a stalwart of the CFR and the Trilateral Commission, was attempting to coerce Ford into making him a "co-President," rather than merely the Vice President, while both Jimmy Carter and his running mate Walter Mondale were entirely created and owned by the Trilateral Commission.

The program for these Trilateral candidates was laid out by the CFR in a series of studies known as "Project 1980's," which presented quite openly the policies we called "fascism with a democratic face": de-industrialization (post-industiral society); controlled disintegration of the economy (a phrase coined by Carter's eventual Federal Reserve chairman Paul Volcker); an open call by Harvard's Samuel Huntington to eliminate the influence of democratic constitutency organizations in America; and rabid demands for de-population world-wide. The anti-growth, "environmentalist" movement was being institutionalized.

After a tour of the Middle East in 1975, LaRouche countered with a program called the International Development Bank (IDB), the first of many proposals by LaRouche for global financial reorganization along the lines of the long-forgotten American System. We began working out detailed programs for the industrialization of Africa, Asia, and Ibero-America, always demonstrating that such programs were eminently feasible, but required the replacement of the decrepit IMF-based financial infrastructure with something like the IDB.

★ ★ ★

LaRouche's IDB proposal burst into international prominence at the 1976 meeting of the Non-Aligned Movement (NAM) in Colombo, Sri Lanka. The NAM, which took its inspiration from the historic Asian-African Conference in Bandung, Indonesia, in 1955, led by such figures as Sukarno, Jawaharlal Nehru, Gamal Abdel Nasser and Zhou Enlai, had enormous potential to shatter the controlled environment of the bi-polar world defined by the "Cold War" and the "détente" process. The developing nations of the mid-1970's were not willing to passively accept the fraud of "post-industrial society," since they had been prevented from achieving the status of an industrial society under the forced backwardness of the colonial yoke. To be told by their ex-colonial masters that the New Age required them to forgo industrialization in order to "save the environment" or to meet the demands of "free trade," did not sit well with nationalist leaders who had won their freedom from colonial domination, often in bloody wars of independence, in order to escape backwardness and poverty. LaRouche was already well known, either directly or indirectly, to the leaders of many of the NAM nations, who recognized the seriousness of his warnings against the IMF as a potential new colonial master.

One of these leaders, in particular, took up Lyn's call for a global solution to the impending financial crisis: Fred Wills, the Foreign Minister and Ambassador to the UN from Guyana. I had known Fred Wills during my Peace Corps years in Guyana, as an outspoken, articulate, and much-beloved statesman for his newly independent nation. (His popularity was not harmed by the fact that he moonlighted as the radio announcer for the national cricket team in Guyana, where his wit and humor reached across the racial tensions which had been aggravated by the British to destabilize the country before independence.)

Fred met with our representatives at the UN, and eventually met with Lyn, where there was a meeting of minds. Fred had been educated as a lawyer in London, one of the "colonials" intended to be trained as a faithful wog to administer the colonies for the Crown, armed with British ideology and British economics. But, Fred loved Classical English culture—he knew Shakespeare, much of it by heart, from the inside, with the passion of one who shared Shakespeare's battle for truth. His years in London taught him to despise the bestial nature of the British oligarchy and their ideology. He often related how he considered every day of his life a victory over British colonialism, since the average lifespan of a colonial male was but 45. (Fred, by 1976, had reached the ripe old age of 47. He died in 1992.)

As Guyana's representative to the Non-Aligned Movement meeting in Colombo, Fred Wills decided that he would speak not only for his own small corner of northeastern South America, but, in league with LaRouche, for all citizens of the world. He proposed to the conference a debt moratorium on all Third World debt, warning that the debt crisis would soon explode if such urgent measures were not adopted at once. He outlined the nature of the crisis and the idea of a new banking system to replace the IMF, based on real development. The Non-Aligned leaders there recognized Fred's proposal as that of Lyndon LaRouche; some lent their support, others quietly took note, but they did not forget.

As to Fred Wills himself, he soon discovered that he had acquired some very powerful enemies, and that Henry Kissinger, in particular, had let it be known that Fred was not appreciated in certain circles. His life was threatened and he was forced to leave Guyana. Except for some help from us, he might not have made it out alive. He came to New York and became a close friend, teacher, and collaborator of LaRouche and the organization. Besides sneaking a few moments here and there to sing Guyanese folk songs together, Fred and I shared many joyful hours in discussion of politics, music, and poetry, in the years before my incarceration.

Vote Fraud

Carter's election victory was not really a victory; it was a Trilateral Commission coup, carried out through blatant vote fraud. If the election were allowed to stand—as we knew it would without our input—the result would be a probably irreversible take-down of the U.S. economy under Trilateral/CFR direction, and potentially a rapid escalation of the tension in Europe towards nuclear war. In the months preceeding the election, Trilateraloid Henry Kissinger and his British allies had orchestrated plans for forward positioning of nuclear missiles in Germany, perceived by the Soviets as a kind of reverse Cuban Missile Crisis. The NCLC launched its first emergency national mobilization, including the mass distribution of leaflets on the danger of the provocation, while Presidential candidate LaRouche directly warned the nation in a national television address, that a vote for Carter would be a vote for nuclear war.

The night of the election the margin of victory was so close that if any one of several large states had gone the other way, Gerald Ford would have emerged the winner. Two of those states, New York and Ohio, had urban concentrations where fraud would have been relatively easy, using large numbers of falsely registered "ghosts." At first, President Ford questioned the outcome and suggested a legal challenge. But, later, during the morning after election day, he conceded. Several sources reported to us that Nelson Rockefeller and Henry Kissinger had demanded that he concede, against his own better judgment. That, more than anything, convinced us that a strenuous and unpopular effort to prove vote fraud was necessary.

I was on the Bronx organizing squad. About a dozen of us took the voter lists from the various burned-out areas of the South Bronx—one of the most devastated urban hell-holes on the face of the Earth. We drove through the city, attempting to verify each address and confirm residence. The results were astonishing. For block upon block, the old tenement buildings were deserted, either boarded up, burned-out, or already a pile of bricks. Yet, hundreds of people had been registered to vote, and *voted* from these non-existing addresses, apparently chosen so as not to duplicate a real voter, or, perhaps, under the assumption that no one would risk entering these neighborhoods to challenge the registration.

I knew the neighborhood well from driving a cab, but I had never combed through the miles of ruins in the South Bronx, as I did on this project. Where a building was still standing, I would go in to determine the registered residence, even if the building appeared to be deserted. In building after building, I found people living in the semi-rubble, even though the buildings had been condemned and lacked even water and electricity.

When I lived in Thailand, I once visited the slums of Bangkok, where people lived in shacks built over swamp-land, near the docks on the Chao Phraya River, without electricity or water or even an outdoor septic system. It was an experience which has remained indelibly in my memory, never failing to arouse a sense of anger that human beings were forced to suffer such degradation. Discovering that thousands of Americans lived in relatively comparable squalor, aroused at least as much anger and a great deal of shame.

Despite the exterior dilapidation of most of the Bronx buildings, the apartment interiors were generally well kept. In some areas the voter registrations were accurate, and the residents were proud to confirm that they had voted. But many registrants did not exist. Nearly everyone warned us to get out of the neighborhood and to "leave it alone."

When the results of our fraud investigation were tallied across the five boroughs of New York, the number of nonexistent voters far exceeded the margin of Carter's victory in the State of New York! A reversal of the result in New York meant reversing the outcome of the national election. When we presented our evidence in court, the judge agreed that we had successfully demonstrated the existence of the relevant number of fraudulent votes. *But*, he ruled, since we could not establish for whom those votes were cast (since one's vote in America is confidential), he would not overturn the election results. Sadly, and with dire consequences for the nation, the Trilateral Commission had its President.

[5]

Campaigning

We acted upon our enhanced role in national politics by expanding our presence across the country. I was asked to set up an office in Westchester County, the suburban county north of New York City, and to run for the office of County Executive in the 1977 election. Three of us took an apartment in Ossining, on the Hudson River, near the famous Sing Sing State Prison. "Dope, Inc.," our exposé of how the London-centered financial oligarchy controlled the drug trade, was about to be published, and we would soon launch the National Anti-Drug Coalition. The following year, I made a run for the U.S. Congress as part of a national slate of U.S. Labor Party Congressional candidates.

★ ★ ★

We spent most of 1977 doing the groundwork to establish our political presence in Westchester, setting up tables in the urban centers (usually in front of the Department of Motor Vehicles or major post offices), selling papers at selected traffic intersections, and conducting door-to-door walking tours in the evenings. My campaign for Westchester County Executive provided a forum to address dozens of organizations across the county, both in private meetings and in public debates with the Republican and Democratic Party candidates. I was the first, and I believe the last, associate of Lyndon LaRouche to receive extensive and totally straight coverage in the *New York Times!* The *Times* invited the three candidates to their editorial office for a joint interview, which resulted in a full-page spread in the suburban section of a Sunday edition of the *Times.* Local press coverage was not quite so even handed, but several radio news broadcasters became quite interested, regularly covering my press releases and taped comments. One show even taped a series of half-hour interviews, covering the world economic crisis, the role of the Trilateral Commission, and LaRouche's proposal for an International Development Bank.

I was, of course, criticized for addressing international issues, rather than the problems facing Westchester County. Several well-meaning critics suggested I should run for Congress, rather than a county office, a recommendation I took up the following year. But my general response was that the problems facing urban and suburban areas—problems of mounting debt obligations, a falling tax base, decaying industrial sectors, and collapsing infrastructure—could only be met by a change in national policy. The biggest local issue was whether or not to build an energy-generating garbage incinerator, and, if not, what to do with the garbage. I insisted that this was, indeed, a garbage issue. Nuclear facilities were required to produce energy most efficiently, not garbage dumps, and funds for efficient incinerators would not be a problem if the industries in Yonkers, the biggest city in Westchester County, were not rapidly closing down under the weight of post-industrialism. But the serious polemical battles in Westchester County were not to emerge until my 1978 campaign for Congress, when I went after the kingpins of Dope, Inc., many of whom held residence in the county.

Drugs

In 1978, the book *Dope, Inc.: Britain's Opium War Against the United States,* was published under LaRouche's direction. It included a brief history of England's use of the drug trade in the 19th and 20th Centuries to finance the Empire, and to enslave their colonial subjects. It presented the astonishing story of England's two opium wars against China, in the 1840's and 1850's, when China's demands that the British traders cease their practice of smuggling opium from India into China, led Lord Palmerston to wage war on the hapless Chinese for their refusal to honor the British right to "free trade."

The focus of the book, however, was the *new* opium war. The drug trade ranked as the biggest business in the world. The sheer size of the operation (at that time approximately $200 billion annually) and the fact that nearly all of the drug money passed through the British Commonwealth banking centers (such as Hongkong, Singapore, and the Cayman Islands), or the London-allied New York banks, was adequate to show where the control of Dope, Inc. was located. It remained to be proven that the British-centered financial establishment was complicit, from the point of production, down to the street sales in Harlem, and in the halls of the country's high schools and colleges.

Dope, Inc. covered the massive expansion of drug cultivation since the 1960's, especially in Ibero-America and Southeast Asia, including the role of the CIA and other "private" intelligence operations in the drug trade during the "secret wars" in Laos, Burma, and Thailand in the 1950's and 1960's. I contributed my photographs of the opium fields of northern Thailand and the donkey caravans which transported opium through the hills, pictures taken on a week-long trip through the Hill Tribe country in 1971, during my Peace Corps years.

A series of pamphlets and centerfolds in the *New Solidarity* prepared the way for the publication of *Dope, Inc.* in 1978. A "National Anti-Drug Coalition," with a monthly journal, *War on Drugs*, was launched. The impact of this offensive reverberated throughout every community and every political institution in the country, far beyond our actual physical presence. It may be hard for some to recall now, but at the time there was no organized resistance to the drug epidemic. In fact, it was LaRouche who coined the phrase "war on drugs," and he did not mean "just say no." The few individual voices of opposition and honest law enforcement efforts had been swamped in a torrent of pro-drug propaganda in the press, from Hollywood, and from political leaders—both the polymorphous perverts (as Lyn called them) of the "New Left" who were now entering politics, and the libertarian fanatics on the "Right," like Milton Friedman, who defended the "freedom" for someone to destroy his or her own mind.

Jimmy Carter's White House was flush with drug-legalization advocates, including his "drug adviser," Peter Bourne, and country music yahoo Willie Nelson, who even bragged about smoking pot in the White House. We published a pamphlet called "Get the Dope Out of the White House," whose title was a classic example of Lyn's delightful use of puns. Everywhere we went we found parents near distraction over their children and the crisis in the schools, frantic for some coherent explanation for the overnight transformation of the country into a "drug-friendly environment." *Dope, Inc.* went through several printings in the first year, each printing selling out as fast as we could ship them to the field offices. The National Anti-Drug Coalition became the motor for a counter-attack against the pro-drug lobby, which was trying to legalize marijuana—or "decriminalize" as they euphemistically called it, an early example of the deconstructionalist nonsense of "politically correct" doublespeak. In the year preceding the founding of the Anti-Drug Coalition, about a dozen states passed "decrim" bills, and it appeared that the country would be swept away in a haze of marijuana smoke. We set a course to reverse the rout.

As in *Dope, Inc.*, the *War on Drugs* magazine presented evidence of both the social and the medical damage done by drugs, but emphasized the political and economic *cause* of the epidemic. It named the names, normally assumed to be "above suspicion," exposing the real drug kingpins who inhabit the board rooms of Wall Street and the City of London, and their political spokesmen, who finance and control the biggest business in the world. Naturally, our enemies were not pleased.

The ADL

The ferocity of the attack against us after the publication of *Dope, Inc.* was not unexpected, but the form of the attack was a surprise, at least to some of us. The nation's press began describing *Dope, Inc.* and LaRouche as anti-Semitic!

Before joining the Labor Committee, I had limited, but significant, personal familiarity with Jews, both at home, and at college. Although the neighborhood in East Cleveland, Ohio in which I had grown up had only a handful of Jewish families, we were just "down the hill" from Cleveland Heights and Shaker

Heights, two predominantly Jewish suburbs. My father's closest friend throughout my youth, Fred Sharp, was Jewish, and his son Brian had been my brother Joe's closest friend for much of their childhood.

I was unaware of anti-Semitism in our community or in our schools, but I recall vividly an incident involving my Dad and his friend, Fred. Dad came home furious one night after an evening at a private club he belonged to, the Hermit Club, which was the Cleveland version of the Lamb's Club in New York—businessmen who were also musicians, using the club for both purposes. My father, who had earned money during college playing saxophone and clarinet in a jazz band, played in the Hermit Club jazz band and in a saxophone quartet. The club was generally racist—all the members were WASPs and all the waiters black—and my mother was uncomfortable there. My father did not consider himself racist, and he was not, but he never accepted my mother's criticism of the club, insisting that, "The waiters are well paid and they're grateful for the positions," and, since the club was located in the inner city, "it would be wrong to not hire local black residents."

That opinion changed when the club rejected his proposal that Fred Sharp, who was a highly skilled jazz guitarist as well as a successful businessman, should fill the spot opened up by the death of another member. "No Jews," he was told, "and no exceptions." Dad was enraged and discussed quitting the club altogether, but he decided to fight it out. As best I can recall, they partially relented, granting Fred some sort of associate membership.

Soon after that incident, while I was in junior high school, I read the novel *Exodus* by Leon Uris. Besides vague references to the Holocaust in textbooks, this book was my first introduction to the story of the Nazi horror and the story of Israel. I was deeply affected, and could think of little else for months afterward.

Trinity College had many Jewish students and professors. Three of my fellow classmates and I became something of a foursome, rooming together, and remaining friends throughout our college years. One of them, Matt Rubin, was a Jew from West Hartford, the only "local" of the group. We all got to know his family quite well, joining them for Passover and other holidays.

They were "survivors," many of their relatives having been lost in the Holocaust, and at one holiday, Matt's father related terrifying stories of the persecution in Europe before the war.

However, it was not until I joined the Labor Committee that I became associated with such a large number of Jews. At least one-third of the membership was Jewish, and several had studied for the rabbinate or had lived on a kibbutz in Israel. The passionate commitment of the organization, and of LaRouche personally, to identify the economic and political roots of fascism, and to fight, above all, to prevent its recurrence, made it seem quite natural that so many Jews would become associated. Being in New York, Jewish humor and Jewish lifestyles were ever-present, and the internal social interaction among the members tended to take on the ambience of New York Jewish culture.

Immediately following the publication of *Dope, Inc.*, we were hit with a barrage of slanders and attacks from the Anti-Defamation League (ADL). The ADL is officially part of B'nai B'rith, the Jewish Masonic order. However, unlike the B'nai B'rith, the ADL is not a membership organization, but is composed entirely of its carefully selected staff. It functions as a protection racket for organized crime, and is historically linked to the networks around gangster Meyer Lansky. The ADL has never been shy about its organized crime connections. As recently as 1985, they proudly presented an award to mobster Moe Dalitz, the founder of the Purple Gang and an associate of Meyer Lansky. Other recipients of the ADL awards include the likes of pornographer and drug promoter Hugh Hefner, and junk bonds scam artist Michael Milken. The honorary National Chairman of the ADL, and one of its major funders, is Edgar Bronfman, head of Canada's Seagram's whisky empire. The Bronfman clan wealth came directly from the "Bronfman Gang" of the 1920's—the primary source of Canadian liquor to organized crime in the U.S. during Prohibition. The Bronfmans had branched out into Hongkong heroin traffic, before buying "legitimacy" after the repeal of prohibition, with the help of several leading lights of the Zionist movement.

Kenneth Bialkin, the National Chairman of the ADL in the 1970s, was the controller of the infamous Robert Vesco, who looted millions from the drug-laundering apparatus called Investors Overseas Service. Vesco fled to Cuba, where he coordinated

Colombia's Medellín Cartel cocaine traffic into the U.S. Although the courts found Bialkin responsible for Vesco's crimes, he continued in his position of honor in the ADL without disruption.

One ADL "investigative study," called "Brown Shirts of the 1970's," opened with a quote from LaRouche: "You don't have to wear a brown shirt to be a fascist. You just have to be one." This truthful statement was presented as evidence that LaRouche had pronounced *himself* to be a fascist! The ADL line on LaRouche took the following general form: LaRouche, a self-proclaimed Marxist, turned from the far Left to the far Right, adopting a classic fascist, anti-Semitic ideology, blaming an imagined world economic crisis on a combination of Freemasonry, the Jews, and the communists.

Various ADL stringers were hired to write slanders on LaRouche. One, Chip Berlet, wrote an article for *High Times*, the slick monthly magazine published by the pro-drug lobby, which is filled with pornography, advertisements for drug paraphernalia, and articles on the sources and methods of consumption of every drug imaginable. This degenerate magazine could be purchased on any newstand in America's major cities! The article, titled "Lyndon LaRouche: Sinister Master-Mind of the National Anti-Drug Coalition: They Want To Take Your Drugs Away," was a general incitement of the drug culture, and the more violent Leftist and anarchist groupings embedded within the drug culture, to take actions against LaRouche and people organizing in support of his ideas.

Dennis King, who was picked up by the ADL from a Maoist outfit, published a full-length book titled *Lyndon LaRouche and the New American Fascism*, financed by foundations linked to the now infamous money-bags for right-wing fanatics, Richard Mellon Scaife.

It was during this period that the national media adopted a standard characterization of LaRouche. An NBC reporter, in covering *Dope, Inc.*'s extensive documentation of British financial control over the flow of international drug money, and the interface of British royalty and British banking, used the ridiculous formulation that "Lyndon LaRouche says the Queen of England pushes drugs." Henceforth, the name of LaRouche could not appear in print, no matter what the subject, without the tag, "who says the Queen of England pushes drugs . . . ."

Dope, Inc. and *War on Drugs* magazine documented that the primary sources of support for the pro-drug lobby were the same institutions and individuals advocating free-trade economics. The oh-so-conservative Bill Buckley, from the *National Review,* bragged about his pot habit, and promoted legalization. Milton Friedman, the guru of free trade and economic libertarianism, is a life-long supporter of legalized drugs.

LaRouche co-authored a book entitled *The Ugly Truth About Milton Friedman.* The book traced the history of Friedman and his Mont Pelerin Society to the fascist economic theories of the so-called Vienna School, associated with Friedrich von Hayek and Ludwig von Mises. While there were various factions among these European networks, and some had opposed the political policies of Hitler and his National Socialists in Germany, they all shared the fascist ideology; that the right of the powerful to profit by any conceivable means constituted the true meaning of the term "freedom"; and that this "freedom" was not to be disturbed by bothersome government intervention or moral niceties.

Milton Friedman never fails to promote his vision of an ideal society: the British Crown colony of Hongkong! *Dope, Inc.* documented at great length the role of Hongkong, from the time of its seizure from China by the British East India Company as spoils of the Opium War in the 1840's, continuing through to its return to China in 1997, as headquarters for the control and financing of the international drug trade. It has never failed to amaze me that Americans could passively accept the promotion of the Hongkong model as the ideal society, since the colony was an overt dictatorship, run jointly by London's hand-picked Governor and a committee of representatives of the leading banking houses, primarily the Hongkong and Shanghai Banking Corporation, the "Hongshang." All the leading banking institutions descended from opium traders of the 19th Century. The official criminalization of opium in the 1920's had no effect on the banking houses, since the "law" of Hongkong allowed the keeping of secret accounts and secret books!

The potential power of the book *Dope, Inc.* was demonstrated in 1979, when the Hongshang took steps to purchase New York's

Marine Midland Bank, which would be the largest takeover of a U.S. bank by foreign interests in history to that point. We acted to prevent the takeover altogether. We provided the Superintendent of Banking in New York State, Muriel Siebert, with our documentation of the Hongshang's continuing role in laundering drug money, warning that the takeover of a leading U.S. bank by a British drug bank would escalate the drug crisis in America into an unmitigated disaster, while creating a speculative bubble of hot money in the heart of the U.S. banking system.

Much to the horror of London and her allies in New York and Washington, New York State banking Superintendent Siebert, openly acknowledging her debt to the material in *Dope, Inc.,* ruled that the takeover of Marine Midland would not be permitted, unless the Hongshang agreed to open its secret books for inspection and could prove that drug-money laundering was not tolerated by the bank's directors!

I was in our New York office on West 29th Street when the news broke of Seibert's decision. I happened to take the call from a field team who first saw the news in the press, so that I had the great pleasure of notifying the office of the decision. The response was euphoric, throughout the entire organization. Not that the decision in itself would solve anything, but the truth regarding the enormity of the crimes of British banking, and its threat to the U.S., had finally forced an act of sanity within the halls of power, entirely due to our persistence in shouting the truth, as boldly as possible. Through the strength of vigorous intelligence, and by focussing all our limited resources on a primary, vulnerable flank of the enemy, we could defeat the most powerful forces in the world.

Ultimately, however, the Hongshang succeeded in the takeover of Marine Midland. This was in 1979, the year that Carter's Federal Reserve Board Chairman, Paul Adolf Volcker, raised the interest rates to 21.5%, launching the "controlled disintegration of the U.S. economy," which he had first proposed in the CFR's Project 1980's study. Superintendent Seibert's action against the drug bank takeover threatened to disrupt Volcker's plans for the U.S. banking system. Throwing aside all regard for the law, Volcker granted the Marine Midland a *national* charter to replace its New York State charter, thus removing the bank from Superintendent Seibert's jurisdiction! He promptly discarded Seibert's demands for the Hongshang to open its books, and personally granted the takeover in 1980. Consequently, the British Opium War against the U.S. moved into high gear.

Candidate for Congress

The Congressman for Westchester County was Richard Ottinger, a soft-spoken liberal who struck me as an aging flower child from the 1960's. He was active in the anti-nuclear movement, soft on the drug culture, and generally supported the policies of the Carter Administration—a perfect target for one of our candidates. We gathered petitions to put me on the ballot for the 1978 Congressional election, a task that required a daily deployment of organizers from New York to join our small team in Westchester. We succeeded in gathering the required signatures, but the Democratic Party challenged our petitions, thereby demonstrating that they took our campaign seriously. We were forced to spend endless hours searching the files of registered voters, looking for the registrations which the Democratic Party claimed were not there. We obtained a court order forcing the Board of Elections to remain open in the evenings to allow us the time required. In a hearing before a judge, I testified to both the validity of the signatures and the legitimacy of our method of collecting them. I rather enjoyed taking the stand (something I would never be able to enjoy in my criminal trials). The judge concurred, and I got on the ballot.

The Republican candidate Michael Edelman, a young lawyer, then approached me with an "offer." Drop out of the race, he proposed, and if he won, he would "consult" with me on issues, assuring me a "voice" in his office. I proposed, instead, that he join with me in exposing the Trilateral Commission agenda behind the zero-growth, anti-nuclear, pro-drug policies of Congressman Ottinger and the Carter Administration. He was not interested.

I soon discovered why not. Edelman was a protégé of New York Senator Jacob Javits, who was both a friend of the ADL and a proponent of legalized drugs! Since 1968, as Senator from New York, representing the financial center of America, Javits had sponsored national legislation to decriminalize marijuana. In 1977, just a year before my Congressional campaign, Republican

Javits personally intervened in the New York State Legislature to ram through a decriminalization bill, backing up Democratic Governor Hugh Carey. Our Anti-Drug Coalition had thrown our full weight into the New York State fight over decrim, rallying the population and holding up the drug pushers in the legislature to public scorn. The bill passed by one vote, but also forced the criminals to expose themselves. The furor over the battle was heard around the country, and, as a result, was the last successful decriminalization bill to pass in any state, while most of those that had already passed were eventually rescinded. (In 1997, with millions of dollars from mega-speculator and drug-pusher George Soros, the decrim movement was revived under the guise of the supposed "medical use" of psychotropic drugs. President Clinton—unlike Carter—has strongly opposed the drug bills, and will probably get them overturned in court.) Edelman was not likely to join my attack on Congressman Ottinger as "soft on drugs," let alone expose the increasing control of Wall Street by Dope, Inc.!

To the contrary, I soon found myself to be one of the most visible targets for the ADL. In the summer of 1978, before the ADL had launched its national assault against LaRouche and the NCLC, I participated in a debate sponsored by the League of Women Voters in a Westchester residential area. Following the opening presentation by the three candidates, a man, whom I subsequently learned was a major real estate mogul and a member of the ADL, stood up with the first question. "I want to protest," he said, "the presence of a known and self-confessed anti-Semite in this race, in the person of Michael Billington. I have here a magazine that he is selling as part of his campaign, which is openly supporting the fascist Lyndon LaRouche, who claims there was no Holocaust, and blames Jewish bankers for every evil in the world. He claims he is not attacking Jews, but only Zionism, but we all know that that is the oldest trick in the book for fascists to hide their anti-Semitism. Billington should be excluded from this debate, and all others." I was stunned. Before I could respond, Edelman leaped up to say that he, too, was very upset that anti-Semitism had been introduced into the campaign, that he had read the horrible things that Billington and some of his associates had said about some of the leading citizens of America, "and even about the esteemed Senator Javits, who, I am proud to say, has endorsed my campaign." He said that it appeared that the only fault of the people I attacked was that they were Jewish, and that there was no place for such "bigotry" in America.

I finally got up to speak. There was even an effort, by some people, to stop me from speaking, but I insisted, telling the moderator, "I'm sorry, but your debate has been rudely disrupted with vile accusations against me, and I must respond." Facing the audience, I went on. "No one has introduced anti-Semitism into this campaign except this man, the questioner, who has filled this hall with filth! Nothing in any of my literature, or that of Lyndon LaRouche, promotes anything other than our lifelong dedication to preventing a recurrence of fascism, and ending racism of any sort. To accuse me of anti-Semitism, because some of the people I have denounced for their policies have Jewish names, is absurd. Hitler said that anyone who opposed National Socialism was anti-German. It's no different to say that opponents of Zionism are anti-Semitic—and just as wrong." Pointing at the real estate mogul, I said, "I think you owe the League of Women Voters an apology for reducing this event to lies and slanders."

I had been totally unprepared for the attack, since this incident preceded the outburst of slanders proceeding from the ADL. In fact, I didn't really know much about the ADL at the time. We had published historical attacks on the British creation and manipulation of the Zionist movement, and certainly condemned the extremists in Israel, but we had never supported the Arab rejection of the existence of the State of Israel. In fact, LaRouche had met publicly with several Israeli leaders. I knew that Israel's first Prime Minister, David Ben Gurion, had denounced the extremist followers of Jabotinsky as being no better than the Nazis, and that Nahum Goldmann, a senior statesman of the Zionist movement, had warned openly that there was a fascistic faction within the Zionist movement. I knew also that LaRouche and Nahum Goldmann had enjoyed friendly relations. How could such hideous slanders and lies against LaRouche be justified, in light of his clearly stated views? It was obvious that I had a lot to learn.

As my Congressional campaign unfolded, so did the national ADL slander campaign. The ADL deployed spokesmen to each of my public debates, but I learned to preempt their attacks during my initial presentation. Mr. Edelman, who had tried to bribe me out of the race, paid dearly for his role in the ADL ambush against me. I learned that he enjoyed the financial and political support not only of Senator Javits, but also of Edgar Bronfman himself. At each event, I presented the details of the role played by these two gentlemen in pushing drugs in America—including the use of New York State as a guinea pig for the decriminalization of marijuana. (A legislative investigation found that the use of pot increased by 300% in New York after the passage of Javits's decrim bill!) I challenged Edelman to denounce drugs and to return the contributions he received from these tainted sources. He, of course, defended Javits and Bronfman, but he never again dared to accuse me of anti-Semitism, nor did any ADL plants in the audience. Congressman Ottinger, who consistently refused to attack me personally, won the race by a landslide. I emerged with only a handful of votes, but we developed an extensive network for the National Anti-Drug Coalition, and a wide subscription base for our publications.

This would not be my last toe-to-toe battle with the actual drug kingpins of corporate and political America. Years later, I found myself staring down the barrel of Colonel Oliver North's cannon, as he was most unhappy at my role in exposing his collaboration with Vice President George Bush in running drugs into the U.S. under the cover of the "Contra" affair in Central America. But that is a later story.

[6]

The Morality of Science

The Fusion Energy Foundation (FEF) was founded by a number of scientists from around the world, on the initiative of Lyndon LaRouche. As a non-profit, tax-exempt foundation, the FEF, with its journal, Fusion, was the only institution in the world which unabashedly defended the necessity for massive expansion of scientific research and development, and the full application of advanced technologies in global nation-building. The leading science journals of the day, such as Scientific American, had become apologists or outright advocates of pseudo-scientific frauds, including the anti-nuclear, anti-DDT, and similar anti-growth manias which controlled the New Age, "post-industrial society" policies. More importantly, FEF was dedicated to creating a political fight among scientists and within the population as a whole, for the revival of the scientific method of hypothesis—the method which had generated all significant discoveries throughout history, but which had practically disappeared in the 20th Century. Fusion magazine grew to 140,000 subscribers by 1987, and became the third-largest circulation science magazine in the United States.

In 1987, however—and this is the reason my description of the FEF has been in the past tense—the FEF became the first science foundation to be shut down by the government of the United States, along with its magazine, Fusion. Under the guise of an "Involuntary Bankruptcy" provision, which had never previously been used against either a scientific or a political organization, the Department of Justice seized and closed the Fusion Energy Foundation, and Campaigner Publications, the publisher of New Solidarity newspaper and The Campaigner, our theoretical journal. That abuse of power, the imposition of scientific and political censorship upon the most outspoken opponents of the policy direction of the nation, together with the simultaneous criminal indictment of LaRouche, myself, and dozens of others by a multi-jurisdictional "Get LaRouche Task Force," stands, still today, as a mark of tyranny and shame for America before the eyes of history.

The question of scientific method—the method of hypothesis—is at the very root of the ideas which have sustained LaRouche's organization, and my own original work. So it is only natural to digress from my narrative, and discuss the concept of scientific method, before returning to the events of the 1980's which led up to the government assault on the organization, and my incarceration.

★ ★ ★

Hypothesis

My collegiate introduction to Kurt Gödel came in my sophomore year in logic. Before introducing Gödel, Professor DeLong had assigned a textbook which discussed logical systems of varying complexity, but which were all, ultimately, extensions of Aristotelian logic. Aristotle's famous syllogisms (variations on arguments of the type: "All men are mortal, Socrates is a man, therefore, Socrates is mortal") are all based on the so-called Law of Contradiction—that a statement cannot be both true and false at the same time. This, of course, seems quite obvious to common sense. A proof by contradiction depends on this most obvious fact: If we make an assumption, but then show that the assumption leads to a contradiction, then we have proven that the assumption is false.

Gödel's proof, however, showed me that, although Aristotle's logic could have some practical application, it was nonetheless practically useless in regard to the most interesting and important questions. Since any system of logic, like any mathematical system, is built on a set of axioms, Gödel's proof showed that such a system were necessarily incomplete—that there are true statements which cannot be derived from the axioms.

What I did not know at the time, was that Kurt Gödel was a confirmed "Platonist," whose life was dedicated to defending

Platonic ideas against Aristotelianism. Years later, in 1992, I had the good fortune to meet with a most fascinating man, Dr. Wang Hao, at Rockefeller University in New York City. Dr. Wang had worked closely with Kurt Gödel at Princeton, and wrote a biography of his esteemed colleague. Dr. Wang was himself recognized as one of the world's leading logicians, and was working on a refutation of Aristotelians of our own day, the positivists Bertrand Russell, Ludwig Wittgenstein, and their school. He explained to me that Gödel was a passionate Platonist, which caused Dr. Wang considerable difficulty in his biography, since he admitted that he, himself, did not fully understand Plato! The problem was even worse, he explained, in regard to Leibniz, the foremost Platonist of the modern era, whom Gödel held in awe, but whom Dr. Wang found incomprehensible.

One might make the mistake of presuming that Dr. Wang's difficulty arose from the fact of his Chinese heritage and education, since such a cultural difference from "Western thought" may have caused him difficulty in grasping the "foreign" ideas of Plato and Leibniz. Ironically, the opposite is the case. Dr. Wang was educated during the 1930's and 1940's in China, under the influence of what was known as "The May 4th Movement," a transformation of education in China based on the influence of none other than Bertrand Russell and his American cohort, John Dewey! As a result, Dr. Wang's education was not only based in part on the Aristotelian, positivist notions of the Western enemies of the Renaissance (and the enemies of the American System), but he was also systematically denied a thorough education in the Chinese classics of Confucius, Mencius, and Chu Hsi!*

By the time I met Dr. Wang, in 1992, I had studied and written about Leibniz's great interest in, and debt to, these Chinese classics. I attempted to help Dr. Wang understand the source of Gödel's genius, by providing him with Leibniz's, and my own, work on the relationship between Western Renaissance ideas and those of the Chinese classics. My efforts were cut short by my return to prison in 1992, and Dr. Wang's death in 1995.

* Transliterated as Zhu Xi in the recently standardized Pinyin system.

What are the issues between the irreconcilable world views of Aristotle and Plato, a conflict which is at the core of every major advance, or collapse, in world history, including, in a slightly different form, the history of China?

Aristotle, a hireling of the aristocracy, posed a view of man's mind as a *tabula rasa*—a blank slate, upon which sense perceptions registered specific images, like marks on a slate, or data input in a computer memory. Man, for Aristotle, is born in this "blank" condition, neither good nor bad, with the same needs and instincts as the beasts, enhanced by a mind capable only of logical deductions, or inductions from the data of the senses. In the Aristotelian system, "deduction" refers to the syllogistic form mentioned above, drawing specific conclusions (such as "Socrates is mortal") from a general premise (such as "All men are mortal"), where the general premise (like the program in a computer) is accepted as self-evident. "Induction" is the compilation of multiple sense perceptions of a similar sort, as the basis for inducing a general concept. Of course, the conclusion of induction is prone to a fallacy of composition—that something is true many times over is not a proof that it is always true. More importantly, the result of deduction is only as valid as the truth of the premise. Aristotle claimed that general premises should be those which are generally accepted as true without need of proof. For example, everyone dies, so it is self-evident that "All men are mortal." How, then, would Aristotle deal with the immortality of the human soul? I, for one, can attest to that immortality, since Socrates has, on more that one occasion, kept me up very late at night challenging my assumptions, forcing me to examine the implications of my beliefs, and guiding me in the formulation of new ideas. I would say, in fact, that he's been one of my closest friends over these past several years in prison.

"Dead words," says Aristotle. "You're only reading dead words. Ideas are only what the words mean, and nothing more—like a mathematical equation. Ideas have no life of their own, just as there is no such thing as a 'soul', much less that foolish thing Plato invented called The Idea. All there really is in the world is what you can see, touch, smell, or taste. You dare not challenge my general premise that 'All men are mortal,' unless you can see Socrates, or touch him."

"But, Aristotle," I'd have to reply, "I can see him with my mind's eye; I can touch him with my heart. I reject your hypothesis!"

"Bah!" roars Aristotle. "I have no hypothesis! I only accept the obvious, and you are talking poetry! It's not real!" Then, from across the centuries, the mystic Sir Isaac Newton, rises up to support his beloved Aristotle. *"Hypothesis non fingo!"* ("I make no hypothesis!"), he declares. "It is obvious to anyone with common sense that the universe is a large, empty box in which little hard balls bounce up against each other. That's all there is! Don't bother me with Kepler's silly Platonic notions about the harmony of the spheres or the 'Golden Mean.' That's all religious stuff. It's fine for Sunday morning appearances, but it has no place in science!"

But, of course, both Aristotle and Newton do have an hypothesis—no one, not even an Aristotle, can say or think anything which is not based on some collection of assumptions about the world, some set of axioms. The problem with Aristotle is that, by denying that the mind can create and change its own hypotheses, by reducing the mind to a linear computer-like machine, based on sense perceptions, he thereby refuses to change those axioms that constitute his flawed hypothesis—i.e., he refuses to think.

Plato, on the other hand, recognized that what we see with our eyes is only a reflection of reality. LaRouche often references the discovery by Eratosthenes, in the Third Century B.C., of the curvature of the Earth, as a clear example of Plato's concept of an Idea, which is the unseen reality underlying what we see with our eyes. The Earth appeared flat, from any perspective on Earth. It would be another 2,200 years before man rose far enough above the Earth's surface to see the curvature directly from space. And yet, even in ancient times, it appeared certain (from, for instance, eclipses of the Moon), that the Earth was round. How could one measure what could not be seen?

What Eratosthenes did was to place gnomons (poles which cast a shadow) several hundred miles apart, but on the same latitude, in Alexandria and in Aswan. He then observed the different lengths of the shadows cast by the two gnomons at the same time of day, from sun rays (which are relatively parallel owing to the great distance between the sun and the Earth). From simple geometry, the difference in the angles made by the shadows must be the same as the angle at the center of the Earth, between the radii drawn from the center to the two cities. By using the known distance between the two cities, Eratosthenes easily calculated the circumference of the Earth. His result was 24,500 miles—about 50 miles from the figure we know today!

The creative thinking in this process took place not in the data of observation, but in the conceptualization of the experiment—to measure the invisible as it is reflected in the visible.

Plato's famous Parable of the Cave conveys the same concept. He likened a person governed by sense perceptions to a man in a cave, with his back to the cave opening, who can only see shadows on a far wall, reflections of that which is passing by outside the cave, illuminated by an unknown source of light. To the cave dweller, the shadows are real, since he knows nothing of the source. It is what St. Paul, in his first letter to the Corinthians, refers to as "seeing through a glass darkly." But since man is blessed with reason, he is not limited, as Aristotle claimed, to logical calculations concerning the statistical possibilities of the appearance of shadows—he can make revolutionary discoveries concerning the reality underlying the shadows, if he is willing, at least mentally, to come out of the cave! In that way, he can also come closer to understanding the source of the light itself.

It is this thinking which led St. Augustine to recognize Plato as the philosopher who came closest to the truth of revelation, as viewed by Christianity—that man is created in the image of God as expressed by the "divine spark" of reason. Reason is most free, and most creative, when governed by a love of truth, of God, and of all mankind, that which both Plato and St. Paul called *agapē*.

In my college days, I was always somewhat disconcerted in my study of Plato by the annoying fact that Socrates, as reported by Plato, would repeatedly engage in dialogues in search of the true meaning of Truth, or Justice, or The Good, but simply refused to come up with the answers! This was, of course, the secret of Socrates' assertion that the only thing he knew was that he knew nothing. In discussions with those who believed that they knew the definitive, fixed, dictionary meaning of such profound ideas, Socrates would take their view as a premise, work through its logical implications, deriving a contradiction with other beliefs held by his interlocutors. He then induced a new definition of the concept from his dialogue partner, which appeared to alleviate the contradiction, only to see the revision subjected to the same treatment. Socrates' unstated message was that knowledge does not lie in any one, fixed definition or concept, but in the process of formulating a more perfect hypothesis, or a higher hypothesis. It is through that process, and *only* through that process, that we can know truth, or beauty, or justice—not perfectly, but ever less imperfectly. The perfect form of such concepts (Truth, Beauty) which Plato called the Idea, exists as the universal boundary of the cognitive, creative process itself.

Plato's goal, as expressed by his Socratic dialogues, was not only to teach the method of the higher hypothesis, but to perfect that method. Only by considering an entire series of higher hypotheses and observing the method of perfecting each higher step, each transformation to a higher, more perfect set of axioms, and by mastering and perfecting that process—do we reach what Plato called Hypothesizing the Higher Hypothesis. It is this process which Plato knew as The Good, a concept fairly compared to the God of Christianity. That man is capable of reason, understood in this way, is what, to Plato, proves that man is good by nature—unlike the morally neutral being of Aristotle's *tabula rasa*. Not surprisingly, Plato viewed *all* mankind, regardless of class, race, or gender, as capable of reason, while Aristotle laid the basis for racism and oppression by viewing certain people to be born as slaves, others as masters.

Kepler

It is the Platonic method of hypothesis which laid the basis for the scientific and cultural explosion in the Golden Renaissance, and every significant breakthrough in the past 550 years. Plato sought universal characteristics in things and phenomena as a basis for investigation, rather than the accidental characteristics of sensual appearance, such as linear measure, scent, or color. He recognized that there is a higher order of geometry in the real, physical universe than in the closed, axiomatic structure of Euclid's *Elements*. (Actually, Euclid himself stated forthrightly that the totality of his *Elements* were idealized exercises of the mind, since neither points nor lines exist in the real universe. The entire exercise, while useful in itself, had only one ultimate purpose—to lay the groundwork for the investigation of the real bounding conditions of the physical universe.)

Plato and his school recognized that, in nature, everything which is living or is the creation of a living presence (such as a seashell), is characterized by a certain ratio in its geometric construction, known as the Golden Mean, or the Golden Section. This is the ratio of self-reflexive growth, as observed in the ratio between successive, expanding ridges of a spiral seashell, the rings in the cross section of a tree, or the spacing of leaves on a flower or branch. Those things which are not created by a living process will never reflect the Golden Mean as a general characteristic. This ratio can be precisely calculated, but in nature, the ratio is never exact—rather, the Golden Mean is the bounding condition of the process of growth.

The Golden Mean, however, is best understood as a concept rather than as a number. It is an expression of the fact that, in nature, the biological process of growth takes place as a "one"—i.e., growth is not a linear extension, where the body grows out in one or more "directions," but growth takes place in the body as a whole, as a unified, single entity. The bounding of the measure of the parts (the "many") by the measure of the whole (the "one") is the Golden Mean. This is a concept derived entirely from the laws of nature, not from the axioms of any geometry, Euclidian or otherwise. Rather, the Golden Mean is a "marker" in the physical universe, indicating the existence of life.

Since biological growth, the characteristic of life, is a non-entropic process—i.e., biological growth is not characterized by the dissipation of the energy of the organism, but by the opposite, the tendency towards greater order and higher levels of energy-density throughput—therefore, the Golden Mean can be thought of as a "marker" for "anti-entropy."

To Plato, the crucial centerpiece of geometry was the proof that there exist only five regular polyhedra which can be constructed in space—the so-called five Platonic Solids.* Rather than

* The five Platonic Solids are the tetrahedron (four triangular sides), the cube (six square sides), the octahedron (eight triangular sides), the

seeing this merely as a numerological or geometric oddity (as many cabalistic and related cultists are wont to do), Plato recognized that the existence of five, and only five, regular solids in space constitutes a boundary condition on space itself. There is a shape to space. Space is not simply undifferentiated extension in three directions, but, rather, is defined by those things and phenomena which constitute the universe, and those phenomena conform to a certain higher geometry, or what was later called curvature. Also, since the Platonic Solids can be constructed from the Golden Mean, they are variants on the same bounding conditions which define life and the curvature of space.

(I should note here that, while I earned a Bachelor of Science degree with a major in mathematics at a prestigious New England college, I never even heard of the Golden Mean, nor of the Platonic Solids, throughout my four years of mathematics courses. Even my philosophy professor, Dr. DeLong, who guided my study of Plato and, more vigorously, the Platonists Cantor and Gödel, never mentioned this most profound and scientifically crucial matter in our study of the philosophy of science and mathematics. A most relevant comment on the state of education in America. . . .)

The fact that Plato's concept of the boundaries of space is not just "numerology" is most beautifully demonstrated by two major discoveries—one in the Renaissance, and one quite recently, in the 1980's.

The first of those two great discoveries, based on the Platonic hypothesis concerning the curvature of space, was that of Johannes Kepler, in his 1596 publication, *Mysterium Cosmographicum.*

Kepler, the greatest astronomer in history, was engaged in the study of the solar system, which would later lead him to his three famous planetary laws. It was Kepler who discovered that the planetary orbits were elliptical, rather than circular, such that the curvature of their motion was not constant, but always changing. He also discovered the laws of motion of the planets—laws

---

dodecahedron (12 pentagonal sides), and the icosahedron (20 triangular sides). Euclid's *Elements* culminates in the proof of the uniqueness of these five Platonic solids.

which subsumed the law of gravitation (later falsely credited to cabalist Sir Isaac Newton). Kepler was most interested, from his earliest studies until his death in 1630, in finding the *reason* for the structure of the solar system—not just the laws of motion, as important as they were, but also why the orbits are where they are, rather than someplace else, and why the planets move in the way they do. Believing absolutely in the Platonic hypothesis of The Good, and, as a devoted Christian (although always engaged in fierce polemics with the Aristotelians within his own Lutheran church), he believed that God's creation must express the most beautiful harmonies possible. Far from being a religious "limitation" on his scientific world-view, as the empiricists are quick to describe his religious belief, it was this Platonic/Christian world view which was the bedrock of Kepler's earthshaking discoveries, and of his scientific method in general.

Kepler hypothesized that the reason for the location of the planetary orbits must be found in the boundaries, or curvature, of space, as discovered by Plato in the geometries of the Platonic Solids. Kepler constructed a model of the five Platonic Solids, circumscribing one within the other, with the octahedron at the center, the icosahedron circumscribing the octahedron, followed by the dodecahedron, the tetrahedron, and the cube. He hypothesized that the planets would "fit" in this structure, one on each of the circumscribing spheres between the regular solids—Mercury on the innermost sphere, Venus on the sphere circumscribing the octahedron, the Earth on the sphere circumscribing the icosahedron, and so on, to Saturn on the outermost sphere circumscribing the cube. Calculating the ratios of the radii of the circumscribing spheres in this nested structure, Kepler compared these ratios to the ratios of the orbits of the six known planets, discovering, to his great delight, a close correspondence. Although the first publication of his discovery, in 1596, used calculations for the planetary orbits considered as circular, he reworked his findings following his discovery of the elliptical shape of the orbits, obtaining a more complex, but even more beautiful, correspondence.

The known universe was thus shown to be not empty, infinitely extended space, but a bounded space, with a structure—what would later be called quantized space, with a non-constant curvature. Certain places in the structure of the solar system were more conducive to becoming planetary orbits than others, reflecting an harmonic ordering consistent with the structure of the five Platonic solids, such that when the planets were formed—however that happened—they tended toward these specific orbits. They could be called "least-action" orbits, since there was a tendency to find a stable orbit at these particular locations. To Kepler, his discovery was a demonstration of the infinite wonder and beauty of the Creation, and a further proof that the truths of this infinite universe were accessible to man through the power of reason.

It is of note here, that when Sir Isaac Newton plagiarized Kepler's planetary laws, in formulating his law of gravitation, he actually weakened Kepler's discoveries, by discarding precisely these beautiful symmetries, thereby removing the *cause* for the structure of the solar system—and, by implication, the cause for the structure of any gravitational field—in favor of a linear, algebraic equation. Newton's equations were useful in mechanical calculations within the system discovered by Kepler, but were incapable of explaining crucial anomalies in the system, and were stripped of that power in Kepler's discoveries which would be useful for further discoveries. The Higher Hypothesis, God and Truth, were removed.

Dr. Moon's Platonic Model

Kepler's discovery, that the solar system is governed by the curvature defined by the Golden Mean and the Platonic Solids, has a most intriguing, and crucial, implication. Since the Golden Mean is a "marker" for living processes within the biophysical realm on Earth, and since nonliving matter does not reflect this "marker," it must be concluded that the realm of astrophysics (the measure of "outer space") is in some sense a "living" process! Putting aside the question of whether or not there exist forms of life beyond the earthly realm, it is generally the case that planets, asteroids, stars, and other matter in the physical universe are non-organic—and yet, the geometry of the evolving physical universe as a whole conforms to a lawful principle which is a fundamental characteristic of life! We can go further. Not only astrophysics, but also *microphysics*, the physics of atomic particles, has the characteristic "marker" of life, although atomic particles are certainly not organic. I was a witness to a most beautiful discovery of a proof of this fact in the 1980's, in Leesburg, Virginia.

One of the primary scientists responsible for the successful development of nuclear fission reactions in the famous Manhattan Project of the 1940's, Dr. Robert Moon, emeritus professor from the University of Chicago, became a close and dear friend of Lyndon LaRouche and many of his associates during the 1970's, and remained a close collaborator in all our political, scientific, and cultural endeavors until his death in 1989. Dr. Moon, in collaboration with Lyn and Larry Hecht, was to extend Kepler's astrophysical discovery to the micro-physical domain, by developing a model of the atomic structure of the elements of the periodic table, based upon nested, interlocking configurations of the Platonic Solids! (Larry Hecht, one of my close friends and collaborators, was also one of my co-defendants in the Virginia "show trials" against the organization. He was incarcerated in the Virginia prison system for 5½ years, and is now free on parole.)

I first met Dr. Moon at a lecture he presented for the organization's membership in New York City in 1976. This old, wild-looking scientist, with pure white hair flowing over his shoulders, was always accompanied by his wife, a victim of multiple sclerosis. Slumped over in her wheelchair, but mentally alert, she would be wheeled by Dr. Moon to the front of the auditorium for any conference he attended, with a display of love which had a deep and lasting impression on all around him.

On that day in New York, in 1976, he spoke on his own scientific work and ideas, and his admiration for LaRouche's dedication to a renewed scientific renaissance. But what I recall most were his final remarks, approximately as follows: "I must add here, in closing, that I recognize in this organization, and in each of you whom I've met, a quality of love for the truth which is sadly lacking in the world today—not only among scientists, but wherever you go. That places an enormous responsibility on your shoulders. Our future, the success or failure of our civilization, will rest disproportionately on you few individuals. This makes me believe it necessary to say something that I know many of you don't want to hear. Many of you think that religion is a tool of those who are opposed to science, who want to keep people down. You may think that there is no God, or that there's no place for God in politics or science. But let me tell you that what we have been discovering is God, and that I know He lives in us through our love of truth, and our search for the principles that govern the universe. Please think about it, and don't just laugh at this crazy old man for talking foolishness."

We all laughed with him, but there was no one who was not deeply moved by his impassioned appeal. It was this speech which rekindled my own long-ignored interest in mastering the principles of science, and provoked a reconsideration of the "free-thinker" mentality of many of us who had accepted the atheism or agnosticism of the 1960's counterculture.

After we moved our operational headquarters from New York to Leesburg, Virginia, in 1985, Dr. Moon spent much of his time in Leesburg, staying at the home of Larry Hecht and his wife, Marje, the managing editor of *Fusion* magazine. There, in the evenings, they explored Dr. Moon's hypothesis, that the beautiful symmetries of the periodic table of elements could be made intelligible—that a reason for the symmetries could be found—by demonstrating the coherence between the number of electrons in the electron orbits of each element, and a nest of circumscribed Platonic Solids, precisely as Kepler had shown for the structure of the solar systems. Together, Larry and Dr. Moon constructed wire-mesh and cardboard models of the solids, placing the electrons of each element of the periodic table on the edges or vertices of the figures, building up from the hydrogen atom to the heaviest elements. Every day, when Larry came into the office, he would bring with him some new configuration of cubes, octagons, etc., and excitedly relate the new developments in Dr. Moon's hypothesis. They ultimately completed a model, called the Moon-Hecht model, which demonstrated the reason for the various special relationships between certain elements, and groups of elements, which had long been known from observation, but without an understanding of the causes. The potential that this discovery could open doors to the still unsolved problems of physics—including especially the most fundamental questions regarding the nature of the atomic particles—was exhilarating.

More broadly, the discovery meant that, in addition to the geometry of astrophysics, the geometry of microphysics also cohered with the "marker" of life—the Golden Mean and the Platonic Solids. The physical universe as a whole, as also the "stuff" of microphysics, although not composed of living substance, nonetheless is "living" in some sense, reflecting the universal characteristic of self-developing, anti-entropic growth.

This also says something fundamental about the inanimate objects in the world: Although, as we've seen, non-living matter does not reflect the Golden Mean "marker" of anti-entropic life in its own visible geometry, it nonetheless is part of the anti-entropic process of the astrophysical universe as a whole.

Inanimate objects also reflect an anti-entropic process on the microphysical scale, at the level of the invisible, subatomic structure. Thus, when things in the physical universe are viewed with the mind's eye—as part of the whole universe, considered in its totality, rather than considering merely the visible sense-certain aspects of things—then we see that anti-entropy is a fundamental law of nature. Maxwell's Second Law of Thermodynamics, the so-called Law of Entropy, bites the dust.

I must mention here, in anticipation of my later work in comparative studies of Eastern and Western science and philosophy, that the "accepted" scholarly histories since the Enlightenment have viewed the above conclusion—that astrophysics and microphysics reflect the negative entropy of life—as an anti-rational, mystical, religiously motivated delusion. Confronting such "experts" with the scientific evidence confirming this conclusion usually has no effect in correcting their mere opinion, since they are so unwilling to acknowledge that they are functioning according to axiomatic assumptions which blind them to such demonstrable scientific evidence.

[7]

Airport Organizing and LaRouche's SDI

My sister Margaret finally joined the organization in 1978. On an earlier visit to Cleveland, Margaret had played a Brahms intermezzo for me on the piano, which bowled me over. I was, at that time, not so familiar with Brahms, but she played with great clarity and grace, and I was deeply moved. I told her that she should put aside her self doubts, since anyone who could convey profound ideas through music could easily find the intellectual strength needed to master any other discipline. She had been studying our literature and attending some local meetings, but I encouraged her to move to New York with me, and to join our organization. She agreed.

She approached her first organizing deployment with a certain trepidation, uncertain she was prepared to defend the ideas when challenged by strangers. She joined me and my Westchester co-organizer, Patricia Noble, at a card table in front of the Department of Motor Vehicles in White Plains, one of our regular sites in Westchester County. The deployment was focussed on our "War on Drugs" work. After about an hour, I noticed that Margaret had wandered down the sidewalk with a woman she'd met, engaged in a very long conversation. Pat and I joked about it, since it was a common problem in organizing, to get caught up in unproductive arguments with people who liked to talk, but not necessarily to think. We decided to let her learn the hard way, and allowed her go on for nearly an hour.

She finally returned, with a sprightly gait and a beaming smile. Not only had she sold a subsciption, but she had recruited a renowned pianist, Bodil Frolund, a Dane who had once accompanied the great Danish tenor Axel Schötz, and who still performed professionally. Mrs. Frolund would become one of our closest musical collaborators and friends, playing concerts and helping in our projects for many years. Margaret not only got over her initial fright, but found a friend, a teacher, and a political ally for the organization, in her first day "on the job."

After a few weeks, Margaret was confident enough to move to New Jersey, away from brother Mike, to organize full time in the New York/New Jersey region. She soon caught the eye of one of the leading members in the New Jersey organization, Elliot Greenspan, and by 1982 they were man and wife. Not for that reason alone, Elliot would become one of my closest friends and comrades over the subsequent years.

Another historic change occurred during this period—the marriage of Lyndon LaRouche and Helga Zepp in December 1977. At the time, I knew of Helga only as the head of our organization in Germany. She was to have a dramatic influence upon the organization, both through her joint work with Lyn on world affairs, and through her intervention into the intellectual and cultural life of the organization. She would also have a particularly profound impact on my own life and work.

Helga's education, in Trier, had led her to a deep love of the great German poet Friedrich Schiller, and to a study of the person largely responsible for launching the Golden Renaissance in the 15th Century, Cardinal Nicholas of Cusa. Both of these giants of Western civilization had been practically removed from history books in the United States—even though, as we would learn, Schiller had earlier been adopted by the generation of the American Revolution, and for over 100 years thereafter, as the poet of the Revolution, "The Poet of Freedom." Later, in 1984, under Helga's leadership, a new institution was founded, the Schiller Institute, to promote the political, scientific, and cultural alliance of sovereign nations, as captured by Schiller's insistence that one must be, at once, both a patriot of one's nation and a citizen of the world.

Although I was otherwise unfamiliar with Schiller, I knew that Beethoven's Choral (9th) Symphony, which had played such a major role in my life, was set to Schiller's poem "An die Freude" ("Ode to Joy"). Imprinted in my heart forever are the words from the first stanza, which always evoke within me a joyful memory of the entire symphony, as if peformed in a single moment:

> Freude, shöner Götterfunken,
> Tochter aus Elysium,
> Wir betreten, feuertrunken,
> Himmlische, dein Heiligtum.
> Deine Zauber binden wieder,
> Was die Mode streng geteilt.
> Alle Menschen werden Brüder
> Wo dein sanfter Flügel weilt.

(My translation, perhaps not the best, but the one I carry in my mind: "O, Joy, beautiful spark of God / Daughter of Elysium./ Drunk by fire, we enter / Thy heavenly sanctuary. /Thy power binds together / That which custom pulls apart. / All men are brothers / Where thy soft wings abide.")

The Schiller Institute adopted, as its theme, the famous "Rütli Oath" from Schiller's play *Wilhelm Tell,* taken by compatriots of the cantons of Switzerland in revolt against tyrannical rule. The oath clearly reflects Schiller's great debt to the American Revolution:

> No! There is a limit to a tyrant's power,
> When the oppressed can find no justice, when
> The burden grows unbearable—he reaches
> With hopeful courage up unto the heavens
> And seizes hither his eternal rights,
> Which hang above, inalienable
> And indestructible as stars themselves—
> The primal state of nature reappears,
> Where man stands opposite his fellow man—

As last resort, when not another means
Is of avail, the sword is given him—
The highest of all goods we may defend
From violence.—Thus stand we before our country,
Thus we stand before our wives, before our children!

One concept of Schiller's which Helga emphasized above all others was that of the "beautiful soul" ("*schöne Seele*"). Schiller spent much of his short life refuting the reigning philosopher of his era, Immanuel Kant, the spokesman for the Enlightenment. Genius can not be explained, argued Kant—in fact, reason itself can not be comprehended except as a form of formal, Aristotelian logic. Kant, at least, opposed the extreme libertine forms of ideology, such as those of Thomas Hobbes and Jeremy Bentham, who rejected morality altogether. But Kant located morality only within a formal sense of duty, an intentional suppression of the sensuous in favor of a submission to duty defined as a kind of "*Zeitgeist*," a spirit of the times—like today's "political correctness." In other words, he saw freedom and necessity as opposed to each other, and he could perceive of necessity only as a giving up of freedom. As Helga once quoted Heinrich Heine: "Kant's problem with understanding genius was that he wasn't one himself!"

Genius can, in fact, be understood, and even "taught." It lies in the *equality* of freedom and necessity, in the equality of truth and beauty. Schiller showed that the spiritual realm of creative genius, which is granted to all mankind as a potential, is part of our sensuous nature—that the human soul is at the same time spiritual and sensual. (This is the essence of the Christian notion of the Trinity, in which Christ partakes of both a divine and a human nature in one person, connected by *agapē*, the Holy Spirit.) Schiller ridiculed Kant for wanting to separate the spiritual from the sensual, to treat the physical, material realm as filthy, corrupted, inherently evil. That was the gnostic view, the view of the ancient Manichean and Nestorian heresies which St. Augustine and his followers battled in the 4th and 5th Centuries.

Schiller ridiculed the Kantian "imperative" to duty as lacking totally the creative spark of reason, which alone makes man truly

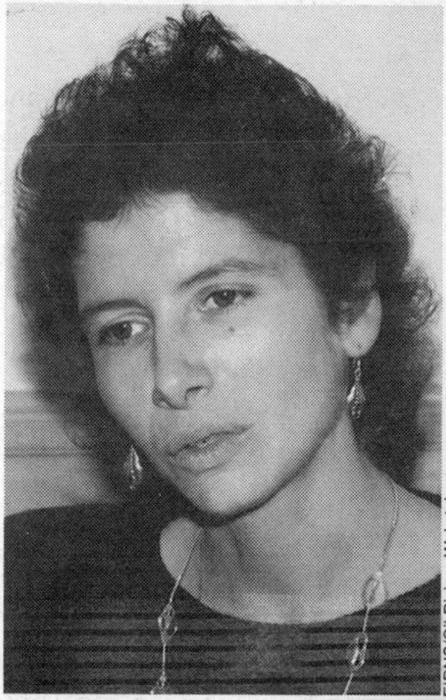

EIRNS/Gil Riviere-Wekstein

These are the two pictures I have taped to the prison wall over my desk: my wife Gail, and Rembrandt's painting "St. Paul in Captivity." The photo of Gail was taken during a press interview in Paris in January 1990, and, from the pucker of her lips, she is clearly speaking French.

Rembrandt van Rijn, "St. Paul in Captivity" (1627). This is my postcard copy, and the scratches and tape marks have accumulated over years in prison.

National Archives

President John F. Kennedy greets Peace Corps volunteers at the White House, August 1962.

Peace Corps days in Thailand, 1969-1971.

Courtesy of Michael Billington

That's me, tinged by the counterculture . . .

. . . and as a young mathematics instructor.

Courtesy of Michael Billington

Courtesy of Michael Billington

"I had absolutely no doubt that, should the U.S. back away from the kind of global development policies which were identified with JFK, it would be both morally reprehensible for the U.S., and disastrous for the Third World."

Courtesy of Michael Billington

Ruth O'Mara Billington

Joseph Alford Billington II

Mom and Dad, c. 1945.

The 1950's Billington clan: Al and Ruth, with (l. to r.) Dan, Pete, Joe, Mike, and Margaret.

Courtesy of Ruth Billington

Christmas in East Cleveland, 1961. Left to right: Joe, Pete, Mike (rear); Marg, Dan (front).

Courtesy of Michael Billington

Marg shows off for brothers (l. to r.) Pete, Dan, and Mike.

Alan Richards/Courtesy of the Archives of the Institute for Advanced Study

Mathematician Kurt Gödel (r.) receives the Einstein Prize, delivered by Albert Einstein, in March 1951. My interest in philosophy was sparked in college by Gödel's refutation of the work of Bertrand Russell.

Library of Congress

Bertrand Russell. Lyndon LaRouche calls him "the most evil man of the 20th Century." I ran into him decades later, in my study of China.

Political organizing in New York City, 1973-1975.

Welfare rights activist Jeanette Washington, and NCLC members Tony Chaitkin (center) and Leif Johnson (far left), march in their campaign for City Council President, Mayor, and Comptroller.

EIRNS

EIRNS

Gathering signatures at a New York City unemployment center.

EIRNS

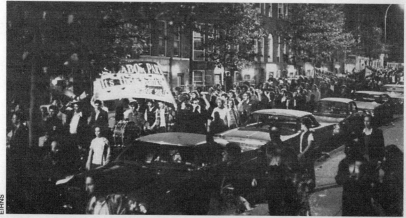

Torchlight parade through Harlem. Our slogan was, "It's the banks, or us!"

United Nations/T. Chen

Dr. Frederick Wills, then Minister of State for Foreign Affairs of Guyana, addresses the U.N. Security Council, June 5, 1975.

EIRNS/Carlos Wesley

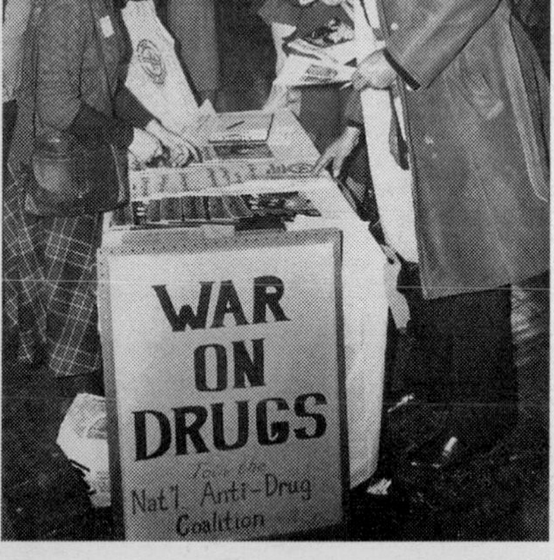

EIRNS/Carlos de Hoyos

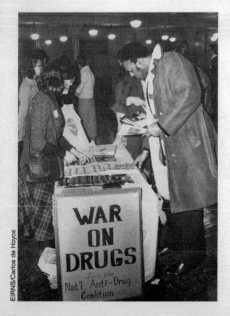

The National Anti-Drug Coalition was launched in 1979, and "War on Drugs" magazine in 1980. Here are organizing scenes from the early 1980's in New York City (left), West Orange, N.J. (above, with my sister Marg), and Brooklyn, N.Y. (facing page).

Control of the drug trade by the London-centered banks was documented in EIR's exposé "Dope, Inc." The book went through many printings and editions, in both English and Spanish.

EIRNS/Stuart Lewis

Campaigning outside Sterling National Bank, February 1982. The sign says, "Drug Links Exposed!"

EIRNS/Stuart Lewis

EIRNS/Dave Peterson

Above: Airport organizing, Boston, 1987. My friend Mike Leppig devised the famous slogan, "Feed Jane Fonda to the Whales!"

I was emcee at Marg's wedding to Elliot Greenspan in June 1982. Right: Directing an impromptu chorus. Elliot is in the center, with Marg behind.

Courtesy of Margaret Greenspan

Courtesy of Margaret Greenspan

Abscam target Senator Harrison "Pete" Williams delivers a prophetic toast: "I have seen how Elliot, like many others who work with LaRouche, has demonstrated the kind of courage and selfless commitment to the truth that is needed to get our nation back on track. . . . Keep it up, and I assure you, you'll be indicted!"

Courtesy of Margaret Greenspan

Marg plays piano four-hands with her teacher Bodil Frolund. Mom is seated at the left.

Maestro José Briano.

EIRNS

Courtesy of Margaret Greenspan

That's me as a fledgling chorus conductor . . .

. . . and chorus member, in the 1980's.

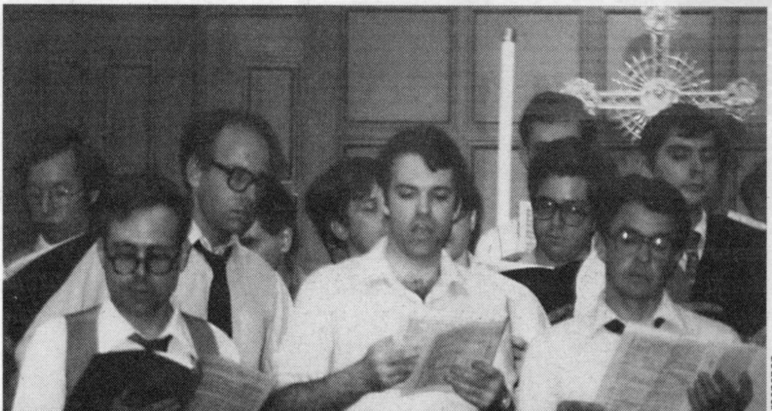
Courtesy of Margaret Greenspan

Courtesy of Margaret Greenspan

Gail and I were married on Dec. 2, 1984. Elliot was Best Man, and our friend Linda de Hoyos was Matron of Honor. Since the wedding was held at the Columbia University Chapel, I thought it only appropriate to adopt the old revolutionary pose of the 1968 Columbia Student Strike.

human, and alone can change the world for the better. Rather than throwing off the sensual nature, to make the spiritual more pure, Schiller insisted that the sensual must be brought into unity with the spiritual, must unite most intimately with "the God within us," in Schiller's words. The "beautiful soul," said Schiller, finds joy in the dictates of reason.

The scientist, like the statesman, must be guided by the same passion for truth as the artist, since only that unquenchable passion can guide the mind towards the discovery of principles of nature and of man. The mind works according to the laws of the universe—in fact, it is the highest expression of those laws within the physical universe. Therein lies beauty, the glorious harmony of human reason with the laws of the universe, both known and unknown, which makes possible man's mastery of the universe, and is the source of true joy—"*Freude, schöne Götterfunken, Tochter aus Elysium.*"

Schiller's inspiration is heard in the final couplet of John Keats's "Ode on a Grecian Urn." "Beauty is truth, truth, beauty, that is all/Ye know on earth, and all ye need to know."

He who acts on the basis of this passion for truth, is Schiller's beautiful soul. Like the Good Samaritan, he does not do good to achieve a reward, nor to conform to duty in the sense of "popular opinion," but because, Schiller said, "he has taken God into his will."

Helga taught us to love Schiller, and called on us all to strive for the *schöne Seele.*

★ ★ ★

In 1978, we began sending some of our field teams to the major airports around the country, setting up booths, or literature tables, with a set of signs, calling on travellers to subscribe to *Fusion* and EIR (*Executive Intelligence Review*), our weekly intelligence journal. Soon after my November 1978, Congressional election campaign, I was asked to join these "airport squads." I primarily worked at the three New York City airports, but occasionally I'd travel around the country, opening new sites in major cities where we had no offices.

I soon found myself in a semi-permanent "partnership" with another organizer in the New York local, Michael Leppig. Mike is an extremely energetic fellow with a strong sense of the dramatic—including an astonishing ability to provoke laughter with pungent irony, breaking through nearly anyone's mental blocks. Tall and lanky, with big eyes, a broad grin, and a tendency to talk with his whole body, he'd often have people in stitches in the process of getting them "on board" with a subscription. In 1995, when I first saw a film with Hollywood wacko Jim Carrey, I thought out loud to myself: "There but for the grace of God goes Mike Leppig."

Mike was the creator of many of our most famous slogans from the late 1970's and early 1980's. These were the days of the anti-nuclear antics of Jimmy Carter, Jane Fonda, and Ted Kennedy (Ted, at least, has more recently corrected himself), and the emergence of "politically correct" liberal posturing, as the 1960's counterculture generation moved into positions of prominence in "acceptable society." Many of Mike's pithy slogans rapidly captured the American imagination: "More people have died in Ted Kennedy's car than in nuclear power plants"; "Feed Jane Fonda to the whales"; "Warning: I don't brake for liberals." We began a thriving bumper sticker business, although we stuck to a policy that the bumper stickers were strictly for the purpose of "bribery"—no subscription, no bumper sticker, no matter how much money was offered. We were building a political machine, so making people read and think was more important than sloganeering, or income. But humor challenges assumptions—the first step in the thinking process. And we had a lot of fun in the process.

Fusion magazine was our first line of attack, demanding that science be treated as the most important *political* issue in the nation. Mike Leppig and I would sell, on an average, about eight to ten subscriptions to *Fusion* each day, and perhaps one or two EIR subs.

Mike and I occasionally spent a few weeks out of town, at the Houston or Denver airports. There was still money being made in the domestic oil business in those days, and Volcker's policies had not yet destroyed the western farmers and ranchers. People literally crowded around our booths, desperate for someone who could make sense out of the escalating destruction of the economy, and who was willing and able to fight for a revival of American System ideas and policies. We had days in Denver where up to 40 people would sign up for *Fusion*.

The airport deployments were my primary assignment for more than two years, between 1979 and 1981—and I enjoyed every minute of it. All of our political organizing—even the hot, dirty, exhausting deployments selling newspapers at traffic islands—was exhilarating work, demanding the kind of continual creative engagement, with all types of people, which stimulates the spirit and satisfies the soul. But the airport organizing, I must admit, was so much fun that I occasionally felt a bit guilty. We pushed ourselves very hard, sunrise to well after sunset, and there were tedious days, provocations and other aggravations. But we met fascinating people—businessmen, farmers, politicians, artists, prominent statesmen from around the world, scholars, and, of course, many average citizens. Humor and irony were our primary weapons. As in all organizing, the best and most lasting results came from successfully challenging fundamental assumptions, leading people to confront personal prejudices, while also forcing them to recognize that something *must* be done to change the direction of national policy, and that effective solutions *do* exist.

We struck a nerve with this "airport" offensive. Our campaigns appealed to the traditional, pro-growth conservative business layer in America (including the right-wing nuts, although they couldn't think past the bumper stickers), but it also captivated a layer of middle-class Americans, including many Democrats, who were increasingly disgusted with the takeover of "traditional" politics by the counterculture ideology of the 1960's.

We soon established a broad layer of Americans as a functioning network, who would stop by regularly at our tables around the country, and take material to distribute to their friends and associates. Foreign diplomats and businessmen met us at the airports and spread our literature through the corridors of power on every continent.

We also set up a more rigorous operation to recontact the flood of new subscribers by phone. New contacts at the airport were told to read the **EIR,** in particular, and to expect a call. This let them know we were serious. We learned over time that the vast majority of our new contacts had indeed read the material by the time we reached them for follow-up.

In retrospect, I recognize that during that period there was a last, desperate attempt by many who thought of themselves as American patriots and traditionalists, to return the U.S. to a position of leadership, in nation-building, scientific excellence, and moral responsibility, but without wanting to change the entire system. Some of these people thought back to Franklin Roosevelt, or at least to John Kennedy, as the last representatives of that ideal. Most Republicans were nostalgic for the days of Eisenhower and Nixon, but many also acknowledged that the memory only "seemed" good in comparison to the "Dope in the White House," Jimmy Carter. There was a non-partisan impulse towards constructing a new, pro-growth conservatism, which converged in 1980 to elect Ronald Reagan.

Our focus throughout that period was to demonstrate to Americans that the idiocies of the Carter Administration were not simply a Democratic Party problem, but that these "post-industrial-society" policies were created and supported by the Rockefeller wing of the Republican Party as well—the Anglophile "fiscal conservatives" of the CFR and the Trilateral Commission, who controlled Paul Volcker at the Federal Reserve Bank. We tried to orient people's thinking towards the battle for science, development, and education, against the "New Age" leadership of both parties. This, we emphasized, required that people join our intelligence network, beginning with subscriptions to our publications.

★ ★ ★

Our impact on world politics escalated through the early 1980's. LaRouche's economic forecasts and proposals were closely followed in Washington and other capitals around the world. In several cases, his ideas influenced critical policy decisions by nations in crisis, such as the nationalization of the banks by Mexican President José López Portillo in 1981. LaRouche's proven authority in economics was coupled with his strategic warning, that the unfolding economic breakdown would bring the world to the brink of World War III, despite the diplomatic fantasies and media hype about "détente" and "disarmament."

In 1977, LaRouche initiated a proposal to address both the economic and the strategic crises, simultaneously, through a massive research and development project for a new kind of strategic defense, centered on space-based "beam weapons." The beam weapons program would be based on the same principle as JFK's Apollo Project—while achieving a strategic objective (in Kennedy's case, reaching the Moon), the project would also push forward on the frontiers of human knowledge.

The political fight for LaRouche's idea took off during the 1980 New Hampshire Presidential primary election, when Democratic candidate LaRouche introduced the idea to Republican candidate Ronald Reagan. During the next two years, President Reagan became convinced of the necessity of LaRouche's proposal, leading to his famous address to the nation on March 23, 1983, announcing the SDI (Strategic Defense Initiative). That historic decision, and the Soviet rejection of the offer to collaborate, led to the collapse of the Soviet empire, despite the fact that the SDI itself was sabotaged by Bush and his allies within the Reagan Administration.

★ ★ ★

Although California Governor Ronald Reagan had a significant base of support as he entered the New Hampshire primary, he was being painted with a right-wing brush by the Eastern Establishment wing of the Republican Party, the so-called Rockefeller Republicans. Their preferred choice was George Herbert Walker Bush. Bush, who had never been elected to anything in his life, was entirely the creation of the Averell Harriman banking empire. His father, Prescott Bush, had been a partner in Brown Brothers Harriman in the 1930's and 1940's, when that firm was instrumental in bringing Adolf Hitler to power in Germany. Young George was carefully groomed, and appointments were arranged—a vacant Congressional seat, head of the CIA, and a diplomatic post in China—for the banker's boy.

With Jimmy Carter a certain loser on the Democratic ticket, the Eastern Establishment wanted one of their own on the Republican side, to keep things "in the Families." However, if the discredited Carter/Mondale Administration could be shown to have been carrying out Trilateral Commission and CFR policy, then George Bush would be vulnerable on the same account. This, LaRouche accomplished, with an uncompromising exposure of the fact that Carter and Bush had the same "mother," while counterposing his own vision of an American System approach to rebuilding the nation's strategic, economic, and moral strength.

Over time, we were able to bring Bush's Trilateral connection into public focus, despite desperate efforts in the media to ridicule the issue as a "conspiracy theory" from "fringe candidates." The attempt to portray Bush as the "safe," more moderate alternative to the "radical" Reagan, fell apart.

Reagan himself, although he would not publicly attack the Trilateral Commission, did not allow himself to be baited into denouncing LaRouche. At one of the joint candidate debates, LaRouche and Reagan sat together at the speakers table, engaging in dialogue throughout the event. Soon afterwards, Reagan was given a loaded question at a press conference, about "fringe candidates." Reagan shocked the media hounds by stating clearly that, while some of the "minor" candidates were not serious, others, "such as Lyndon LaRouche, for instance," were making a very important contribution to the political debate, which was of great value to the democratic process. Although the press, as expected, blacked out this response, the radar screens at the London and Wall Street establishment institutions registered a major penetration of their controlled election environment.

Reagan's New Hampshire victory convinced Republicans (and many Democrats) across the nation that he was a viable candidate, and that speaking openly in support of progress, science, technology, and morality had not yet been fully abandoned in America.

Just as important, George Bush was crushed in New Hampshire, and the LaRouche method was widely recognized as the primary cause. The Trilateral Commission stood badly bruised by our exposure, and neither the Eastern Establishment nor their boy George would ever forgive LaRouche for spoiling their party.

The remainder of the campaign period was marked by a concerted drive by the establishment to contain Reagan, and to force a compromise on the question of his Vice Presidential choice. Their success in getting Bush on the ticket would prove to be decisive in President Reagan's ultimate failure in the White House.

Despite Reagan's personal limitations, he possessed a healthy dose of the scientific and moral optimism which once governed the thoughts and actions of most Americans. The belief that man could meet any challenge and solve any problem, carried with it a rejection of the cynical "hedonistic calculus" of the British liberal philosophers, those who treated man only as a beast of passion and desire, governed by no higher goal than the attainment of personal pleasure and the avoidance of pain. In Reagan's case, although he knew little about British philosophy, he recognized the danger inherent in the moral indifferentism and hedonism in the liberal ideology of the Eastern Establishment, and in the "me generation" of existentialist baby boomers who had turned California into a psychedelic play-pen for counter-cultural freaks.

Unfortunately, this worthy sentiment did not extend to an understanding of economic science. Reagan's view of entrepreneurial capitalism was shaped by his friends in the retail business, who thought only in terms of "buy cheap, sell dear," and the free trade shibboleths of the London and Wall Street monetarists. Such a "merchant" mentality had nothing to do with the problems of building and maintaining an industrial economy or the national infrastructure required for a modern nation-state. Trapped in the false choice between "laissez-faire, free trade, and deregulation" on the one hand, and "socialist, big government welfare state" on the other, he chose the former.

Nonetheless, LaRouche's ideas on space-based laser and particle-beam missile defense, and on some other issues, had captured Reagan's imagination.

Following the election, several members of Reagan's transition team provided an open door to LaRouche, and to a small group of our intelligence staff whom LaRouche called on to represent him in discussions with the government-to-be.

While LaRouche hammered away at the economic questions, administration officials were most anxious to get LaRouche's input on two specific issues: strategic missile defense and drugs. On drugs, the Reagan team was very much aware that our Anti-Drug Coalition, together with EIR's publication of *Dope, Inc.*, had shut down the stampede of drug legalization legislation across the country, while focussing attention on the role of the British and the international banks in controlling the drug trade. Reagan created a new office of "Drug Czar," and, over the coming years, followed our intelligence closely, especially in regard to Ibero-America.

The administration moved tentatively on two crucial fronts in the War on Drugs: Support for nationalist forces in Ibero-America against the narco-terrorist armies and their international backers; and, secondly, efforts to identify and prosecute drug-laundering in the banking system—including U.S. banks and their branches overseas. We were at the center of this effort, providing crucial intelligence and direction, while trying to convince the President that success required a no-holds-barred offensive against the Anglo-Canadian drug bankers and their American partners. The board of directors of Dope, Inc., which included several members of Reagan's cabinet (Don Regan, in particular, had been CEO of Merrill Lynch), were not pleased. As we shall see, George Bush, Henry Kissinger, and their favorite Section Eight, Col. Oliver North, ran a protection racket for the drug cartels in Ibero-America, while Don Regan and the corrupt bureaucracy in the Justice Department ran cover for the international drug banks. Not surprisingly, these were the same individuals who ran the political and legal witch-hunt against LaRouche and the NCLC. President Reagan's anti-drug efforts were to be defeated, and ultimately degenerated into Nancy Reagan's pathetic "Just Say No" sloganeering.

President Reagan was even more enthusiastic about LaRouche's ideas on beam-weapon defense. To convince him to adopt it as official policy, we needed to organize significant portions of the U.S. population, of other governments, and of the scientific community.

LaRouche's beam defense proposal took aim precisely at the potential to break the British-controlled "condominium" of the Cold War. Both the Soviet "Marxist" economy and the Western "free-market" economy were heading rapidly towards collapse and depression, he warned, and thus, also, towards war. The MAD ("Mutually Assured Destruction") doctrine could, at best, postpone such a military conflict, but could not prevent it. Were U.S. and Soviet scientists to join forces in the development of beam weapons, to mutually defend against nuclear war, the science-driver aspects of the renewed dedication to technological progress and optimism would simultaneously contribute to solving the economic crises on both sides.

We presented forums on the beam defense proposal in Japan, Europe, Ibero-America, and throughout the U.S. At one such forum in New York City, in 1981, I was manning the literature table outside the conference room when two young Russians came out of the room and began asking me questions.

"Why shouldn't we consider this beam weapons proposal to be a threat to the Soviet Union?" one of them asked me. I asked who they were, and they somewhat hesitatingly told me they were from the Soviet Embassy.

I explained that if both sides had such defense capabilities, then the threat of war through strategic miscalculation would be eliminated. "Rather than the current impotent posturing about disarmament," I said, "which you know is meaningless in regard to the potential for war, why not mutually develop technological defenses? Then we can both get on with the application of the new technologies which will emerge from the project to achieve what we both need—global development."

"Why should we want to see the U.S. develop its economy? Why should we trust the U.S.? What if the U.S. developed them first, pinned down our missiles, and threatened to attack? Why not agree to not build space-based weapons?"

Their questions came rapidly, and with increasing intensity. Never had I been so conscious of our role as international statesmen, speaking for the long-lost tradition of America as nation-builder. I concurred with them that trusting the U.S. was difficult, after years of Kissinger's duplicity about peace and disarmament, covering for IMF destruction of economies worldwide. Only mutual commitments to science and technology, not promises to *limit* science and technology, could serve as a basis for actual trust.

Although I was intrigued by the attention from Soviet diplomats (or intelligence agents), I recognized the seriousness of the exchange, and asked them to wait while I invited the appropriate spokesman to meet with them. They readily agreed.

I later learned that during this period LaRouche was engaged in a series of formal meetings with a high-level spokesman for the Soviet government, acting as a "back channel" between the Reagan Administration and the Soviet leadership on the issue of beam defense.

LaRouche has publicly described the last of these meetings, in February 1983. The Soviet official reported that he had conveyed LaRouche's proposals in detail to the Soviet government, and that, although they concurred on much of the analysis, and on the importance of both beam defense and research on new physical principles, the Soviet Union still would not agree to the proposal. The U.S. enjoyed an advantage in technological potential and funding availability, the Soviets believed, and any attempt to keep up with the U.S. pace would bankrupt their economy. It were better to ban such development, through a continuation of the disarmament process. In any case, he told LaRouche, the Soviets had been assured by their contacts within the Democratic Party that the beam defense policy would never be adopted. Besides opposition in the Congress, he said, there were those within the administration who would prevent Reagan from implementing the proposal.

But on March 23, 1983, President Reagan did adopt the policy, and in precisely the form proposed by LaRouche—despite extensive maneuvering within the White House to prevent the President from including the proposal in that historic, national live telecast to the nation.

The March 23 SDI speech marked a singularity, a discontinuity in the course of history. The preconditions were met for a total transformation of the economy, ending the post-1966 devolution into a "post-industrial society," and reviving America's technological optimism. The battle now moved to the economic sphere—would President Reagan extend his collaboration with LaRouche into the realm of economic policies? Would the President respond to the emerging financial crash by creating a new national credit mechanism to replace the bankrupt Federal Reserve System, and mobilize other nations to hold a new "Bretton Woods" conference, to replace the IMF and the World Bank?

We had reached what Friedrich Schiller called the "*punctum saliens*"—the salient moment in Classical tragedy where the protagonist is confronted with a crucial decision, in which courageous and resolute action can bring victory, but where the failure to make the required change, to break from his own failed preconceptions, at that singular moment, would lock in certain doom.

Were Ronald Reagan better trained in Classical tragedy, and less in Hollywood westerns, he might have been capable of carrying through on the enormous potential of the SDI initiative.

Following President Reagan's March 23 speech, the organization set out to educate and activate the population, keeping in mind the lessons of Classical tragedy. The *punctum saliens* was upon the human race, and while the crucial decisions would be made by a few leading figures, everyone had a role to play in this real-life drama.

For the first 24 hours following Reagan's announcement, the enemy was in disarray, caught off guard by the President's unexpected independence of action. When the media scrambled to find out who could provide the background on this surprising development, they were told by many officials, truthfully, to look to the Fusion Energy Foundation. As a result, the press barraged the FEF office with inquiries, shattering (temporarily) the media-wide blackout rule against LaRouche. One national network sent a TV crew to the FEF offices. Paul Gallagher, Executive Director of the FEF (and later one of my co-defendants, now serving a 34-year sentence in the Virginia prison system),* was given national TV and radio coverage explaining the details and potentials of the President's program. Across the country and around the world, calls of congratulations poured in, from political leaders and average citizens, who had followed our efforts for over six years to implement the beam weapon policy.

The oligarchy went ballistic. Within 24 hours a full-scale containment policy was in place, and counter-measures were launched, against President Reagan, and against us. Over the next five years, there was an unrelenting international deployment against LaRouche and against "Star Wars" (as its detractors dubbed it), which came from London, Moscow, and numerous institutions of the Eastern Establishment in the U.S., using their control of the national media.

* Paul Gallagher was released on parole June 21, 2000.

One of their first tasks was to disassociate the name of LaRouche from SDI, and to break all ties between LaRouche and the Reagan Administration. The order spread rapidly through the press sewers of America: *No one* was to interview LaRouche or the FEF concerning the SDI, nor was the name LaRouche ever to be mentioned in regard to the program. In all subsequent coverage of LaRouche himself, it was to be alleged that he had opportunistically "supported" Reagan's SDI in order to ingratiate himself amongst conservatives. And, of course, these orders by the powers that be, were strictly followed by America's "free press."

At the same time, the "correct line" on the SDI was formulated and circulated for popular consumption. It was "Star Wars," a "right-wing, militaristic adventure," pronounced the media, "dreamt up by unreconstructed Cold Warriors out to launch World War III," with "Ronald Ray-guns" at the command.

For those who could not be dissuaded from supporting the idea, it was considered necessary to construct an imagined source for Reagan's SDI—someone other than LaRouche and the FEF. This was found in the person of Lt. Gen. Danny Graham, a retired chief of the Defense Intelligence Agency. Graham, a stooge for the Heritage Foundation and other libertarian think-tanks spawned by London's Mont Pelerin Society, concocted a "cost-effective" proposal for a space-based anti-missile defense system, called "High Frontier," which was nothing but a collection of off-the-shelf technologies, variations on anti-missile missiles, super-guns, and gimmicks. Not only would such systems fail to defend against a missile attack, but the expense of building a defensive missile would be greater than the cost of the missile itself. The only "savings" would be in the scrapping of all basic research and development! By ruling out the use of "new physical principles" of precisely the sort called for in LaRouche's beam-defense proposal, Graham's High Frontier eliminated the "technological spin-off" and "science driver" dimension of the SDI, and (not the least of the problems) the damn thing wouldn't work.

And yet, the entire conservative apparatus suddenly unleashed a massive propaganda barrage for High Frontier, either outright lying, or cleverly implying, that this was identical with President Reagan's SDI!

These were classic British methods, peddled through their Mont Pelerin Society apparatus within the U.S. While striking a macho, conservative pose, the actual purpose was to undermine the American commitment to fundamental scientific progress among conservative layers of the population. I would run into this disease over and over again in discussions with self-defined conservatives, who received tons of junk mail from the Mont Pelerin-linked organizations selling High Frontier. The disease attacked the weak link in an otherwise healthy, patriotic mind—the preoccupation with "my money." Anti-missile defense was necessary, the argument went, to beat them damn Commies, but we shouldn't waste our precious tax dollars on long-term, untested pie-in-the-sky boondoggles, when we can just place lots of orders for existing anti-missile missiles and get the same result. The treatment for such a virus required repeated, extended discussions on the indispensable role of long-term R&D, on American System economics, on the actual basis of long-term peace, and on the outright treasonous lies of the "Conservative Revolution" honchos.

The "gang, counter-gang" debate between macho right-wingers around Danny Graham, and the New Age anti-science mob, who opposed any version of missile defense, was essentially a diversion. The oligarchy knew that their most serious problem lay in the potential for further collaboration between Reagan and LaRouche. Soon the press and the airwaves, both in the U.S. and in the Soviet Union, were filled with hateful diatribes against LaRouche, and dire warnings to President Reagan to disassociate himself from LaRouche—or else.

[8]

Abscam, Music, and Freedom

By this time, I was beginning to feel my wings, and found myself searching out new pathways to explore with my new sense of intellectual freedom. I hit some rough weather here and there, but I took on a new role in the organizing which was more challenging, providing the opportunity to engage contacts from around the country in intensive discussions over time. Then Maestro Briano entered my life, leading me to discover a new singing voice, and a new degree of aesthetical freedom. Perhaps not coincidentally, I met my wife Gail at the same time, and began to bring my intellect and my emotions into harmony. Ironically, this new freedom would lead me, eventually, to prison—but it was a true freedom, which would never leave me.

★ ★ ★

In the summer of 1981, I requested a transfer from the airport deployments to the newly developing phone teams. I sensed that as our influence expanded, our capacity to develop the far-flung networks of supporters met at the airports and other sites would provide the crucial leverage for national campaigns, while expanding our sales and fundraising base. I'd been told that spending long days glued to a telephone was tough—and certainly nothing like the rapid-fire pace of airport deployments—

but I was anxious to get beyond the initial discussions, to grapple with ideas in greater depth, than was possible in initial contacts at a field site.

I began working in Bloomfield, New Jersey, with three or four others on the sales and fundraising staff. We called the new contacts met at the airports, and worked through the subscription lists for *New Solidarity*, EIR, and *Fusion*, recruiting people to our ideas and our campaign, and renewing subscriptions, especially to the EIR newsweekly.

With the new contacts, I quickly learned that if someone had read the literature, then there was an almost inevitable polarization—either he or she would be totally hostile, or totally intrigued. With those who were hostile, we could sometimes turn them around, but generally just asked them to read carefully and watch our track record, and not to listen to slanders (since most hostile responses reflected either direct or indirect media reports with the programmed lies about LaRouche). For those who had not read the literature, I found it was best not to launch into a political briefing, but to ask them to read it, and call back later. Unless someone knew that we were not just an "adversary group," promoting a few hot items, but rather, that we were political fighters, searching out the root causes of the global crisis and confronting the "powers that be," then they would have no basis for supporting us beyond a small contribution, as they would to any "good cause." We needed people to become active and to give generously, which requires that people change the way they think. In giving up an opinion which had been accepted out of ignorance or prejudice, a person rightfully believes himself to have become somehow *better*, and usually wants to help, politically and financially, in getting our ideas out to others.

Although we refused to become advocates of any single-issue campaigns, it was nonetheless necessary to confront people on various popular issues, in order to force them to question their acceptance of popular opinion. When I joined the phone team in 1981, the airwaves were inundated with anti-nuclear propaganda. At the same time, a massive Department of Justice sting operation, supported by the DOJ's obedient "mainstream" press, was targeting certain Democrats in the Congress, as well as key labor leaders. The sting was called Abscam (for Arab Scam) and Brilab (for

Bribe Labor). This was to be our first serious confrontation with the new style of justice in America, where the suspect is chosen first, and the crime concocted thereafter.

There were multiple connections between the anti-nuclear campaign and Abscam/Brilab. The Justice Department had targetted for destruction precisely those Congressmen and labor leaders who still retained at least some semblance of belief in the old "American System of political economy" and Henry Carey's "Harmony of Interests" between working people, industry, and government. Sometimes known as "labor Democrats" or the "smokestack Democrats," these Congressmen worked with labor to carry out the FDR and JFK tradition of nation-building, scientific progress, and an increasing per-capita quality of life for all Americans. With occasional help and occasional hindrance from the Republicans, they built industries during and after the war, and built our cities, ports, transportation systems, nuclear plants, schools, and hospitals, from the 1950's to the 1970's.

To the "post-industrial-society" ideologues, such nation-building was ridiculed as "boondoggles," "corruption," and "cronyism."

Abscam and Brilab aimed at eliminating any potential resistance to the "post-industrial" ideology, from either the Congress of the United States or the organized labor movement. By running stings and frame-ups against a number of prominent "labor Democrats" in the House and Senate, and threatening the rest with the same treatment, the witch-hunt practically destroyed the Congress as a politically effective force in America. Although there certainly was corruption in the Congress, and organized crime in the labor movement, cleaning out such corruption was not the intention of the Justice Department's attack, as demonstrated by their blatant disregard for the law or justice in bagging their pre-selected victims. The old FDR labor-minority coalition in the Democratic Party was to be destroyed. In its place, the Democratic Party would emerge as a New Age amalgam of self-interested "constituency groups," no longer united by a common interest in progress, but only by the desire of each alienated constituency to impose its often irrationally self-defined self-interest upon the rest of the nation.

We emerged as virtually the only institution attacking the outrageous and illegal methods of the Department of Justice (DOJ) in the Abscam and Brilab prosecutions. The witch-hunt was run by a nest of criminally corrupt officials in the DOJ, functioning as a "permanent bureaucracy," with tenures of 30-50 years, who wielded far more power than the political appointees. Those same individuals, including especially John Keeney and Mark Richard, would turn their full fury on us a few years later, at the behest of Henry Kissinger. Besides the "Get LaRouche" operation, Keeney, Richard, and their cohorts systematically targetted virtually every black elected official across the country for prosecution, and eventually turned their guns on the Presidency itself, with the "Get Clinton" escapade.

Our closest collaborator in the fight against Abscam was Sen. Harrison "Pete" Williams of New Jersey, who was one of those framed, but who decided to put up a fight. Most of the DOJ's targets were pressured to admit guilt in exchange for a light sentence—those who refused were hounded ruthlessly by the DOJ and the media jackals, who served as the judge and jury long before the cases came to trial—a process which has become all too familiar today. Truth was rapidly becoming irrelevant in the American justice system. Even those who fought and won their cases in court often found themselves financially bankrupt and their careers destroyed. Most of the Abscam targets succumbed to the pressure and struck a deal before going to trial. Senator Williams soon realized that we were the only organized force with either the courage to fight for truth and justice, or the capacity to carry out a national and international defense—the only defense which could possibly succeed against an oligarchy which utilized an international apparatus of think-tanks, foundations, and the media to carry out the assault.

The Williams case was exemplary of the criminal nature of Abscam itself. An FBI agent disguised as an Arab sheik arranged a meeting with Sen. Williams to discuss plans to invest in a large business venture in New Jersey—something which is a large part of a Senator's job, seeking out and encouraging investment in his or her state. A covert videotape showed Senator Williams strenuously refusing a bribe offered by the "businessman" at the end of their discussion. He was nonetheless convicted of corruption by a jury!

Senator Williams was then censured in the U.S. Senate. Even his closest friends and associates in the Senate, who knew he was totally innocent, voted for censure, under threat of getting the same treatment themselves. It was argued by the prosecution that the meeting with the imposter showed a "susceptibility to corruption" by the Senator, which was adequate to sway a jury already convinced by the media.

In fact, ever since, the criminal elements within the DOJ, in league with their official and private allies, have run roughshod over the Constitution, including the "Get LaRouche" attack—which former Attorney General Ramsey Clark described as a "broader range of deliberate cunning and systematic misconduct over a longer period of time, utilizing the power of the Federal government, than any other prosecution by the U.S. government in my time or to my knowledge." Every opportunity, and there were several, for the U.S. Congress to carry out its responsibility to investigate illegal operations by the DOJ has been passed by. Not many people realized it at the time, but the Pete Williams case marked the death of justice in America.

In 1982, my sister Margaret married Elliot Greenspan, the head of our political support staff in New Jersey, who had worked closely with Sen. Williams throughout the Abscam trials, and would become one of my closest friends and collaborators over the years. Their wedding reception was a wonderful event, filled with joyful music, good humor, and good wine. Among the guests were Sen. Williams and his wife. Our vocal quartet, which included myself, performed selections from Beethoven's opera *Fidelio*. The bride played a Beethoven variations for four-hands with her recruit and teacher, Bodil Frolund, and many others performed *Lieder*, Beethoven Bagatelles, poetry, or presented colorful stories from the wedding couple's history.

Towards the end of the evening, Sen. Williams proposed a toast: "I'm absolutely amazed," he said, "to see how all of you, who work harder than any people I've ever known, who seem to be pushing forward with insight and enthusiasm when others become discouraged and lose faith—how in the world do you find the time to also become accomplished singers and artists?

This has been a most beautiful evening, an appropriate event to honor this wonderful couple. I have seen how Elliot, like many others who work with LaRouche, has demonstrated the kind of courage and selfless commitment to the truth which is needed to get our nation back on track. I can tell you, Elliot, and all of you—keep it up, and I assure you, you'll be indicted!"

This was precious. Like all good jokes, the ironic surprise captured a higher truth. Everyone in our society is faced with the contradiction between the real source of joy, in the often risky pursuit of truth and beauty, and the banal, common notion of security and popularity. With a single, simple shift of context—a "phase shift"—the Senator captured the emotion involved in the love of great music and poetry, the love between man and wife, and the love of mankind as a whole, which leads people to fight for justice despite great personal risk. This is the emotion of creative discovery, of reason, what Plato and St. Paul called *agapē,* which makes life so beautiful.

Phone Team

Organizing, selling literature, and raising funds on the telephone is extremely hard work. It requires working through difficult ideas with an unseen person, figuring out the millions of different ways that various people block on reality (starting with yourself!), and overcoming those blocks. Over the years, some of our most talented and most experienced organizers were drawn into the sales and fundraising work on the phones, and most people in the organization spent at least part of their time helping out.

I found the work to be far more trying than I had expected, very different from my previous organizing experiences, and I had a very slow start. I also found that several of my associates had a tendency to suppress the problems they had in the work, with an unhealthy dose of machismo. Much of the advice I received was in the form of dramatic posturing, which I did not appreciate. Everyone was well-intentioned, but they often seemed more concerned with their "performance" than with the difficulties involved in conveying ideas.

My sister Margaret and I discussed it later on, comparing it to the problem in musical performance. Most performers are more concerned with what the audience thinks of *them,* of their skills, their technique, rather than trying to convey the ideas of the composer. The passion of the performance is faked, trying to create an effect on the senses, instead of uplifting the mind and soul of the audience. Conveying profound ideas, be they in music or in politics, requires *agapē*—not just technique.

Throughout 1982, I alternated with a few other members of the New York regional phone team in month-long trips to Boston, where the region was in need of additional manpower. Although I was hesitant to leave New York, I finally agreed to move there permanently in January 1983.

The Boston region was run by Mike Gelber, using his house as an office. There were eventually six of us working either full time or part time on the phones, and all six of us were eventually indicted in the Boston Federal case, the first of the multiple prosecutions against LaRouche and his associates brought by the "Get LaRouche Task Force."

The work was a bit rough around the edges in Boston, owing in part to the lack of an office. But Gelber was undaunted, and our influence in the region expanded. As part of the project to restore the true history of America, one of our members had researched the history of Harvard University, and its early takeover by the British Tories who ran the infamous "Vault" in Boston, the name for the inner elite of the Boston Brahmins. While the Boston Tories had joined the British in the 19th-Century Asian opium trade, they also ran various efforts to break up the United States—first the Essex Junto and the Hartford Convention, trying in 1814 to split New England off from the nation, and then, when that failed, moving South to set up the Confederacy.

Harvard, after the destruction in the 1870's of the American System faction there under Louis Agassiz, became the center for British-instigated psychological warfare on all fronts. We had put together profiles of some of the most egregious of the racist, genocidal, and traitorous operations run out of Harvard. We intervened in and around the Harvard campus—our favorite slogan: "Before Hitler, there was Harvard." The role of geneticist Robert Shockley, a typical Harvard professor teaching Nazi race science, "proving" the inferiority of blacks through sociological and psychological clap-trap, became a major national issue at the time. Then-Congressman George Bush praised Shockley as "courageous" in the U.S. Congress, and entered Shockley's fraudulent statistical theories into the *Congressional Record*. Our Boston organizers had fun exposing this and similar filth at Harvard, providing the rest of the country with valuable intelligence on the enemy operations in Cambridge on the Charles.

Later, the story of the Boston Brahmins would be filled out in Anton Chaitkin's 1984 book, *Treason in America*. This political bombshell exploded the myths of the "Eastern Establishment," tracing the British roots of every effort, throughout U.S. history, to undermine the republican advocates of the American System. To live in Boston was to live in the true capital of the Confederacy—even more so than my later days in Virginia. Perhaps that provides the best explanation for why the first "Get LaRouche" judicial witch-hunt against the NCLC took place in Boston.

Years later, Mike Gelber and his wife, Debbie, visited me at my Virginia prison, in a joyful reunion after ten years of separation. We laughed recalling how we exposed the dirty laundry of the untouchable Eastern Establishment. Mike had also served a brief prison term, but was by then back at work, sparking the organization in the New Jersey office with his tenacity and good humor. A few weeks later, I painfully learned that Mike had been killed in an auto accident. My memories of Boston will always be filled with memories of his infectious optimism, and the sound of his cackling laughter.

I Become a Tenor

Although my colleagues were busy raising hell in the city, I actually never saw much of Boston. I worked out of one of our home/office apartments, seldom leaving the immediate area except to catch a plane back to New York, which I did every weekend. This was awkward, but it was essential that I continue my work as director of the New York/New Jersey regional chorus. We had begun a local chorus (distinct from the main chorus in the National Center which John Sigerson directed) in 1982, in our Brooklyn office. Our original group came to be known as "The Straphangers' Chorus." We would meet at the end of a long day of organizing, often ending our rehearsal close to midnight. We'd then all pile onto the A-train (most of us lived in Washington Heights, in northern Manhattan). With song still in our hearts and minds, we'd occasionally sing on the subway, hanging onto the straps for dear life as the A-train rumbled under the city—thus, "The Straphangers." Our major accomplishment was a four-part setting of the Beethoven song, from the Gellert *Lieder*, called "Die Himmel Rühmen des Ewigen Ehre" ("The Heavens Proclaim the Eternal Glory"). Despite the very ragged nature of the individual voices, we had great enthusiasm, and we brought the house down at the 1982 year-end National Conference of the NCLC.

A very moving encounter took place at our only other public performance of the Beethoven piece. The scene was Elliot Greenspan's house in Bergen County, New Jersey, at the reception following the marriage of Elliot and Margaret. Mrs. Greenspan asked me to be the master of ceremonies at the crowded gathering, composed of about 25 of Elliot's relatives, another 25 Labor Committee friends, and my mother. (The public reception for all the Labor Committee members, with Sen. Williams, was held after the family's private reception.) Elliot's mother asked me to be Master of Ceremonies, so I donned a yarmulke and did my best at introductions and toasts. "The Straphangers" performed "Die Himmel Rühmen," crowded into the stairwell leading upstairs, to the delight of Elliot's family. When we finished, an old man introduced himself to me as Elliot's Uncle Isaac. He was absolutely beaming and spoke with a heavy accent as he grasped my arm: "Beautiful, beautiful. It takes me back many years, to my Gymnasium in Poland." He began singing the piece in Polish, then continued almost crying: "There was beauty in those days. I'm so happy you still learn this music. It seems to be lost now."

We wanted to sustain "The Straphangers," so I became a weekly commuter on the Eastern Shuttle between LaGuardia and Logan Airport in Boston. We started a chorus in Boston as well, although it was actually a men's glee club, except for Mike's wife, Debbie. Although we did manage to recruit one new female member, and encouraged our contacts to join the chorus, it remained heavily dominated by the "Boston bachelors."

Our music work was about to be totally transformed, however, by our association with Maestro José Briano, a distinguished professor from the Autonomous University in Mexico City, and the impulse his ideas gave to LaRouche's genius. Maestro Briano had become a friend and collaborator of our organization in Mexico. He travelled to New York in early 1983 to meet Lyn and present his ideas to the American membership. Although he spoke virtually no English—he required a translator for his lessons—he spoke a universal language in music. The concepts were conveyed with only the minimum of verbal exchange.

The Maestro's brilliance lay in his conviction that every single human being, except those with actual physical damage to the vocal chords, can learn to sing with the beautiful, penetrating, vibrated tone of a Classical "*bel canto*" (beautiful song) vocalist. While every voice is different, there is no natural hindrance to mastering the *bel canto* method, nor is there any such thing as a person who is "tone deaf." Those who appear to be tone deaf, have simply never learned how to place a tone correctly (which is usually the result of not having a musical environment as a child). The same is true for those who can sing, but whose voices—like my own—were throaty and unattractive. Once the proper method for placing the tone is learned, then all voices can attain the natural beauty which is one of the gifts of Heaven to every newborn child. In fact, the Maestro often referenced the wail of a little baby to prove that we are born with the capacity to project the voice with the intensity of a laser beam!

Briano had made a difficult decision in his own life. He had a promising career as a bass singer—something rather rare, since only a small percentage of men have a true bass voice. But he had learned the Classical Italian method of *bel canto* singing, and had developed a methodology based on the old school, which proved to be extraordinarily successful in both improving the capacity of trained singers, and in teaching total novices to quickly master the technique. He also recognized that the Classical method was practically extinct, as the world of professional musicians and teachers appeared to have lost all sense of the importance of the science of vocal expression, searching instead for quick methods and the most dazzling effects. The Maestro decided to dedicate his life to reproducing the Classical scientific method wherever possible, with the included goal of creating choruses throughout the world, even with people who may never have sung before.

My first meeting with the Maestro was one Saturday afternoon in the spring of 1983. I had been told to prepare a song or an opera aria to sing for him, and I chose "Se vuol ballare" from Mozart's *The Marriage of Figaro,* a famous bass baritone aria sung by the opera's Figaro. After an introductory explanation and some preliminary vocal exercises, he asked me to sing the aria. He stopped me immediately with several instructions:

"Open your mouth." (Almost no one opens the mouth adequately when singing.)

"More nose." (Almost everyone sings "in the throat" without using any of the head cavities.)

"Sing on 'no' instead of the words, to get more nose and rounded sound." (The use of "no" as a syllable is an exercise which facilitates nasalization, an open mouth, and a rounded sound.)

I plodded ahead. But not far into the aria, Figaro suddenly leaps to a high G (in the third register), as he imagines he is telling the Count (who is trying to finagle a night in bed with Figaro's betrothed) how he intends to teach the scoundrel a lesson. Since I had no idea how to sing such a note properly, I had the choice of shouting it raucously, or singing a thin note in falsetto. I chose the latter, and Maestro Briano broke into a huge laugh. He walked around the room, roaring, holding his belly, unable to talk over his laughter. When he finally calmed down enough to speak, he said, "Figaro; Figaro; it's Figaro, not Figaretta!" We all laughed.

Briano made it clear that I would have to change almost everything in my singing technique. My ultimate success in discovering my true singing voice is a useful object lesson in the method itself—an example I used with many of my own students over the years. My breakthrough came while working with John Sigerson, my old friend and singing partner, who had mastered Maestro Briano's method very rapidly.

John thoroughly delighted in his newly discovered teaching skills. I set a schedule to catch the 5:00 a.m. shuttle out of Boston's Logan Airport every Saturday morning, proceeding directly to John's apartment by 7:00 a.m. for an hour-long lesson, before starting the organizing in the New York office. John worked me through the basics: opening, rounding, connecting the resonance, relaxing. Soon my voice began to unfold, with a clear, unforced vibrato, and, to my great joy, a pleasing tone quality which, I had once despaired, was beyond my capacity. Still, I had no third register. As a baritone, Briano had me pass into the third register on the E-flat above middle C, but I would only force my second register up, clearly shouting, disrupting the otherwise well-placed sound. John worked with me on the Beethoven song "In Questa Tomba" ("In this Tomb"), written for a baritone, with only one note—but, of course, a very crucial note—in the third register.

On Maestro Briano's next visit to the U.S., I had the opportunity to sing this song at a seminar of about a dozen of our better singers, those whom we thought could most quickly master the method in order to become singing teachers themselves. Everyone was excited by the transformation in my voice, despite my flubbing the third-register note. Briano spent some time specifically trying to help me place this "E" correctly, but to no avail.

At my next lesson with John, he played a hunch. As we worked up the scale with arpeggios, instead of stopping when I could not even shout out the F or the F♯ above middle C, he continued up the scale. Suddenly, on the G (a note I could never sing), my voice literally popped into a booming, rapidly vibrating, penetrating tone, which made my entire body resonate and my head ring. John simply continued up the scale. G♯—more of the same. A, A♯—it was a glorious feeling. Only on the B did my voice crack. John laughed. "That's it. You're a tenor. Always have been. Actually, I'm beginning to recognize that most self-described baritones are probably lazy tenors!"

We tried some other exercises, and there was no question. Once I'd found my third register, there was no longer any chance of losing it, nor any question of where my voice passed—as a *tenor*, not a baritone.

A few weeks later there was a chorus rehearsal, held in a hall with a very high ceiling near the office. John warmed up each voice part as a group. ("Group lessons" were an important part of the Maestro's method, allowing each person to work through both their own problems and those of others.) He called me up with the tenors for the first time, and when we reached the third register, my voice boomed out, filling the acoustically expansive room like a cannon shot. There was an audible gasp throughout the hall, then a big laugh from John. "We're going to find a lot more tenors out there!"

This discovery was certainly one of the happiest moments of my life. It was a sort of liberation—a new freedom to create beauty. I could not sing enough after that. Not that my transition to tenor was easy. It required some straining and some pushing, since it takes enormous energy to place these higher tones—especially the top part of the second register. But a passing remark by the Maestro, that my voice was similar to that of Jussi Björling (by far my favorite tenor), left me both ecstatic, and determined that I would master any problems, despite my late start in life.

I immediately began applying this new discovery, this marvelously simple method, to the members of my New York and Boston choruses. Word about Maestro Briano's assistance spread rapidly throughout the organization, which encouraged those who had not sung before to give it a try, to see what all the commotion was about. People who were convinced they were tone deaf—the type whose second-grade teacher finally, in desperation, told him or her, "please, just mouth the words"—suddenly discovered how to produce a tone scientifically, and thus to *know* it. One of my New Jersey students had been unable to even match a tone. If I played a G, she'd sing a D, or something equally distant, and would not even "hear" the difference—or so we thought. A few years later, she would perform Bach's "Bist du bei mir" for me in a lovely, pure *bel canto*.

Teaching became an exciting adventure. Maestro Briano insisted that a good chorus required that each member sing with the rounded, elevated tone of a well-trained singer—every member a soloist! This was opposite to the generally accepted practice with choruses, which usually discouraged *bel canto* singing, since a well-placed voice would stand out among the "normal" breathy, colorless tonal production of the untrained singers.

As to my own singing, I began to monopolize my sister Margaret's every spare moment. We had worked together over the years on some Schubert and Schumann songs, in the baritone range. It was fun, but the product was not "marketable," as the yuppies say today. With my newly discovered voice, we began to work in earnest, switching to the tenor (original) setting of the German Lieder. John Sigerson had performed the Schubert song-cycle, "Die Schöne Müllerin" ("The Lovely Miller's Daughter"), perfect for his light but strong high tenor. Margaret and I had worked through that cycle as well, but we soon found ourselves more intrigued by the somewhat weightier Schubert cycle, "Winterreise" ("A Winter's Journey"), Schubert's last cycle of his tragically short 31 years. The somewhat somber character of the songs was more appropriate to my rather heavy voice, although I soon learned that the songs were only apparently somber. The cycle, based on poems by Wilhelm Müller (who also wrote the poems in "Die Schöne Müllerin"), portray a young man who imagines himself to be suffering every conceivable torture over his lost love, certain that his grief can lead only to death. As all his fellow men, and even nature itself, seem to desert him in his desperate state—only the carrion crow circling overhead will remain faithful unto death, expecting a good meal at the end!—he finally resigns himself to the graveyard. But even the graveyard rejects him! "No room," it says!

At this point in the song-cycle, any performer with any brains—i.e., anyone not totally brainwashed by the Romanticism of virtually all music after Brahms—must realize that the morose quality of all the songs is entirely ironic. The performer must engage the audience to join Schubert in looking over the young man's shoulder, smiling at his youthful romantic excesses, capturing in the music both the pathos of the romantic wanderer, and the humorous, ironic reality visible in the mind's eye. When the youth ponders the road to the graveyard ("Eine Strasse muß ich gehen, die noch Keiner ging züruck"—"I must take a road from which no one has ever returned"), there is a beautiful *double* irony, for the young man is clearly clinging madly to the failed path of self-pity, which is familiar to him, rather than breaking off into the real world of the unknown, which actually frightens him so. Müller and Schubert were, in fact, ridiculing the then-popular romantic stories of the wandering youth, living out a fantasy life, which the great Heinrich Heine also attacked with such penetrating irony. The last song of the "Winterreise" proves the point. The youth comes across *true* pathos—a poor organ-grinder standing barefoot in the snow, with dogs barking at his heels, and passersby ignoring his empty bowl. This sharp dose of reality breaks the lad out of his self-pity, forcing him to consider something and someone outside of himself. He asks the "wünderlicher Alter" (the amazing old man) if he could join him, and if he would "play your organ to my song."

Margaret and I fell in love with these songs. We listened to various recordings, but none even tried to capture the irony. We had to work out our own approach, based only on Schubert's genius, Margaret's poetic power on the piano, and the wonderful freedom provided by my new-found vocal instrument.

My weekends in New York became marathon adventures. Following my lesson with John, I joined the New York office staff in a day of organizing on the phones. In the evening, at about 9:00 p.m., the chorus would meet for as long as two hours, and almost the entire regional membership now joined in. Then I retired to Elliot's and Margaret's apartment, where we stayed up all hours of the night working on "Winterreise" and other *Lieder*. Sunday was often another day of organizing, before I'd catch an evening flight back to Boston. Tiring—but delightful.

Gail

And then, soon, my weekends in New York became even busier, with the *most* welcome addition of a new love. A longtime member of the NCLC, Gail Kay, whom I had known only slightly, had recently been divorced, and, while working herself through that difficult process, she began spending a few days per week in the regional office, in addition to her work as an editor in the National Center. I couldn't help but notice her. She's a striking woman—thin, with sharp, elegant features, intense eyes, and graceful in her composure.

All I really knew of Gail was the famous story of her "infiltration," (as the *New York Times* called it), of the Council on Foreign Relations (CFR) in the 1970's. She had answered an ad in the *New York Times* for the job as secretarial assistant to William Bundy, one of the partiarchs of the Anglo-American Establishment, and editor of the CFR journal *Foreign Affairs.* She got the job, and began working as an assistant on *Foreign Affairs,* while doing secretarial work with Bundy in planning conferences and other events.

At a certain point in 1979, after the wide circulation of articles by LaRouche with such titles as "Rockefeller's Fascism with a Democratic Face," someone at the CFR found out that Gail was a member of the NCLC. Bundy went ballistic and raked her over the coals. The *New York Times* described the incident as a major security breach, an espionage coup by LaRouche against the Eastern Establishment!

"Among the secretary's duties last year," wrote the *Times*, "was to attend the sessions of the Bilderberg Society, an exclusive organization of the world's industrial and foreign-policy elite that meets annually for confidential discussions of economic policy and world trends. 'I'm absolutely floored by this,' said William P. Bundy. . . . 'It's like the CIA getting an agent into the Politburo.' " Super-spy, however, was not exactly Gail's M.O.

I made a few hesitant, tentative efforts to speak with Gail in the office, during my weekends in New York, but she was sticking strictly to business. However, since I definitely needed this new female voice in the Straphangers, I asked Elliot and Richard Black to see if she would join our chorus. They somehow surmised that I may have been interested in more than a stronger soprano section, and set about conspiring on how to convince her to sing with us. The less than subtle campaign succeeded, but not without tipping off Gail to the fact that something strange was going on (as she later informed me).

I was in my late thirties, but felt like a teenager afraid to ask that special girl out for a date. Finally, with some cajoling from a few friends, who gratefully played busybody, I invited her to a local opera company's performance of *Il Travatore*. We went on to enjoy a delightful courtship, built around the poetry of Dante, recordings of Jussi Björling, Thai and Italian food, good wine, long-distance phone calls, and *very* late nights on my weekends in New York. There were some ups and downs, but before long, I asked to be transferred back to New York, and not long after that we announced our wedding, for Dec. 2, 1984.

For more than half of our married life (as of 1999), Gail would be a prison wife, living alone, with occasional visits, over great distances, in sterile, noisy prison visiting rooms, while trying to maintain a relationship through 15-minute, tape-recorded phone calls. She was to bear the burden with strength, becoming a leading world spokesman for the organization, while demanding justice for LaRouche, her husband, and the other LaRouche defendants. I thank Heaven for the blessing of such a beautiful marriage.

[9]

Breakout—And the 'Get LaRouche Task Force' Counterattacks

LaRouche announced his candidacy for the Democratic Presidential nomination in September of 1983, identifying himself as the Democratic candidate for the SDI, and against the "nuclear-freeze" nonsense of the New Age Democrats. We began devoting part of our time to raising funds for "The LaRouche Campaign," or TLC, as we called the campaign committee. In January of 1984, Lyn decided to produce the first of many one-half-hour national TV programs—a format he had already made famous in 1980. The subject would be the strategic implications of SDI, in the context of the mounting global financial crisis. It required a legal fight with the networks (as it had also in 1980), to force them to follow the law, making time available to the campaign at special candidate rates of between $100,000-$200,000 for a half-hour, coast-to-coast broadcast. By the end of the campaign, LaRouche would have addressed the nation in 16 separate half-hour TV shows.

Fundraising for these broadcasts was arduous. Being a Federal election, all aspects of the fundraising were regulated and monitored by the Federal Election Commission (FEC). No individual could give or loan more than $1,000, and all records of contributions had to be submitted to the FEC for inspection and public disclosure. The leadership of the major parties found ways to get around these restrictions—"soft money," which went to the party, rather than individual candidates, was less restricted. But LaRouche could expect no support from the Democratic Party leadership, which was, at the time, firmly in the hands of the

Trilateral Commission apparatus—including the annointed party candidate-to-be, Walter Mondale.

★ ★ ★

Raising the millions of dollars needed for 16 TV programs required expanding our base of support dramatically—a process which was politically necessary in any case, for other than financial reasons. Every supporter, every subscriber to our publications, was asked to act on the window of opportunity for reversing America's decline and the global descent towards depression and war. The combination of President Reagan's adoption of LaRouche's SDI proposal, and LaRouche's ability to break through the media blockade as a Presidential candidate, created the preconditions for breaking the "post-industrial society" paradigm shift of the 1960's, and mobilizing the American population for a new era of American System nation-building throughout the world. We insisted that anyone who even partially understood this situation as a *punctum saliens* in history, must find a way to give or lend the legal limit of $1,000 to pay for the TV broadcasts. At the least, he or she should give $250, which was the maximum per individual which would be matched by the Federal government's "Matching Funds" program for Presidential campaigns.

At the same time, we had to maintain the income required for our publications and for all our other political work. In addition to a rapid expansion of our subscription base, we supplemented our sales efforts with numerous books and exclusive, high-priced Special Reports. We asked supporters to purchase copies both for themselves and for their political representatives. EIR subscriptions and Special Reports soon spread across Capitol Hill and through the state legislatures. We asked those who were able, to give or lend large amounts to support special publishing efforts, conferences, or other specific activities.

I moved back to New York at the beginning of 1984, living with Gail in a small house in Astoria, Queens. I worked in the New York regional office, which had moved from Brooklyn to upper Manhattan, but continued calling our contacts in the New England area, while keeping in close touch with our Boston office.

This lasted until July of 1984, when my engagement to Gail required a change of assignment for one or the other of us. The National Center of the organization had scheduled a move to Northern Virginia, nearby to Washington, D.C., in 1985. Couples needed to consolidate jobs in one place or the other. I moved to the National Center.

Gail had worked for years in the publications editorial department. She had, however, recently moved into Asian intelligence, concentrating on the Philippines. The entire Asia sector was being overhauled under the leadership of Gail's friend, Linda de Hoyos, who asked Gail to participate. As I would later learn through my own work with Linda, behind her stern appearance and famous scowl, she has a wonderful sense of humor and an insightful grasp of events as "world history in progress," as well as a deep compassion for the suffering brought upon the world's nations by the ravages of the British imperial mind-set. Gail was glad to join her friend in taking responsibility for over half the world's population.

There was a second reason for my move to the National Center in July 1984—nearly a year before our planned move to Virginia—namely, to help in getting the National Center more involved in the sales and fundraising effort. My addition was welcomed, since no one there had any significant experience in sales or fundraising. A team of experienced members had been assembled for the National Center phone team, beginning with Anita Gallagher, who had significant phone organizing experience from her work on political operations and political intelligence in the U.S. sector, and Christian Curtis, who had worked in Ibero-American Intelligence. (Chris was brought up in Brazil, where his father was a State Department career diplomat. His wife, Guida, was Brazilian.) Chris had also been the editor of *War on Drugs* magazine. I joined them in July 1984.

One member of the National Office staff who helped part-time with the phone team was Larry Hecht (of the Moon-Hecht model of the atom), one of the original Labor Committee members from 1968. Larry so much enjoyed the direct, one-on-one organizing, after years of editorial work, that he requested a permanent assingment to the phone team. Larry had always taken an active part in the science work in the organization, and his wife Marje was the managing editor of *Fusion* magazine. Larry would continue in his scientific work, making several major original contributions over the coming years, both during his time on the phone team, and later as a political prisoner in the Virginia prison system.

In addition to the four of us, Paul Gallagher, Anita's husband and the director of the Fusion Energy Foundation, undertook part-time work with the phone team during 1985-86, helping to lead the national sales efforts for our publications, while continuing his FEF responsibilities. Aided by Paul, we four led the National Center phone team, which, over time, became the "flagship" phone organizing operation in the country—and a primary target of the "Get LaRouche Task Force." Eventually, four of us—including Paul and his wife Anita—would be incarcerated. Curtis would escape prison only by selling his soul to the devil.

We took responsibility for a group of mostly rural states which were the most distant from our regional centers around the country, and arranged with the regions that we would call the subscribers in those states. We also purchased lists from political organizations, and began calling people "cold," to sell subscriptions to *New Solidarity* or EIR. Our intelligence sectors also had many contacts overseas, both foreigners and Americans abroad, whom we contacted for subscriptions to EIR and other literature sales.

We worked intensely throughout 1984, often until 10:00 or 11:00 p.m. at night (and often for seven days a week!). Our efforts, and those of others in other locations, contributed to a dramatic expansion of our literature distribution, and the spread of our ideas across the country.

There was a raging battle taking place around the world, across the U.S., and in the White House, over Reagan's SDI proposal, and we were at ground zero of that battle. Special Reports, a book called *Beam Defense,* as well as regular coverage of the SDI in our press, flowed into every policy-making center in the world. EIR and FEF sponsored conferences in Europe, Ibero-America, Asia, and throughout the U.S., bringing together scientific and political leaders for in-depth briefings and discussions with LaRouche and others in the organization.

Because of the fierce counter-measures against the SDI from within the Reagan Administration, our work with Republican leaders and supporters became especially volatile. In the National Center, we purchased lists of traditionally conservative political contributors, which directly intersected the internal battle in the White House. The Kissinger coterie was fully mobilized to break President Reagan from both the SDI policy and his connection to LaRouche. This included a massive mail solicitation operation targetting conservative Americans, to direct attention away from the real SDI, onto Danny Graham's phony "High Frontier." These conservative networks, we found, were easily taken in by such garbage, but were often shocked and angry when we provided them with detailed briefings on the fact that the High Frontier "flying junk" program was a Trilateral Commission instigated hoax to wreck the SDI. Presented with LaRouche's (and Reagan's) science-driver concept, situated within LaRouche's economic forecast, our *War on Drugs,* and our commitment to building a cultural renaissance, many of these traditionally stalwart sponsors of conservative issues began to give us serious support, as they began to re-think all their political assumptions—much to the dismay of the establishment, and especially the Mont Pelerin-style conservatives.

The 'Get LaRouche Task Force'

The slanders began in earnest in January 1984, with several high-profile, hysterical diatribes in the media against LaRouche and his influence in the Reagan Administration. We were aware that these slanders were in preparation, since we had been tipped off to a meeting in the spring of 1983, sponsored by Wall Street investment adviser and intelligence asset John Train. According to our source, the meeting was called to plan a national media smear campaign against LaRouche. Much later, we learned that the Train meetings, of which there were several, spawned a "Get LaRouche Task Force" composed of government agents, private organizations, and selected media. Besides coordinating dirty tricks and media attacks, the Task Force worked directly with the Department of Justice and various state Attorneys General in a politically driven judicial witch-hunt. Much of the following account of this "Get LaRouche Task Force" was pieced together only *after* our convictions in Virginia and New York, through the Freedom of Information Act (FOIA) and other investigative measures. Most of it was denied in court by those involved, before we had obtained the evidence—in other words, the prosecution teams blatantly perjured themselves, and illegally withheld crucial exculpatory evidence during the trials. This is now a matter of documented facts—facts which have been systematically ignored by the corrupt judicial system in the United States of America.

The first meeting of the "Train Salon," as we called the planning sessions at John Train's apartment, took place on April 23, 1983. Our initial tip described this gathering, but when we tried to follow up, people denied involvement or knowledge—including reporters for NBC, who responded with half-truths and lies when questioned under oath. We were finally able to assemble the cast of characters after the ADL's Mira Lansky Boland spilled some of the beans in court testimony in the spring of 1990. Attending were: Richard Mellon Scaife, who has subsequently been exposed as the moneybags for nearly every British-sponsored act of treason against the United States connected to the Bush/Ollie North/ Newt Gingrich "Conservative Revolution" gang, including the "Get Clinton" operation; Roy Godson, a consultant to the National Security Council (NSC) and the President's Foreign Intelligence Advisory Board (PFIAB); John Rees, a long-time FBI stringer in right-wing groups; Mira Lansky Boland, an "ex"-CIA employee, who had taken over the ADL's Fact-Finding Division in Washington, D.C.; several journalists, from NBC, *Readers Digest, Business Week, New Republic,* and *The Wall Street Journal;* and other spooks with various "government credentials" in the Bush and Kissinger networks. The Smith-Richardson Foundation, a long-standing U.S. intelligence community proprietary, funded a major piece in the smear campaign launched against LaRouche at the meeting.

The theme of the meeting, besides preparing the lies and slanders about LaRouche to be broadcast uniformly by America's "free press," was the need to manufacture a "foreign connection" to LaRouche, especially the implication that he was "KGB-linked." This was intended to trigger an official investigation of LaRouche and the NCLC under Executive Order 12333. E.O. 12333 had been carefully drafted by the Bush apparatus in the administration, and signed by President Reagan in December 1981. It established an institutional structure, under the National Security Council, called the Special Situation Group, reporting directly to Vice President George Bush. In any situation that could be vaguely called "special," this Bush-directed group had virtually unlimited power to do whatever they wished, whether within the law or not. E.O. 12333 authorized illegal, covert operations, not only by government agencies, but by a host of private organizations and people in the media, under the direction of Vice President Bush. Sometimes referred to as "Project Democracy," the apparatus utilized many of the old intelligence hands floating around since the 1970's, when the Carter Administration's CIA Director, James Rodney Schlesinger, "down-sized" the agency, putting many agents off the official payroll, but not necessarily out of work. Such "ex"-CIA agents became known as the "asteroids."

Besides running such things as Ollie North's Iran arms sales and his Contra drugs-for-guns deals, this Bush-run structure also coordinated the covert side of the operations against LaRouche. But first, a background review of the government efforts to destroy LaRouche and his organization, beginning in 1969, is necessary, in order to understand the nature of E.O. 12333 and the Train Salon.

Cointelpro

The FBI, under its Counter Intelligence Program (Cointelpro), with direct input from the Criminal Division of the Department of Justice, began covert operations to disrupt and destroy the Labor Committee, virtually from the day of its creation—including efforts to assassinate LaRouche. Documents received through FOIA, after years of court battles to force their release under the law, exposed a number of these illegal operations.

In April 1969, the Director of the FBI wrote to the New York FBI agent-in-charge, authorizing the distribution of a wild slander against the Labor Committee amongst the various factions of the SDS in New York, "designed," the memo stated, "to cause disruption within the Columbia University Chapter of SDS. . . . As such a leaflet may cause dissension between two New Left groups, the mailing by New York is being authorized." It is of note that this disruption was done on behalf of the Mark Rudd faction against LaRouche's associates—the same Mark Rudd faction, which then proceeded, with Ford Foundation financing, to build the Weathermen and other terrorist organizations.

Then, in November 1973, came the FBI directive to use the Communist Party USA to "eliminate" LaRouche, which I described earlier. This was followed by a failed assassination attempt against LaRouche in December, run by a combination of U.S.- and Puerto Rico-based networks of the Communist Party.

In 1975, the U.S. Labor Party initiated a lawsuit against the Department of Justice, demanding an end to its illegal campaign to destroy the LaRouche movement and, in particular, LaRouche's 1976 Presidential campaign. But before the suit could get into full discovery, the FBI and the DOJ announced in 1977 that they were ending the "domestic security" investigation of LaRouche and the NCLC. This was a full two years after Congress had already shut down Cointelpro and exposed widespread illegalities on the part of the FBI and other intelligence agencies. The strange continuation of Cointelpro solely against the NCLC, did not escape public notice. In 1977, investigative reporter Carl Stern announced on NBC nightly news that, despite FBI denials, Cointelpro was continuing, and its target was Lyndon LaRouche and the National Caucus of Labor Committees.

But the FBI merely went on to replace its open disruption program with a covert one. The spy apparatus which had assisted in the pre-1977 investigation—the ADL, the International Division of the AFL-CIO, the Heritage Foundation—took over the major disruption efforts against us. Simultaneously, the DOJ and FBI launched a series of secret operations, whose details are still classified to this day. Perhaps the lawsuit launched in 1975 (*LaRouche v. Freeh*), which is still in court as of 1999, will finally reveal major aspects of the establishment's secret war against LaRouche.

In 1982, with Henry Kissinger watching in horror, Lyndon LaRouche and elements within the Reagan Administration developed an increasingly close working relationship. Kissinger fired off a memo to his friend William Webster, Director of the FBI. Dated Aug. 19, 1982, Kissinger's letter told Webster that Lyndon LaRouche and "these people" had become "increasingly obnoxious," and that Kissinger had instructed his lawyer, Bill Rogers, to meet with Webster to plan a strategy against LaRouche.

It is important to note that Henry, at that time, was a private citizen, holding no public office of any sort, and, in particular, had been conspicuously excluded from the Reagan Administration. His friend, FBI Director William Webster, was in no way restrained by such mere formality, and placed this government agency at Henry's service.

On Jan. 12, 1983, Webster wrote to the head of FBI counterintelligence, Oliver "Buck" Revell, instructing him to respond to the numerous complaints from "Americans in public life (who) had been the subject of repeated harassment by LaRouche," and wondered whether the FBI had a basis for investigating these activities "under the guidelines or otherwise." This chilling phrase, in fact, served as the basis for the "Get LaRouche" operation, a clear, blatant, self-described *criminal* campaign, carried out by those supposedly responsible for the protection of liberty in America, at the behest of the private Anglophile elite.

Webster's letter to Revell also made reference to a meeting of the President's Foreign Intelligence Advisory Board (PFIAB), in which members David Abshire and Edward Bennett Williams had "raised the question of the sources of funding for these U.S. Labor Party (*sic*—the U.S. Labor Party had been disbanded in 1978) activities." Webster added, "In view of the large amounts obviously being expended worldwide, the question was raised whether the U.S. Labor Party might be funded by hostile intelligence agencies."

This formulation was the required code to activate the carefully constructed E.O. 12333, authorizing the non-official "asteroids" to go to work, in any manner they saw fit (i.e., the "or otherwise" in Webster's terminology), using the full power of the media, Wall Street, corrupted law enforcement, and the private institutions in their employ. Thus was born the "Get LaRouche Task Force."

It is important to note that the first meeting of the Train Salon fell exactly one month after President Reagan's March 23, 1983 announcement of LaRouche's SDI proposal! Only ten days before the Train meeting, LaRouche had keynoted an FEF conference in Washington, D.C. on the SDI, attended by 800 representatives of the administration, the Congress, and business and foreign diplomatic circles.

While the "Get LaRouche Task Force" proceeded to paint LaRouche as KGB-linked, the Task Force was itself heavily KGB-linked! Through multiple operational interfaces, the attack on LaRouche and the LaRouche/Reagan connection was jointly carried out by both the "Get LaRouche Task Force" and the Soviet intelligence and media outlets. In May 1983, an official Soviet delegation of 25 KGB, and Soviet media (i.e., more KGB) officials came to Minneapolis, Minnesota for a "peace conference," prominently attended by the Trilateral Commission Democrats around Walter Mondale. The Soviet delegation was led by Georgi Arbatov, head of the Soviets' U.S.A./Canada Institute. Arbatov knew of LaRouche's meeting with the Soviet representative over the previous year, but had rejected that representative's effort to set up a meeting with LaRouche immediately following President Reagan's March 23 speech.

Arbatov instead took the opportunity of the May conference in Minneapolis to declare war on the SDI, in league with the Democratic Party leadership. We monitored this conference carefully, and broadcast the blatant Trilateral/Soviet collaboration through all our publications. In the fall, both the KGB and the Democratic Party went public with attacks on the SDI and LaRouche.

In Moscow, the journal *Literaturnaya Gazeta* declared the SDI a "casus belli," a justification for war, in an article authored by Fyodor Burlatsky, a KGB journalist who had attended the Minnesota conference. The government paper, *Izvestia,* wrote a long report on one of our SDI conferences in Rome, describing it as a "Sabbath of Troglodytes," ominously warning that "the get-together showed that both Reagan and LaRouche have followers in the Old World." *Pravda* called our Paris conference "A Colloquium of Murderers." *Izvestia* also demanded that Reagan break all ties with LaRouche, describing the association as a "scandal." Not to be outdone, Henry Kissinger told a public conference of his Wall Street friends that "I will do everything in my power to break the links between LaRouche and the Reagan Administration, and you can quote me!" Democratic Party National Chairman Charles Manatt publicly denounced the SDI, and said that all Democratic Presidential candidates in 1984 would oppose it.

The public attack against LaRouche provided us with enormous organizing leverage. The previous policy of "containment" against us by the U.S. press, based on preventing any reference to LaRouche's existence whatsoever, had made it very difficult for the average "other-directed" American to understand the crucial nature of our *ideas* in the real world. Reports of the Soviet denunciations actually served to convince many such doubters both that our ideas *could* change history, and that the U.S. media was massively lying to the American people by blacking out LaRouche and his impact on history.

Containment was clearly not working, so "The Big Lie" method went into operation, beginning with NBC and *New Republic* slanders in early 1984.

NBC-TV's "First Camera" ran a half-hour segment on LaRouche by Pat Lynch and Brian Ross, both participants in the Train Salon. They accused LaRouche of plotting the assassination of President Jimmy Carter, by remote control bomb. It suggested mysterious foreign sources of our finances, and called for an IRS investigation. It interviewed Reagan Administration officials who acknowledged collaboration with LaRouche. In fact, NSC economist Norman Bailey described EIR as "one of the best private intelligence services in the world." This, NBC warned, constituted a severe threat to the security of the United States! The *New Republic* magazine expanded on these fabrications, and further threatened President Reagan himself. Its cover read: "The LaRouche Connection—Since 1981 the leaders of a lunatic movement have conferred repeatedly with top administration officials. Their aim: to win respectability and to influence Reagan's Star Wars plan. They succeeded."

Within hours of the NBC slander, Democratic Party Chairman Charles Manatt held a press conference in Chicago, expressing his "shock" at the "revelations" concerning LaRouche's influence in the Reagan Administration, and demanding that Reagan break all ties immediately. Manatt was seconded by the Soviet government's *Izvestia*, which called the NBC lies a "scandal" which "the White House does not even try to deny."

Ten days after the "First Camera" broadcast, Army Colonel Oliver North, who had been personally recommended by Henry Kissinger to represent the military on the NSC, intervened to block a crucial communication between LaRouche and Reagan. Although Reagan had refused to let Kissinger anywhere near his administration during his first few years in office, the Bush apparat eventually succeeded in getting Kissinger appointed as head of a commission on Ibero-America, the Kissinger Commission. LaRouche wrote a private memo to the President, warning that Kissinger would work to destroy U.S. economic and security interests in Ibero-America, while creating diversions from the necessary war on drugs required across the continent. (This was, of course, exactly what the Bush/North "Contra" support operation proceeded to carry out!) North intercepted LaRouche's memo, instructing that no response should be made.

Every available means was activated to threaten President Reagan, demanding that he break his contacts with LaRouche. Kissinger went public, telling the *Washington Post* that he was shocked at the revelations of the LaRouche connection, implying that Reagan would get the "LaRouche treatment" if it continued. Richard Morris, a member of Reagan's National Security Council, testifying on LaRouche's behalf at our 1988 Federal trial in Alexandria, Virginia, told the court that LaRouche and his associates were engaged in regular and intense discussions with the administration over SDI and several other subjects. One faction within the NSC, Morris said, led by Train Salon member Roy Godson, was determined to break the LaRouche input to the President, calling LaRouche "fascist," "communist," or "KGB," depending on who was listening. Godson and his cohorts were to be key operatives in North's subsequent criminal enterprise, running guns and drugs in Central America.

Unfortunately, Ronald Reagan did not have the internal strength of character to withstand this barrage.

Presidential Campaign

Over the course of the 1984 campaign, millions of Americans watched one or more of LaRouche's national broadcasts. However, even the existence of the broadcasts went almost entirely unreported in the nation's media. I spoke with many hundreds of people over the next few years with stories approximately like this:

"Have you ever seen LaRouche?"

"Nope, never heard of him."

"He did 16 half-hour broadcasts during the election."

"Oh, you mean that guy who talked for about an hour on Star Wars?" (or, "on the cartels stealing the farmers' crops?," or "on the Trilateral Commission running Bush and Mondale?" or, etc., etc.).

"Yes, that was Lyndon LaRouche."

"My God, that was amazing. I called Mable and the kids in to watch it. We called our neighbors, but they missed it. So we looked for the story in the morning paper. Damned strange, they didn't even mention it. I know I didn't just imagine it. Can't understand why they didn't cover it. That was the most interesting speech I ever heard. Why did he drop out of the race?"

"He didn't drop out. He ran in the Democratic primary, and then, when they nominated Mondale, he ran in the November election as an independent Democrat."

"Why, then, that's *really* strange. They didn't say anything about him on the news. I'd have voted for him if I'd known. You ought to tell him to stop hiding! We need someone like him out here."

While we can blame the media for their criminal malfeasance in disrupting the electoral process by blacking out LaRouche's ideas (not to mention spreading the "Get LaRouche" slanders), nonetheless, the bigger problem lies with the American people. Many, perhaps most, will tell you that they despise and distrust the media, but then turn around and swear that they *know* such and such is true because they heard it on the news! Lyn loves to tell the story of the average American who gets hit by a truck, crawls home, and turns on the TV news to see if it really happened.

The vicious lies in the media frightened some people, but they also served us as a basis for highly effective flanking attacks against the enemy. I had on my desk at all times copies of the slanders, both those in the U.S. and those in the Soviet press. I read them to virtually every supporter I reached—*especially* the most outrageous parts. Nothing could more clearly demonstrate that the Soviet and the U.S. media were running an operation in tandem against LaRouche, against President Reagan's policies, and against his collaboration with us. We knew the Train Salon to be the source of the fabrications. "Do you want Henry Kissinger, the KGB, and NBC dictating policy to the President?" I asked,

"Or do you think you ought to help us expose this treason and mobilize Americans to support the SDI and LaRouche's other proposals?"

The TV broadcasts, each of the 16, conveyed a conceptual whole to the audience, locating the particular subject within a universal reality. The viewer, accustomed to "sound bites" rather than real political dialogue, was suddenly confronted with a paradox in current world history, and led to understand that he or she was responsible for the solution, and the consequences, of that paradox. One show, "Great Projects vs. Henry Kissinger's Genocide," presented Kissinger's war on the "over-populated" nations of the Third World, with graphic displays of the death and destruction wrought by his policies. Counterposed to that, Lyn described the Great Projects: vast rail and canal development in Africa and China, bridging of the Bering Strait, nuclear desalination of water to green the deserts of the Mideast, and so forth. He showed that the Great Projects were totally possible, but only by replacing the bankrupt IMF with a new international monetary system, while the Great Projects themselves (like Alexander Hamilton's "internal improvements" approach) were the assurance that the new system would function and prosper.

Other shows focussed on the collaboration between the Soviets, the British, and the Kissinger circle in sabotaging the SDI; on the emerging worldwide financial collapse; on the coming food crisis in America. The food crisis show, beautifully produced to Vivaldi's *Four Seasons* concerti, demonstrated the destruction of the family farm under the growing power of the grain cartels, and the productive collapse this was creating in the agricultural sector. There was a virtual deluge of mail from across the nation following that broadcast, from farmers who simply couldn't figure out what was happening to them, and were thrilled to find someone who could explain it, and who knew what to do about it.

While LaRouche emphasized the crucial importance of Reagan's adoption of the SDI policy, he did not let the President off the hook for his slavish adherence to the Volcker dictates from Wall Street and the Federal Reserve. One broadcast was called "Reagan's Hoover Recovery." Mocking all the talk of "recovery," Lyn showed that the Volcker measures were creating a financial bubble through speculative looting of the productive sector of the economy. Not only were industrial and agricultural output shrinking, when measured as per capita of the work force, but we were also failing to make the necessary investments in maintaining and expanding the nation's infrastructure. He compared this to Herbert Hoover's "prosperity," which had been based on the same process.

In "What Is the Soviet Union Today?," shown to the music of Mussorgsky, LaRouche provided a psychological profile of the imperial mentality which had seized the Russian leadership following their rejection of LaRouche's proposal for collaboration on SDI. He traced the paranoid outlook of the Russian peasant in the village, the *mir*, through the nihilist protofascism of Dostoevsky and the Russian followers of Friedrich Nietzsche. He acknowledged the opposite scientific tradition in Russia, from Peter the Great through to the great Mendeleyev and other Russian "Riemannians," but insisted that the Soviet leadership was preparing for war on a purely chauvinist, imperial basis.

In October, LaRouche produced a broadcast exposing Democratic candidate Walter Mondale's open collaboration with the Soviets, including the infamous KGB delegation in Minneapolis in 1983, where the war on SDI had been announced. "I am thoroughly convinced," LaRouche said, "that if the KGB asked Walter Mondale to lick the floor, he would promptly do precisely that."

Fundraising for the LaRouche campaign was a question of volume, and the response was tremendous. People knew, through reflection upon their own reactions, the importance of the LaRouche broadcasts, breaking through the controlled environment created by the U.S. media. Thousands of people who had never taken an active part in elections before, gave or loaned what they could. After the Democratic Convention, when LaRouche announced that he would continue campaigning as an independent Democrat, we set ourselves a double quota each morning for the special election funds—some for the primary election campaign fund, in order to retire debt, and some for the new Independent Democrats for LaRouche fund, to continue the TV broadcasts.

An incident at the Democratic Convention in San Francisco demonstrated how hysterical the Democratic Party leadership had become concerning LaRouche. We succeeded in gathering nominating signatures from more than enough convention delegates to place LaRouche's name officially in nomination, following the party rules and the rules of the convention down to the fine print. This meant that LaRouche would be allowed to address the convention! But when the signatures were presented to the appropriate committee, Party Chairman Charles Manatt rejected them, insisting that he—not the delegates, and not the voters of the United States—would decide who could, and who could not, be a Democratic Presidential candidate. LaRouche, he said, was absolutely out.

We took them to court. Their lawyers argued that the Democratic Party is a "private club," and has the right to ignore the voters, its own members, and its own rules and to choose as candidates whomever its leaders so desired. This, despite the fact that the Federal elections of the world's leading "democracy" were structured around the two-party system, and that millions of taxpayers' dollars paid for the primary election process! They can change the rules midstream, the Democratic Party lawyers argued, and all questions of basic rights or free elections be damned. The judge agreed. We got an early taste of the "LaRouche factor" in the U.S. judicial process—we, and the American Constitution, lost.

The most blatant recurrence of this tyranny occurred much later, in the 1996 Presidential election. LaRouche won delegates to the Democratic Convention in several state primaries, but Democratic Party Chairman Donald Fowler ruled that no delegates committed to LaRouche would be seated at the Convention! This blatant effort to disenfranchise American voters was not only un-Constitutional, it was an overt, intentional breach of the greatest legislative victory of the civil rights movement—the Voting Rights Act of 1965. When we challenged them in court, the Democratic Party lawyers argued that the Voting Rights Act should be annuled, rather than allow LaRouche's votes to be honored! Thus has the Democratic Party deserted the policies of FDR, and Martin Luther King, returning to its racist roots in the Confederacy and Woodrow Wilson's Ku Klux Klan.

Crimes of the DOJ

The momentum of the LaRouche Presidential campaign escalated through the fall of 1984. Despite President Reagan's increasing tendency to compromise, or outright capitulate, to the Kissinger/Bush wing of the Republican Party, our own independent credibility and authority were reaching a critical mass. LaRouche authorized his campaign committee to literally take over the airwaves on election eve, purchasing a half-hour spot on each of the three major networks. Not only was LaRouche's message shaping the entire political climate, much to the consternation of the families of the establishment, but there was a definite potential that LaRouche would receive a significant vote of his own. The "Get LaRouche" folks foresaw a disaster. Their timetable was radically moved forward.

Boston became the first point of attack for the "Get LaRouche Task Force." In addition to the historic tradition of "Tory" control in Boston, the DOJ also had one of their top blue-blood "Bush babies" on the job as United States Attorney: William Weld. Late in October 1984, Boston's major TV station, the NBC-affiliate WBZ, launched a three-part series, claiming that the LaRouche campaign had made false charges on contributors' credit cards. The reporter on the story was Dan Rae, a long-standing media conduit for the FBI. The same story appeared on the TV news in other cities around the country. The day after the last segment aired on WBZ, U.S. Attorney Weld announced the opening of a grand jury investigation—only days preceding the Presidential election! Had it been anyone other than LaRouche, the overt political nature of the assault would have provoked an outcry from all the cackling hens of the "human rights" lobby, who so readily demand economic sanctions, or even military operations, against targetted Third World countries, on the basis of "anti-democratic" actions against opposition candidates.

The "investigation" moved with lightning speed. Within hours, the bank accounts of the national LaRouche campaign were shut down, after the bank was contacted by the FBI, forcing the cancellation of an election eve LaRouche Presidential broadcast. Supporters began receiving calls from banks and FBI agents, in which they were ominously warned that association with LaRouche was "trouble," and urged to "charge back" their credit card contributions to the campaign. Then, in December 1984, the bank accounts of every entity associated with LaRouche were completely shut down, following a new round of calls to the banks by the FBI.

LaRouche's political campaign committees went to court to challenge the seizures of funds by the banks. In February 1985, a New Jersey Federal judge found the seizures to be illegal, but his ruling received no coverage in the media. Instead, through the terror campaign conducted against our supporters, and the press leaks orchestrated by U.S. Attorney Weld, the LaRouche campaign was convicted in the media of "credit card" fraud, long before any trial—indeed, even before the two-year grand jury investigation, which Weld eventually conducted, was even under way.

We immediately launched a counter-punch on the legal (actually illegal) operations against us. We already knew a great deal about the source of the operation—Kissinger, and the Train Salon. The U.S. Attorney leading the investigation in Boston, William Weld, was already known to us as a member of a family which was at the center of British drug-trafficking, going back to the Weld family's interests in clipper ship trade in China at the peak of the British opium wars.

Weld was an heir to the White Weld banking empire, which interfaced Crédit Suisse in Switzerland, Merrill Lynch, and First Boston. In February 1985, just a few months after the launching of the legal witch-hunt against us, Crédit Suisse was caught laundering over a billion dollars in hot money through the Bank of Boston. Over a thousand separate incidents of illegal transactions were identified. The Bank of Boston had earlier been caught laundering drug money for the organized-crime Anguilo family, but Weld had allowed them to apologize for their "honest mistake" without prosecution!

However, the billion-dollar Crédit Suisse caper was too big to simply ignore in that manner. Instead, U.S. Attorney Weld struck a plea bargain with his family friends: the thousand-plus felony counts were collapsed into a single count, the Bank of Boston pled guilty, and a fine of $500,000 was imposed. That amounted to 0.05% of the laundered money. The Bank made a fortune in (confessed) criminal activity as part of Dope, Inc., while paying a pittance in "protection money" to their inside man at the Feds.

Not only did Weld refuse to put anyone in jail for this billion-dollar dope business, but he established a precedent that was controlling in future money-laundering cases against banks. While the *bank* can be held liable for the crime, no *banker* can be criminally charged with the bank's activity! Drug enforcement officials over the years complained bitterly to us, and to the Congress, about this "Weld precedent."

While Weld was protecting Dope, Inc., he was simultaneously using his powers to crush its enemies in the LaRouche movement. Political persecution was not new to Mr. Weld. He had spearheaded a vicious campaign against the machine of Boston Mayor Kevin White, winning a conviction in a poisoned climate against the mayor's top aide. The Federal Appeals Court threw out the conviction, however, and compared Weld's tactics to Soviet legal practices! A national law journal called Weld's actions "a textbook example of prosecutorial abuse of power to control the political process."

With these qualifications, the Get LaRouche Task Force believed Weld was the man for the job.

★ ★ ★

Develop Africa with SDI

Our political response to the legal assault was to escalate the offensive. Lyn and Helga jointly declared that we would mobilize across the country for a major march on Washington in honor of Dr. Martin Luther King, Jr., on the newly established "Martin Luther King Day," January 15. The march would be sponsored by the Schiller Institute, and besides honoring Dr. King's achievements, would also honor his spirit and his method. The theme would be the urgent necessity to "Develop Africa with SDI Technology!"

By emphasizing the "science driver" concept underlying LaRouche's SDI proposal, the march aimed to establish several crucial political points. First, the spin-off technologies of the SDI, as with Kennedy's space program, were the necessary means for generating the huge technological transformation required to develop the African continent. This exposed the evil of the IMF's "appropriate technology" policy toward Africa (and all of the

Third World), which held that advanced technology was wasted on such backward economies, and that only those technologies "appropriate" to their primitive standards—such as picks and shovels—should be allowed.

Second, by showing the connection between the science of the SDI and the development of Africa, we also exposed the fraud of the Leftist argument that "the people" should oppose the space program (and other great projects) as a rip-off by the "ruling class"—the greedy business leaders and scientists.

Third, it provided a context for reminding the citizens, black and white, that Dr. King worked to unite all people around the common interests of mankind as a whole.

To the conservative layers we had recruited in support of our SDI work, the idea of the march came as both a surprise and a revelation. Many of them had been filled with the venom of "Gay" Edgar Hoover's campaign to destroy Dr. King, labelling him a "communist" because he willingly collaborated with the Communist Party and other Leftists who supported the civil rights movement. We took the opportunity to simply read excerpts from King's writings to them, demonstrating his extraordinary love of humanity and his profound understanding of both Christianity and the Platonic method.

We wanted to bring ten thousand people to Washington for the march. Our locals on the East coast, and as far away as Pittsburgh, organized dozens of busloads of supporters, many from the black community. On the phones, we told everyone about the march as the only method of combatting the collapse of the SDI policy under the pressure against Reagan from within his own administration. One call I made at that time was of particular significance, as it was the beginning of a relationship which put me personally at loggerheads with a deranged Lieutenant Colonel by the name of Oliver North.

The call was to Barbara Newington, a resident of Greenwich, Connecticut. She had contributed $1,000 on the very first call from Chris Curtis, who got her name from a list of contributors to some conservative cause. She was mailed a packet of literature, including a pamphlet describing the Schiller Institute. When I called, she immediately expressed her delight that we were combining a fight for the SDI with the necessity of a cultural renaissance. The Schiller poetry from the pamphlet, especially the "Rütli Oath," she said, "gave me hope that there may be a chance for this country yet."

I briefed her on our plans for the march. She, like many others, fed back to me the FBI lie on Dr. King as a communist, but listened intently to my rebuttal. "King's dream must be the dream of all of us," I told her, "that all God's children can march hand in hand in support of a better future. President Kennedy understood that the Moon shot was a necessary and essential prerequisite for his ambitious plans for the industrialization of Africa, Ibero-America, and Asia, as well as sparking the potential of the American economy. King also understood that. Reagan's SDI—which is LaRouche's SDI—is based on the same concept, as the engine for development. You must back the aspirations of those who have been relegated to backwardness. Their development is development for everyone. And imagine the scene in Washington on King's birthday, when 10,000 white and black Americans march with signs saying 'SDI technology to develop Africa.' "

"What do you need?"

"We estimate that the buses and the other logistics will cost about $30,000. We're hoping a few people could cover that with contributions of $5,000 or $10,000, so we can maintain our normal operations otherwise."

"I'll do thirty-five," she said. Long pause.

"You'll do thirty-five thousand dollars?" I asked.

She laughed, obviously enjoying my surprise. "Yes, I want to make sure that Washington looks exactly as you described it on January 15. And I want poets to be running it."

After letting my head clear, I thanked her, and told her that we should meet. She agreed.

I travelled the next day to her beautiful estate in a specially secured area of Greenwich. She was the widow of a Gulf Oil executive who had been a major figure in right-wing circles. He and Congressman Larry McDonald had co-founded an organization called Western Goals, which supported conservative causes both in the U.S. and in Europe. McDonald had also taken over the rabid right-wing John Birch Society a year or so before he boarded the Korean Air Lines flight 007 on Sept. 1, 1983, the ill-fated flight which was shot out of the air by Soviet Migs when it veered over Soviet air space.

There were other important officials on board KAL 007, but the right-wing was convinced that the Soviets' primary purpose was to murder Larry McDonald. This was one of the first things Barbara told me when we met—that she was certain the Soviets and their agents in the U.S. were trying to kill Reagan and all leading "patriots" (meaning the right-wing) in the U.S.

Barbara was an elegant woman in her fifties, who was a descendant of one of the leading painters of the "Hudson School" of American artists, Jasper Cropsey. Cropsey's studio in Hastings-on-Hudson in Westchester County had been turned into a museum under Barbara's tutelage, filled with many of his major paintings and sketches. There were several grand pianos in her home and in the museum, where Barbara and her sister had performed music for two pianos in earlier days. We would discuss this cultural heritage, as well as our political campaign for a cultural renaissance, for many, many hours during the next few years. At one later point, she opened the museum for a concert for some of our musicians—a string quartet and several vocalists, including myself—attended by some of her closest friends and family members.

On that first day, we spoke for several hours about her own role in conservative circles, our intelligence about the nature of the split in those circles over the SDI, and the broader strategic crisis required to understand that dynamic. I made clear to her that we were opposed to nearly all of the right-wing "rhetoric," but, as demonstrated by our influence in the Reagan cabinet, we knew we could orient the patriotic sentiment of many conservatives to the higher perspective we represented—neither "Left" nor "Right."

I knew several things about the circles she worked with and supported financially. When she told me about her connection to Larry McDonald, I told her quite bluntly that the John Birch Society was way off base, and that McDonald's office had been hostile to us, but that the source of that hostility was not McDonald himself. One John Rees, who had attended the "Get LaRouche" meetings in John Train's apartment, worked in McDonald's office, spreading lies about LaRouche there and across the country. I told her that Rees must be viewed as an agent of not only the "Get LaRouche Task Force," but the broader Kissinger and Soviet-linked apparatus dedicated to killing the SDI.

Our discussion otherwise focussed on the financial crisis, and the fact that the split among conservatives resulted from the fact that Wall Street was no longer interested in industrial progress, scientific advance, or strategic defense. Short-term profit, keeping the bubble growing through speculation and looting, had become the only concern of the financial oligarchy. She admired Reagan, was suspicious of Bush, but had no idea how intense the internal strife within the administration had become.

We talked for hours. When I decided I should leave, she again asked, "What should I do?"

I had not considered asking her for more money. I had a $35,000 certified check in my pocket. I thought for a moment, and said, "You should get a copy of our special report on beam weapons into the hands of every U.S. Congressman and Senator." She went upstairs and returned with another check for $50,000.

Barbara contributed well over two million dollars over the next two years, making possible many special campaigns and projects, while providing a crucial margin of support through several periods of intense political harassment. As we shall see later, and as Barbara subsequently revealed in her testimony before Congressional committees investigating the Iran-Contra affair, she was a major funder of Iran-Contra operations also. Ollie North and his minions did everything in their power to stop her support for our work—including direct instructions to cut us off, in favor of North's drug- and gun-running scams.

★ ★ ★

In the midst of this chaos, the annointed day of our wedding came rushing down upon us. I had proposed on a summer evening in a small Italian restaurant on Manhattan's East Side. Gail not only accepted, but was ready with a date: December 2, 1984. When that date arrived, postponement was out of the question, despite the political turmoil, since my mother, my brother Joe, Gail's parents and her brothers, John and Lee, were all descending on New York, from points as distant as Austin, Dallas, Cleveland, and Pittsburgh. Not that we wanted a postponement—there had been some hesitation along the way, but we were revelling in our mutual commitment. The political climate assured that any thoughts of a honeymoon would have to wait—for many years, as it turned out. Several of our friends who had been married during the frantic days of the early 1970's, told stories of leaving a *New Solidarity* distribution site at a plant gate about noon, getting married at City Hall, and then proceeding to an intervention at some event that evening. My first marriage, as well as Gail's, was of that general variety. This time, however, we planned an all-day affair—a wedding at the chapel on the Columbia University campus, and a grand reception for the entire membership in the same church hall in Washington Heights where Margaret and Elliot had held their reception.

The wedding was idyllic. Gail was elegant, and I even bought a new suit to replace the blue polyester rag which had been my only suit for about eight years. The minister read I Corinthians 13, using "love" as the translation for "*agapē*":

> Though I speak with the tongues of men and angels, and have not love, I am become as sounding brass, or a tinkling cymbal. . . . And though I bestow all my goods to feed the poor, and though I give my body to be burned, and have not love, it profiteth me nothing. . . . For now we see through a glass darkly; but then face to face; now I know in part, but then shall I know even as also I am known. And now abideth faith, hope, and love; but the greatest of these is love.

Gail's brother, Jon, read from Milton's *Paradise Lost*:

> Hail wedded love, mysterious Law, true source
> Of human offspring, sole propriety
> In paradise of all things common else.
> By thee adulterous lust was driv'n from men
> Among the bestial herds to range, by thee
> Founded in Reason, Loyal, Just, and Pure,
> Relations dear, and all the Charities
> Of Father, Son, and Brother first were known.

Of the pictures we took on the chapel steps, the most memorable shot was of Gail, me, our best man Elliot Greenspan, and the matron of honor, Linda de Hoyos. As we posed, I was recalling the famous events of 1968, when the SDS Labor Committee led the occupation of Low Library, just across the yard from the chapel. I raised a fist in memory of those earlier days, and in honor of our new pledge of mutual "militancy," in love and war. It was a wonderful moment of history, joy, and good humor.

The reception was a much-appreciated respite from the intensity of our political battles. Gail and I sang several duets, from *Don Giovanni, The Magic Flute,* and *Il Trovatore.* Many others recited poetry, sang, played the piano, made toasts—and, of course, we waltzed. We were very happy, and it was clear that our friends and families were delighted. No one objected when we showed up a bit late at the office the following morning.

[10]

Toe to Toe with the Oligarchy

With LaRouche now at the center of critical policy-making in Washington and several other capitals around the world, our organizing was also approaching a breakthrough level, with mass political action an immediate potential. In my own daily work, calling supporters around the country, I found that my associates and I were intersecting a broad layer of people who were being inundated with mail and calls from the pseudo-conservative networks (the so-called "neo-cons"), who were directly organizing against LaRouche's influence in the Reagan Administration. This included various spin-offs of the Heritage Foundation's "High Frontier" fraud, and the Mont Perlerin Society's crusade to deregulate everything—especially drugs. Barbara Newington was not the only supporter who began telling these British-inspired soliciters that LaRouche was exposing their game. As I would soon discover, George Bush and Col. Ollie North were among those most displeased by this exposure. I would soon feel the brunt of their enraged response.

★ ★ ★

The organizing for the Martin Luther King Day march in Washington was extremely successful, with singular developments in the minority communities in several Eastern cities. The linking up of the fight for scientific progress with a revived civil rights movement must have sent shivers through the bluish veins of the social planners amongst the oligarchy. In the days leading up to the march, the *Washington Post* ran a three-day, ten-thousand-word diatribe against LaRouche and our influence in the Reagan Administration—without mentioning, of course, the planned ten-thousand-man march in Washington. The article repeated the general line of the previous year's *New Republic* and NBC slanders, but they added in the new ammunition of extensive "leaks" (all distorted, as well as illegal) from William Weld's grand jury in Boston, claiming all sorts of criminal activity by a nefarious LaRouche machine.

The *Post* interviewed each of the people in the administration who had worked with us, who had met with Lyn, who had conveyed our ideas to the President; and also those who hated us and were hell-bent on breaking our input to the President. While the *Post* had to concede Lyn's influence on the SDI decision, they painted this as a wild, right-wing, war-mongering policy, which the saner elements within the administration were attempting to contain. Henry Kissinger was prominently featured. He expressed his shock and dismay at the "news" of LaRouche's influence over Reagan, and openly threatened the President that "if it is true," he had better break the connection, or pay dearly for such insubordination to the real powers that be.

In spite of Weld and the *Washington Post*, the March on Washington was a tremendous success. Buses rolled in from Boston, New York, New Jersey, Philadelphia, Pittsburgh, and Baltimore. Several car caravans drove from more distant areas, as far as California. Despite 9° weather, the marchers were exuberant, displaying precisely the kinds of slogans I'd discussed with Barbara Newington: "America Has a Dream: Feed Africa and Build the Beam"; "SDI Technology for African Development"; "Kennedy, King, LaRouche: Peace Through Development." The shivering but enthusiastic crowd displayed the optimism that a new mass movement in America was a possibility. The keynote speech to the outdoor crowd was given by Helga, with another stirring presentation by a remarkable heroine of the civil rights movement in America, Amelia Boynton Robinson.

Amelia, then in her seventies, was known, loved, and respected by all those who had participated in the struggle of the 1960's. In fact, she and her husband were active already in the 1930's, registering blacks to vote and giving them a voice in the Jim Crow environment of Alabama. In 1965, when the struggle for justice in her hometown of Selma reached an impasse against entrenched racial exclusion, it was Amelia who called on Dr. Martin Luther King to come to Selma, where her home became the headquarters for that famous confrontation. On March 7, 1965, the community began a march to the state capitol, crossing the Edmund Pettus Bridge out of Selma. State troopers were unleashed in a police riot against the peaceful marchers, in what became known as "Bloody Sunday." Across the world, the picture of Amelia Boynton lying on the side of the road, left for dead by Alabama State troopers, became a symbol of the evil of America's apartheid, and the courage of those who were determined to end it.

Amelia spoke at the 10,000-strong Martin Luther King Day March on Washington in 1985, as she has many times since, about Lyndon LaRouche as the man who has taken on the mantle of Dr. King, and about Helga, her "adopted daughter," as the inspired leader of the fight for a new renaissance. The rally was, by far, the largest in the nation that day.

As could be expected—no less disgusting because of its predictability—the nation's entire media blacked out the existence of this historic event. National coverage of Jesse Jackson speaking to a few dozen people, and coverage of the King family, made it appear that nobody except King's family and Jesse Jackson, with little following, were keeping Dr. King's spirit alive. The "LaRouche factor" was in play—any event with a LaRouche connection didn't happen, or, if it couldn't be blacked out, it was slandered and denounced. Again, America's "free press."

★ ★ ★

Gail and I moved to Virginia, along with the entire staff of the National Center, in April 1985. Our new abode, Leesburg, the county seat of Loudoun County, was in the middle of the "horse country" of Northern Virginia, rural and idyllic, about one hour from Washington, D.C. What we had not anticipated, however, was that the county is the site of ranches and farms owned by some of the bluest of the blue bloods. At the top of the register is Sir Paul Mellon, who entertains the Queen herself when she visits her ex-colonial holdings in the Americas. It included Averell Harriman (until his death in 1986), and his wife Pamela Churchill Harriman, daughter-in-law of Winston Churchill by her first marriage, and countless others of "high breeding." There were also a large number of "spooks" from the various branches of U.S. and British intelligence services residing in Loudoun.

Gail and I lived in a newly constructed cardboard townhouse of the sort which sprang up throughout the area during the 1980's and 1990's, the sort in which you could hear the toilet flush three houses down the row, and the mortgage had a longer life than the structure.

We were very happy, nonetheless. Gail's grandmother in Tulsa, Oklahoma, had bestowed both her 1973 Oldsmobile and a wonderful old baby grand piano upon her favorite granddaughter and new husband, just before our move to Virginia. We needed a car in Virginia—something we had lived without in New York City—and the piano was a godsend. I had begun playing while I was in Boston, on the Gelbers' piano, reaching back to my childhood lessons from the lady down the street. I read music very slowly and had no technique, but I took great joy in working through the Bach two-part inventions and the easier Mozart sonatas. I developed the habit of playing a little bit every day, which I have continued ever since, except for some of my prison years when I had no access to a piano. It has been food for the soul, a delight which no child should be denied.

We took several steps to assure that our presence in Loudoun County contributed to the local cultural life, both because that's the kind of people we are, and because we knew we needed to create a "reality buffer" against any potential slander in the small-town environment. We presented regular public concerts, and invited the public to join our musical work.

As a "town warming" gift to the community, we presented Mozart's magnificent *Requiem Mass,* complete with chorus and orchestra, in a local high school auditorium, on the July 4th weekend of 1985. Our chorus had been preparing the work since the previous fall in New York City, under John Sigerson's direction, with regular guidance from Maestro Briano on his regular visits from Mexico. In the week preceding our National Conference on the July 4 weekend, we brought together our best instrumentalists from around the world, and devoted two days to final preparation for the combined chorus and orchestra. Maestro Briano sang the bass solos, with professional singers (friends of the Schiller Institute) from the U.S. and Mexico on the other solo parts.

It was a grand performance, before a full house, including many of the local community leaders, and was warmly received by our new neighbors. Despite a few incidents of petty rumor-mongering, our initial reception was one of cautious interest. As we would soon learn, however, the lords and ladies of Loudoun's horsey set were busy preparing their attack.

★ ★ ★

In late 1984, while still in New York, I began calling on Dennis Small, one of the directors of our work in Ibero-America, to brief my contacts over the phone on the War on Drugs, both on the ground in Ibero-America and in the corridors of power in Washington and Wall Street. We found that Americans, while horrified by the apparently unstoppable drug epidemic across the country, felt totally impotent and discouraged about ever being able to seriously combat it. This sense of defeat bred pessimism in regard to the other mounting problems in the country. But when Dennis provided a picture of the courageous and increasingly effective fight of our members and our political allies in Ibero-America, together with an exposé of the individuals in the Western banking establishment who ran Dope, Inc., people became less cynical and far more optimistic, while properly focussing their anger over drugs on the "people above suspicion" who were actually responsible. The likes of Henry Kissinger and William Weld were easily shown to be the facilitators of the narco-armies of Peru and Colombia. Without the lax international financial mechanisms and a corrupt Justice Department, the likes of drug lords Carlos Lehder or Pablo Escobar could not survive.

By 1984, we had an extensive presence in Ibero-America. We had offices in Mexico, Colombia, Peru, and Venezuela, with networks of collaborators in most of the other Spanish- and Portuguese-speaking nations south of the U.S. border. We built up our membership through tough, scrappy fights against the IMF policies towards Ibero-America, demanding debt moratoria as the necessary precondition for development, and to prevent the "Africanization" of Ibero-America. Besides the entrenched local oligarchy, who despised our exposure of their cozy relationship with their foreign mentors at the IMF, we were also attacked by the emerging phalanx of NGOs (non-governmental organizations), sponsored by European royalty and the Anglo-American family foundations. This was a globalization of the New Left "swamp" from 1960's America. These NGOs simply retailed the slanders against our organization as "right wing" and "anti-Semitic," adding in occasional zingers, like "LaRouche sponsors Latin-American death squads." To such self-proclaimed "progressives," hiding behind Leftist rhetoric, the enemy was not the IMF conditions, the Malthusian depopulation policies, nor the bankers who had turned their countries into cocaine plantations. Rather, their enemy was precisely those institutions which were capable of defending national sovereignty, especially the military and the Church. This was the "secret" which explained the total agreement between the financial oligarchy and the narco-terrorists: on the one hand, drug money, and on the other, the desire to destroy any institution capable of offering political or moral resistance to the IMF. The Church and the military were the primary institutions with that potential.

Were the institutions of the Church and the militaries corrupt? Absolutely. But the same international institutions which contributed to that corruption were now sponsoring "anti-corruption" campaigns, demanding not only the *reform* of the Church and the military, but their *destruction*.

A handful of courageous prelates spoke out, in league with Pope John Paul II, against both the bloody hell of the narco-terrorist brigades and the rapacious looting by the international financial institutions. But many of the Church leaders said nothing, or outright supported the narco-terrorists.

Under the guise of "liberation theology" and "Marxist-Christian dialogue," a radical existentialist (pagan) movement was created within the Church, aimed both at its subversion, and its use in fostering insurgency. It was a short step for the "liberation theologists" to endorse and sponsor the "indigenous" drug producers' violent defense of their "way of life."

Simultaneously, the Western press and the NGO's mounted international campaigns denouncing Ibero-America's national military institutions. When Peru's bloody *Sendero Luminoso* (Shining Path) fanatics entered a village, lined up the adults, shot every teacher, nurse, or political representative connected to the government, impressing the rest into service to "the revolution" (usually as forced labor on the coca plantations), not a word would escape the lips of the "human rights" organizations. But every act of the military to combat such narco-terrorism was blasted as an abridgement of human rights, and as proof that the "brutal Latin American dictatorships were oppressing 'the people.' "

Debt Bomb

Our importance in the battle in Ibero-America had escalated dramatically in 1980 and 1981. The combination of Volcker's high interest rates, the contrived oil crisis of the 1970's, and the accumulating effect of IMF conditionalities, had created a debt bubble which was about to explode. The oil crisis had generated a flow of billions of dollars out of the real economies of both the advanced and the underdeveloped nations, through the oil nations in the Gulf, and into the coffers of the Anglo-American financial institutions, who were the bankers to the Arab sheiks. This money was then loaned to Third World nations, at exhorbitant rates and with stringent economic and political conditions, to meet their massive oil debt, thus giving the international banking establishment a new colonial hold on most of the Third World.

LaRouche coined the phrase "debt bomb" to describe the bubble of Third World debt, warning that this imminent explosion would take down the Third World and the advanced sector with it. He wrote a proposal for global financial reform, called *Operation Juárez,* calling for debt moratoria, industrialization, and the integration of Ibero-America, aimed not only to save Ibero-America, but to save the U.S. as well, as potentially the primary supplier of the machine tools and advanced industrial technology required for continental development.

Although LaRouche's *Operation Juárez*'s proposals were not reported in the U.S. press, the term "debt bomb" was soon recognized as an apt and unavoidable metaphor. It even turned up on the cover of *Time* magazine—without credit to LaRouche, of course.

The greatest financial problem was in Mexico. President José López Portillo had followed Lyn's analysis closely, and had met often with our national leadership in Mexico to discuss the crisis and our proposals. In 1982, President López Portillo invited LaRouche to visit him in Mexico City. Following a lengthy private meeting, the President called together the entire world press corps at the Presidential Palace, with no pre-announcement of his purpose. Before the stunned gathering of national and international reporters, many of whom had gone to great lengths to assure their readers that LaRouche was a non-entity or a kook, President López Portillo personally introduced LaRouche, explaining to the press that LaRouche's ideas on the crisis, and his solutions, were worthy of careful consideration by all nations. He then turned the press conference over to his guest. This press conference went unreported in the U.S. press.

Later, in the summer of 1982, López Portillo dropped the debt bomb, announcing a moratorium on the servicing of Mexico's foreign debt. Speaking before the Mexican Congress, he implemented a package of emergency measures to stop the speculative destruction of the economy, including the nationalization of the banking system. On the way out of the Congressional building, the President stopped to greet the head of our Mexican organization, Marivilla Carrasco, saying, "Well, I did it!" He knew the fight had just begun.

Our efforts to win support for Mexico and for the *Operation Juárez* program from both the Reagan Administration and the other nations of Ibero-America, were generally unsuccessful. As mentioned earlier, Kissinger pushed frantically to insert himself into the administration as "Latin American Advisor," while LaRouche's reports to President Reagan warning him against Kissinger's appointment were intercepted by Oliver North. Kissinger succeeded. The result was economic disaster and Ollie North's guns-for-drugs business.

In Ibero-America itself, the problem was one we would come up against time and time again—the utter corruption and outright cowardliness of most political leaders across Ibero-America. With few exceptions, they had reached their positions of power through a willingness to compromise with the powers of the IMF. Always promising the electorate that just one more round of IMF conditionalities, one more tightening of the belt, would create the conditions for future jobs and prosperity, these leaders were sitting on a pressure cooker, hoping to buy off any threat to their power with occasional crumbs from the IMF. Now that the "debt bomb" was exploding, we called on each nation to come to the defense of López Portillo, and to replicate his actions against international speculation. The answer was universal: "Our situation is different. We've been assured by our friends at the IMF that they won't let things get that bad here, that we're doing very well so far on our own structural adjustment program, and that very soon we'll be getting a flood of new investments. We can't afford to risk sticking out our necks in defense of Mexico."

Such cowardice, both North and South, left the nations of Ibero-America weak and divided, subject both to the numerous drug armies and the emerging "globalization" process, which has now rendered Ibero-America an economic basket case.

The Drug War

The battle lines in Ibero-America shifted to the Andes nations in the mid-1980's, as our War on Drugs organizing engaged the enemy both in the advanced sector and in the producing countries of South America. As cocaine, and later crack, became the "drug of choice" in the U.S., the coca plantations of the Andes, and the armies protecting them, took on increased importance in the international battle. In Colombia, Bolivia, and Peru, the narco-terrorist armies were far better funded, and better armed, than the national armies. We were determined to convince the Reagan Administration to attack the drug problem both militarily and through prosecution of the drug-money-laundering banks. We also supplied the governments in Ibero-America with the global intelligence they required to effectively counter the narco-terrorists and their international NGO and "human rights" support structures.

Dennis Small, in our joint calls to our supporters, emphasized two things: first, the personal courage of our members on the ground in the "narco-democracies" in Ibero-America; and, second, the fact that the crucial handful of nationalist leaders in those nations who were battling for the combined power of the drug armies and the IMF looked to us as their only reliable source of intelligence on international matters, and as the one hope that there was some sanity in the United States. Several of our friends amongst these nationalist leaders were killed by the narcos. Our own members were under constant threat and, in one case in Colombia, a leading member was kidnapped and narrowly escaped death.

We emphasized in all our work that the narco-armies and the various "revolutionary" gangs using Marxist rhetoric were actually what we termed "narco-terrorists." This issue became a crucial litmus test in the coming years, as the Bush/Oliver North apparatus covered up for the drug traffickers (including themselves!) by insisting that the "communists" were distinct from the "drug-traffickers," and that the primary concern of the U.S. should be that of fighting "communists."

Later, when Oliver North was illegally extracting millions of dollars from Barbara Newington, while coercing her to stop her support for us, he told her that the Contras were "good" drug-runners, while the Sandinistas were "bad" drug-runners. To "draw the line against communism," he said, meant turning a blind eye to the drug trade. In fact, he was covering up his own direct involvement in the drug trade—his notebooks from 1985 and 1986 are replete with references to his knowledge that the planes used to supply arms to the Contras were also loaded up with dope. His gallant, patriotic, anti-communist crusade was *directly contributing to the primary means of support for the Marxist insurgent organizations across Ibero-America!*

My work mobilizing Americans to support our campaigns in Ibero-America taught me something about the American people. The general interest in countries south of the border was minimal, as was the general level of knowledge of the history and culture of our southern neighbors. The fact that these nations, too, were being destroyed by drugs, was blurred by the image of "banana republic dictators" which was conveyed equally by Hollywood and the national media. But our briefings put a name and a face on those who were risking their lives on the front line of the War on Drugs. The War on Drugs became more than a legislative issue, and, although people were shocked at the military, political, and financial power of the narco-terrorists, they also began to grasp that this war could be *won,* if the U.S. were to join in the manner outlined by LaRouche—a military blockade of air and shipping routes against unscheduled transport, and a full criminal prosecution of the London and New York banks of Dope, Inc.

Our influence in Ibero-America expanded rapidly in 1984. We completed a Spanish translation of *Dope, Inc.*, adding chapters on the Ibero-American situation. But when we were suddenly stripped of our bank accounts, we were forced to postpone publication. While we scrambled to brief all our supporters on our emergency needs to combat the assault from the "Get LaRouche Task Force," we could not afford to let new initiatives and publications be stalled by the enemy attack. Dennis Small and I discussed the problem. He agreed to brief a few of our better contacts in depth on the overall situation and on the urgency of publishing *Narcotráfico S.A.*, the Spanish-language edition of *Dope, Inc.*, without delay.

I called several supporters who had already responded generously to the crisis created by the financial warfare and the media slanders, and explained to them the general parameters of the dangerous but crucial battle on the ground in Ibero-America. I told them that Dennis wanted to speak with anyone who was willing to consider a large contribution or loan to finance the publishing of *Narcotráfico S.A.* and an organizing blitz across Ibero-America. By pre-arranging the call for Dennis, I allowed those who simply did not have the means to make such a large contribution to tell me so directly, while those who considered it a possibility could hear Dennis's briefing with a clear sense of what we were asking them to do, and what their support would achieve. The response from nearly everyone was extremely positive.

We had learned over the years that virtually every American had some personal experience with the effects of drugs—some relative or close friend whose life had been ruined by Dope, Inc. Dennis often told the story of his own brother, who had been destroyed by cocaine and other drugs, and was battling to regain his mental balance. We were disturbed, but not surprised, to learn that even the most stable and conservative families from small towns in Iowa or South Dakota were not free from the deadly psychological and physical effects of the drug epidemic. Our supporters were not only willing to contribute to the fight, but they often came to believe—quite rightly—that it was one of the most important things they had done in their lives.

Years later, in courthouses in Boston, New York, and Virginia, the prosecutors of the "Get LaRouche Task Force" would present these calls to our supporters as vile tricks played upon unsuspecting victims. I was described as a "set-up man," who lured the naive, vulnerable target into the trap, where Dennis barraged them with fanciful stories and half-truths, ruthlessly coercing them into relinquishing their life savings to our "money machine."

Banned in Venezuela

We succeeded in getting *Narcotráfico S.A.* published in January 1985, at about the same time as our 10,000-strong Martin Luther King Day march on Washington. Within days of its release, the oligarchy responded. In Caracas, Venezuela, the political police raided our office, seizing every copy of *Narcotráfico S.A.*, and arresting four non-Venezuelan representatives of EIR, who were deported the next day. This iron boot treatment did not come from the government, but directly from the head of the Venezuelan oligarchy, Gustavo Cisneros, who officially filed a complaint and demanded the seizure. Within a few days, one of the judges beholden to Cisneros banned all distribution of *Narcotráfico S.A.* within the country, the first—and last—political book to be banned in Venezuelan history!

Why Venezuela? Mr. Cisneros and his family had indeed earned their place within the pages of *Narcotráfico S.A.* As the leading oligarchical family in the region, with influence far beyond Venezuela, the Cisneros clan were the closest of friends with the royal families of Europe and the would-be royalty in the U.S., such as Henry Kissinger (now *Sir* Henry), and George Bush (now *Sir* George), who were the Cisneros's personal guests on their frequent visits to Caracas. Together, they oversaw the implementation of IMF and Dope, Inc. policies in Ibero-America. The role of Venezuela as both a location for laundering drug money and as a center for orchestrating IMF colonial policies throughout Ibero-America was severely threatened by *Narcotráfico S.A.* and our intelligence capacity generally. The Cisneros gang, with full support from the Kissinger gang stateside, tried to crush the danger through jackboot methods.

Across Ibero-America, the release of *Narcotráfico S.A.* became a rallying point for patriots in the fight to save their countries from the drug lords and the drug bankers. In Peru, a leading newspaper, *El Popular*, serialized the entire book. In Colombia, when the drug cartel-linked newspaper *El Tiempo* ran a multi-part attack on LaRouche and our movement, targetting *Narcotráfico S.A.* for "slandering" prestigious figures, President Belisario Betancur stood his ground in defense of our role in the struggle. President Betancur also held a high-profile meeting with President Reagan, declaring joint collaboration and mutual dedication to winning the war on drugs.

However, by the end of 1985, the Reagan Administration had largely capitulated to the Kissinger policies towards drugs, and towards Ibero-America generally. One sign of this came from FBI Director William Webster, who issued a public statement that there was no such thing as "narco-terrorism"—that there was no connection between the "revolutionary" organizations and the drug cartels. I was astonished at FBI Director Webster's pronouncement. I had, for two months, been briefing all my contacts on the narco-terrorist wars in Peru and Colombia, and the director of the FBI then pretends that this highly publicized war didn't exist! Webster's lie confirmed that the Bush/Kissinger faction in the administration was going public with their overt support for drug-running. Further proof came with the Nicaraguan "Contra" operation, which was breaking into the open during the early months of 1986.

Sparring with Ollie North

We had been monitoring the mounting U.S. support for Nicaragua's Contras for years, and Lyn had repeatedly warned against it. Several officials from the NSC, the CIA, and other intelligence agencies had called on the organization to support their overt and covert operations against the radical Marxist Sandinista regime in Nicaragua, arguing that the Sandinistas were both terrorists and drug runners, and that LaRouche would certainly agree with their scheme to support the armed opposition which called itself the Contras. The only problem was that we knew all too well that the

Contras, the remnants of the old Samoza regime, were themselves deeply involved in drug trafficking—including direct collaboration with the narco-terrorists of the Medellín and Cali cartels in Colombia!

We did everything we could to convince our friends in the administration that supporting the Contras was a pre-programmed disaster. The Sandinistas were not an isolated, contained phenomenon that could be defeated by traditional military means. They were but one piece of a global narco-terrorist operation, with connections into Castro in Cuba, the Colombian drug cartels, the oligarchy's "human rights" organizations, and the global Dope, Inc. financial institutions. Either the U.S. adopted a comprehensive policy to attack this unified Dope, Inc. apparatus, including those parts within the U.S.A. itself, or we were doomed to lose the war.

There was also a particularly putrid stench arising from the entire "Contra-supply" program. We were familiar with Col. Oliver North, and his involvement in a number of covert operations, including security operations in Ibero-America, and secret wheeling and dealing in Middle East arms markets. Ollie had been brought into the NSC as a military liaison (at the request of Henry Kissinger, we would later learn), but his operations were being run *independently*, as semi-private enterprises. Such semi-private and semi-official operations were intended to allow activities which could circumvent Congressional oversight, bypass legal restrictions on government agencies, and provide for a "plausible denial" capacity when things went wrong.

As the world would soon learn, with the breaking of the Iran-Contra scandal in 1986, the Contra policy was a crucial part of the *defense* of Dope, Inc., including the fact that Ollie and his boss, then-Vice President George Bush, were themselves running tons of dope into the streets of the U.S. on Federally protected transport planes, exchanging guns for drugs in Central America. They were also spending a great deal of their time and energy trying to cut off LaRouche's influence in Ibero-America and in Washington.

My regular contact with Barbara Newington in Connecticut put me directly in the middle of this fight. Throughout 1985 and 1986, in addition to her sponsorship of our Martin Luther King Day March on Washington, Barbara contributed to most of our major campaigns and publications. I spent hours with her, discussing history and ideas, and also arranged background briefings from Dennis and others on specific projects. She was also supporting other organizations, including Western Goals, which she told me was foundering since her husband's and Larry McDonald's deaths. She asked if I could propose anyone who might take it over, and that she had recently met a man named Spitz Channell, who represented certain other conservative causes, who was anxious to take it over. She doubted he could provide the necessary leadership—certainly not the kind of comprehensive, global policy initiatives that we carried out—but, she said, he was "very well-connected."

Indeed. Spitz Channell was Ollie's hit-man for the massive illegal fundraising operation, which paid for the logistics of the North/Bush guns and drugs business, while also keeping a nest of fundraisers well-heeled. Spitz was also part of the "homintern," the nest of (mostly conservative) homosexuals connected to Henry Kissinger, British intelligence, and the Soviet/East German Stasi apparatus. Spitz's "friend" Terry Dolan, the head of the National Conservative Political Action Committee (NCPAC), would later "come out" as a homosexual activist before he died of AIDS, to the shock of many of the arch-conservatives who had plied NCPAC with millions of dollars over the years. Particularly disturbing to many was the discovery that much of their money had passed through NCPAC into "conservative" gay-rights organizations. Spitz's assignment from the Bush/North network was to take over Western Goals, which represented a large number of the wealthiest conservative political contributors in America, while also breaking LaRouche's connection to members of the group.

Barbara told me that Spitz, and others, were advising her not to support LaRouche, trying various tacks about our being "soft on Communism" or "anti-American." She told them that such accusations were nonsense, and tried to get Spitz to work together with us, but to no avail. We were, in fact, in touch with several people in the Western Goals office, who told us they considered Spitz a snake, and that Spitz was spreading venomous slanders against us.

Barbara was supporting the Contra supply effort through Spitz Channell, although she never mentioned Oliver North's name to me, nor told me how much money they took from her. Nor did she tell me of her trips to Washington, where she was entertained by Ollie, and even had two brief "thank you" meetings with the President at the White House. All this was eventually revealed in Barbara's testimony before the Congressional Committee investigating Iran Contra.

Also revealed in Barbara's Congressional testimony was further evidence that North, and his immediate boss, Vice President George Bush, were coordinating their Contra scam as a direct counter to LaRouche, and to our program for an effective war on drugs. She reported that the most pious Colonel North, while employed as both a military officer of the United States and as a representative of the President's National Security Council, instructed her to cut off all support to LaRouche organizations, and to funnel all her contributions through Spitz Channell and his homosexual "partner" Richard Miller, into North's operation.

On May 4 and 5, 1986, Ollie and his wife, together with Spitz and his "partner," spent the weekend at Barbara's home in Greenwich, Connecticut. Two most interesting developments emerged. First, Ollie told Barbara, that the enemies of America may well be watching her, and that he would arrange for a "sweep" of her phones to assure that there were no wiretaps. Of course, they also discussed LaRouche, and the fact that I called and briefed her on a regular basis. It seems to me most probable that whiz-kid Ollie was planting a tap on her phones in order to monitor our calls. Strong circumstantial evidence for that conjecture emerged years later, when we received through the Freedom of Information Act a telegram that had been found in Ollie's safe, dated May 6, the day following his weekend at Barbara's estate. The telegram, from North's cohort, Gen. Richard Secord in Texas, read, in part: "Lewis has met with FBI and other agency reps and is apparently meeting again today. Our man here claims Lewis has collected info against LaRouche—let's see how polygraph goes. Regards, Dick." (This gem showed up, in the midst of our Federal trial in Boston, in 1988, while the government's prosecuting attorneys had been repeatedly telling the judge that our contentions concerning government operations against our political work were fantasies, delusions, and lies designed to cover up our "crimes." The memo provoked the judge to order a thorough search of government offices, including that of Vice President Bush, and contributed to the breakdown of the Boston prosecution.)

Yet another piece of the puzzle emerged with the release of North's notebooks during his own trial, further demonstrating how much LaRouche was on the "saintly" demon's mind that first week of May. On April 30, 1986, only a few days before his weekend in Greenwich, North spoke with Spitz about a meeting with Nicky Arundel, one of the Lords of Loudoun who ran the local *Loudoun Times-Mirror* newspaper. The *Times-Mirror* served as the voice of the "Get LaRouche Task Force" in our hometown area. Given Nicky's penchant for slandering LaRouche, there can be little doubt about the subject matter of his meeting with Ollie.

Ironically, North's overt, confirmed, criminal fundraising practices went unpunished, along with all his other crimes, while our totally legitimate sales and fundraising were used as the excuse to throw us in jail! It was firmly established that North lied to Barbara, and several others, telling them that their contributions were tax deductable—"charitable" contributions, supposedly for the purchase of helicopter gun ships (!), although that, too, was most likely a lie. North didn't really need the millions of dollars gathered from Barbara and a few others. He had access to enormous amounts of slush funds from arms and drug deals internationally.

The "fundraising" effort had other objectives. First, to bring this traditional layer of political conservatives into support for the narco-terrorist apparatus run from London and Wall Street, under the guise of fighting communism in one country. Second, to end the growing support among conservatives for our war against Dope, Inc., both in Ibero-America and here at home. The fact that these conservative layers were also strong supporters of the LaRouche/Reagan SDI made it all the more imperative, in the eyes of the Bush/Kissinger apparatus, to break their ties to us. That aspect became even more apparent in the fall of 1986, when the Soviets and their Western allies tried to "Bushwhack" President Reagan at the U.S./Soviet Summit in Reykjavík, into deserting his commitment to the SDI; while, virtually simultaneously, over 400 Federal, state, and local law enforcement officers, heavily armed, with helicopters and armored personnel carriers, raided the offices of the LaRouche-connected organizations in Leesburg, Virginia, New Jersey, and Boston, and carted me and others off to jail.

[11]

Targetted

Throughout 1985 and 1986, the DOJ and U.S. Attorney for Boston William Weld were desperately trying to put together a case against us. They used the subpoena power of the grand jury, and the right to impose fines for anything they deemed to be non-compliance with their subpoenas, to disrupt our political work. Tons of documents were subpoenaed and turned over, while several members were dragged before the grand jury and grilled for weeks on end over minutia pertaining to our fundraising.

We learned quickly from our contacts that a team of FBI agents had been deployed on an harassment detail, a "fishing expedition," calling all our supporters with questions along the lines of: "We've learned that the LaRouche organization has been calling people under false pretenses, soliciting money for various causes, and putting charges on people's charge cards, and that you are a victim of their scheme. Did you know that they are racist and anti-Semitic? That LaRouche lives a life of luxury in a mansion from all this money from their scheme? You can get your money back if you report it to the charge card company as an unauthorized charge." Later, as they prepared for trial, they also lied to people that if they would testify against us, the government would help them get some money back. They had no such intention—their only purpose was to shut us down by any means necessary.

★ ★ ★

Things began to get nasty in October 1985. My brother-in-law Elliot was the record-keeper for our primary literature distribution company, and was therefore called before the grand jury to turn over documents and answer questions. At one point, he was asked repeatedly to identify people who were referred to only by first names on organizational phone lists. He explained that he would not speculate on things he did not know. The prosecutor promptly asked a judge to throw him in jail. The judge was most willing, and Elliot was "in the slammer."

This was not Elliot's first time in jail. In fact, at the tenth anniversary party for the founding of *New Solidarity,* Elliot had been presented with a nailfile mounted on cardboard, as "The Most Arrested Member of the NCLC." He had been a favorite target of the 1970's Cointelpro operations against us, which had included petty harassment by cooperating local law enforcement, detaining political organizers for "disrupting pedestrians," "soliciting without a license," and similar ridiculous excuses. Such charges were inevitably dropped, but only after a night in jail, lawyers' fees, etc.

Elliot's jailing in Boston was a clear warning that the illegal legal assault was escalating. We "counter-punched," by hitting on a flank. My sister Margaret was, by coincidence, in Colombia when her husband was thrown in jail in Boston. She had travelled with John Sigerson to present a series of concerts and classes on classical *Lieder* and musical tuning in Peru. When the news arrived, our local in Bogotá immediately arranged a press conference for Margaret. The wife of the political prisoner struck a compassionate chord in Colombia. As soon as he was released, Elliot flew off to Mexico, and then to Peru, speaking before the national press and large forums in each country, on judicial tyranny in America and the abuse of power used to destroy political opposition—i.e., Dope, Inc. vs. LaRouche. Mexicans, Colombians, Peruvians, and, in fact, nationalists all over the world, who were repeatedly accused by Americans of "human rights violations" against political opposition parties, were interested indeed in Elliot's story. The extensive press coverage in Ibero-America generally went unnoticed by the American public, but the Kissinger networks in the State Department and within the administration knew exactly how much damage we were doing to their hypocritical campaigns in the Third World, complaining about a lack of "democracy and human rights" every time a narco-terrorist was captured.

Another blow from the grand jury process hit in March 1985. A court imposed fines of $10,000 per day on each of the four organizations under investigation, for supposedly failing to turn over documents. Truckloads of documents, of course, had been turned over, but some material was being contested legally. These legal challenges, and arguments, were totally appropriate, but the four organizations were slapped with huge fines nonetheless. Over the next two years, these fines accumulated, with interest, to several million dollars against each of the four organizations!

U.S. Attorney William Weld, was not satisfied with the results of the Boston grand jury witch-hunt. We learned years later, in documents obtained through FOIA, that Weld had sent a series of letters to the DOJ demanding a wider investigation, a national task force with broader scope. When the first Boston grand jury expired without indictments in January 1986, Weld called a meeting in Boston, inviting both Federal officials and known LaRouche-haters from state and local law enforcement agencies around the country, trying to paste together a "national conspiracy" case.

Also in 1985, the first steps in the amazing case of Lewis du Pont Smith unfolded in a court in Chester County, Pennsylvania. I had met Lewis, by phone, in 1983, while I was in Boston. He was an outspoken, opinionated young teacher in a private school, who was intrigued by *New Solidarity*, but full of criticisms of our "style." I learned later that he was one of the heirs to the DuPont fortune. He became a close supporter, and began to organize with us, speaking out as a member, as well as making a large contribution to the campaign against Dope, Inc. His blue-blood family went bonkers. Lewis's father, Newbold Smith, found a compliant judge, who declared Lewis mentally incompetent to manage his financial affairs. (Newbold went even further, joining forces with the "Get LaRouche Task Force" in financing and planning overt crimes against the organization, including a kidnapping of his own son! In that case, however, he got caught, and later stood trial in Federal court as a kidnapper.)

The harassment of supporters was stepped up as well. In December 1985, a woman in Florida, Audrey Carter, with whom I had been in touch for several months, was visited by the FBI. She was scared, and reluctant to tell me about it, but eventually told me most of the story after a front-page article in the *Tampa Tribune* appeared, describing her as a brainwashed dupe of the LaRouche cult. It turned out that she had been sending some of our literature to her son, both to share the intelligence and to try to get his support for our efforts. The son knew his mother was very active in politics, although limited by her health to phone conversations, financial help, and organizing her friends and family. But when he learned that she had loaned money to our campaigns, he moved to stop it. He called the FBI and an acquaintance at the *Tampa Tribune*, resulting in an article which characterized Mrs. Carter as a confused old lady.

The press smears against us shifted at that point, to "LaRouche Bilks Little Old Ladies." It became clear that the Task Force was targetting older people, seeking out seniors on our list of contributors, calling their *children*, soliciting greed under the guise of protecting senior citizens. The fact is, I would have been glad to seek out senior citizens—which we did not, except to the extent seniors were a relatively high percentage of those on the "political contributors" lists we purchased—since there was unquestionably a *moral superiority* in those over the age of 70 at that time. This was not a question of *age*, but of *generation*. Those born before about 1915 were young adults during the Depression. They remembered from their youth, and also through their parents and grandparents, an America which still had a moral purpose, which believed in principle, in inalienable rights, and which was optimistic that science and technology, with a lot of love, could create a better world. But this generation also learned that speculative exuberance leads to disaster, as it did between 1929 and 1933. And, they knew that the consequence of depression is war. Their children, many of whom displayed great courage in fighting fascism in World War II, fell for the post-war myth that "built-in stabilizers" would keep the economy prosperous forever.

The over-70 generation was generally repulsed by the mindlessness of the counterculture, but even more incensed that the generation then governing the institutions of state (that is, the generation of their children) was doing nothing to counter the descent into post-industrial society, Sodom-and-Gomorrah decadence, and 1920's-style speculation. Many of that older generation saw in LaRouche and in our work, a hope that someone in America was committed to reviving the idea of progress, with the courage to fight evil, rather than the "I'm okay, you're okay" moral anarchy of the Pepsi generation.

The increasing pace of slanders in the national media had some impact in frightening our supporters and prospective supporters, but our constant exposure of the operation served to counter the lies in most cases. Rather than downplaying the legal witch-hunt against us, LaRouche emphasized that every attack was an opportunity to expose those *behind* the attack. Nearly every *New Solidarity* carried front-page stories—often blaring headlines—of the accusations against us. In our calls, we kept the accusations against us up front, taking people through the chain of events (as we knew them at that point) which had provoked this high-powered combination of forces to go to such extremes to stop us.

It wasn't until January 1986—14 months after the first FBI (illegal) seizure of our bank accounts—that I learned that I was one of the targets. I was sick with the flu when our bell rang one morning at about 6:00 a.m. Gail answered, to find two FBI agents asking for me.

"He's sick. You'll have to come back," she told them. They made threatening noises, but she closed the door and told me what was going on.

"You call security—I'll guard the cats!" I said with a smile. (We'd had a good deal of fun over the years at the expense of "Gay" Edgar Hoover's known perverse proclivities.) Gail called someone on the security staff, who said they'd be over to check things out. A few minutes after the agents left, we received a call from the growling and snarling FBI Agent in Charge, Dick Egan, threatening horrible things if I didn't answer the door. Sure enough, the agents returned. I answered the door, but demanded to see their identifications and take a few notes before confirming who I was and accepting a subpoena, while an associate who had arrived recorded the exchange on film. Overall, we were most polite, while the super-sleuths were most "uptight."

The FBI wanted handwriting samples and voice exemplars, indicating they were investigating me for some criminal activity. I was more amused than disturbed, since I knew I had never done anything even bordering on criminality. Nonetheless, I proceeded to find a lawyer, the first of many I would have to deal with, and spent a day at FBI headquarters in Alexandria, writing names and speaking into a tape recorder.

'LaRouche Killed Palme'

In February and March of 1986, LaRouche and the organization burst again onto the front pages of the world press, following two extraordinary developments: the first, the assassination of Swedish Prime Minister Olof Palme on Feb. 28, 1986, and a massive international attempt to blame LaRouche for the crime; and, the second, the election victory three weeks later of two LaRouche associates in the Illinois Democratic primaries, for the offices of Lieutenant Governor and Secretary of State.

The Palme assassination was a shock. He had dismissed his security staff early one night and gone to a movie with his wife, only to be gunned down on a public street by a killer, who simply ran away. As in all such political crimes, the course of the attempted cover-up was, and continues to be today, the primary clue to the solution of this as-yet-unsolved murder. The primary thread which can unravel that cover-up is the attempt to pin it on LaRouche.

Scandinavian press were the first to cry "LaRouche did it," quoting leaks from the investigation that the prime suspect was connected to the "right-wing extremist, Lyndon LaRouche." Right on cue, NBC-TV's Brian Ross put together a story for the Evening News accusing LaRouche, and interviewing the "expert" Irwin Suall, head of the ADL's Fact-Finding Division, pontificating on how likely it was that LaRouche would do such a thing. The supposed suspect, a man who had merely purchased some literature from our Swedish organization at public events, was quickly found to have had no involvement in the murder, and was released. This did nothing to slow the pace of the international "exposé" of LaRouche as the assassin.

Most importantly, the Soviets produced a documentary called "Who Killed Olof Palme?," which I had the opportunity to view.

Complete with actors portraying the sinister, Nazi-like LaRouche and his killer assistants, the moderator portrayed LaRouche and his movement as the re-emergence of fascism in Europe.

Meanwhile, Irwin Suall and his ADL associates presented a series of spectacles for U.S. newspapers and television, culminating in another NBC special, claiming "inside information" that LaRouche had ordered the assassination of Henry Kissinger. Suall travelled to Sweden to "help the Palme investigation," although he was generally ignored and even ridiculed by the Swedes. In the fall, after the spectacular Oct. 6, 1986 raid on our Leesburg offices, NBC's Nightly News reported "new evidence" of LaRouche's role in Palme's murder, pointing to notebooks seized in the raid—full of the notes of our investigation into the assassination!

Three years later, after the fall of the Berlin Wall in 1989, a high-ranking official of the East German intelligence service (Stasi) went public with his role in the disinformation campaign following the Palme assassination. The official, Herbert Brehmer, told the Swedish press that his assignment in 1986 had been to cover the tracks which led from the Palme assassination into Stasi covert operations and East German arms deals. He revealed that *he had created* the story that "LaRouche killed Palme," using intelligence networks within the Swedish Social Democracy and in the Western press. The leading role of the ADL in this Big Lie was of particular interest, in light of the fact that ADL leader (and bankroller) Charles Bronfman, the organized-crime, dope, and booze kingpin of Canada's Seagram's Co., was exposed as a close personal friend of the bloody dictator Honecker, who even awarded him communist East Germany's "Order of the East German State" in 1988. The ADL interface with every layer of the criminal "Project Democracy" arms- and drug-dealings of the Bush-Thatcher networks should have made absolutely clear to anyone with any sense—if it wasn't clear before—why the ADL went to such lengths to slander and disrupt our organization. The Nazi "Big Lie" tactics served the ADL quite well.

Victory Means Defamation

On March 18, 1986, a totally unexpected (by the oligarchy) event forced the Task Force to escalate its campaign. Two LaRouche

Democrats, Mark Fairchild and Janice Hart, won the races for Lieutenant Governor and Secretary of State in the Democratic primary in the State of Illinois. The winning candidate for the Governor's race was Adlai Stevenson, Jr., son of the famous Democrat and party-standard bearer in the Eisenhower years. The victories by Hart and Fairchild meant that the official Democratic Party ticket in the November elections, which the Democrats had a good chance to win against the incumbent Republican Administration, would be Stevenson, Fairchild, and Hart—a stunning demonstration of the rapid expansion of the LaRouche faction of the Democratic Party among the electorate.

We were elated, and well prepared to launch into a new phase of responsibility for mobilizing and educating the population. The "Families," however, were shocked and hysterical—including most of the Democratic Party leadership. They should not have been shocked. Not only had our thousands of candidates across the country done increasingly well in both local and statewide races—including 19% for U.S. Senate candidate George Gentry in Oklahoma, and 26% for Steve Douglas running for Governor in Pennsylvania—but even the Democratic Party's own pollster, one Mike McKeon, had been reporting for months that the LaRouche organization in Illinois was out on the streets across the state, gathering considerable support from a disgruntled population. As it turned out, not only was this honest appraisal ignored by the press, but to their own peril, by the party leadership as well.

We expected to receive all the attention from the press that we'd been denied up until that point. For the first 24 hours or so, there was stunned but somewhat straightforward coverage. Headlines across the nation reported the upset. Adlai Stevenson himself appeared, at first, ready to negotiate a working relationship with us. Hart and Fairchild, who had promised during the campaign that they would roll the tanks down State Street, if that's what it took to drive the drugs out of Chicago, did exactly that. With an armored personnel carrier loaned by some friends, they led parades and demonstrations through the streets of Chicago, while activating networks across the state to escalate on all fronts. LaRouche was suddenly in great demand on the talking-head circuit, appearing on Nightline, Good Morning America, and other shows. Nightline's Ted Koppel tried to instruct LaRouche on the necessity of talking in "sound bites" to accommodate the media; LaRouche took the opportunity to inform Americans of the fact that *nothing* they hear in "sound bites" can even begin to approximate the truth. Koppel asked LaRouche at the end to express the message he believed most important for the American people. Lyn said to look to the stars, that the effort to go to Mars was both a scientific necessity, and also the program which would rekindle hope in America, to revive scientific and cultural optimism, especially among our youth.

One would expect, in a normal world, that when a new political force proved itself in a democratic election, that the policies and ideas of that new force would be explored by the media for the benefit of an informed population. But the Task Force was not about to let LaRouche, or his ideas, have a fair hearing in America.

The key-and-code phrase "Political Extremist" suddenly became a permanent fixture in front of Lyndon LaRouche's name, in every newspaper across the nation. This phrase has no content, but sounds somehow ominous. It became a virtual title, like "Dr." or "Professor." The name LaRouche *never appeared*, except as "*political extremist* Lyndon LaRouche."

Simultaneously, "leaks" from the grand jury began showing up at every turn, making it "common knowledge" that "LaRouche scams money off charge cards," or that "LaRouche bilks little old ladies." ADL spokesmen were quoted and interviewed more often than LaRouche himself or any other members of the organization, probably about 1,000 to 1, to "explain" to the population how this anomaly in Illinois took place. The pollster Mike McKeon's predictions of our successful organizing were totally buried, while instead it was reported that the voters did not know that Hart and Fairchild were associated with the "Nazi, anti-Semitic, racist" LaRouche, but only voted for them because their names were more "American-sounding" than the Eastern Europeans who ran against them with the party leadership's endorsement! Nothing more sophisticated than that. When I first heard this, I realized in what low regard the population was held by the social planners—not that they thought people voted by the sound of names, which they knew was a lie, but that they considered the population to have become so passive, so terrified, so politically correct, that most people would *tolerate* such a banal, ludicrous explanation.

An aerial view of the large house where LaRouche lived (identified as "LaRouche's palatial mansion") appeared in *Newsweek,* and in newspapers around the country, ignoring the fact that the rented house served many different functions for EIR, and that only two rooms were put aside for LaRouche's personal use. *Newsweek*'s cover story called the organization "one of the most bizarre cults in the history of the United States."

Adlai Stevenson's initial caution was contrasted to the hysteria from the national Democratic Party leadership. Democratic National Committee Chairman Paul Kirk welcomed the new, hard-working, victorious faction into the electoral process most "democratically," by denouncing our victory and declaring the entire movement to be a "cult"—an increasingly prevalent ADL slander. Kirk toured the country, speaking on the need to fight "extremism," and retailing stories about our "bilking the elderly."

Senator Paul Simon (D) of Illinois, one of the ADL's own, led an assault on Adlai Stevenson for being too soft, demanding that Stevenson and the State Democratic Party *self-destruct,* rather than run on a joint ticket with the LaRouche faction candidates. Stevenson capitulated, announcing that he would run as an independent—deserting the ticket chosen by the electorate, assuring that neither the official ticket (with our candidates), nor the independent ticket (with Stevenson and party-selected running-mates), could possibly defeat the Republicans in November.

U.S. Attorney William Weld, meanwhile, was rewarded for his witch-hunt against LaRouche, by receiving an appointment as head of the Criminal Division of the DOJ. He assured the Congress that he would personally pursue the LaRouche prosecution—the press reported that he had "thrown a grenade into the DOJ" to get action against LaRouche.

The impact on our organizing was devastating. I called all our closest supporters with the good news on the election victory, but with few exceptions, they were scared half to death by the incredible barrage of "Big Lie" slanders on virtually every front page and evening news in the country. Some of the older supporters were furious at the lies, but nonetheless frightened, with memories of the McCarthy witch-hunts destroying lives in the 1950's.

The younger supporters were stunned, but no matter how much they insisted they didn't trust the media or the "establishment," many were nonetheless terrified. There were exceptions, of course, and those who rode through the storm were much stronger as a result, while most of those who fell away came back after things cooled down a bit.

Our relations with new contacts were even worse. A call to a new person inevitably ran into a massive wall of fear—sometimes an invisible wall, in that a person would not admit that he or she was responding to the slander, but would manufacture political "disagreements" to justify doing nothing. If some of our organizers had not understood it previously, it became abundantly clear in 1986, that to reach someone's mind, one must first peel away all the garbage about LaRouche that has been piled on through the media.

"Well, I agree with what you're saying about drugs, but I just don't go along with your approach."

"Oh, I see you're accepting what they're saying on the news about LaRouche."

"Oh, no, not me! I think for myself! I never take what they say on the media at face value."

"Well, perhaps you think drugs are run without the knowledge or control of the international banks which launder the money?"

"No, no, they're involved—got to be. You couldn't have that much money in the system without having a say in it."

"You're right. That's why we're going after the people at the top—very powerful people, by the way, people considered to be above suspicion, but whom we've shown are the controllers. What don't you like about our approach?"

"Well, you know, that bit about the Queen of England pushing drugs—that's too far out for me."

"We didn't say that—NBC said we said that. What we said is that the British political/financial institutions, which answer to the Queen and her Privy Council, have run the drug business since the opium plantations were created in colonial India and the Opium Wars forced dope on the Chinese—and they *still* control it, through Colonial Hongkong, Singapore, and offshore banks in the Caribbean."

"Yeah, I can believe that."

"Okay, now, let's talk about why the establishment and their media outlets are so anxious to slander LaRouche, and what you can do to help win this war. Or do you think we'd be bilking you, as NBC says, if you buy our literature or contribute to our campaigns?"

A good laugh at that point means it's possible to *start* talking about reality, and how the population's ability to think has been destroyed by "popular culture."

Things were very difficult for several months after the Illinois victory, even though we strengthened the membership in the process. Finances collapsed. Our vendor bills were stretched to the limits, and we lost our phones in various locals, while debt accumulated. Our loan repayment schedules were blown sky high. We contacted our lenders by phone and by letter, making clear that nothing would deter us in our fight, that we would not fold up and disappear, or declare bankruptcy, leaving our task undone, or our supporters in the lurch. We asked patience, and a renewed commitment to our cause. Some lenders were upset, some angry. The DOJ moved rapidly to locate the weakest amongst them, to turn them against us. They were not very successful, however, until far more drastic measures were taken against us over the following year.

Recovery and Desertion

We worked ourselves ragged during those difficult months. Fourteen-hour days became the norm, rather than the exception. I took only one brief break that entire year (not counting the "break" I was to spend in jail in the fall), when Gail and I travelled to Philadelphia to the wedding of my brother Joe. His wife, Claudia Cortez, had been in the organization for years, and I was delighted to hear they had hooked up. There was a beautiful wedding in one of the famous old black churches in the city, and I had the honor of singing a few pieces, accompanied by the church organist. There was a grand party in the Philadelphia office, with song, drama, and good humor. It was clear the membership shared in the not-so-young couple's joy—a joy that has grown and flourished over the years.

But we all returned quickly to the battlefront. Each conversation with our supporters required intense concentration, and a determination to address forcefully, but lovingly, the illusions that govern people's thinking about "how things work." We had to locate those illusions, and the fear that was created by the McCarthy-like attack against us, in order to turn the slanders into an object lesson in mass cultural brainwashing. Only then could we force reflection upon unconscious assumptions—which is the starting point of discovery.

We learned from the process, and by the mid-summer we began to put our finances back into some semblance of stability, including to start catching up on overdue debt payments. The priority was to get the publications out, without fail. We often didn't have enough money to mail the *New Solidarity* subscriptions on schedule. This was self-destruction, since the literature was our primary weapon. To allow subscriptions to fall behind, was like disarming the troops in the face of an enemy attack.

Our own stipends were last on the priority list, and we went without pay a great deal of the time. Since the stipends were already at the bare minimum to meet people's essential payments, things got very tight, including some people's nerves. Some, who had lost their sense of moral commitment, who had begun to "settle in" to routine, or "personal" or "family life," used the opportunity of crisis to drop out.

Amongst the dropouts was my phone team colleague Chris Curtis. Chris had always been blocked emotionally, finding it very difficult to engage supporters at the level of ideas, rather than issues. I worked closely with him for nearly two years, as did the others on the phone team, to improve his creative insights, by seeking out tough, philosophical problems in the minds of his contacts. Chris was not dumb, and he occasionally did good work, but he was intellectually lazy. He thought of himself as a salesman, and often talked about finding someone's "button," meaning the issue which excited him or her, as if that were the way to get the person to buy something or make a contribution. That drove me nuts.

I told him a million times that people won't *change*—they won't become better people—if you're only looking for *agreement* with them. "Find out if they're racist. See if they think the Third World is living off handouts from the U.S. Ask them if they think industrial progress is bad for the environment. Don't worry about what they're right about—find out where they're wrong, and *educate.* Figure out how to show them that their false beliefs about certain things simply don't fit in with their own best understanding of mankind. Force a conflict in their minds, and let them solve it. Unless they're outright lunatics, you can lead them to new discoveries, and they'll be happy for it. They'll be glad to help *for that reason,* not just to support some single issue. We've got to build patriots of the nation and citizens of the world."

But Chris didn't change. In May, after about two months of particularly hard work and few stipends following the Illinois victory, he quit. Dennis Small and I went over to see him. Dennis had worked closely with him when he was in the Ibero-American intelligence sector, and they had collaborated on fundraising. Chris, with backup from his wife, insisted that there was no disagreement with us, but that he just couldn't take the pace and the pressure, and that after a rest and an attempt to get a regular job, he might come back to organizing. We tried to convince him to reconsider, that he would deeply regret turning his back on the world just because of personal hardship. He said he'd think about it, and that he'd never do anything to harm the organization.

Chris continued doing political cartoons for *New Solidarity,* and his wife continued working in our business office, well beyond the time he began collaborating with the FBI and the Virginia State Police to destroy the organization—something he did in exchange for his own freedom from prosecution and a few petty bribes.

★ ★ ★

Although the original SDI program announced by President Reagan on March 23, 1983, as proposed by LaRouche, had been drastically watered down by the influence of the Bush networks in the administration, nonetheless the President was fully committed to the program in some form. Moscow, and its allies in Washington, appeared to be convinced that the combination of Soviet denunciations and anti-"Star Wars" hysteria in the U.S., would force Reagan to capitulate and abandon the SDI program at the upcoming summit scheduled for Reykjavík, Iceland, on October 8, 1986. Gorbachov, the "peace-loving" man of *perestroika* and *glasnost*, would be meeting President Reagan to advance détente and disarmament. LaRouche forecast that there would be a showdown over the SDI, and that the Soviets would threaten and cajole President Reagan to give up SDI, if he wanted any progress in peaceful coexistence, or face Soviet belligerence if he would not.

The U.S. think-tanks and media sewers were in high gear in the fall of 1986, insisting that the SDI was a non-issue. Their lies took various forms: some said the SDI was dead, anyway, since the U.S. population was against it; others said the Soviets wouldn't bring it up, since other issues were more important. LaRouche alone perceived that there was an attempt to "bag" President Reagan, by building up expectations of a breakthrough on U.S.-Soviet relations at the summit, then confront him with an ultimatum on SDI. If he refused, he would take the blame for "spoiling" the summit, and putting the world on a course of nuclear confrontation.

We published LaRouche's analysis in all our press. We also sent a team to Reykjavík, to intervene against the total media blackout on the emerging confrontation. The world press corps gathered there scoffed at our "alarmist" publications, insisting to our organizers that SDI would not even come up at this supposed U.S.-Soviet lovefest in the making.

There was an additional basis upon which LaRouche and his representatives at Reykjavík were supposedly "discredited." One day earlier, on Oct. 6, 1986, some 400 armed men from the FBI, IRS, Secret Service, Marshal's Service, state and local police forces, with armored personnel carriers, helicopters, Uzi machine guns, and God knows what else, had raided the offices of the organizations associated with Lyndon LaRouche. The entire spectacle had been broadcast live around the world.

In Reykjavík, the journalists were all buzzing with the story of the "LaRouche raid." At one point, when about 1,000 journalists were waiting for a closed session to end, CNN entertained the "troops" with a video rerun of the entire raid. Meanwhile, the reporters continued to ignore the SDI question altogether.

My friend, co-worker, co-defendant, and fellow inmate, Paul Gallagher, prepared a timeline of the Soviet participation in the Get LaRouche campaign. His report showed the following pattern in 1986 leading up to Reykjavík:

• A disinformation campaign, including two Soviet TV broadcasts, accused LaRouche of the Palme assassination.

• Two articles in *Sovetskaya Kultura* denounced LaRouche's influence over the Reagan Administration, accusing him of fraud, and demanding that he be prosecuted. "Why isn't the IRS interested?" the Soviets asked.

• The Soviet magazine *New Times*, published in most major languages around the world, slandered LaRouche as a warmonger and called for a criminal investigation in the U.S.

• On September 24, in a pre-summit press briefing in Copenhagen, Georgi Arbatov, head of the U.S.A.-Canada Institute in Moscow, and a top aide to Gorbachov, was asked a question about SDI by EIR representative Poul Rasmussen. Arbatov became visibly shaken, denounced EIR as "LaRouche fascists," and closed down the press briefing.

• On October 3, a few days before the summit, Mikhail Gorbachov, speaking in East Berlin, denounced "hidden Nazis, without swastikas," a phrase used by ADL scribbler Dennis King, and picked up by the Soviet press, to refer to LaRouche.

• At a press conference on the first day of the Reykjavík summit, Georgi Arbatov again shouted, "fascists, LaRouche fascists" at our correspondents, when queried on the SDI. That was, it turned out, the only question he received concerning the SDI.

Together with the constant news coverage of the Leesburg raid, this hysteria against LaRouche by the Soviet leadership had created an eerie environment in Reykjavík, when suddenly, on October 12, the last day of the summit, when everyone was waiting for the final communiqué, the whole thing blew up—*over the SDI!* Secretary of State George Shultz called a press conference to announce that a broad arms control agreement was practically ready to be signed, but the Soviets were demanding that the U.S. renounce plans to develop the Strategic Defense Initiative.

As we learned later, virtually everyone around the President was trying to maneuver him into agreement with the Soviet demand—not because they were "communists," but because they were *British in outlook,* in the service of the City of London, and Wall Street, determined to prevent the resurgence of technological optimism, which they knew would accompany the SDI program. But President Reagan stood his ground, much to the distress of his would-be controllers. The Soviets had been assured that the pro-SDI current in the U.S., launched by the "troglodyte LaRouche" (as one Soviet media called him), had finally been taken care of by the judicial suppression of our movement. They were stunned that their ploy had failed.

After 1989, when the Berlin Wall fell and the Soviet Empire collapsed, Soviet leaders acknowledged publicly what LaRouche alone had forecast beginning 1982: that failure to engage in joint development efforts for strategic defense using new physical principles, would lead to the collapse of the Soviet economy within about five years. A decade later, at a 1993 Princeton University conference studying the end of the Cold War, several ex-Soviet officials, including Soviet Defense Minister D.T. Yazov, reported that Reagan's refusal to capitulate at Reykjavík had left them "at wit's end," and that their effort to develop their own SDI had so drained their already foundering productive resources, that the Soviet economy simply unravelled.

[12]

Arrest and Jail

My aesthetical education was about to be tested. It had been easy to accept Schiller's concept, that the path to freedom lay in the pursuit of beauty—but how would that look from the inside of a dingy jail cell?

★ ★ ★

My first-hand perspective on the incredible events of the week of Oct. 6, 1986 was rather limited, since one of the first tasks of the armed force which invaded Leesburg was to drag me off to jail.

That Monday morning, we received a call at home at about 7 a.m. It was Nancy Spannaus, a member of the NEC.

"There's a raid going on at the office," she said. "FBI, state police, and others. Stay at home. I'll call when we have more information."

This was not a total shock, since we had been under investigation and harassment for two years. Nevertheless, they had succeeded in preventing any leaks from reaching us as they prepared for this military-style operation, and we were caught by surprise.

Turning on our TV, we learned that the media, however, had *not* been caught by surprise. Camera crews and reporters were swarming all over town, filming every move by the hundreds of armed Federal and state agents, and interviewing the "man on the street" about how he "felt" about the raid and the LaRouche presence in Leesburg. Of course, these supposedly random interviews just happened to be with the two or three leading yahoos in town who had led the campaign to destroy us. Over the preceeding two years the local paper, Nicky Arundel's *Loudoun Times Mirror*, had prepared the way with articles that included such accusations as: we used a farmhouse outside town for covert military and weapons training (it was actually used as a summer camp for children); we killed the cats of our "enemies" and left them on their porches (anyone who killed a cat in this organization would probably have been skinned alive by some of the cat lovers amongst us, including Gail and me); our "cult" leader had demanded that no one in the organization have children (I guess that helped in describing our children's summer camp as a paramilitary commando center); and, of course, they peddled all the cock-and-bull stories about our policies and ideas. The Loudoun County residents had been carefully psychologically conditioned to accept the virtual military occupation of their county seat for two days in October 1986.

Gail went out to empty the garbage, and noticed several cars and vans parked at the entrance to the dirt road leading back to our house, and a few more in the neighbor's driveway. She called Nancy.

"They're just sitting out there," Gail told her. "They're obviously planning to get Mike, but they seem to be hanging around first to scare the hell out of the neighborhood." Nancy told her that Jeff and Michele Steinberg, two members of our security staff who worked closely with Lyn on our contacts with the government, were also being staked out, and that there was a simultaneous raid on the Boston office.

John and Renée Sigerson, who lived across the street, called over to tell us they'd seen the stake-out, which was hard to miss. "Come on over," I said, "we might as well enjoy the siege."

On the way over, they noticed that a TV van was prominent among the vehicles crowding the roadway. They were stopped by one of the plainclothes officers, but when they said they were coming to visit us, they were allowed to proceed. We all had breakfast together and joked about the ironies of the situation, debating whether or not the FBI gumshoes actually believed all their own hype about the "dangerous LaRouche group." We settled in to watch a videotape of Mozart's *The Marriage of Figaro*, which I had wanted them to see anyway.

We only made it through "Se vuol ballare," when the G-men moved in for their "dangerous" mission. About a dozen of them, all wielding handguns, stealthily surrounded the house, while we stood watching at the door. Gail got on the phone to make sure others were notified. Rather than waiting, I simply walked outside.

"I assume you're looking for me." They were far too hyped up to be civil, however. I was grabbed by the arms and shoved up against a car, frisked, and handcuffed. Gail came out and told the media to get the hell off our property or she'd call the police, or something like that.

They shoved me into the back seat of one of their cars and began the long ride to the Alexandria Federal Courthouse. The FBI agents radioed in to their headquarters that, "Target No. 1 has been apprehended." Real cops-and-robbers stuff.

Jeff and Michele were already at the FBI office when I arrived. We joked about the absurdities of the situation. Jeff said he knew several of the Federal officers who were "staked-out" at his house, from previous contacts and collaboration in our anti-drug and anti-terror work. When the agents stayed "on guard" for so long, without making any move to arrest them, Michele made up a tray with coffee and pastries and took it out to serve her guests. That was too much—out came the Uzis, and the Steinbergs got the same treatment that I had received. After a half-hearted effort to convince us to talk with them without our lawyers present, the FBI agents moved us off to county jails. They found a law having something to do with "dangerous criminals" which allowed them to postpone any bond hearing for four days—so we dug in for four days in the clinker.

I have been in dozens of jails, prisons, holding cells, even jails within prisons (called "the hole"), many of them filthy, cramped, cold, and generally disgusting, but none of those conditions was as despicable as those at Fairfax County Jail those first few days of my incarceration. I was placed in a tiny, cinder-block holding cell, with a bright fluorescent light, the standard jail-cell metallic commode and cold-water sink, and a raised cinder-block platform with no mattress. There were about 30 such cells along the hall, filled with men in various stages of intoxication or withdrawal, whose only means of communication was to shout out of the slot in the solid metal door, to unseen friends or enemies in other cells. The lights stayed on for 24 hours, so it became difficult to tell night from day. Sleep was nearly impossible on the cinder block, and the hall resounded continuously with pure cacophony—shouts and threats between prisoners, several "entertainers" with their own versions of rap or country "music," screams and curses against the guards, who generally ignored everyone, and even totally undecipherable babblings from several poor souls who had clearly gone stark raving mad.

It was quite an experience, more like being in a 19th-Century looney bin, than in jail. We were allowed nothing to read, and were not permitted out of the cells for any reason. Meal trays were passed in through the slot. I assumed that this barbarous treatment was intentional, in order to break people when they first came in. This was confirmed on the third day, when I was finally interviewed for classification. I was still in the same clothes I'd had on when I was arrested. I was terribly sore from sitting and lying on the cinder block for 72 hours, and, as a result, I had had little sleep.

"Have you been feeling suicidal?" the interviewer asked.

"No," I responded without emotion. Pause. Deep stare.

"Are you *sure?* You look terrible."

Many possible responses flew through my mind, a few sarcastic, but mostly enraged.

"Perhaps you'd like to live like this for three days amongst people who are losing, or already have lost their minds, and we'll see how you look," was what came out.

Jeff was too far down the hall for us to exchange information, even by shouting. There was a phone, if one were willing to spend an hour or so shouting over the din to try to convince a guard to bring it over, which I did twice. Gail was able to fill me in on the essentials of what was going on, including the raids and the arrests. Besides Jeff, Michele, and me, my brother-in-law Elliot had been arrested in New Jersey, and Richard Black in Boston. Other arrest warrants had been issued for Paul Goldstein (a member of our security staff who worked closely with Jeff), and for my Boston phone team associates, Mike Gelber, Chuck Park, and Rick Sanders.

LaRouche had not been arrested, but the story of why not is hair-raising. On the day of the raid, the farm where LaRouche stayed in Virginia was surrounded by law enforcement agents and all types of SWAT teams and commandoes—although the latter have never been officially acknowledged. Helicopters criss-crossed the area, while searches of our offices were conducted in downtown Leesburg. According to his subsequent court testimony, FBI agent Richard Egan entered our offices to begin the search, and immediately spied "evidence" which he claimed was grounds to arrest LaRouche. He rushed off to the U.S. Attorney's office in Alexandria to get an arrest warrant. Eight or nine hours later, local television reported there was about to be "an entry into the farm." Associates of LaRouche sent a telegram to President Reagan, noting that since LaRouche had committed no crime, any arrest would only be a pretext to kill him. No arrest warrant was ever served, and no entry was attempted in the tense hours which followed the telegram.

Years later, Sheriff's Deputy Don Moore—the local sheriff used for black-bag jobs and similar dirty operations by the Task Force—was indicted after he blabbed details of a plot to kidnap Lewis du Pont Smith to other Sheriff's Deputies. In the course of the kidnapping investigation, Moore bragged about the strange events of Oct. 6, 1986. He explained that the entire exercise "at the farm" was designed to provoke a shootout with LaRouche's security personnel—a shootout in which LaRouche would be killed. Moore's state of mind comes across clearly in a direct quote from the audio tapes which were part of the FBI's kidnapping investigation: "Shoot to kill. These guys are armed. They have been warned. When the time comes to arrest LaRouche—and I'm a Special U.S. Marshal right now and I'm telling you, if one of those guys goes for his pocket, when I pull up to arrest him, I'm going to start shooting until the screaming stops."

Although some may imagine that these were merely the grandiose fantasies of a deranged mind, and that the actual raiding party could not have contemplated such murderous provocations, it must be noted that the same agencies, and many of the same individuals, who planned and executed the October 6 raid in Leesburg, would later apply their skills against the Branch Davidians in Waco, Texas.

Deputy Moore himself, it should be noted, had been Col. Oliver North's tent-mate in Vietnam. Moore was deputized a Special U.S. Marshal by the Task Force. He went out of his way on two later occasions to *personally* arrest me and parade me in handcuffs before the cameras, perhaps trying to impress his more famous and more successful criminal cohort, Ollie North.

It is not known, at least by me, what President Reagan did in response to LaRouche's telegram. When the Task Force finally succeeded in getting a superceding indictment for LaRouche the following July, his lawyer, Odin Anderson, was duly notified, and LaRouche was called to turn himself in in a civilized manner.

Beethoven

My four days in the Fairfax County Jail were spent largely with music, reviewing in my mind the pieces I had memorized for performance, either as singer or conductor. I was reminded of the weekly show on WQXR, the classical music station in New York, called "Tropical Island," where various famous personalities discussed which few recordings they would wish to have, if they were shipwrecked on a deserted island. The pieces I'd conducted were a source of endless delight and intense concentration, especially the Bach cantata *Wachet auf* and the fourth movement of Brahms's *German Requiem, "Wie leiblich sind deine Wohnungen."*

The Florestan prison aria from Beethoven's *Fidelio* took on a new meaning. I worked through the three levels of that aria, following Plato's concept of the three levels of the soul, the bronze, the silver, and the gold. Florestan, lying in chains in a dungeon, is being starved to death, deprived even of water, by an unknown jailer whom he presumes to be his political enemy, the tyrant Pizzaro. (Beethoven's Pizzaro was modelled on Pitt the Younger of the British Empire, who had ordered the imprisonment of the Marquis de Lafayette. As in the opera, Lafayette's wife dedicated herself to winning her husband's freedom.) Florestan opens the aria with an anguished cry: "God! Such darkness here!" From near hopelessness, he reflects on the severity of the torment imposed upon him in the springtime of his life. But his faith defeats his despair, as he declares that God's judgment is always just, and that he had, throughout his life, lived by a higher calling, of duty to God and to mankind. This "silver soul" is then uplifted to pure gold in the third and final section of the aria, as a lilting oboe line introduces the appearance of a vision of his wife, Leonora, in the form of an angel, whose *real existence* cannot be doubted by anyone who has ever seen the opera and has been transported, as was the character Florestan, by this angel of God, who led him "to freedom in the heavenly realm," carried by the exquisite beauty of Beethoven's genius.

In September 1992, on the eve of my return to prison to begin serving the 77-year sentence imposed upon me by the Commonwealth of Virginia, the New Jersey regional office compiled a collection of poems and reflections for me from the members. Among them was a letter from my sister Margaret, addressed to both Gail and me, with her thoughts on the Florestan aria:

> What is an angel? An angel is the spirit of God coming to you in a real form; a physical result of deep spiritual contemplation of love of God, of truth, and of doing one's duty—which I think must include the sacrifice of self and acceptance of earthly humiliation. The angel is the metaphor for the mind's creative spark, born of true love of God and His divine justice. Is there anything more physically powerful than Florestan's outpouring of joy at the presence of his angel Leonora? And is not the angel Leonora the physical embodiment of God's perfect love; leading not only Florestan, but subsequently all the people to freedom—the heavenly realm—through her equal devotion to duty and her perfect love for Florestan? She appears to him, not as he is thinking about her, or despairing of his fate, but in his deepest devotion to God.

And so, indeed, did I converse with angels in that Fairfax County jail cell.

My extended concentration on the Florestan aria, during those days in isolation, led me to a new understanding of Schiller's concept of the sublime, and to see into the mind of both Schiller and Beethoven in a personal sense. Beethoven was profoundly influenced by Schiller, and this is most evident in *Fidelio*. The

Florestan aria demonstrates, through the interplay of music and drama, how *agapē* ennobles duty, by uniting the passion of creative reason, the universality of wedded love, and the joy which derives from doing good, from acting selflessly on behalf of mankind as a whole. Florestan was not dedicated to duty in the sense of "following orders," but of following *truth*, one's duty to God, even to the point of giving one's life. Schiller defined the sublime as that inner strength, located in the mind of every human being, which leads a person to take the suffering of others totally into his or her own heart, or to face severe personal suffering, and yet to overcome that suffering through the dedication of one's life to a higher purpose. In this universal sense, Beethoven's opera is truly sublime.

Fidelio was to play yet another role in those first days of incarceration. After four days in jail, Jeff, Michele, and I were taken before a magistrate for a bail hearing. At the courthouse, we were placed in a small holding cell outside the courtroom. We all agreed that our love of classical music had been crucial in maintaining strength through the ordeal, and we soon launched into song—only this time, not just in our minds. Although there were but three of us, we did the best we could on the beautiful quartet from *Fidelio*'s first act, "*Mir ist so wunderbar.*" The other prisoners were speechless. We entered the courtroom in high spirits.

The prosecutors, led by the U.S. Attorney for Eastern Virginia, Henry Hudson, and Assistant U.S. Attorney for Boston John Markham, had worked out an elaborate scheme of lies to bulldoze the magistrate into denying bail. Jeff and Michele, as members of the security staff, were described by FBI agent Egan as something akin to cold-blooded murderers and terrorists, referencing the "terrorist training camp" (i.e., our summer camp for the kids), and the fight over weapons permits for our security staff. They were such a danger to the community, Hudson argued, that they dare not be allowed to walk the streets. Our lawyers' efforts to ridicule this nonsense were most convincing, but the magistrate seemed unwilling to counter the overkill mounted by Markham and Hudson. Both Jeff and Michele were denied bail and sent back to jail.

My case was different. I could not be presented as a danger to the community, since I had no connection to our security staff. So F.B.I. agent Egan transformed himself into a psychiatric expert: "Billngton was part of the Boston phone team, but he was considered to be unstable and unreliable, and could not be trusted on his own. So they brought him down to their national headquarters compound, where they could keep a close eye on him. If he is given bail, he will flee."

I laughed out loud, which seemed to upset my lawyer more than anyone else. But this fairy tale was too much even for the magistrate, who granted me bail.

When Gail came later in the day with a bail bondsman to get me out, I told her how touched I was by her dedication to her job—as the person apparently assigned by our security staff to keep me under scrutiny, she'd gone so far as to marry her deranged ward! True devotion to the cause!

Tyranny

Between October 1986 and the following summer, the "Get LaRouche Task Force" went on a tirade. While the media maintained a barrage of slanders, the Task Force carried out more arrests, more raids, forced bankruptcies, and massive harassment of our supporters, culminating in the indictment of LaRouche in July 1987. During the two days of the raid, the Task Force had carted off several truckloads of documents, computer records, and other material from our offices in Boston and Leesburg. Dozens of agents from various state and Federal government departments spent thousands of man-days combing through the material, manufacturing various cases against us over the next three years.

A new grand jury was opened up in Alexandria, Virginia, aimed at creating a tax case against LaRouche. This struck me as particularly laughable, since LaRouche was notorious for living a very simple life. The fact that LaRouche was indicted, convicted, and sent to prison for conspiring to defraud the Internal Revenue Service, is, on its face, the most blatant technical proof that the entire frame-up and judicial railroad had absolutely nothing to do with anything that went on in the real world.

Federal and state agents launched a comprehensive, national harassment of our supporters and contributors to our campaigns, contacting them by the thousands. They concocted various lies about our supposedly devious intentions and practices, fishing for a few weak links.

The October 1986 raid was also the beginning of a fierce competition between me and my brother-in-law Elliot, in pursuit of his coveted title as "the most arrested" member of the Labor Committees. This was certainly not a competition of my choosing, however, and it got to be downright annoying.

I had only been home from jail for ten days, when Gail and I were having a glass of wine before bed at about midnight. I noticed someone in the yard with a flashlight, and walked to the door to see what it was.

"Are you Michael Billington?" the voice behind the flashlight asked.

"Yes. What's up?"

"We have a warrant for your arrest," he said, showing a paper through the glass door.

I noticed that it was a Loudoun County Sheriff's Deputy. "What the hell is this one for?" I asked.

"It has something to do with Missouri. You know anything about Missouri?"

"I've never been there in my life."

"Are you sure? Yep, it says Michael Billington. You're under arrest."

I told him to come on in. Unlike the cops-and-robbers charade during the October 6 raid, the Sheriff's deputies made no effort to handcuff me. Gail went to call our security office.

"Why, in the name of God, are you coming to get me at 12:00 o'clock at night?" I asked. "This is like something out of a Franz Kafka novel, a knock on the door in the middle of the night."

"Well," he stammered, "we had trouble finding where you lived."

"Right, right, sure, after my house and my arrest were broadcast all over the world a few weeks ago, with half your force up here with the Feds, today you can't figure out where I live!"

Arranged conveniently on a *Friday* night, I couldn't be brought before a magistrate for a bail hearing until the following

Monday, leaving me with another lovely few days in jail. This time I discovered the graces of the Loudoun County drunk tank—the cell where the Friday night robbers, drunks, and whatever else pops up, get thrown together until Monday morning. There were about 25 people with 12 beds, although, unlike the Fairfax jail, mattresses were provided for everyone who had to sleep on the floor. There was a TV in the cell, and I received my first trial by fire with the idiot box in jail. It stayed on continuously—as it does in every jail or prison in the country—from the break of dawn until the guards pull the plug at about midnight, and serves to prevent any meaningful activity from taking place in the minds of any inmates. It's not only that they watch the most banal garbage (is there anything *else* on TV?), but that the medium itself is mind-destroying, creating total mental passivity, where even the hyperactive types respond to profile, determined entirely by the controlled environment of the programming and the mode of presentation.

Even more deadly is the electronic nature of the sound of the television. In a crowded room, with noisy inmates playing cards or arguing, one can sit and read or think, closing out the "white noise" of people's voices, even if very loud. But a television or a radio can not be blocked out. The electronic pulse penetrates both earplugs and the most carefully constructed mental wall. I quickly developed a hatred for television, which would grow over the years. I laugh when I hear the "tough on criminals" politicians complaining about prisoners being "coddled" with access to television. The truth is, that the TV is an essential tool of control and pacification in the nation's prisons. I became nostalgic for the "peace and quiet" of my solitary cell in the looney bin of the Fairfax County Jail, where there was no TV to drive me nuts!

I learned that the arrest warrant was indeed from Missouri, where the son of a woman who had contributed and loaned some money to us had tried to stop her by calling in the police. He was contacted by someone on the "Get LaRouche Task Force," who guided him to file *criminal* charges, for some sort of fraud in regard to the loans. I was to be extradited to Missouri, based on the accusation that I had travelled to Missouri to meet the lady and pick up the check—which had never happened. Since I'd never been there, the Missouri officials did not even have jurisdiction to bring charges against me in that state. I was advised, by my lawyer, to fight the extradition order, and told that I'd almost certainly win. I was granted bail, and told that I must wait for the governor of Virginia to sign an extradition order before I could officially file my opposition to it. My lawyer told the court that, when that governor's order came in, he didn't want to hear that I'd been snatched out of my bed at midnight again. The court agreed, and ordered the disappointed prosecutor (the local Commonwealth's Attorney) to notify my lawyer when the warrant arrived, so I could turn myself in. We assumed that my bail would cover me until my legal fight against extradition was completed, but, as I soon learned, I was set up to get bushwhacked when the governor's order arrived in January.

The intervening months, however, were hectic. We attempted to maintain our political offensives, although the raid itself had to be recognized as a crucial feature of everything else going on in the world. It was not only our supporters who had to be convinced of that: many of our members had serious fear reactions as well. Unconsciously, and in some cases quite openly, many members began looking for "what we had done wrong" that brought on this onslaught by the government.

"Perhaps we shouldn't have been so shrill in our attacks on Kissinger," a little voice would whisper in someone's ear. "Maybe we could have explained our disagreements with the ADL more politely," said still another. "Maybe if we didn't ask people to do so much, we wouldn't have gotten into trouble," said a third. Fear—the "little me," reacting in terror to the use of irrational, and apparently uncontrollable, power.

The obvious fact was that the massive assault by corrupt forces within and without government institutions, was due to our having done something *right*—and that they had failed, through covert means alone, to destroy us. They thus chose (as demonstrated by the paper trail later constructed from the antics of Henry Kissinger and his friends) to throw care to the winds, ignore the lack of evidence, railroad LaRouche to prison, and try to shut down the movement.

They had seized all of our personal notebooks and contact cards in the raid, so we had to reconstruct everything from backup subscription lists. I called all my contacts, and many contacts of other organizers around the country, with briefings on the raid, jail, the midnight arrests, and so forth, but keeping the focus on the political warfare which motivated the raids in the first place. LaRouche released a document honoring President Reagan's victory at Reykjavík, for standing up not only to Gorbachov, but also to the media and his Wall Street "advisors," who tried to coerce him into dropping the SDI (while orchestrating the judicial assault on the recognized *author* of the SDI policy).

President Reagan was already showing signs of concentration loss, perhaps early symptoms of the Alzheimer's which has taken his later years. Several of his closest personal associates, such as NSC chief William Clark, had already been driven out of the administration in tandem with the "LaRouche connection" hype of 1983-85, while Vice President Bush brought in his own allies to replace them—including Dr. K. himself. The President also had the old Hollywood ties around his neck, intensified by his stargazing wife. Nancy Reagan not only practiced astrology and other occult fantasies, she even influenced her husband to follow the advice of her astrologer in choosing auspicious dates for official U.S. government events! She also made sure that she and Ronnie maintained close contact with the perverse political networks that set up and ran the virtual whorehouse known as Hollywood.

That President Reagan accomplished what he did, despite his Hollywood history and connections, is remarkable. That he was increasingly marginalized as a figurehead by Bush and the establishment, was no surprise—but it could have been otherwise, if LaRouche had not been cut off from his collaboration with the President.

★ ★ ★

The crimes of the Bush apparatus in the Reagan Administration burst into public view on Oct. 5, 1986, a mere day before the Leesburg raid, when a U.S. covert arms supply plane was shot down by the Sandinista government in Nicaragua. This led to the unravelling of the "Iran-Contra" scandal. Our publications had already exposed nearly all the fundamental "secrets" of the arms-for-drugs deals with the Contras and the Colombian drug cartels, as well as the criminal covert arms supply to Iran via Israeli and East bloc networks, long before the scandal broke. We had also already identified the role of Bush and his asteroid network working behind President Reagan's back, controlling the illegal covert operations. Therefore, in a normal world, one would have expected that the Iran-Contra revelations would have thrust LaRouche and EIR *into the forefront of the international investigations, and press coverage, as the foremost authorities on the entire operation. But instead, LaRouche was the subject of a judicial witch-hunt and feeding frenzy by the press, while Section 8 psycho Ollie North shredded documents and prepared a cover-up for his boss George Bush, and Bush's far-flung criminal apparatus.*

★ ★ ★

The 'Leesburg Hilton'

In early January 1987, I received word from my lawyer that the governor had signed the order for extradition to Missouri, and that I had been given a court date to formally file my notice challenging that extradition. I appeared at the court on the assigned day, expecting to be back in the office within an hour or so. To my surprise, and to the utter shock of my lawyer, who was caught absolutely flat-footed, the Commonwealth's Attorney in Loudoun County, certainly on orders from above, declared to the court that, based on the precedent of the H. Rap Brown case, I should be denied bail! Suddenly, I found myself being treated like an accused cop-killer! Drawing on a legal decision in the trial of the gun-toting black nationalist, who was deemed too violent to be released while contesting an extradition order, the prosecutor argued that the ruling meant that no one contesting extradition may be allowed bail, even if the judge wishes to grant it! My lawyer, who was (of course) totally unprepared for such an argument, assured me that this was absurd, that the Constitution guarantees bail to anyone not a danger to the community or at risk of flight, and presented that basic argument to the court.

The judge, the semi-retired Carlton Penn, took a recess to "study the law." When he returned, looking very ponderous, he told me his hands were tied, that he had no choice but to lift my bail, and send me off to jail! Thus began a month's stay in the "Leesburg Hilton."

It began disastrously, with eight people in a six-man cell, the TV on all day and most of the night, no table, and, since I was one of the two sleeping on the floor, not even a bed to work on. But after a few days I convinced the sheriffs to move me to an isolation cell.

"But, these are for punishment," the guard protested. "Why in the world do you want to be moved there? There isn't even a television!" They were so concerned about the television, that they put one in my cell without my even asking for it! Alone, but, this time, without the cacophony or the 24-hour fluorescent light of the Fairfax jail, I settled in to catch up on some reading. John Milton became my closest companion for that month, while I allowed myself the pleasure of writing some poetry. The passing of Valentine's Day inspired a tradition of "poems from prison" for Gail—a tradition which we both enjoy, while also hoping for its early end.

Outside the jail, the organization staged several demonstrations targetting Loudoun County Sheriff John Isom, who was turning out to be a significant player in the "Get LaRouche Task Force," and a hired hand to the Mellon family circles who reigned in Loudoun County. Our members marched with signs like, "Free Billington, Send Isom To Missouri," and "Missouri Loves Company—Send Isom." Even such a low-key political demonstration was most out of keeping with the genteel Southern veneer of Leesburg. Some reported that the statue of the Confederate soldier which adorns the front lawn of the county courthouse, took on a particularly nasty scowl.

My Missouri ordeal ended peacefully, but in a manner which would become all too common throughout the LaRouche cases. In a hearing held in Missouri, the woman's son presented the "case" that his mother had been defrauded, while the woman herself expressed strong support for our activities! Since the only evidence they had of my presence in Missouri (which was necessary for their jurisdiction in bringing criminal charges) was the woman's vague (and mistaken) memory that I had picked up the check (a supporter in the area had picked it up), the prosecutors quickly moved to drop the charges in exchange for an arrangement to pay back the loans.

I was released after about 30 days, on Feb. 15, 1987. Release from incarceration—even after such a brief period—is an extraordinary experience. I had quickly adapted myself to the totally controlled environment, both the confinement, and the sometimes difficult procedures required to obtain even those simple things which were permitted, such as a daily shower or a phone call. A video camera was pointed into my cell at all times, as a reminder that there was no such thing as a moment of privacy. I had been allowed brief visits with my wife and a few friends, but only through a dirty plexiglass screen, talking on a static-filled phone line. Walking out into the fresh air, embracing Gail and greeting friends, simply walking down the street, was an exhilarating experience. Eating a grilled steak, one of Gail's exquisite vegetable and pasta creations, and her nearly sinful desserts, with a glass of *spätlese*—such a delight quickly extinguished the memory of turkey loaf and cold, canned veggies.

The relief was short-lived. Two days later, on February 17, I ran by the jail to drop something off for an inmate I had met during my stay. When I walked in, the guards jumped up, one nearly running into the back office, returning with the officer in charge. I explained my simple purpose and left, noting their extreme paranoia. I learned later that evening, as I stood once again on the *inside* of a Loudoun County jail cell, that the Sheriffs were terrified that I had discovered the secret of the "big bust" planned for that evening, and for which they had been moving inmates around to clear out a cell large enough to hold all of us listed on the new indictment.

But, in fact, I never guessed the reason for their paranoia, and went about my business. That evening, I was walking back to the office after a late dinner break, when I noticed the office was surrounded by Sheriffs' cars and media crews. I stopped at a pay phone, across the street, and called in. "What's up?" I asked.

"The Commonwealth of Virginia has indicted about a dozen people. You're on the list."

"Oh, great. What did I do this time?"

"It appears you're accused of selling securities without a license."

I had heard of this before. Missouri had described the loans as "securities," and used security laws for their criminal indictment

On the 1980 Presidential campaign trail: Lyndon LaRouche and Ronald Reagan, candidates' debate, Concord, New Hampshire.

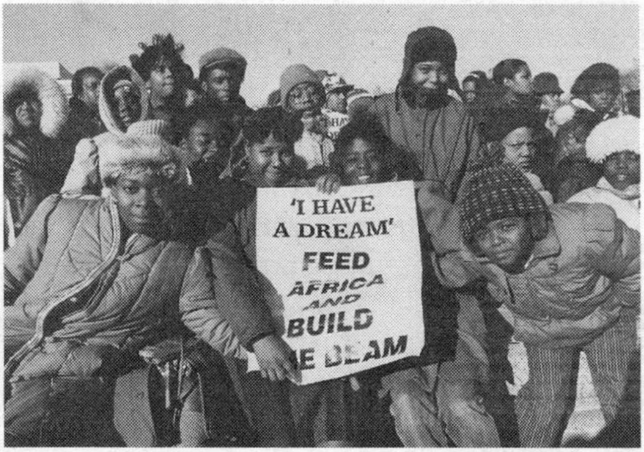

Martin Luther King Day, Jan. 15, 1985: Schiller Institute march to develop Africa with SDI technology. In March 1983, President Reagan had adopted the beam defense policy in precisely the form proposed by LaRouche; earlier, LaRouche had carried on back-channel negotiations with Soviet officials on behalf of the Administration.

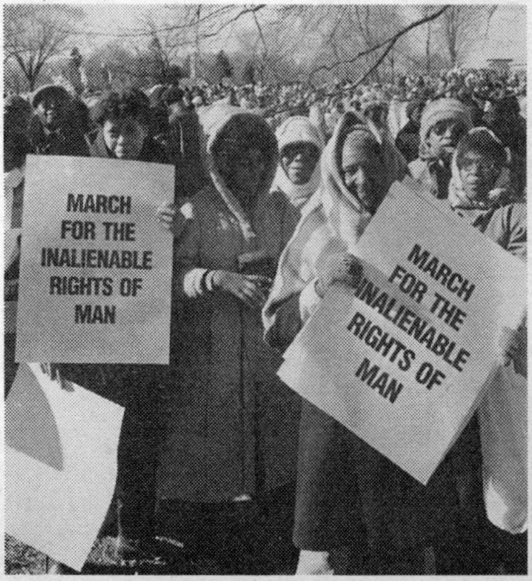

Financial contributor Barbara Newington offered to pay for buses to bring 10,000 white and black Americans to rally for the development of Africa with SDI technology. She told me, "I want to make sure that Washington looks exactly as you describe it on January 15. And I want poets to be running it."

Assault on the LaRouche Movement.

EIRNS/Stuart Lewis

Vice President, later President, George Bush.

EIRNS/Stuart Lewis

U.S. Attorney for Boston William Weld.

EIRNS/Stuart Lewis

Iran-Contra bagman Lt. Col. Oliver North. Later, when he ran in the Virginia Senate race in 1994, our "Son-of-a-Bush" campaign defeated him.

EIRNS/Stuart Lewis

Loudoun County Sheriff's Deputy Don Moore—Ollie North's Vietnam tent-mate—was deputized a Special U.S. Marshal for the Leesburg Raid.

The Leesburg Raid.

EIRNS/Stuart Lewis

Oct. 6-7, 1986, Leesburg, Va. FBI agents, accompanied by 400 armed police, helicopters, and heavy military equipment, raid our national headquarters. An armed standoff at the house where Lyndon LaRouche was staying, was averted. This was the first of my many arrests.

EIRNS/Stuart Lewis

Oct. 6, 1986, Leesburg, Va.

EIRNS/Stuart Lewis

Oct. 6, 1986, Leesburg, Va.

EIRNS/Ernie Fullerton

EIRNS/Stuart Lewis

Under arrest. Above: Richard Welsh (left) and Paul Gallagher, Feb. 18, 1987, indicted by the Commonwealth of Virginia. Left: Nancy Spannaus, March 17, 1987, indicted by the State of New York. Bottom left: Linda de Hoyos (left) and Kathy Wolfe, indicted by the State of New York.

EIRNS/Stuart Lewis

EIRNS/Philip Ulanowsky

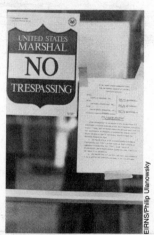

April 21, 1987: Involuntary bankruptcy of LaRouche movement publishing companies.

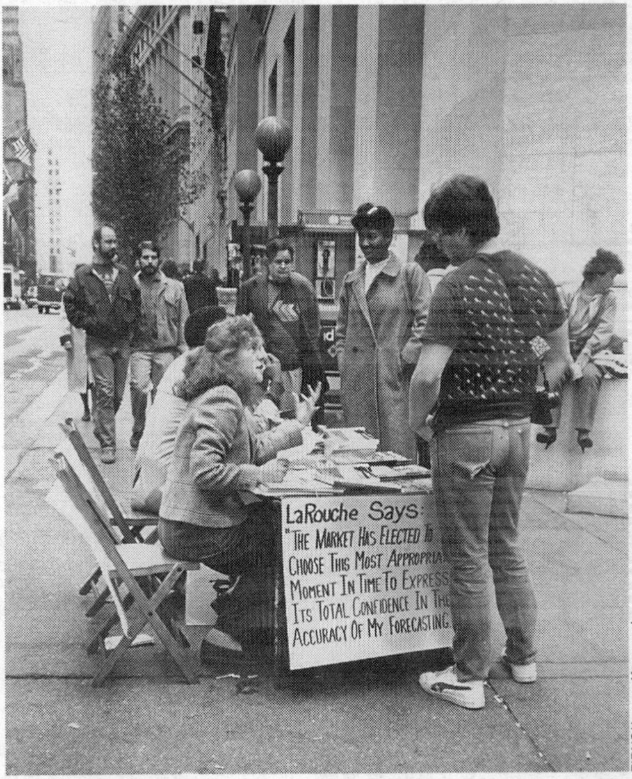

EIRNS/Jeanne Kacprezak

Wall Street, Oct. 20, 1987, one day after stock markets crashed around the globe. Marg's sign says, "LaRouche says: The market has elected to choose this most appropriate moment in time to express its total confidence in the accuracy of my forecasting."

Courtesy of Margaret Greenspan

Just prior to Federal sentencing, I performed Schubert's "Die Winterreise" at an event in New Jersey. Gail and Elliot are to my right, and Mom, Fred Wills, and my brother Joe to my left.

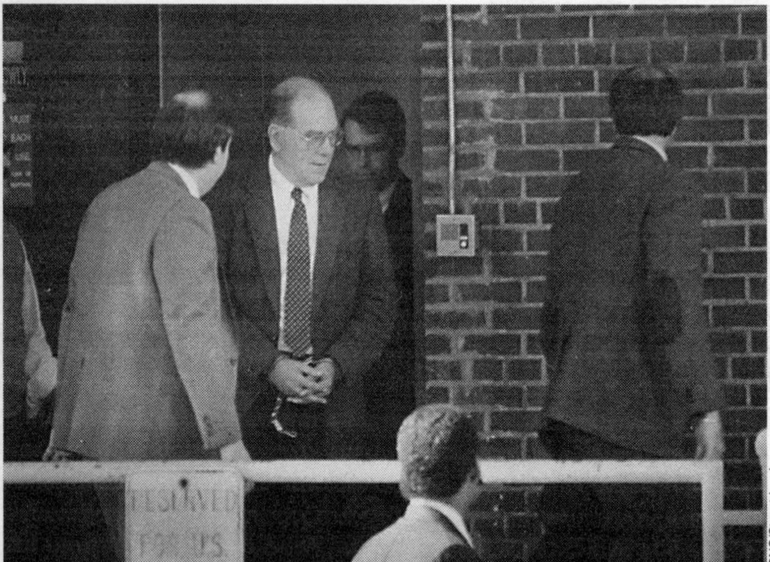

EIRNS/Stuart Lewis

Jan. 27, 1989: After sentencing, Lyndon LaRouche is led out of the Alexandria, Va. Courthouse. I'm right behind him. A crowd of our supporters broke into "Va Pensiero," a song of freedom and hope sung by the Hebrew slaves in Verdi's opera "Nabucco."

Virginia trial: treachery!

Roanoke County Judge Clifford R. Weckstein.

EIRNS/Stuart Lewis

Attorney Brian Gettings.

Virginia defendants Shelley Ascher (left) and Larry Hecht, Paul Gallagher, Anita Gallagher, and Don Phau (below, l. to r.). They all spent years in prison, before being released on parole.

against me. A few other states had also issued temporary restraining orders against our solicitation of loans, using similar securities law to describe our political loans as the equivalent of stocks and bonds. Still, there had been no such restraining order in Virgina.

"Tell them I'll be right over," I said, and walked across the street to the office building. "I believe you're looking for me," I told the officer at the door. "I'm Billington." "Yes. We have a warrant for your arrest," one of them told me, and began to lead me over to his car.

At that moment, however, the man we all came to know as Deputy Dog, Don Moore, who had seen me through the glass door from inside the building, literally ran outside, nearly breaking the door in his haste, grabbed my arm, cuffed me, and paraded me around the building before the media cameras to his own car in the back. Sure enough, the wires put out a picture of brave Deputy Dog, chin thrust out, leading his prey to justice, defending Americans from the "LaRouche Menace." His old Vietnam buddy Ollie North couldn't have done it better.

Sixteen of us were indicted, along with the companies which had borrowed funds. Three of those arrested were in Baltimore, and the rest in Leesburg. Besides those of us on the phone teams, the indictment included two members who worked on finances, and three from the legal staff. We were herded into court the next morning, wearing the bright orange jumpsuits provided by the county jail. The prosecutors tried to deny bail, but it had become too well established by that time that none of us was interested in disappearing. We intended to defeat the (il)legal onslaught through the courts, if possible, and through political warfare. We were each released on a recognizance bond.

We had been arrested with no prior notice or warning that the Commonwealth of Virginia viewed our loans as "securities." In fact, we soon learned that the Commonwealth had not yet determined whether or not such loans could in any way be construed as securities under Virginia law! Only *after* our indictment, did the prosecution approach the State Corporation Commission (the state's securities regulatory body), requesting that they declare our loans to be securities! To make matters worse for the prosecutors, the State Corporation Commission responded that they could not rule without a thorough investigation, since this was a "case of first impression," meaning it was the first time such political loans had been alleged to be securities. Thus, while the Commonwealth's experts had no basis for knowing whether such loans should be treated as securities, *we* were expected to have known, before the fact, that they were securities, and that we should have registered with the Commonwealth as "stockbrokers"! As a result of my "criminal failure" to know what their own experts did not know, I was facing one to ten years on each of nine counts. The Corporation Commission did eventually rule that our loans *could* be considered to fall under the securities law, but only months after our arrest. The head of that Commission, Elizabeth Lacy, was quickly rewarded with an appointment to the Supreme Court of Virginia. (Virginia Attorney General Mary Sue Terry would later run her 1989 re-election campaign, and her unsuccessful campaign for governor in 1993, on the grounds of her "success" in prosecuting the LaRouche organization!)

Our motion to dismiss, on the grounds that the ruling was "ex post facto," was rejected, as were later appeals on those grounds. The fix was in.

I was the only one of the 16 who had also been indicted in the Federal case. I had nine counts: failing to register as a securities broker, selling securities without a license, conspiring to defraud (that count was actually added on at a later date), and six counts of specific cases of "selling securities" to an individual, three to an American engineer in Saudi Arabia, and three to a woman in Illinois. Each count carried one to ten years, so I faced a potential 90-year sentence.

The two individuals named in the indictment surprised me enormously. As to the woman in Illinois, Marie Fincham, although her daughter and her son-in-law had been furious with her for supporting us, she had stood up to them, had tried to organize them to support our ideas, and shared our literature with them. I had first called Mrs. Fincham only a few months earlier, *after* the October 1986 raid. Virtually every call had centered on a discussion of the massive legal and media attacks against us, compared with the actual content of our political work. Not only did I discuss with her the efforts of the "Get LaRouche Task Force," both in the government and outside of it, to shut us down by any means necessary, but I even called her from my jail cell in Loudoun County, to tell her about the Missouri case! Mrs. Fincham even met with Elizabeth Rose, a beautiful old lady who toured the world speaking on the victimization of senior citizens like herself, who were being attacked and denounced as unstable if they supported LaRouche. Mrs. Rose had spoken in Chicago in January, and Mrs. Fincham attended the meeting, and spoke with her. Mrs. Fincham was a wealthy woman, who explained to me that she would only lend us funds which she could easily afford to lose. Nevertheless, I was charged with *fraud* for having somehow misled her as to the risk of such a loan! Imagine the following discussion:

"Hi, Mrs. X. This is Mike Billington. I wanted you to know that what we're doing has provoked our enemies into an all-out effort to destroy us. Henry Kissinger, Vice President Bush, elements of the Justice Department, several state governments, the Russian government, the media, and the drug cartels are all publicly and actively engaged in that effort. In fact, I'm in jail right now. We need your help."

"Oh, that sounds like a wonderful investment. I'll probably make a good profit by lending my money to you, and it would be safer than in the bank. How much do you need?"

Crazy? That is precisely the story line sold to the jury. I could not imagine at the time of the indictment that they could possibly use Mrs. Fincham against me. Although we were forbidden by the court to speak with her, it seemed certain to me that her testimony would bear out the truth.

The other named lender in my indictment, an engineer who was working in Saudi Arabia at the time of his contribution and loans, was also a surprise to me. He was a very serious supporter, who had been reading EIR carefully over a long period of time. When he returned to the U.S., soon after I moved to Virginia in April 1985, he travelled to Leesburg to meet with me and an associate who had been in contact with him most often. He was considering becoming active in our organizing efforts, and attended several of our national conferences over the next year. But he was having financial troubles, and needed his money back. We were then in the midst of the post-Illinois election tailspin with our finances, but we arranged to get him some money. After the October 1986 raid, I was told that he had agreed to roll over his loans. He, too, seemed to me to be a very poor witness for the prosecution.

Then, just one month after the Virginia arrests, before even the pre-trial hearings had been scheduled, the Sheriffs invaded our offices yet again. I was out of town that day. When I called in, I was told that New York State had issued indictments to 15 people from California, New York, and Virginia.

"Where should I turn myself in?" I asked.

"You're not included," I heard from the other end.

"What? Are you sure? There must be some mistake!" I protested.

But, sure enough, I was passed by on this one. Several of my close friends in the New York region were indicted. So was Nancy Spannaus, the editor of *New Solidarity* since its inception in 1968. Her husband, Ed, had been added onto the Federal case in a superceding indictment issued in December (along with other members of our security staff and phone teams). Ed and Nancy, both members of our National Executive Committee, and with two teenage sons, were now both facing long prison terms.

Involuntary Bankruptcy

Then came April. The Task Force surprise for April took the prize for utter and total disregard for law, justice, or the principles of the U.S. Constitution. The government harassment, the legal barrage, the media slanders—nothing seemed to work to shut us down. So, like Soviet Commissars, the corrupt DOJ officials decided to simply move in and take over our publishing companies, and stop those damn newspapers once and for all. Since there were no legal grounds to do so, they created some.

The Boston judge supervising U.S. Attorney Weld's grand jury investigation, Judge Mazzone, had imposed millions of dollars in fines against Caucus Distributors, Campaigner Publications, the Fusion Energy Foundation, and the National Democratic Policy Committee (the political action committee which funded Congressional and local state campaigns for the LaRouche movement), because Weld was not satisfied with the documents these entities produced to the grand jury in response to subpoenas. In what the government acknowledged to be a legal first, the DOJ suddenly moved to collect these fines, which were still being appealed, by imposing an involuntary bankruptcy on Caucus, Campaigner, and Fusion—that is, liquidating the companies in order to collect the fines. In reality, the government already knew that these companies had no real assets. Our financial strength rested entirely on the cash flow from the extensive (and expanding) circulation of our publications. In a Justice Department memorandum obtained years later under the FOIA, the real purpose of the government bankruptcy filing was set forth: "shut them down."

Contacting U.S. Bankruptcy Judge Martin Bostetter in secret, and with a thick stack of pleadings, the DOJ legal team argued that the LaRouche movement companies had to be seized secretly, and padlocked immediately, to prevent them from moving and concealing assets. The basis for this preposterous assertion was an affidavit executed by none other than Deputy Don Moore. But Judge Bostetter complied.

So, as a result of an order issued by Judge Bostetter, on April 21, 1987, the offices in Leesburg were once again occupied. In addition, every office in the country was seized by U.S. Marshals. The companies were turned over to bankruptcy trustees, who shut down their operations. Campaigner had published *New Solidarity*, the weekly newspaper with a circulation of 100,000, as well as a theoretical journal, *The Campaigner*. *Fusion* magazine, published by the Fusion Energy Foundation, had reached 140,000 in circulation, making it the third-largest scientific publication in the U.S.

For the first time in the history of our republic, the U.S. government shut down an opposition newspaper, as well as the only scientific journal which had relentlessly defended scientific progress against the madness of the increasingly hegemonic, radical ecologist movement. The nature of the government action was so blatantly illegal that even the "LaRouche Fix" was not sufficient to allow their action to stand in court forever. Over two years later, after hearing the government's "evidence" in a trial where the companies were allowed to defend themselves, Judge Bostetter dismissed the entire government bankruptcy case—ruling that the government had acted in bad faith, and that their actions in bringing the case amounted to a constructive fraud on the court.

Although Judge Bostetter overturned the bankruptcy, the damage had been done. Not only had the publications been shut down, but, since the companies had been ordered by the court to cease all financial activities, including all debt payments, and to turn over all such activity to the trustees, all our creditors, both business vendors and political supporters who had loaned money to our campaigns, were left high and dry.

In the past, despite our difficulties in making debt payments, we could always assure our supporters that nothing, absolutely nothing, would induce us to shut ourselves down, to desert the fight, or to declare bankruptcy to avoid our creditors. The one thing we did not even imagine, was a court order to stop publications and stop debt payment. Of course, the government, which now ran the defunct companies, had absolutely no interest in whether or not our supporters were repaid.

On the day following the imposition of the involuntary bankruptcy, the *Washington Post* carried the headline: "Federal Raids Effectively Shut LaRouche Organization." We did not see it that way. The entire Leesburg membership met on the morning of the Federal takeover. There were many jokes, but a great deal of apprehension and confusion.

"Well," said Nancy Spannaus, "it looks like we've got to start a new newspaper. I volunteer to be editor! Any ideas for a name?" We had been spared the EIR, since it was not published by any of the bankrupted companies. But we could not transfer subscriptions from *New Solidarity* to a new newspaper, nor those for *Fusion* magazine to a new science journal, nor those for *The Campaigner* to a new theoretical journal. We had to begin anew, selling new subscriptions, starting from zero.

After a few days of discussions, the name *The New Federalist* was chosen for the paper, reflecting our forefathers in the Federalist movement who built the Constitution and the American System. On either side of the masthead would be quotes from the Founding Fathers: "Whoever would overthrow the liberty of a nation must begin by subduing the freeness of speech" (Benjamin Franklin); and, "It was by the press that the morals of this country have been ruined, and it is by the press that they shall be restored" (Alexander Hamilton). *The New Federalist* came out within days of the involuntary bankruptcy, looking very much like the old *New Solidarity*, except for the name.

We set up shop in our houses and apartments, since our offices were permanently sealed off. We tried to reach all of our supporters as quickly as possible. It was very hard for most people to comprehend that our nation had fallen so low, that the government would silence a major opposition voice by force.

The scientific community, not only those who had worked closely with us, but also many who disagreed with the political combativeness of the Fusion Energy Foundation, were nonetheless shocked and angered that both the freedom of speech and the freedom of scientific inquiry and debate had been so abused by government dictate. A public letter of protest, signed by leading scientists from around the world, was published in the *Washington Post* in the spring of 1988. In the fall of that year, we launched a new science journal, called *21st Century Science & Technology,* with Marje Hecht as managing editor.

The Campaigner magazine, our theoretical journal, had also been cut off, but we partially compensated for it with a regular four-page centerfold in *The New Federalist,* called "The American Almanac," which was long enough to print philosophical and historical works by Lyn, Helga, and others—a feature of *The New Federalist* which continues to this day. It was not until 1992 that we finally produced a new theoretical journal, called *Fidelio,* under the editorship of Will Wertz and Ken Kronberg. I had first come to understand the Schiller quote on its masthead—"It is through beauty that we proceed to freedom"—as I lay thinking of the angel Leonora, on the cold cinder block of the Fairfax County Jail.

[13]

The Crash of '87

We struggled through the spring of 1987 to reconstruct the infrastructure of the organization, with diligence and a spirit of resistance against the totalitarian methods thrown against us. But there was also a great deal of fear induced by the terror tactics—the willingness to use the power of the state far beyond the strictures of law to bring down the organization by any means necessary. No one was free of fear in considering this awesome array of power, but some were less able than others to overcome it—including some in our national leadership.

One of the most severe examples was Criton Zoakos, the National Executive Committee member who oversaw our intelligence work.

★ ★ ★

Parmenides and Paralysis

Criton was a Greek expatriate who had been involved in Communist Party activities in Greece in the 1960's. He attended one of LaRouche's classes in New York in 1970 and became one of the early members of the NCLC. Criton had a sharp mind and a quick wit, but sometimes took to impotent blustering when he felt insecure intellectually. This was the case in 1984, when we were under heavy attack both by the "Get LaRouche Task Force," and by the Soviet Union. Criton was clearly agitated about the public attacks on Lyn and the movement. He gave several political briefings which were more macho than reason. Lyn, in a move which I interpreted as an effort to focus Criton's mind through serious intellectual work, assigned him the task of preparing a class series on Plato's *Parmenides* dialogue. The class was a colossal failure. Criton had done valuable work on Plato in the past, including directing an original translation of Plato's *Timaeus*. But he got lost in *Parmenides*, and guided those of us attending his classes into, rather than out of, a maze.

I came to understand the *Parmenides* dialogue years later, partially owing to regular references by Lyn, but mainly because I read some of the works of Parmenides himself, and his student Zeno, and then re-read Plato's dialogue featuring these two contemporaries of Socrates. Plato's dialogue portrays Parmenides, one of the Eliatics (later known as Aristotelians), investigating the question of the One and the Many, proving that if the One exists, then it doesn't exist; if it doesn't exist, then it does exist; and so also with the Many, and that this is the case both in fact, and in appearance: In other words, he "proves" that everything is unintelligible and contradictory!

Plato's point was to ridicule the *method* of Parmenides, as well as his fundamental assumptions. Parmenides's method was that of strict logical argumentation, without questioning the hypothesis underlying the argument. The hypothesis of Parmenides, and of his student Zeno, which was well known to the Platonic school (and should have been known to Criton), was that there is no change in the world—that all change is merely appearance. Reality is a linear, undifferentiated continuum, while matter is composed of unchanging atoms, little hard balls which can not be further subdivided.

It was this hypothesis which led his student Zeno to his famous—and ridiculous—paradoxes. Motion is impossible, Zeno "proved." If Achilles were to try to overtake the tortoise, he would first have to reach the spot where the tortoise began. But the tortoise would have moved forward by then, even if by a small distance. Since the same problem would still exist for Achilles to move to the new location of the tortoise, Achilles could never catch the tortoise—proving, said Zeno, that motion is impossible, a mere illusion.

Similarly, an arrow shot through the air is, at any particular instant (as with a still photograph), at rest, and therefore, argued Zeno, it is *always* at rest. Again, motion is impossible.

What neither Zeno nor Parmenides considered, was that their hypothesis was flawed—that neither time nor space could be measured in a linear way in the realm of the very small, what we call today the micro-physical. Distance is not composed of a collection of dimensionless points, nor is time composed of dimensionless moments (photographs). Nothing is fixed in the real world, but is in a constant state of change, interacting with everything else in the universe. Although the mind can conceive of dimensionless points and "snapshot" moments, they must not be confused with anything real, as Plato's cave dwellers confused the shadows for reality. The arrow never stands still—even the photograph only approximates the arrow at rest, depending on the shutter speed of the camera. Zeno's notion of fixed objects moving in empty space and fixed time—the same flawed hypothesis which guides Newton's incompetent attack on Leibniz and "Continental" (Renaissance) science—can lead only to contradictions, and can say nothing truthful about the real world.

Plato's *Parmenides* dialogue is an extended version of Zeno's paradox. Criton, however, like most of the "politically correct" scholarly studies of Plato which I have seen, seemed to miss Plato's point altogether, and treated Plato as a follower of Parmenides! Parmenides's excruciating deductive logic was described by Criton as the highest expression of Plato's method of the higher hypothesis, and he never discussed the *object* of Plato's parody of Parmenides's thought—that without viewing *change* as the *object* of scientific and critical investigation, nothing can be known.

I have made this digression regarding Criton and his classes on Plato for a purpose, for these were the precise thoughts which flooded my mind in late June 1987, when I watched Criton virtually dissimulate, out of fear, while giving a briefing in the office. The Boston prosecution under William Weld had informed LaRouche that they were preparing to indict him. LaRouche offered, on his own volition, to testify before the Boston Grand Jury, to clear his name. This he did, but the superceding indictment, adding LaRouche to the case, appeared imminent.

Criton burst into the briefing room one morning, having received a report confirming the impending indictment, in a state of pure rage. His performance was a clinical demonstration of "flight forward"—the battlefield syndrome whereby a terrified soldier loses touch with reality, and, in a fit of false bravado, dashes headlong into the enemy lines to certain death. Criton pranced about, shouting that this was fascism, a police state, that we wouldn't tolerate it, that the American people would be called out to the streets, and on and on. I thought for a moment I was back at a student anti-war rally in the 1960's. The indictment was, in fact, strict evidence of America's devolution into a police state, but Criton was fantasizing to believe that the American people were anywhere near prepared to lift a finger to stop it. The sad fact was that the population would, by and large, respond exactly the way the social planners from Tavistock intended—they would rush to dissociate themselves from the "political extremist" who was "in trouble with the law."

And that was, in fact, exactly what Criton, himself, proceeded to do! He began preparing his exit from the organization, setting himself up financially and politically—contacting potential employers in the intelligence and financial community—while constructing an hysterical "theoretical" justification for his break with Lyn.

LaRouche later revealed that Criton had confided in him that the government was threatening him with deportation back to Greece. The terror of going to jail, combined with the unknown dangers of Greek retribution for his earlier radical activities, turned Criton onto an easily manipulated bundle of infantile rage.

The next year, in the winter of 1988, Criton turned up on the government's witness list against us in the Alexandria Federal trial. He was hanging around the courthouse with "Deputy Dog" Don Moore, but the government eventually thought better than to put such an unstable, "loose cannon" on the stand.

LaRouche was, indeed, indicted by the Boston Grand Jury, his name included with the rest of us in a superceding indictment on July 2, 1987. Headlines across the country blared: "LaRouche Indicted for Conspiracy." LaRouche understood that he had been targetted for destruction not for anything he had already accomplished, but in order to prevent those things he was uniquely qualified to accomplish in the future. For LaRouche's ideas for a new economic order, based on the revival of scientific and cultural optimism throughout the world, could, when the crisis reached a critical point, threaten the power of the oligarchy itself.

The proper response to the indictment, therefore, was to continue doing exactly what we were doing. We did not have the strength or the resources to combat the corrupt power of the Justice Department in a head-to-head confrontation, but we knew the nature of the beast of which the Justice Department was but one part. We deployed to hit the enemy on a vulnerable flank.

LaRouche expanded his campaign for the Democratic Presidential nomination in 1988. He travelled widely around the world. Shortly after being indicted, he visited Turkey, meeting with Turkish Prime Minister Turgut Özal, the foreign minister, and others. He lectured and held private meetings in Peru, Japan, Taiwan, and all over Europe.

All of us who had been indicted, including LaRouche, had to spend a certain amount of time meeting with lawyers and planning legal strategy, but our real defense—and the only defense that would be effective against a corrupted judicial system—was to expand our political offensive. By refusing to slow down our campaigns, no matter what the difficulties, we could come out stronger in the end.

★ ★ ★

In the spring of 1987—between the involuntary bankruptcy and LaRouche's indictment—LaRouche issued a forecast that the stock market was almost certainly facing a major collapse, likely to hit in October. He had made other forecasts in prior years, although never one concerning the stock markets. In the 1950's, he had warned of an "Eisenhower recession," caused by the overextension of easy household credit to prop up the explosion in consumer goods production, at the expense of basic infrastructure and heavy industry. Following that recession, he published a long-term projection of a late 1960's breakdown of the Bretton Woods accords, and an end to the era in which the dollar was considered to be "as good as gold"—as indeed came about on Aug. 15, 1971, when Nixon pulled the plug on the dollar. He made strong warnings in 1979 concerning the devastating impact of Paul Volcker's policy of usury at the Federal Reserve. He also warned the Soviets of the collapse they faced if they rejected the SDI proposal of 1983. None of these forecasts was a "prediction," but a warning, in the subjunctive mood, of the form: "If the current policy trends were not drastically reversed, then the irreversible consequences would be. . . ." His spring 1987 stock-market warning was still a forecast, rather than a crystal-ball prediction, but it was far more specific than his preceding ones.

During the 1980's, deregulation of the banking and securities sectors had wiped out much of the local, domestic credit used by farmers, entrepreneurs, oil drillers, and other small to medium-sized businesses. The local banking system in the U.S., and especially the Savings and Loan banks, had been preserved through strict regulation since the 1930's Depression, which prevented interstate takeovers of banks by the Wall Street giants, and separated banking functions from brokerage, insurance, and other financial operations.

The S&L's were already reeling from the 1979 Volcker interest rates, when deregulation hit them in the 1980's. The S&L's and small local banks depended on long-term, low-interest lending, with small but stable profit margins. With deregulation, they were suddenly placed in competition with the big money-center banks in New York, which wanted to get hold of the billions of dollars being "wasted" on relatively low-profit investments in small industry, home construction, and agriculture, and use this enormous cash-flow to prop up the emerging speculative bubble on Wall Street.

I spoke with hundreds of ranchers, farmers, and small bankers around the country throughout the 1980's, who told me countless horror stories of the destruction of family farms and businesses. One banker in Utah described to me his precarious position, brought on by the expanding rate of default and bankruptcy among ranchers and farmers, who had been his major clients. His family had been ranchers in the area for four generations, and bankers for two, and he was doing everything in his power to help his friends and neighbors keep their family businesses afloat through the "hard times." One day, when I called, he was clearly depressed, and I asked what was wrong.

"I've just received a call from the FDIC bank regulators. They're doing an audit of our S&L, part of this national drive to stop the fraud in the S&L's."

"Don't tell me they've accused you of fraud!" I said, since I knew him to be both honest and an extremely dedicated and hard-working fellow.

"Well, I didn't *think* I'd done any thing illegal. But he tells me that the government was not going to allow S&L's to lend money to their friends anymore. That's corruption, he told me. Hell, every one of my clients is a friend, and their daddy'd been a friend of my daddy. I told him that, but he said they wouldn't put up with that anymore, and, besides, they'd checked some of our loans, and found that several of our biggest clients were going under. Yep, I told him, 'but we're doing our best to keep them afloat.' He said, 'Why, that's defrauding your stockholders. They have a right to hold you to making profitable loans, and if you're loaning out the bank's money to friends who are going under, you're liable to end up in jail!' "

My friend was told that a "profitable" way to invest the bank's money was to put it in the money markets in New York! *Some* of the nation's S&L's, such as those owned by George Bush's children, were delighted to leap into the speculative whirlwind, and often robbed their depositors of everything they had when the bubble burst. Others, like my friend in Utah, were not in the least bit interested in deserting their friends and communities. Eventually, many of the S&L's went under, and the large New York banks moved in to buy them up (under the new bank deregulation laws rammed through the Congress), with the taxpayers picking up the bad debts.

When October 1987 arrived, the stock market at first continued its euphoric highs, defying Lyn's forecast. But on Friday, October 16, the Dow Jones took a hefty decline, and worried noises filled the nation's airwaves all weekend. On Saturday, in the office, the phone team formed a little pool, everyone throwing in a quarter and taking a guess at how many points the market would fall on Monday. Now, we're hardly a betting crew, and we usually pay little or no attention to the ups and downs in the market. But we had spent the previous six months explaining Lyn's forecast for an October (or so) crash to our supporters, and it seemed inevitable that reality had finally caught up with the speculators. Nevertheless, we were all rather conservative, guessing that the fall would be in the 50- to 200-point range—except Larry Hecht, who boldly picked 400, which would mean about a 15% fall in one day.

On Monday, Oct. 19, 1987, the crash hit, exactly as LaRouche had forecast. Markets across the globe tumbled, with the Dow Jones falling by over 22%. This was particularly discomforting for the "Get LaRouche Task Force," since LaRouche had once again been proven right, and the "experts" were proven to be incompetent bunglers. Larry collected his quarters.

The following morning, my sister Margaret and a team from our New Jersey office set up a literature table on Wall Street, sporting a sign with a personal message from LaRouche: "The market has elected to choose this most appropriate moment in time to express its total confidence in the accuracy of my forecasting—Lyndon H. LaRouche." A good time was had by all, although they had to be on the lookout for falling bankers!

LaRouche's fame throughout the world took a geometric leap upward, as national leaders and economists pulled out their old EIR's to take a closer look at LaRouche's writings, to see how he knew what was coming, and what he thought would be coming next. LaRouche's response to the crash was to intensify his warning that it was a *systemic* crisis, not a *cyclical* collapse, like that of 1929, caused merely by a speculative bubble. Unless the mid-1960's paradigm shift into deindustrialization, hyper-environmentalism, and unrestrained financial speculation were scrapped, along with the IMF and its "conditionalities" against industrialization in the developing sector, then the '87 crash would appear as just a blip in comparison to the coming disintegration. The IMF related system had become like a cancer on the body of the world economy, leading towards the death of its host.

As we learned soon enough, LaRouche's warnings were ignored in the corridors of power. Instead, the world economic gurus in London and New York launched the "Casino Mondiale"—the transformation of an already sick financial system into a global gambling establishment, with the massive escalation of "derivatives" trading. Henceforth, the majority of money in the markets was not to be investments in the stock valuations of real companies, but, literally, the placing of side bets, called derivatives, on where the values of stock indices, currencies, and interest rates would be somewhere in the future. By 1998, there was over $150 trillion in outstanding derivatives contracts, several times greater than the value of the total product of the world's industry and agriculture! Whereas before 1971, about 75% of the money traded in foreign exchange markets around the world corresponded to the trade of physical goods between nations, by 1997, that ratio was below 1%! More than 99% was pure speculation, making billions in speculative profits for the likes of George Soros and his London mentors, at the expense of real economies and real people.

Along with the derivatives bubble came "globalization." Nineteenth-Century British colonialism had been based on the establishment of mining and plantation agriculture in the colonies, using the native population as serfs or slaves, depending on the circumstances, while pumping opium from colonial India into the other colonies to destroy the population's capacity to resist their oppression. The new colonialism of the late 20th Century would retain the role of opium, but replace the plantations with low-skill process-industries, making such things as textiles, electronics, toys, and tennis shoes for export.

However, in 1987 and 1988, LaRouche believed that the world economy could still escape "the big one," if emergency policies were implemented with due haste. In the year following the October 1987 crash, LaRouche travelled the globe—between court appearances and Presidential campaign events at home—offering programs to unite nations, both regionally and internationally, behind great infrastructure development programs, while there was still time. On four continents, LaRouche's initiatives demonstrated his universal vision: a Pacific Basin Development program; an effort to unite the Ibero-American nations into a United States of Ibero-America; the launching of an international "Food for Peace" program, with a major focus on the crying need for the development of the vast potential of the African continent; a proposal, on the brink of the collapse of the Iron Curtain, for reuniting Eastern and Western Europe, and linking Europe with Asia, through extensive development spiraling out from a revitalized industrial core in the heart of Europe. All of these were dependent upon the replacement of the bankrupt IMF with a new monetary system based on national banking and oriented towards global development.

Great Projects: Asia

Three of our 1988 initiatives would each have a direct effect on my subsequent work: one in Asia, one in Ibero-America, and one in Europe.

In September 1988, Lyn and Helga made their first visit to Taiwan. They met with many of the nationalist leaders, some of whom had worked with Chiang Kai Shek in the "Development Decade" of 1927-37, fought the Japanese, fought the civil war against the communists, and ultimately built Taiwan into a significant modern industrial economy. Lyn and Helga were featured on the cover of one of the political magazines, the "China Flag," which represented the "old-line" Kuomintang Nationalist Party leadership. These people were fiercely anti-communist, but, ironically, shared with the mainland leadership in Beijing a passionate dedication to the unity of China, with Taiwan strictly viewed as a province of that united China. This "One China" policy placed them in functional agreement with Beijing, in opposition to the British efforts (continuous over the past 150 years) to divide China and to sabotage national development. When the reform policies launched by Deng Xiaoping in 1979, began to open up the myopic, closed society of the Mao Zedong era, these Kuomintang nationalists in Taiwan strongly advocated the export of Chinese technological and industrial know-how from Taiwan into the mainland. LaRouche encouraged that approach, while insisting that the program must be placed in the content of a broader policy for the development of the Pacific Basin—a policy LaRouche had explicated in 1983 in a report called *A Fifty-Year Development Policy for the Indian-Pacific Oceans Basin*.

Although this was their first visit to China, Lyn and Helga had made several other trips to Asia in the early 1980's, including especially Japan, Thailand, and India. In India, Lyn and Helga had established a friendship with Prime Minister Indira Gandhi through the course of two personal meetings. Mrs. Gandhi, like her father Jawaharlal Nehru, recognized the crucial importance of the Non-Aligned Movement, which then-Prime Minister Nehru had helped to create. By forging an alliance of developing-sector nations friendly to both "blocs" in the British-instigated Cold War, the Non-Aligned Movement was dedicated not only to defending these generally poor nations against subversion—either from communists or from the Western colonial powers—but also to building a bridge of collaborative development between the superpowers. Mrs. Gandhi shared with Lyn and Helga the belief that nothing short of such a global development perspective could prevent another great depression and a Third World War. Together, the three of them conspired to revive FDR's post-war vision for the mighty nations of Eurasia—China, India, and Russia—together with the United States, to build a century of global peace and development.

Lyn and Helga's 1988 Taiwan visit opened up a new era in our relationship to China, and served as a spark for what would become my focus for many years to come—namely, China's history and culture, and the relations between East and West over the millennia.

Lyn spoke often of Dr. Sun Yat-sen (a name only vaguely familiar to me at the time), the father of the Chinese Republic. He discussed Sun's 1919 book, *The International Development of China,* which presented a massive railroad and water development perspective for China, to be supported by the Western nations. Dr. Sun argued that the enormous productive capacity which had created the means of war in the just-completed "Great War," must be converted to produce the capital goods needed for the development of China. Such an international development of China, he said, would not be merely an act of benevolence by the West towards the world's largest nation, but was *absolutely essential,* if the West were to avoid yet another great depression, and another world war. Like LaRouche, Sun posed these arguments as *forecasts,* in the subjunctive mood, to the purpose of provoking Western leaders to confront reality, and either rise to the historic occasion, or face the consequences. In this, and in many other things, Dr. Sun proved to be devastatingly correct.

We began building networks among the Chinese community

in the U.S., while EIR initiated a monthly Chinese-language newsletter. Over the years, this would develop into one of the most crucial areas of our work, and a major point of leverage in Lyn and Helga's direct contribution towards creating a new world economic order out of the wreckage of the Bretton Woods System. Beginning in 1996, Helga would make several trips to China, and LaRouche's ideas would find fertile soil in a nation filled with optimism and hope for the future.

Great Projects: Ibero-America

In Ibero-America, the year preceding LaRouche's incarceration was witness to a potentially world-shaking development—a movement to invite the nations south of the Rio Grande into a new political union.

In August 1988, delegates from 22 countries in Ibero-America gathered together for four days in Panama City, for a meeting called "Towards a Second Amphictyonic Congress." The title referred to the effort in 1826 by Ibero-American leaders, with the strong support of American nationalist leaders John Quincy Adams and Henry Clay, to unite the nations of Ibero-America, at the First Amphictyonic Congress, also held in Panama City.

The idea of the Congress was to build a United States of Ibero-America. In 1986, we had published (in Spanish) *The Integration of Ibero-America—One Hundred Million New Jobs by the Year 2000*. The book detailed our proposals to unite the economies of South and Central America, in order to jointly combat the demands of the IMF, and the subversion of the narco-terrorists, while unleashing the tremendous productive potential of the Ibero-American population. The legacy of colonialism had left Ibero-America with neither the physical nor the political structures required to carry out bilateral trade or mutual infrastructure development projects. There were no adequate rail or road connections crossing the continent from East to West. Infrastructure was generally either totally inadequate, or in cases of once relatively developed nations like Argentina, in a state of decay. Unified political action against the IMF was needed as the basis for launching the Great Projects required to develop the continent.

The Integration of Ibero-America became the handbook for expanding circles of Ibero-American patriots, many of whom attended the Congress in Panama. There were representatives from political parties, military institutions, labor unions, the Catholic Church, and others who recognized the urgency of this effort. It was this Congress, more than any other particular issue or event, which was the immediate cause for Sir George Bush's hysterical outbursts against General Manuel Noriega, leading to the infamous and disgraceful U.S. invasion of Panama. The personal role of Lyndon LaRouche in uniting Ibero-America in its own defense, and to a higher purpose, was a red flag in the face of the Queen, Lady Thatcher, and the soon-to-be-knighted pseudo-nobility in the U.S., Sir Henry Kissinger and Sir George Bush.

But what about the monotonous headlines and one-liners from Sir George declaring Noriega to be the "Drug Kingpin" of Ibero-America? The easily demonstrated fact is that General Noriega, more than any other leader in Ibero-America, not only waged war against the narco-traffickers, but was the U.S. Drug Enforcement Administration's (DEA) closest and most successful collaborator in their war against the drug trade! Only one year before Bush launched his campaign to label Noriega a "drug kingpin," the DEA released a report on the remarkable success of "Operation Pisces," a three-year, collaborative project between the U.S. and Panama, to track down and arrest the drug cartel operatives from across the continent who used Panama's banking system—both the Panamanian and the foreign banks—as a primary money-laundering center. DEA Director John Lawn sent a personal letter to General Noriega praising him for his leading role in the most successful anti-drug effort in the Western Hemisphere!

Then came the Contra supply operation, run by George Bush and Ollie North. As General Noriega later reported, when Bush sent John Poindexter to Panama, demanding that General Noriega join the covert CIA plan for an invasion of Nicaragua, the General told him to forget it. Bush was reportedly furious.

In December 1989, the U.S. invaded Panama, killing thousands of innocents, kidnapping General Noriega, and placing Guillermo Endara, a lawyer for the Medellín Cartel's Panamanian drug banks, in the Presidency. Although I had been deeply involved in organizing support in the U.S. for the conference in Panama to unite Ibero-America, I could only watch passively on television as Bush laid waste to Panama, since I was by then sitting in a prison cell. In fact, by 1990, all the primary architects of the Amphictyonic Congress were in prison: Gen. Noreiga, a prisoner of war in a U.S. prison; Col. Mohamed Alí Seineldín, convicted to a life sentence by Argentina's British darling, President Carlos Menem; Joaquin Hernandes Galicia (La Quina), framed up in Mexico on weapons charges, removed from the leadership of the oil workers union, and imprisoned; and Lyndon LaRouche, political prisoner of George Bush. Ibero-America was ready for the slaughter—set up to be "Africanized" by the IMF and Dope, Inc.'s narco-terrorists.

Great Projects: Europe

The most important of LaRouche's initiatives during 1988 occurred on October 12 in Berlin, only a few weeks before our conviction in the Alexandria Federal trial. In a press conference which was videotaped and included in a national TV broadcast a few weeks later, Presidential candidate LaRouche forecast the near-term fall of the Berlin Wall, and explicated a program to bring about peace and prosperity out of the impending dissolution of the Soviet bloc. Reflecting back on this today, with the vivid memory of the sudden collapse of the Iron Curtain and the communist governments of Eastern Europe after 1989, the average observer may fail to recognize the shocking nature of LaRouche's message at that Berlin press conference. I, for one, found it hard to believe. Despite my intimate involvement in the political work and analysis which led LaRouche to his forecast, and to his formulation of the necessary policy required to meet the pending transformation of history, I could not imagine the fall of Soviet communism, except as the result of a cataclysmic military confrontation, which seemed unlikely in the near term.

It was a question of clinging to the axioms of my upbringing, even though I didn't recognize them as axioms. Even those of us who consciously rejected the libertarian degeneracy of "popular culture" in the post-1960's era, still retained some of the mindset of the Cold War—the bi-polar world of Bertrand Russell's "condominium of super-powers." LaRouche could not have made it more explicit to all of us, as he had to his Soviet dialogue partners in 1982, that the Soviet economy could not survive, except by adopting his proposal for joint U.S.-Soviet collaboration on relativistic beam defense systems—but "understanding" does not become "knowledge" until a person replicates, in his or her own mind, the discovery of principle which led to the conclusion.

The power of Lyn's proposed policy, as laid out in detail in his national TV broadcast, stands as testimony to his vision: The Berlin Wall will fall soon, he said, owing to the inability of the Soviet empire to sustain the looting of the satellite nations of Eastern Europe at a rate required to prop up the crumbling Russian economy. The task for the West, in tandem with the new, united Germany, is to initiate a development perspective towards the Soviet bloc which will be of such obvious benefit for them, and for the world, that the transition will be peaceful, and contribute to ending the economic disintegration facing both the East and the West. In addition, a "Food for Peace" agreement between East and West should be negotiated, to meet the mounting food crisis in the Soviet Union, in exchange for collaboration in the development of Poland and the other satellite countries.

This dramatic proposal would grow in scope and detail over the coming months and years, assuming various forms and names, such as the Productive Triangle, the New Silk Road, and the Eurasian Land-Bridge. But the core concept was already there in Lyn's Berlin press conference: Break the axiomatic assumption of irreconcilable confrontation between the "communist East" and "capitalist West," through collaboration on Great Projects essential for both.

Subsequent events once again proved that LaRouche was right, from the dramatic fall of the Berlin Wall, to the utter disasters of the 1990's, when the West failed to implement LaRouche's development proposals for Eastern Europe. The shock therapy and globalization imposed on Russia and the former COMECON nations during the 1990's have proven to be total failures, bringing on both a global depression and the threat of global war. The misery of the past decade was far too heavy a price to have paid, because people did not do what they should have done at the historic juncture of 1989.

[14]

Trials

In the middle of the dense array of international diplomacy and Presidential campaigning in 1988, Lyndon LaRouche stood trial in the Federal Court in Boston, before Judge Robert Keeton. The trial lasted for six months, from December 1987 to May 1988, and showed signs of going on indefinitely, as we succeeded in forcing multiple revelations about government misconduct at every stage of the investigation and prosecution. Only a declaration of mistrial ended what was a devastating exposure of the "Get LaRouche Task Force" as a criminal operation from top to bottom. As we discovered later in 1988, when the entire Federal prosecution was moved to the controlled environment of the Alexandria Federal Court, the Task Force realized that, in Boston, any even remotely fair hearing of the evidence in the LaRouche cases threatened to explode the entire corrupt structure of the U.S. judicial system. Henceforth, the Task Force was instructed to stick to the "Old Boys" network in the Virginia judiciary, where extraneous elements such as truth and justice would not interfere with the task at hand.

★ ★ ★

The Boston case was a classic post-Watergate political prosecution—the supposed criminal act, in this case "credit card fraud," was primarily a pretext for concocting a charge of "obstuction of justice," and pinning that on LaRouche. Lyn was not charged with any involvement in the "fraud," but instead, he and the leaders of the security and legal staffs were charged with obstruction of justice for allegedly *covering up* the crime.

But what about the "crime," the charge of credit card fraud brought against me and my fellow Boston phone team organizers? As I joked with our supporters over the years: "What kind of idiot would try to scam his own political supporters, unless he were planning to disappear, to enjoy his ill-gotten gains? There are many in positions of power and influence who wish we *would* disappear, but, to their deep regret, we never have, and never will, give up or sell out."

Although I looked forward to proving my complete innocence, I was not to stand trial in Boston. The prosecution conceded their evidence against me was weak, so my lawyer secured a severance of my case, with the expectation that I would be tried later, once the main trial was completed.

The main trial began with the government presenting its allegation of credit card fraud. They called Richard Welsh, the campaign committee's assistant treasurer, as a witness. Despite their efforts to rattle him, Welsh was able to present the jury with a detailed history of financial warfare operations against the LaRouche movement, including the statement of Henry Kissinger, that he planned to settle his score with LaRouche after the November 1984 elections.

Following Welsh's testimony, the obstruction of justice case also began to evaporate. We had submitted motions asserting that a "secret government" operation in the White House was behind LaRouche's indictment, and had demanded that the government produce the evidence in their possession which would prove it. These motions were ridiculed by the prosecutors as an "Orwellian fantasy." But, during Welsh's testimony, a document that had been obtained by the Iran-Contra Special Prosecutor from the safe of Col. Oliver North, was obtained by our defense team through an FOIA request. This document, the telex I reported earlier, states: "Our source reports that terrorists plan to use airfield near Texas border. . . . Lewis has met with FBI and other agency reps and is apparently meeting again today. Our man here claims Lewis has collected info against LaRouche—let's see how polygraph goes. Rgds., Dick."

"Dick" was Richard Secord, North's partner in the arms- and drugs-trafficking "enterprise." Lewis was Fred Lewis, an intelligence community stringer with direct ties to George Bush. Lewis, along with his associate Gary Howard, had tried to infiltrate the LaRouche movement in 1984. In fact, it was based on phony allegations made by Lewis and Howard that an investigation of the LaRouche movment was launched under secret counterintelligence guidelines during the fall of 1984 period—the same time that Weld's criminal investigation was being put in place.

These and other revelations in classified FBI documents spurred Judge Keeton to convene a series of hearings into government misconduct, in the course of which he ordered searches of Vice-President Bush's office. Eventually, Judge Keeton ruled in our favor that the government was illegally hiding exculpatory material concerning an agent-provocateur, Ryan Quade Emerson, sent into the LaRouche movement, who played a key role in the government's obstruction of justice case. It was revealed in the hearings that the prosecution had instructed Emerson to make certain statements to our security staff, knowing that these would be diligently recorded in their notebooks. The government then seized the notebooks. In his opening statement to the jury, the prosecutor quoted these very statements—which he had dictated to Emerson to begin with—as proof of the defendants' intent to obstruct justice!

The jury was not present during the misconduct hearing, but when Judge Keeton called them back to tell them that the trial would now have to go on for a much longer time period, several jurors could no longer continue. After six months, their lives had already been totally disrupted, and the judge ordered a mistrial.

The following day, May 5, 1988, the *Boston Herald* ran an article headlined, "LaRouche Jury Would Have Voted 'Not Guilty.' " The jury foreman, Roman Dashawetz, told the *Herald* that, after being dismissed, the jurors took a vote in the jury room, agreeing unanimously that they would have acquitted all the defendants, even though they had only heard the government's side of the case. According to Dashawetz, "There was too much question of government misconduct in what was happening in the LaRouche Campaign."

Further backing up this charge, Judge Keeton himself ruled, a few months later, that during the hearings into the government handling of the case, he had discovered "institutional systemic prosecutorial misconduct."

The government's response? Get the hell out of Boston and start over again in Virginia.

A parting recollection of the Boston trial: I sat in for a few days when the prosecution called poor old Chris Curtis, the drop-out who had sold his soul to avoid prosecution. Curtis had aged about 15 years between 1986 and 1988. We had received the "302's"—FBI reports on their numerous meetings with Curtis. At the beginning, he had insisted that, to his knowledge, nothing illegal was ever done by him or anyone else. Over time, under threats that he would be prosecuted if he failed to provide "evidence" against us, he slowly manufactured a story, which grew over the years, from trial to trial. In Boston, his lies were relatively mild, of the sort that "the pressure for money was so intense that they'd do almost anything," and that we (I, in particular) called our supporters "pigs and swine." Even bigger fish tales would emerge in Curtis's testimony at later trials.

When Chris left the stand, he walked out through the courtroom, accompanied by Marshals. He stopped when he saw me. "How you doing, Mike," he said. He had his same goofy grin, but I saw that his eyes had become hollow.

"Much better than you," I replied.

Alexandria

The declaration of a mistrial in Boston, rather than an acquittal, was a disappointment for us. But, the "Get LaRouche Task Force" had been badly bruised by the exposure of its use of the judicial system for political purposes. We were left with little breathing room, however: the Virginia cases were pending, prosecutions and investigations were ongoing in New York, California, and perhaps elsewhere, and the "Feds" (as the Federal system is called in prison) were preparing another case in Alexandria, Virginia. The Justice Department announced that it would re-try the case in Boston, but that was a lie, as we soon discovered; behind the scenes, the Task Force was getting together to ensure that the truth would never again be allowed to interfere with the railroad.

The courtroom of Judge Albert V. Bryan, Jr., in Alexandria, Virginia, was their chosen venue.

Judge Bryan was not an ordinary judge. He was one of several designated Federal judges who could oversee national security cases requiring secret proceedings. He was one of the "Old Boys" of the Virginia judiciary, with political and business connections into the intelligence community. The Federal Courthouse in Alexandria is named the "Albert V. Bryan Courthouse," after Albert Jr.'s father. Around the corner from the Courthouse is a huge warehouse, part of Interarms, Inc., a company which Albert, and his father, had helped create and administer. Interarms serviced the intelligence community, providing the weapons for the bungled Bay of Pigs invasion and other similar exploits. Judge Bryan would demonstrate in our case that it was to the "secret government" that he paid allegiance, and not to the U.S. Constitution.

We knew that the Alexandria U.S. Attorney, Henry Hudson, was planning an indictment, but we had been led to believe it was limited to a tax charge of some sort. In the months following the Boston mistrial, however, frantic memos and meetings were held by the prosecutors to try to solve their timing problems: the Boston trial had failed to knock LaRouche out of the 1988 Presidential race. Vice President Bush had already made known, on national television, that he wanted LaRouche in prison immediately.

The Task Force decide to indict LaRouche and others for a broad conspiracy to defraud our supporters through the failure to repay loans, in addition to a tax-related charge against LaRouche individually. The new Federal indictment in Alexandria was rushed to completion in time for the November Presidential election. As in 1984, when, a few days before the election, the closing of our bank accounts placed LaRouche in the national news as a suspected criminal, so in 1988, on October 14, two weeks before Election Day, LaRouche and six associates were splashed across the headlines as indicted scam artists, conspirators, and income tax cheats.

Imagine for a moment the headlines in the U.S. press if, on the eve of a Presidential election, a nation on the State Department's "hit list" had arrested and indicted the most outspoken Presidential candidate opposing the existing administration:

"Brutal Dictatorship Squashes Opposition," "Democracy Mocked, Sanctions Discussed In UN," and so forth. But, of course, there was no such outpouring of indignation over the LaRouche indictment. In America, after twenty-five years of Tavistock brainwashing, the oligarchy was confident that, if something were in the national news, then the population would accept it as true. *After all, LaRouche wasn't REALLY a Presidential candidate . . . .*

I was notified only a few weeks before the indictment came down, that I was a target. The plan was to accuse four of us involved in fundraising—Dennis Small, Paul Greenberg, Joyce Rubinstein, and me—of conspiracy to defraud our supporters; two National Executive Committee members—Will Wertz and Ed Spannaus—of conspiring to carry out the fraud; and Lyndon LaRouche, of leading the conspiracy, with an additional count of conspiring to "impede and obstruct" the functioning of the IRS. We were notified in a more civil manner this time—no knock on the door at midnight—with notification through our lawyers to appear for arraignment on a certain date. It was clear from the beginning that this prosecution was on a different track. I prepared for the worst.

Judge Bryan made two astonishing pre-trial rulings, which even years afterwards continue to astonish me. First, he ruled that *no evidence of government misconduct would be allowed in the trial*—that all of the evidence that had essentially proven our innocence in Boston, was to be forbidden in his courtroom! His justification for this atrocity would make the infamous Nazi Judge Roland Freisler blush: He said this evidence would divert the attention of the jury from the issues of the case, which were, pure and simple, a scheme to defraud people, virtually unrelated to any political considerations! (This would be the theme of the prosecution throughout. The first words of the prosecutor's opening statement were: "This case is about money!")

As for the government-imposed bankruptcy, Judge Bryan ruled that, although we could tell the jury that there was a bankruptcy, *we were forbidden to tell the truth,* that the bankruptcy had been *imposed,* against our will, by the same government prosecutors who were prosecuting us in criminal court! We could not tell the jury that we had been *ordered* to stop all payments to our lenders; nor could we tell the jury that we were contesting the bankruptcy. The judge had thus ordered that the jury be intentionally misled, to believe that *we* had declared bankruptcy, in order to avoid payment of our debts, while the government actions against us were hidden behind his robe.

Judge Bryan's district was known in the national legal community as the "rocket docket," because he ran cases at such a pace that careful examination or consideration of government conduct and misconduct was impossible. True to form, at the arraignment he assigned a trial date a mere 37 days away! By comparison, the Boston trial had taken 14 *months* of pre-trial preparation before it began, and the Virginia state cases were about the same. This was a case with literally millions of documents, and years and years worth of activities which had to be investigated and understood. Although some of our lawyers (not all) had been involved in the Boston or Virginia cases, the schedule guaranteed that the lawyers would have no time to prepare anything, outside of filing the necessary pre-trial motions. The die had been cast, and *nothing* was to interfere with Judge Bryan's pre-determined outcome.

My lawyer, Jim Clark, was a young Alexandria attorney, with little political experience, but with a reputation for being willing to fight. Actually, as I learned later in the Virginia prisons, he was known as one of the best lawyers for getting drug dealers a "good deal" on plea-bargains. But he was a nice fellow, who tried his best. He would later admit to me, when I was getting ready for my state trial, that he didn't consider himself capable of waging an aggressive defense, going after the government misconduct. But, as part of the team of seven defending us in Alexandria, he seemed to be all right, as lawyers go.

Of course, "as lawyers go" is a loaded phrase. Besides all the normal problems lawyers have with looking at things from an Aristotelian standpoint—according to *appearances*, rather than truth—the Virginia lawyers in our case proved to have an even more serious problem. They were terrified of the Virginia judiciary. It seemed as if the Virginia lawyers were preoccupied with the fact that they were going to have to make their livings before this court in the future, and they were not willing to rile it. The truth would have to take second place.

The legal team of seven was headed by Odin Anderson, who had been LaRouche's personal lawyer for several years, and who, alone amongst the lawyers, had some understanding, and some passion, for the ideas we represented. But there was no time to prepare a competent joint defense, and Odin, as Lyn's lawyer, had to prepare the defense against the ridiculous tax charge. Otherwise, he was unable to do much more than concentrate on a few crucial aspects of FBI entrapment and misconduct.

None of the lawyers had time to prepare their defendants to testify; although, as LaRouche pointed out, the real problem was that *we* didn't have time to prepare the lawyers.

A good example of the "rocket docket" at work was the selection of a jury. In Boston, jury selection had taken several weeks, as each prospective juror was carefully questioned by both the prosecution and defense for prejudice picked up from the enormous media hype over the years. As that process demonstrated, many people were only vaguely aware that they had acquired such prejudices, and would deny it when first questioned, only to reveal it when more fully probed. Such is the power of the media to create presumptions within the population, which are not considered to be presumptions at all, but "well-known facts." "Well-known facts," like, "LaRouche is a racist," or, "LaRouche is a communist," and other even more lurid fantasies.

But, in Judge Bryan's courtroom in Alexandria, jury selection took about two hours!

Our attorneys were not permitted to examine the potential jurors at all. The judge asked all the questions, addressing them to the jury pool as a whole. Only those potential jurors who raised their hands when asked if they had read articles about the case which had influenced their opinions, were then asked individual questions, and even then, there was little discussion. We later discovered that over one-quarter of the jury pool were government employees (one of the reasons the DOJ wanted Alexandria as its venue for the case).

For the remaining questions asked about bias, the judge required the jurors to repond by raising their hands only if the answer were "yes." Buster Horton, who later became jury foreman, never raised his hand, including when he was asked whether he had been connected with a law enforcement agency. Horton's juror information card described him as a U.S. Department of

Agriculture employee, but post-trial investigation determined that he was Deputy Chief of Emergency Programs at the USDA—a position which placed him on an elite inter-agency task force, coordinated by the Federal Emergency Management Agency (FEMA) and the National Security Council, with the function of ensuring "continuity of government" in the event of a national emergency. Horton's job brought him into regular contact with the law enforcement and intelligence community. Along with other members of this inter-agency group, Horton had Top Secret clearance, and direct access to FBI investigative data on all criminal and foreign counterintelligence matters. And, in fact, the individual who shaped this "continuity of government" task force was none other than Col. Oliver North, under the direction of the Bush-run national security apparatus in the White House!

Trial

We rented a few furnished apartments near the courthouse, where Gail and I shared a suite with Dennis Small and his wife Gretchen. Evenings were spent poring over material, trying to put together ideas on how to deal with the witnesses. I met with my lawyer, Jim Clark, several times, and wrote out my recommendations for his cross-examination of Chris Curtis and the "lender" witnesses. I was very anxious to testify.

As it turned out, the lawyers were totally dumbfounded as to how to talk about our loans, without being allowed to explain that we had stopped making repayments because of the government's imposition of involuntary bankruptcy. This, combined with the general terror which the lawyers exuded before Judge Bryan, led them all, with the exception of Odin Anderson, to recommend that none of us testify, but to rely instead on a refutation of the government's charges through cross-examination of government witnesses, a few defense witnesses to provide technical material on our finances, and an *attempt* to situate the case in its political context, within the confines of the judge's gag order. I very reluctantly agreed. I certainly concurred that there was no time to prepare. I recognized that a proper preparation would require a review of virtually every document the prosecution might have chosen—which was many thousands from among the millions of documents seized in the Leesburg raid—and a thorough review of my relations with each of the dozens of witnesses.

But the real reason I agreed not to testify, was that my lawyer simply didn't understand the scope of the political reality surrounding the case, and was not really willing to *try* to understand it. As it turned out, none of us testified. And even though it was clear at the time, that "the fix was in," the fact that we couldn't properly testify removed any lingering hope for acquittal.

The lender witnesses were paraded before the jury, each acknowledging that payments had been made, albeit irregularly, up to the March 1986 election in Illinois, when the victory by Janice Hart and Mark Fairchild set off the explosion of slanders and dirty tricks against us in the press and by the various branches of the "Get LaRouche Task Force." Our letters explaining the situation to lenders, were presented not as expressions of honesty and good intent (since, rather than declaring bankruptcy and ducking out, we were determined to put things back together), but as a cover-up, a stalling tactic. The prosecutors never tried to explain why we needed to write to our lenders at all, if we were not planning to repay them.

One after another, the prosecutor asked the lender witnesses: "And after the payment of such and such a date, did you receive any more payments?" "No." "And *up until today,* have you received any more payments?"

Each time I heard this, my blood boiled. Judge Bryan *never once* accepted our objections to this question, which clearly conveyed that we were, as a *continuing practice,* refusing to pay debts—whereas we were forbidden to tell the jury that for *over one and a half years,* we had been under court order not to make any payments, and that the seized company's accounts were out of our hands, having been turned over to government appointed trustees. A year after the trial, when Judge Bostetter ruled that we had, in fact, *not* been bankrupt, and that the court order had been obtained through a fraud by the government, the prosecutor's repeated question, *"And up until today . . .,"* burned in my memory.

Chris Curtis was carefully primed for his performance. The prosecution drilled him before the trial on his Boston testimony, and on his earlier interviews (some of which they had been forced to show us), since shadows of the truth had been allowed to slip through. He constructed stories to plug those holes. When my lawyer, for instance, questioned him on his earlier statements, on the record, that none of us had ever done anything illegal, and that he knew me to be passionately committed to the ideas and goals of our political work, he now "explained" that he'd *meant* to say that we were all purposely playing blind to the criminal nature of our operation, and that he'd *meant* to say that I was a zealot, who would do *anything* for the organization, that I would "fall on the sword." Executive Committee member Will Wertz, whom Curtis had always referred to as "the General" in a joking but respectful tone, was transformed by the glassy-eyed Curtis into "Darth Vader."

To a certain extent, Curtis described some of his *own* problems, which had been the subject of our criticisms over the years, as if these were things we *taught* him to do. His constant neurotic appeal to a supporter's "button"—a single issue he or she was interested in—was described on the stand as "our method." The detailed briefings we'd arrange for supporters from our national leadership, describing our projects in regard to the SDI, drugs, AIDS, and so forth, were described as "set up" calls in which any story could be made up to convince the supporter to contribute. He said, for instance: "I'd call someone and say something like: 'My friend Dennis Small just came back from South America where he met with roomfuls of generals, working on the War on Drugs. I'd like you to talk to him to see if you'd be willing to support the campaign.' "

This was said by Curtis in a totally flippant manner, as if it were a story made up out of thin air. That Dennis *did,* in fact, make dozens of trips to South America, *did* meet with numerous generals (and Presidents, and Bishops, and trade union leaders, and so forth), was transformed into a "ploy," a scam constructed to con people out of their money. Throughout the trials, these "set-up" calls would be presented as the ultimate proof of our conspiracy to defraud.

The facts of the *actual* conspiracy—that of the DOJ with the media, private institutions, and the intelligence community, to defame and destroy LaRouche—were repeatedly denied by the prosecution in pre-trial hearings, and *totally excluded* from the trial itself. We were not permitted to call witnesses to confirm the "Train Salon" meetings between Wall Street, the ADL, the National Security Council, the FBI, and others, which planned out the "Get LaRouche Task Force" campaign. Nor were any questions permitted of any witnesses about government or private operations to destroy us, even when witnesses were part of those operations.

Richard Morris, a senior National Security Council official who had been one of our primary contacts within the Reagan Administration, testified concerning the importance and the scope of LaRouche's input to policy in the early years of the Reagan Administration, and about the fierce campaign to eliminate that input by other individuals in the intelligence community. But neither he nor any other witness was permitted to answer questions concerning the illegal, covert operations against us under Executive Order 12333, operations which the prosecution claimed did not exist. (Six months later, the FBI confirmed it had an E.O. 12333 file on LaRouche.)

We also called several character witnesses, to try to establish LaRouche's role in affairs around the world. Amelia Boynton Robinson, one of the true heroines of the civil rights movement, testified on LaRouche's role in picking up the mantle of Dr. Martin Luther King; General Paul Scherer, head of German intelligence for many years, testified on LaRouche's crucial contributions in regard to the still-festering Cold War, and the violent propaganda campaign against LaRouche by Soviet intelligence; General Luis Anez Rivera, former chief of the Bolivian Armed Forces, described the critical nature of his meetings and discussions with Dennis Small and LaRouche in regard to the War on Drugs.

But these and other witnesses were limited to describing LaRouche's good intentions, without any references to the public or covert operations against him. The prosecutors' only questions to each of them: "Did you ever lend any money, or know about the lending practices of these defendants?" After all, *"This case is about money . . . ."*

Perhaps the most absurd part of the entire case was the tax charge against LaRouche. He was not accused of tax evasion, but of conspiring to impede and obstruct the IRS. LaRouche had precisely followed the advice of his tax attorney, that in his particular circumstances, there was no need to file a tax return. Reliance on such professional advice should have served as a full defense to the tax charge. In fact, LaRouche had publically reported these circumstances, and the IRS had never requested an audit of his personal finances, before bringing the criminal indictment. Nonetheless, the Railroad was on, and neither a corrupt judge nor a runaway jury would allow the facts or the law to slow it down.

Sentencing

On Dec. 16, 1988, we gathered in the Albert V. Bryan Courthouse to hear the jury verdict. With Christmas carols drifting in from the surrounding shopping district of downtown Alexandria, jury foreman Buster Horton, Ollie North's associate at the Department of Agriculture, read out the "guilty on all counts" decision. Sentencing was set for Jan. 27, 1989, only days after the scheduled inauguration of President George Herbert Walker Bush.

I spent the next month trying to reach as many of our supporters as I could, while also taking care of all my personal affairs with Gail, who was about to begin her long ordeal as a prison widow. There was still the possibility that Judge Bryan would grant bail pending our appeal, but we were quite certain (and correctly so) that he wanted LaRouche in jail immediately, as Bush began his Presidency. On our final night together, Gail and I had dinner at a Thai restaurant, just as we had on our first date in New York City six years earlier. This final evening was a memorable, but hardly joyous occasion.

Judge Bryan let it all hang out at sentencing. First, the DOJ announced that they were dropping the Boston case (which *we* wanted to pursue, to prove our innocence and the DOJ's guilt). The reason given was that they were satisfied, now that LaRouche was going to prison, and our companies had been placed into bankruptcy "and their assets seized." (This in itself was most interesting, since the government had sworn in court that the bankruptcy was totally unrelated to the criminal prosecution!) Judge Bryan blustered: "Someone should tell [Boston] Judge Keeton that he owes me a cigar." Actually, Judge Keeton owed Judge Bryan a lesson on the criminality of prosecutorial misconduct.

But Judge Bryan was just getting warmed up. He was ready to address the question of the government's misconduct, which had caused the breakdown in the Boston trial: "The defendants have repeatedly raised this idea that this is a politically inspired, politically motivated prosecution. I reject this as arrant nonsense. The idea that this organization is a sufficient threat to anything that would warrant the government bringing a prosecution to silence them is—just defies human experience."

This was not Judge Bryan's "opinion." He had before him the multiple public and private demands by Henry Kissinger, and others with enormous power, that national-security measures be used to create a pretext for shutting down the activities and influence of Lyndon LaRouche. He had the Soviet intelligence diatribes with a similar message. Judge Bryan was not evaluating the evidence—he was simply lying. Joseph Goebbels would have been proud.

LaRouche, in his allocution to the court, did not bother countering the judge's lies, but exposed a higher reality guiding the proceedings in the courtroom. Only shortly before the Railroad (as the trial came to be known), LaRouche had been given a message from a high-ranking member of the British oligarchy, Mr. Kenneth Hugh de Courcy. De Courcy offered LaRouche a deal—if he were to desist from attacking certain named capabilities of the oligarchy, including Henry Kissinger, the case could be "arranged" to go in his favor. LaRouche explained why he refused the offer: As Christ taught at Gethsemane, a dedication to truth is a higher freedom than physical liberty. Nonetheless, LaRouche had absolutely no doubt that the offer was real, and that de Courcy could deliver if he so desired. The judge was not pleased, but the matter was not actually in his hands anyway—he was doing what he was told, as any good fascist does.

I was sentenced to three years, along with the other three defendants involved in sales. Will Wertz and Ed Spannaus, both NEC members, were given five years. Lyndon LaRouche got fifteen. For a man of 66, fifteen years was practically a life sentence. Under the Federal law then in effect, a convicted felon had to serve two-thirds of his sentence (provided he served with good behavior), but was eligible for parole after one-third. LaRouche would thus be eligible for parole in 1994, with a mandatory release in 1999. Politically, this assured that he would be locked up for the 1992 Presidential election, and possibly also the 1996 one, depending on the parole process. This fact was certainly in the forefront of Judge Bryan's calculations.

After fingerprinting and other formalities in the courthouse basement, we were lined up by the parking lot exit to be marched out, in handcuffs and leg irons, to a waiting van for transport to the Alexandria County Jail. A large crowd had gathered outside the courthouse, including many of our members and supporters, but also many press and unfamiliar figures of questionable intentions. The U.S. Marshals carefully placed Lyn in the front of the line to march out before the crowd—an obvious security threat of frightening proportions. I casually moved to the front of the line, nudging Lyn back to my No. 2 spot, but the Marshal in charge immediately grabbed my jacket and pulled me back, forcing Lyn back up to the front. Luckily, there was no incident outside.

As we shuffled out in our leg irons towards the van, our members in the crowd broke into song, singing "Va Pensiero," from Verdi's opera *Nabucco,* a song of freedom and hope sung by Hebrew slaves during the Babylonian captivity. *There is joy in the sublime in even the greatest tragedy.*

★ ★ ★

For the next six months we were held in the Alexandria County Jail, while we worked together to prepare our appeal. Joyce was separated, of course, but the six men were placed together in a large cellblock with prisoners of every stripe and color. We set up a routine for maintaining our political work, as best we could. The Morning Briefing was prepared in a special audiotape version for us. Besides preparing the appeal, we compiled a comprehensive accounting of the lies of the prosecution, before and during the trial, which we published as a pamphlet called "149 Lies of the Prosecution." A book on the trial, called *Railroad! U.S.A. vs. Lyndon LaRouche, et al.*, was set in motion, and published in 1989.

The other prisoners in the cellblock were fascinated with this unlikely crew of bespectacled intellectuals in their midst. Lyn would respond to their questions in the same way he did with everyone else—lots of jokes, and extended lessons in political history, culture, and science.

A few years later, while I was at Raybrook Federal prison in upstate New York, a young Italian-American from one of the New York "families" arrived after a year at the Rochester, Minnesota prison where LaRouche was being held. He described in glowing terms how every day, after lunch, a group would gather on the benches in front of the cellblock, and Lyn would walk back and forth, telling jokes and teaching. One skeptic accused Lyn of making things up, and started taking notes and checking out every historical reference in the library, but never caught an error. If someone new joined the group and was wasting time with foolish comments or trying to disrupt, the others would tell him to "shut up, and you'll learn something."

My own relations with fellow prisoners have been generally constructive, with no physical confrontations of any sort. At each new location (there have been ten altogether) I would seek out the most politically conscious leaders of the prison community—which tended to be the leaders of the Muslim community or the Nation of Islam—and introduce myself, share my ideas about the world, and show them our literature. In most cases, these people already knew a fair amount about LaRouche, and had respect for him. The few times I was approached in an intimidating manner—one fellow offered "protection" while showing me a shank (a homemade knife)—I launched into a political briefing as to who I was, what I did, and who had put me in prison, and why. This tended to intimidate *them*, or at best, provoke curiosity. I came to be friends with some very unusual people.

★ ★ ★

China

A few weeks before sentencing and my departure for prison, I had met with Linda de Hoyos, my old friend who ran the Asian intelligence sector for EIR. I told her I'd like to study Asia, as one of the things I could do while incarcerated. She sort of gasped, as if someone had hit her in the stomach. "China," she said. "China."

"What do you mean?" I asked.

"You'll do China. It's perfect. It's so big. And we don't have anyone working on China. It's perfect."

So that was it. I had thought more of Japan and Southeast Asia, which I had worked on previously, but China was obviously the key to Asia. I took into prison with me a number of books on China, and everything I could find by Sun Yat-sen and Confucius, which seemed like the right place to start. Various people in the organization had studied the history of the Maoist era, but no one had seriously studied the Chinese classics, nor the works of the father of the Chinese Republic, Sun Yat-sen. That would become my task, and my passion.

In prison, I began receiving by mail a daily, book-size collection of Chinese press and radio broadcasts, translated into English and published by the Foreign Broadcast Information Service (FBIS) at the State Department. I'd compile reports on developments in China once or twice per week, and send them in.

I also began studying Chinese, but it was very difficult to develop a speaking facility in the language, with no one to talk to. I listened to tapes and practiced speaking to myself, but never developed fluency, as I had in Thai in less than a year by living there. (Of course, one advantage of talking only to myself in Chinese, was that I always understood everything I said!)

Even in reading, the going was very slow. In Chinese, each word is a separate character, and the shape of the character has almost no relationship to the way it is pronounced. It is thus an extremely tedious process, requiring memorization of thousands of characters. I developed a working knowledge of the language, so that I could read the classics (with a dictionary) in the original, and make informed judgments on the widely diverging interpretations by both Chinese and Western scholars of the highly poetic classical Chinese.

One of the books I read in the Alexandria jail was *The Natural Theology of the Chinese*, written by Gottfried Leibniz in 1716. The fact that Leibniz had spent much of his later years in close collaboration with the Jesuit missionaries in China was a wonderful surprise to me, and Leibniz was to become my friend and guide over the coming years. The thrust of his book on China—one of the last things he wrote—was that his study of the classics of Confucianism confirmed his belief that there is but one God, one

Truth, and that that Truth is (as St. Paul said) "inscribed in our hearts." He saw in Confucianism the same fundamental view of man as in Christianity—that each man reflects the power of the Creator through the creative capacity of the mind, guided by love for truth and justice, a love (*ren* in Chinese) which is the natural characteristic of man, provided as a gift from Heaven to every newborn child.

Leibniz also devoted much of his life to the task of building bridges between Europe and Asia—both intellectual bridges, and physical bridges, in the form of opening up the overland connections between the Atlantic and the Pacific, through Russia, and the economic development of the regions in between.

I set for myself the task of picking up where Leibniz left off, in building those spiritual and material bridges, over time and space, between the great nation and culture of China, and the Renaissance tradition of Western civilization.

My time was limited in those first months of 1989 in the Alexandria jail, since my Virginia trial was scheduled for July. But, as fate would have it, in April, China suddenly leaped onto the front pages of the world press, and became the 24-hour-a-day focus of CNN news. Hundreds of thousands of Chinese youths had occupied the central plaza in Beijing, known as Tiananmen Square.

Our intelligence on the particulars of the student demonstrations was sparse. However, we knew that China was flirting with disaster by opening the country to the "globalization" process. LaRouche and others had published warnings in EIR that, despite the benefits of the reform process in China in the post-Mao era, the apparent boom in the several Chinese coastal cities designated as Special Economic Zones was actually creating a dangerous speculative bubble. Investment had been diverted from the interior to the Zones, leaving vast armies of unemployed peasants to flood into the coastal cities in search of low-paying, low-skill jobs in low-tech export industries. There were estimates of up to 100 million peasants—called the "blind flow"—wandering about, being cycled in and out of the process-industry sweatshops, then replaced and sent back into the flow. The agricultural sector faced an explosion as well, as peasants were being paid with scrip for their crops, and local bankers and party officials spent the money speculating in land or in low-tech factories.

It is important to note that the post-Mao reform launched by Deng Xiaoping in 1979 was absolutely necessary, and must be credited with saving the country from imminent collapse. The story of the Great Proletarian Cultural Revolution in China, from 1966 to 1976, has been told in gruesome detail in countless books, articles, and films; but, like the Nazi Holocaust, the story of this Chinese Holocaust can and must be retold and retold, and its sources ever more deeply investigated. There is no question, but that the Chinese look back at that ten-year nightmare with the same horror as the German people feel in regard to the Nazi era. As I studied the heart-wrenching accounts of terror, humiliation, torture, and cultural collapse, I came to concur.

The problem was that post-Mao China was "opening up" to an era of Thatcherite monetarist madness, every bit as dangerous, potentially, as the Cultural Revolution—as was to be soon proven in Russia and Eastern Europe, where "shock therapy," imposed by the IMF, brought chaos and death to the already weakened nations after the collapse of communism. In China, an earlier version of "shock therapy" was pushed on Beijing by the British and the Paul Volcker crowd in the U.S. While foreign investment was picking up steam, quick money was to be made in the "new colonialism" of process-industries and speculation. Spokesmen for free trade and globalization, from Milton Friedman to quacks like Alvin Toffler, were crawling all over China, pressing the globalization process to gullible takers on both sides of the Pacific. After one trip to China, Toffler wrote about China in glowing terms as a country which could pass from the First Wave (agricultural society) directly to the Third Wave (information society), without the need to pass through the dirty, polluting Second Wave (industrial society). Toffler, later to be one of Newt Gingrich's gurus, painted an image of China's future: A peasant, half-naked, up to his knees in mud in his paddy field, talking on his cellular phone to his derivatives broker!

A financial bubble, and a social explosion, were becoming unavoidable. Very few believed LaRouche's forecast, until the phenomenal explosion in Tiananmen Square in the spring of 1989.

I wrote a series of articles from my Alexandria jail cell, drawing on the cram course I had done on Chinese history and Sun Yat-sen. I emphasized that the demonstrations were composed of angry people, generally with only a vague idea of what they wanted, but who were groping for something better, and for their roots in Chinese history—a history which had been distorted or totally hidden during the dark days of radical Maoism. Lyn's insight, after watching several weeks of the demonstrations on CNN in our cellblock, was that one could see in the eyes of the young people that they were searching for their souls, souls that had been lost when their youth and their education had been stolen from them during the Cultural Revolution.

There were many positive images presented by the demonstrators—images of China's cultural greatness, such as quotes from Confucius and Sun Yat-sen, as well as images of universal culture, such as Beethoven's Fifth Symphony played over the loudspeakers, and quotes from the Gettysburg Address on placards.

I wrote a profile of Sun Yat-sen for *The New Federalist*, showing that his Three Principles of the People, the guiding principles for Sun's vision of a constitutional republic, were drawn directly from Abraham Lincoln's concept of government "of the people, by the people, and for the people." Sun was not blindly "pro-American," however, but pro-*American System*. He taught the Chinese people about the British system of colonial looting, their Darwinian hatred of humanity, their drug dealing, and their genocide. He also taught them the history of the American System of Washington, Hamilton, and Lincoln, of nation-building, universal education, and global development. He distinguished between American System advocates within the U.S. and their opponents, pointing to the promotion of the Confederacy by the Anglophile bankers of New York and Boston. I later learned that Sun Yat-sen had been educated in Hawaii by close associates of economist Henry Carey and his Philadelphia-based circle. Sun's program for the "International Development of China" was not only a program for China, but part of the global organizing effort to extend American System industrial development to all of the Eurasian continent, and beyond.

My work was also translated into Chinese, as part of EIR's recently launched Chinese-language newsletter. After the June 4th debacle in Tiananmen Square, when the tanks were brought in to crush the demonstrations, we made a concerted effort to build networks among the overseas Chinese, including the thousands of newly exiled youth who fled their homeland. We focussed on Sun Yat-sen as a unifying force in 20th-Century China, and LaRouche's "Productive Triangle" program, for rebuilding Eastern Europe through a revitalized European industrial heartland—showing that the spiral arms of the development triangle would extend all the way to China. Lyn's Productive Triangle proposal from Berlin, in October 1988, was eventually expanded into the concept of rebuilding the old Silk Road, and reviving the "Eurasian development" ideas of Leibniz in 1700, and Sun Yat-sen in 1920. I was thrilled to be at the center of this process, despite my rather "restricted" circumstances. Unfortunately, I had another trial to attend to.

[15]

Treachery

The story of my Virginia trial, had it not been captured on video tape and in a transcript, would be impossible to believe. Many jurists from around the world who have reviewed the record, are simply dumbfounded that such a spectacle could take place in an American court. The level of treachery, not only by the prosecutors, the judge, and their allies in the "Get LaRouche Task Force," but also by my own lawyer, was more in keeping with a Soviet or Nazi show trial.

It is almost universally accepted that an accused has the right to have his interests represented by an attorney. My attorney, however, joined forces with the "Get LaRouche Task Force" on the eve of trial, both to convict me, and to discredit my political organization—and the Court congratulated him on a job well done!

In many, many instances, citizens and statesmen who were angered by the railroad of Lyndon LaRouche, but who held lingering doubts that there could really be political prisoners in America, upon reviewing my case, and the outrageous 77-year sentence, became convinced that the entire LaRouche prosecution was both unlawful and entirely political in nature.

★ ★ ★

In a sense, I was anxious to go to trial, in the hope that the conditions would be less onerous than those in Judge Bryan's courtroom, and that I might be allowed to present the truth before a jury. I knew that the structure of the trial would be essentially the same as in the Federal court, even though I was the only defendant. By putting on a full defense, including not only my own testimony, but also that of LaRouche, Dennis Small, and others, I thought we could convey the story which had been hidden in Alexandria, and had only begun to emerge in Boston.

I was the second Virginia defendant to go on trial. The first, my friend Rochelle (Shelley) Ascher from our Baltimore office, went on trial in Leesburg, just days before our sentencing and incarceration in Alexandria. I had the opportunity to sit in on a few sessions of jury selection. Although this was not Judge Bryan's "rocket docket," the results were similar. Judge Penn (the same who had locked me up two years earlier on the "H. Rap Brown" precedent) presided over an individual *voir dire* of prospective jurors, which was truly mind-boggling. One example will suffice (this is a paraphrase, but captures the essence of the exchange):

"Mr. X, have you formed any opinions about Mr. LaRouche or his organization?"

"Yes, your Honor, I believe that LaRouche is a fascist, a Nazi, that if he were ever to be President, it would mean the end of civilization."

"Do you think that you can put aside your views of Mr. LaRouche, and judge impartially the evidence presented in this court about Rochelle Ascher, knowing that she is dedicated to LaRouche's ideas?"

"Yes, your Honor."

Mr. X was seated on the jury.

The outcome of Shelley's trial was thus a foregone conclusion. Any hope that my trial would provide an opportunity to rectify the abomination of the Alexandria trial appeared ever more remote. Nonetheless, I diligently prepared a box of material on my case, which I took with me to prison.

Our legal staff began mapping out the material needed by my lawyer to prepare both an exposure of the illegal government operations at every point of the process, and a comprehensive presentation of who we really were and what we actually did. We could only hope that the truth would break through the massive psychological conditioning against us in the media.

The results of *not* presenting the whole story were evident from Alexandria—especially when compared with Boston. Nothing but an extensive documentation of our rapid growth, our mounting influence in the U.S. and around the world, our methods of sales and fundraising, and an accounting of how we used the funds, as well as the full story of the "Get LaRouche Task Force," could cut through the lies in the Virginia indictment—namely, that we had used money we raised for purposes other than those we had presented to our lenders (i.e., that our politics were just a huge ruse created to raise money for ourselves), and, secondly, that we took loans with the intention of not paying them back.

The outcome of Shelley Ascher's trial in Loudoun County confirmed my certainty that only such a "full exposure" approach could win. Shelley did take the stand in her own defense, but she and her lawyers were not able to build a positive defense, as Judge Penn would not allow testimony concerning the political motives for our activities. Then, the judge delivered jury instructions which ensured a guilty verdict. It was not necessary, he said, to prove intentional fraud or misrepresentation, only that non-payment was a foreseeable consequence of taking political loans. Shelley was convicted on all counts, getting a jury-imposed sentence of 86 years! I'm sure the juror paraphrased above would have preferred the guillotine.

In Virginia, the jury sets the sentence on each count of the indictment, but does not decide whether or not to impose the different counts concurrently—that is up to the judge. In Shelley's case, Judge Penn imposed one ten-year sentence, with the others served concurrently, and added a ten-year probation at the end. This was perhaps Judge Penn's view of being reasonable—acknowledgment that he had seated one of the most overtly prejudiced juries since the old Jim Crow days (which, by the way, was not that long ago down in "Ole Virginie," where lynching was only officially outlawed in the late 1920's).

Judge Penn made a further concession after the trial, announcing that he did not believe *another* impartial jury could be seated in Loudoun County (while never admitting that Shelley's jury was an abomination), and that all the subsequent defendants would therefore be granted a change of venue. We soon learned that our trials would be held in Roanoke County, in the town of

Salem (not officially related to the witch trials), under Judge Clifford R. Weckstein.

I had another problem to solve first. My lawyer, Jim Clark, had been very forthright in telling me that, while he understood my view on why I needed to mount an aggressive defense, he personally felt unsure of his ability to carry it through. Our legal staff began looking for another attorney. It clearly had to be someone who had worked on our cases already, since time was short. The most likely candidates were not available. The only possibility was one of the Alexandria lawyers, Brian Gettings, who had represented Will Wertz in the joint defense before Judge Bryan, and was also representing one of my Virginia co-defendants, Richard Welch.

I was not anxious to hire Gettings. During discussions in preparation for Alexandria, he had tried to convince the defendants and the other lawyers to concede the government's characterization of the organization as a single, monolithic entity, with everything run from the top by Lyndon LaRouche. The prosecution's purpose for this misrepresentation, portraying Lyn's political and intellectual leadership as that of a bureaucratic controller of corporate entities, was to justify Lyn's indictment as the "conspirator" responsible for all the alleged misdeeds in the sales process. We corrected Gettings on that issue, but he retained a very formal view of our work. I also had been disturbed by a blustering presentation he'd given in closing arguments in Alexandria, which had been more bark than bite.

Nonetheless, Brian Gettings was willing and able to put up a fight in a courtroom. In some of the pre-trial hearings, he had forcefully confronted several of the sheriffs and other officials who had ignored the law, and forced some concessions as a result. I decided that if he were willing to spend a good deal of time with me, and meet with LaRouche and Dennis Small while we were all together in Alexandria, then he could possibly do the job. I knew that our own paralegal staff, which did most of the background work for the lawyers in all the cases, would be able to provide Gettings with extensive support along the way.

Gettings met with me in the Alexandria jail together with Jim Clark. We discussed at length my desire to testify before a jury, to call Lyn and Dennis (and many others) as witnesses, and to counter every prosecution claim vigorously. Gettings made clear that he understood, and that he could do it. Jim Clark, with whom I remained on friendly terms, would later testify at my Federal hearing on my claim of ineffectiveness of counsel against Gettings, telling Judge Williams that he had heard Gettings confirm absolutely that he understood and agreed with my approach to the defense, which was, after all, the only reason I was changing lawyers. Gettings simply lied, even against his fellow attorney Jim Clark, that he had never agreed to such a defense.

Money was a part of Gettings' treachery, but, although it was a large amount of money, it was not likely the largest factor in his subsequent behavior, which is still not clearly understood. As to the money, we had an outstanding bill from Gettings from the Alexandria trial, which he demanded be paid in full, in addition to an $80,000 retainer to take my case. We had little choice, so word went out around the country for special contributions to the Constitutional Defense Fund (CDF), which was covering my legal costs.

The three of us—Brian Gettings, Jim Clark, and myself—appeared in the Roanoke County Courthouse before Judge Clifford Weckstein in June, to get the judge's approval for the change of lawyers. Jim Clark explained to the judge that, although he and I had excellent relations, he was not prepared to proceed, owing to differences over fundamental questions of trial strategy, and recommended that Brian Gettings take over as my lawyer. Gettings explained that he had a scheduling problem which required postponing the trial date a few months, to September 1989, which did not particularly bother Judge Weckstein. However, Judge Weckstein was most concerned that no further conflict would arise between me and Gettings, and asked Gettings directly if there were any potential problems other than scheduling.

Gettings responded: "I do not have any problem with Mr. Billington that would, you know, that I would be seeking relief on these grounds."

That was as clear as could be. Of course, in the Wonderland of the Virginia judicial system, things mean whatever the "Old Boys" want them to mean.

I expected that Gettings would spend many hours with me while I was in the Alexandria jail (just a few minutes from his office), and that he would also have extensive meetings with Dennis and Lyn. Once we were moved to our intended Federal prisons, he would be an airline flight away. However, we had only a few, relatively brief meetings. He told me there was plenty of time, that he'd visit me at my prison (which he never did), and that I'd be brought down to Roanoke a week or so before the trial, where we would meet at length. He arranged one meeting with Dennis, and acknowledged after that discussion that Dennis's testimony would be very useful and important in the trial. He never once met with LaRouche to discuss his testimony. When I questioned this, he said he'd fly out to visit him at his prison. That also never happened.

On one of Brian Gettings's brief visits, at the jail, he told me that he'd been given a plea-bargain offer from the prosecutor, Assistant Attorney General John Russell.

"If you plead guilty," Gettings said, "Russell can arrange for you to be sentenced to about five years, which could be served concurrently with your Federal time. You'll get off with no additional time." For the small price of lying, on the record, that I was guilty of committing fraud, and of conspiring to commit fraud, against our supporters!

"Take it, Mike," said Brian. "It's up to you, but it's everything you could hope for."

"Forget it, Brian. It's everything the 'Get LaRouche Task Force' could hope for. Can't you just see the headlines? 'LaRouche Aide Confesses To Fraud And Conspiracy.' I'm not going to lie, and sell out everything I've done with my life, in response to their threats. I'm innocent, and I'm going to prove it."

Gettings was not pleased, but he accepted it as my decision, and didn't bring it up again.

I spent much of my time reviewing my own files and records, writing out voluminous reports on each perspective witness, including my expectations of how they would respond to various lines of questioning. Most of this would end up being ignored by my attorney.

In July, I was moved to the Federal prison in Allenwood, Pennsylvania, without yet having spent any significant time with Gettings. LaRouche was sent to Rochester, Minnesota, a medical prison facility connected to the Mayo Clinic. The others were all sent to separate low-security camps (like Allenwood), although they allowed Will Wertz and Ed Spannaus to be placed together, at a camp in Petersburg, Virginia, so that Marianna Wertz, who has a disability, could travel with Nancy Spannaus to visit their husbands.

For the next two months, my contact with Gettings was limited to a few short phone calls relating to pre-trial motions. He refused to visit. I sent my reports and analyses to him, but received no response. He insisted that we'd have time in the week preceding the trial in Roanoke County. He also assured me that he was arranging with the court and the prison to have Lyn and Dennis sent to Virginia as witnesses—arrangements which were never made.

LaRouche did get an opportunity to testify in New York, in the summer of 1989, just two months before my trial in Roanoke. The New York case had proceeded very slowly, while the charges against all but four of the 17 defendants were dropped in pre-trial hearings. The judge in New York, Stephen Crane, while not as overtly hostile to us as the Virginia crew, still allowed the prosecution to withhold exculpatory evidence and to lie in court. Full presentation of the defense was hampered by constant judicial intervention, particularly concerning the role of the John Train salon, the Democratic Party, and Henry Kissinger in operations against LaRouche. There *was* a difference, however, because Judge Crane gave the defense a shot at presenting its case, while barring some of the most egregious and false prosecution "evidence."

The difference in judges became even more apparent after the trial. The jury acquitted one defendant, convicted one defendant, and split its verdicts on the remaining ones. Judge Crane gave out sentences of six months to one year. (Need I draw the comparison to my 77 years?) However, after nearly five years of post-trial investigations and hearings, Judge Crane overturned the entire prosecution on the grounds of gross prosecutorial misconduct! The conduct of the prosecutors, he said, "raises an inference of a conspiracy to lay low these defendants at any cost both here and in Virginia."

But we were not to find such honesty on a Virginia bench. In the first week of September, I was transported to the Roanoke County Jail from Allenwood. Pre-trial hearings were scheduled for the week of September 11, and the trial was to begin on Monday, September 18. I was placed in an isolation cell in the middle of the jail house, with no windows, and a single, bare light bulb hanging in the middle of the dingy, cinder-block cubicle. When I was taken to court, I was escorted through an underground tunnel connecting the jail and the courthouse, shuffling about 200 yards, up and down several flights of stairs, in leg irons. I was not to see a tree for three months.

I was only granted one or two phone calls per day, which required calling for a guard, getting his approval, and giving him the number to dial. He'd then dial and stick the receiver through the food slot in the door. I had to sit on the floor by the door to talk. It was not the best of working conditions. Naturally, they put a TV in my cell!

The next week was filled with pre-trial motions. There were several serious issues, but the most important was a motion to dismiss the case outright on the grounds of double jeopardy. The prosecutors only made a half-hearted effort to argue that my charges were different from the Federal charges, since they were so obviously identical, despite using different statutory names. The Federal indictment was for mail fraud, using the Federal laws against using the mail to commit fraud—our letters acknowledging the loans were called an illegal use of the mail to commit a felony. The state charge was security fraud, using statutes against selling securities without a license—this time, the letters acknowledging the loans were labeled "securities"! The activity was the same, the "conspiracy" was the same, and the witnesses were generally the same.

But, the state argued, they had started their investigation first, and therefore it didn't matter that I'd already been tried, convicted, and sentenced on the same charges by the Federal court. This cute little trick is called "dual sovereignty," a leftover from States' Rights days, still much admired in Ole Virginie. Of course they were lying about starting first—the FBI had been investigating loans from the get-go, as proven by many documents on the record.

Gettings presented the double-jeopardy argument, and Judge Weckstein gave us our first glimpse of his style. He explained that he had "considered the arguments at great length, and found much merit in your case for double jeopardy, but, owing to such-and-such a technicality, and such-and-such a refined point of law, this fundamental, Constitutional guarantee doesn't hold in your case," or words to that effect. Thus would every argument of any consequence be lost before Judge Weckstein.

I was, meanwhile, getting a bit frantic about the fact that Brian Gettings had yet to discuss the case itself with me, nor to meet with any other witnesses, nor arrange for Dennis and Lyn to be transported to Roanoke from their Federal prisons. My understanding was still that Gettings would definitely call Dennis, and that he would also call Lyn, but only after a substantial period of time in preparation. Gettings kept telling me not to worry, there was plenty of time.

On the Thursday before the Monday, September 18 trial date, Gettings came to see me at the jail, together with Gail, who was part of the legal staff assisting on the case, and three other members of our legal staff, including Warren Hamerman, the NEC member who directed our legal work. Gettings told me that the judge had encouraged him to recommend that I waive my right to a jury, and let Judge Weckstein be judge and jury—a so-called "bench trial." Gettings said he knew I wanted a jury trial, but he wanted me to know that he thought Judge Weckstein had shown himself to be an insightful judge, even though he had turned down the double-jeopardy motion. Gettings believed that it would be easier to put on the kind of defense I wanted before the judge rather than before a jury. His main concern, he said, was that Judge Weckstein had told him that he never reduces jury sentences, unlike the judges "up north," such as Judge Penn, who had reduced Rochelle's sentence from 86 years to 10 years. If the jury gave me 90 years, I'd get 90 years. Gettings said he knew my only concern was proving my innocence, not getting a "better deal" on the sentence, but for all these reasons, he thought I should waive my right to a jury.

I didn't dismiss it out of hand. At the time, I generally trusted that Gettings was trying to represent me as best he could, despite my serious concern for his lack of preparation for trial. "The threat of a long sentence from the jury is not a consideration," I told him, "and I'm not convinced that your other reasons amount to much. I don't think we can judge the judge from the little we've seen, whereas, if we can present the whole case before a jury, like we started to in Boston, we may find some jurors willing to stand up against popular opinion. But I'll think about it." I told Gail and the others to see what my co-defendants thought, as well as the other lawyers. Warren was flying out to Minnesota to visit Lyn over the weekend, so I asked him to get Lyn's ideas.

Gettings seemed pleased, and told me he'd stop back in the morning, and try to repackage his argument, leaving out the question of jury sentencing. He did so, but he didn't have any better reasons than he had the night before. He tried to "pitch" me, saying that if I agreed on the spot, he could probably get the judge to postpone the trial a few days, and that he would go to Alexandria and try to arrange a "work release" for me for the duration of the trial, so I could be free to work more closely with him on preparation.

I felt like I was being sold a used car. The idea that I could possibly get work release was preposterous, but I didn't hold it against him. I would not agree on the spot, as he wished, but told him I'd keep it open over the weekend, and consider what the other lawyers and defendants had to say. "But," I told him, "we should get ready for a jury trial on Monday." Gettings nonetheless went off to Alexandria for the weekend.

I didn't know it at the time, but he apparently told the judge, and his law partners, that he had persuaded me to forgo the jury and take a bench trial! The trial, he thought, would be much shorter, which may have been his primary financial concern. But whatever else went on that weekend between Gettings and anyone else, we still don't know.

Over the weekend, I received reports from my co-defendants, who certainly had a stake in the outcome of my trial. The Alexandria case was on appeal, and several Virginia co-defendants remained to be tried. Some of my co-defendants thought I should take a bench trial, others thought it would mean throwing away a chance to win. Several said that their own lawyers had told them that a bench trial was the closest thing to an admission of guilt, especially in Virginia. Lyn was skeptical about Gettings' comment that Weckstein was a good judge, noting that Weckstein sounded like the type of "yeah, but" judge we had run into before in Virginia—"you guys are right, *but* we're turning you down."

In addition, Lyn noted that jury sentencing, and the fear of its consequences, was used to frighten people into giving up fundamental rights. He reiterated his support for my effort to put on a full political defense. Nothing my co-defendants said changed my desire to proceed. I decided to stick with a jury, and asked my associate Martha Quinde to convey this to Brian.

Then, all hell broke loose.

About midnight, the night before the trial date, a guard told me to go downstairs for a legal visit! Apparently, Gettings had been trying to get in to see me for hours, but an inmate had hanged himself in his cell that evening, and they wouldn't let Gettings in until things were settled down.

When I arrived, he was pacing about the room, red-faced and furious. He had heard of my decision, and had it in his head that I had been all set to go with a bench trial until LaRouche "instructed" me to go with a jury. I explained all the events of the weekend, including the report from the other defendants and lawyers. I tried to calm him down, and assured him that I had confidence in him to proceed to trial, although I thought we had a lot of work to do.

But he was nearly delirious. He began ranting at me, saying I was brainwashed, that I was crazy to go against his advice on this. I asked him to explain why he was now so insistent, when we had determined months ago that I'd have a jury trial, and he'd agreed. What changed? He would give no coherent answer, but only became more and more abusive. This continued for over an hour, until he finally left. I asked him to get some sleep. "Let's get to work in the morning."

But Brian Gettings was in outer space. At about 7:00 a.m. the next morning, I was called down again. Brian was there with a statement which he said he was going to introduce into court that morning. It read: "Comes now Brian P. Gettings, counsel for the defendant Michael O. Billington in this case and moves to withdraw as such on the grounds that irreconcilable differences of opinion now exist between them as to how to proceed in defending the case. These differences are fundamental. Counsel was retained to defend Michael Billington not an organization with a political agenda to advance in this case. Counsel perceived that his duty is to Michael Billington, but now has reason to believe that he can not discharge that duty because Mr. Billington's free will is so impaired that he cannot intelligently assist counsel in making decisions as to how best to try the case."

"Brian, this is nuts," I said. "Don't do it. Let's get ready for trial."

"*You're* nuts," he responded, "and I'm going to do it!"

"But it's not true. You know I'm perfectly competent to assist you with the trial. What possible basis could you make for such a ridiculous statement? Certainly not because I chose to go with a jury. The judge himself told us that was entirely up to me. What's your reason?"

"That's enough of a reason," he shouted. "You didn't make that decision—LaRouche makes your decisions for you."

"So we're a cult now, Brian? Lyn didn't make any decisions for me, but what could possibly make you think that he wouldn't have a great deal to say about a trial which is, after all, as you argued in the double-jeopardy motion, a virtual retrial of the LaRouche case in Alexandria? You know it's our political movement that's on trial. That's why I hired you."

But, as I would learn, Gettings would never again tell the truth about what had happened between us before that midnight freak-out.

We went to court, and Brian presented his motion. I asked the judge to let me speak. I explained what had happened, that I was nonetheless prepared to go to trial right up until that morning. "But now that Mr. Gettings has introduced this motion and shown such incredible animus towards me, I can only concur with the motion—to let him withdraw as my counsel—while denying absolutely the charge he makes about my incompetence."

John Russell, the prosecutor, then stepped in, and I quickly realized that he and Gettings—and probably the judge as well—had already worked out the little drama being carried out in the courtroom. Russell refused to accept Gettings's motion to withdraw, but suggested that I should be given a psychiatric exam to determine my competence! Gettings immediately concurred.

I objected. "Your Honor, may I speak?" It was hard to know how to address the court, since my lawyer was now my accusor! Judge Weckstein let me speak—this time.

"This is ridiculous, Your Honor. There is no reason whatsoever for me to undergo a psychiatric exam, and Mr. Gettings and Mr. Russell certainly know that."

As if trying to prove LaRouche right, the judge came back with another "Yeah, but. . . ."

"Mr. Billington, I tend to agree with you that there is no purpose served by this, but I believe that your lawyer's motion automatically requires that I grant the request for psychiatric examination."

And so began my ordeal. That evening, Dr. Daum, a local shrink who regularly did examinations for the court, came to the jail for about one and a half hours. He said that he'd been briefed by both Mr. Gettings and Mr. Russell. His questions seemed to be an effort to intimidate me about the length of sentence I'd receive if found guilty by a jury. He asked me to calculate the maximum (90 years—ten years on each of nine counts), going over and over the fact that this judge was known for never reducing jury sentences. But Dr. Daum was otherwise a reasonable fellow, and asked intelligent questions when I explained our political work, LaRouche's anaylsis of the bulging speculative bubble and its effect on the U.S. and on the world, and a brief history of my own reasons for joining the organization.

Court was scheduled for the next afternoon. In the morning I called the legal office we had set up in Roanoke, and learned that the morning newspaper, *The Roanoke Times* (which I discovered later, was run by members of Judge Weckstein's wife's family!), carried a prominent article on the case, headlined: "LaRouche Aide Trial Delayed—Billington To Undergo Mental Test." They went all out, getting a personal interview with the ADL Washington Bureau chief, Mira Lansky Boland, who was the ADL case officer for the "Get LaRouche Task Force." The LaRouche movement was a dangerous cult, Boland pontificated. The members have no control over their lives, LaRouche runs everything, etc., etc., *ad nauseam*.

There was more. Brian Gettings had been staying in an apartment/office complex we had set up in Roanoke County, where he could work with my associates, who were assisting in putting the case together. He packed up all the case files, which we had carefully assembled for him, and moved into a local hotel.

And there was still more. The sheriffs at the jail suddenly informed the legal staff that none of the three paralegals working on my case would be permitted to visit me again, although they had been allowed in regularly up to that point. The excuse was that two of them were co-defendants in the case, and the third, Gail, was my wife. Of course, there was no *rule* against co-defendants or wives working as paralegals, but who needs rules? The walls were closing in on me.

The staff had contacted various other lawyers, both for advice and to see who could take over for Gettings, assuming the judge would let him withdraw. John Flannery, who had been Shelley Ascher's lawyer in the first Virginia trial, was shocked and disgusted by Brian Gettings's antics, and offered to help immediately. I spoke with him, and told him I would write up a full report. All the other lawyers were equally shocked, and considered Brian Gettings's actions to be wildly unethical and, in a word, nuts.

That afternoon I was called to court, where Dr. Daum was to give his report. I would receive yet another lesson in how the rules are changed by those who control the game, when things don't go their way. As I arrived at the courtroom, Assistant Attorney General John Russell and Gettings were coming out of the judge's chambers.

Gettings sneered at me: "There's going to be another examination." He would say nothing further.

A very uneasy Dr. Daum was called to the stand. He carefully explained his analysis, but it became apparent that his unease was caused by the fact that his own judgment had been run over by the Railroad. He testified that he had been specifically asked to determine if I were under the control of a cult. He said he had some experience with the problem of "shared delusional disorder," when a person is unduly influenced by others, or picks up beliefs of others who are "not psychologically sound."

"In my opinion, he does *not* suffer from a shared delusional disorder," Dr. Daum said. "That's my judgment—but there certainly is a great deal of controversy here, so I would welcome a second opinion. I'm not an expert on cults, so if they want a second opinion, they should get one."

"For God's sake, Brian," I said quietly, "the guy says I'm fine. Give it up."

Another snarl: "You're getting another examination."

Brian and the prosecutor, John Russell, were by then working together in lock step. Russell got up: "I'm still troubled. Dr. Daum lacks experience with cults. Even though it will mean a further delay, I believe Mr. Billington should be examined by experts in cults. I know just the place—the Institute of Law, Psychiatry, and Public Policy at the University of Virginia. I've already called them, and they could do the exam next Monday."

I was not allowed to speak for myself, but had to go through my "lawyer"! I told Brian to tell the court that I did not agree, that I objected to this nonsense about cults, and that I certainly wanted the right to investigate this Institute before accepting an examination. Brian got up and lied flat out: "To cut it short, Mr. Billington does not object to the examination, but he wants to reserve an objection to the person doing the examination." The judge was clearly in on the staging of this act of the drama, and gave his approval, postponing the trial a week to allow the examination.

When the judge left, I turned to Gettings: "Brian, you're creating the ADL's dream. Out of the blue you've manufactured a fiasco. You're not only poisoning our political work, but you're poisoning the environment for my trial and for all my co-defendants."

Brian responded: "I'm doing what I think is right for you. Whatever the effect on the organization or the other defendants, I just don't care."

That evening, the screws were tightened another notch at the jail. Sandy Roberts, one of my associates who had worked with Gettings on the case, was neither a co-defendant nor a relative, and therefore we presumed he would be allowed to visit me. He drove down from Leesburg. Later, I was called to go downstairs for a legal visit, but the elevator stopped between floors, and returned me to my cell. A guard told me there was a new rule: no legal visits after 8:00 p.m.

The next day, Brian came to visit with Sandy, bringing along a young fellow from his law office, Mark Thrash, whom he had brought down to help him. Thrash was totally inexperienced, and tried to make friends by telling me stories about the clients he'd seduced. Gettings had carefully worked out a strategy to defend his insane actions, by rewriting the history of our attorney-client relations before the explosion. He had *never* intended to call Lyn, nor Dennis, he said, and never thought I should testify, either. "Brian, that's absurd," I responded. "That was the only reason I hired you, and you said so before Jim Clark, and even before the judge."

"Look," Gettings said with his eyes blazing, "we have totally different views on a lawyer's responsibility to his client. Moral questions just can't govern here."

He also said that we were out to get him. Nancy Spannaus had held a press conference outside the courthouse that morning, primarily focussing on the fact that the ADL was all over this incident, including all the press coverage, demonstrating the totally political nature of the entire bizarre affair. Gettings complained that Nancy was attacking him, and that other, unnamed members of the organization were out to get him. Actually, we refrained from publicly denouncing him throughout that first week, hoping he'd regain his senses. Lyn's response, in a note to the legal staff, recommended that Gettings should be treated "charitably"; that he'd made a bad mistake, but perhaps it was only a mistake, rather than an intentional political attack. Gettings later introduced that message to the court as a "threat," comparing it to a mafia Don conferring a kiss of death!

Gettings also ran a little scam to discredit me before the court. He told me that I should officially fire him as my lawyer, which, he said, would make it easier to get a new lawyer to take over, which we both wanted. That sounded reasonable to me, so I wrote out a brief note, dictated by Gettings, saying I was terminating his services. This turned out to be a set-up, when we next appeared in court, on Thursday, September 21.

I spent that Wednesday talking to lawyers on the phone about representing me. Several were willing to come in, and all expressed shock and disgust at Gettings's behavior. I asked them about representing myself (*pro se,* in legal terms), if the judge refused to allow Gettings to resign, but they all strongly advised against it.

I received a telegram from my close friends and co-defendants, Paul and Anita Gallagher: "Dear Mike, It never fails to amaze us to what lengths you are willing to go to remain the most famous member of the phone team. Love, Paul and Anita."

Our security staff launched an investigation of the University of Virginia Institute of Law, Psychiatry, and Social Policy, the site of my scheduled full-day psychiatric examination. The first quick pass revealed some disturbing signs. The director was Richard Bonnie, whom we knew very well as the godfather of the movement to legalize drugs! Bonnie had been the keynote speaker just two years earlier at the national convention of NORML (the National Organization for the Reform of Marijuana Laws—i.e., the pot lobby). It was the NORML-linked *High Times* magazine which ran the scurrilous slander of LaRouche: "He Wants To Take Your Drugs Away!" We had been in several head-to-head clashes with Bonnie, including a fight over a bill to decriminalize marijuana in the State of Washington. Bonnie was featured in several of our newspapers and leaflets as a drug pusher, and it was widely and bitterly acknowledged by our enemies that our mobilization against Bonnie and the pot lobby had turned the tide on the decriminalization movement in the 1970's. The idea that Bonnie would be an "impartial examiner" was absurd.

Another person who had until recently been a member of the institute, Paul Dietz, had been a part of the team at the Quantico, Virginia, FBI center which specifically ran operations against us. This Quantico team gave rise to the crew which carried out the raid in Leesburg on Oct. 6, 1986 (and later ran the horrible murder of the Branch Davidians at Waco, Texas, and the murder of a mother and her young son at Ruby Ridge, Idaho).

These were only indications of a potential problem, but enough that I wanted to take a much closer look. I told the staff to contact Gettings and tell him to see me or call me before the next court appearance, so I could tell him how to explain the problem to the judge. He neither showed up nor called.

When we went to court on Thursday, he sprang his trap on me. "Your Honor," he said, "I didn't expect to have to address this issue again today, but Mr. Billington has now sent me a note firing me as his lawyer. I don't have anything to say, but I wanted the court to know."

The judge responded as I'm sure Gettings knew he would: "It's not going to happen, Mr. Billington. I'm not going to allow any more gamesmanship in this case. Mr. Gettings has acted competently in your defense, and I will not let you fire him and further disrupt this trial." I was forbidden to speak.

I quickly briefed Gettings on what I had learned concerning the Institute for Law, Psychiatry, and Social Policy, and told him to tell the court of my objections. Gettings acted annoyed that I was bothering him with this, and conveyed that annoyance to the judge. Judge Weckstein responded in kind, saying, "You *will* take this second examination, Mr. Billington."

When the court session ended, I told Gettings I wanted him to file two motions for me—one to the Court of Appeals, asking them to intervene to allow Gettings to be replaced, on the grounds that there was irreparable damage done to the attorney-client relationship; and second, to appeal the order for me to take the second examination.

Gettings refused. "I'm going back to Alexandria. I'm not going to waste my time with your appeals. All you're doing by all this is giving me more grounds for proving you incompetent!" I concluded that Gettings was now totally hostile towards me. He seemed driven to facilitate the railroad—defending himself rather than defending me. He even admitted this in a discussion with John Flannery, who was ready to come in as my lawyer. Gettings told Flannery that it was obvious, that whatever the outcome, there would be an appeal over his conduct, and he would have to reach out to the Commonwealth to support himself against me—so he could not afford to alienate the prosecution while defending me!

I received a message of support from Ramsey Clark. The son of Supreme Court Justice Tom Clark, Ramsey had been the Attorney General of the United States during the Lyndon Johnson Administration—the highest position in the criminal justice system of the nation. Although we had roundly denounced him for many of his political activities (such as his support for Ayatollah Khomeini's revolution in Iran), and he was very much aware of our very public criticism, Ramsey had nonetheless stepped forward, after the Alexandria trial, to support LaRouche and his co-defendants in the appeal process. He was appalled at the blatant political nature of the case from beginning to end. He had several meetings with LaRouche, and one meeting with all of us at the Alexandria jail. He played a major role in the appeal process, and testified in public hearings on the crimes of the DOJ, that the LaRouche cases were the worst case of prosecutorial misconduct in his experience, or in his knowledge of the history of U.S. jurisprudence!

Pro Se

I had no choice but to begin writing motions *pro se*, since Gettings refused to defend me. The most urgent was a motion to stop the psychiatric examination. Further investigation had turned up an annual report of the Institute for Law and Psychiatry, which bragged that they worked in close collaboration with my prosecutor, Virginia Attorney General Mary Sue Terry, and the FBI Behavioral Sciences Unit at Quantico. They could hardly be considered a neutral party.

I wrote a motion to the court, objecting to the examination in general, as being completely without cause. I described Brian Gettings's psychotic behavior, his lying to the court, and his refusal to file the motion on my behalf. I also described the history of my organization's political warfare with those who were now being called upon to judge my sanity, and quoted from the Institute's annual report, showing their connections to my prosecutors. I left the handwritten motion for Gail to pick up from the Sheriff. She typed it, and dropped it off at Judge Weckstein's house over the weekend.

I hoped he would read it and cancel the examination. But on Monday morning, the Deputies chained me up and transported me to the Institute, at the University of Virginia in Charlottesville. The Deputies told me I'd be there all day, and perhaps even stay overnight in a local jail so that they could continue the examination the next day!

When we arrived, Gettings's assistant Mark Thrash was there to "represent me." I told him his boss had subjected me to this, so he was hardly qualified to represent me. Thrash had a canned speech prepared, obviously scripted by Gettings: "If your purpose is to distance your organization from the accusation that it is a cult, this is your chance. I have no doubt they'll find you're competent to stand trial—and that will prove it. I've thought a lot about it this weekend. This is *my* thinking, not necessarily Brian's."

But I had already decided that I would refuse the examination, regardless of the contempt of court charge that would surely follow. I imagined various headlines in the nation's press if I'd permitted the examination: "Experts Rule LaRouche Lieutenant Delusional—Shares Psychosis Of Cult Leader LaRouche," or, perhaps, "Billington Is Nuts, But He Can Stand Trial."

I did not know it at the time, but we learned later through investigations, that both Gettings and Assistant Attorney General Russell had briefed the Institute's examining team at great length on what they wanted out of the exam. Russell even gave them the business and home phone numbers of Mira Lansky Boland, ADL case agent, advising them to contact her as the expert on the LaRouche movement! (This from a prosecutor who swore to the court and the jury that this is *not* a political case!) Russell added a proviso in his briefing to the shrinks: "Whatever you do, don't tell Billington that you talked to the ADL!"

When I was taken in for the exam, I told them I would not allow it. The team of three shrinks came in and sat down with me, asking if I had any questions.

"No, no questions."

"Why won't you take the exam?"

"I've explained it all in a motion to the judge, which will be on the record. You can read that," I explained. I was polite, but would not be drawn into a discussion.

The stage was set for one of the most bizarre courtroom scenes in history.

[16]

Three Prosecutors

ROANOKE COUNTY COURTHOUSE, SALEM, VA., Sept. 6, 1989—When the deputies bring me into court, there is a stranger sitting next to Brian Gettings at the defense table. Brian introduces me: "Mike, this is Harvey Cohen, my law partner at Cohen, Gettings, Alper, and Dunham."* Harvey shakes my hand without smiling.

"Why is he here?" I ask Brian.

"He's going to speak for me on the question of my withdrawal from the case," he responds.

"Wait a minute," I say, a bit incredulously. "You mean you're allowed to have a lawyer come in to represent you against me, but I'm not allowed to have another lawyer come in to represent me against you?"

The judge enters before he can answer. I learn quickly that Mr. Cohen is already cozy with Judge Weckstein. Gettings introduces Cohen to the court, and Weckstein says, "Yes, of course, Mr. Cohen, I recognize you from your executive position within the Trial Lawyers Association. I'm honored to have you in my court." So much for Gettings's rights versus my rights.

* The dialogue of these events is recounted to the best of my recollection.

Gettings tells the court that John Flannery is in the courtroom and is ready to substitute as my lawyer. The judge says he wants everything on the table before he rules on substitution of counsel.

Harvey Cohen takes the floor. The facts in this situation are bizarre, he says, leading to a complete and total breakdown between Gettings and his client. "The fact is, the relationship was made unreasonably difficult by the client. We've reviewed the *pro se* motion filed with the court this weekend, against taking the psychiatric exam, which he refused to take, without even waiting for your ruling. You can read between the lines of that petition to see the paranoid mind of Mr. Billington. Brian Gettings, in Mr. Billington's view, is now part of a grand conspiracy, and has become his enemy. This is absurd, of course, but the important thing is that *Mr. Billington believes that*.

"Perhaps it was a set up. Mr. Billington is looking back at his attorney's past work with the FBI, and as a prosecutor, and he's decided that Mr. Gettings has shined off his badge and joined a conspiracy against LaRouche and his organization. Billington sincerely believes that."

I'm practically gagging, and almost stand up to intervene, or at least voice an objection. Who is this guy? Is he supposed to be part of *my legal defense team?* If so, is he peddling these total lies on the court in *my name?* All I've said, both to Gettings himself and in my motion, is that Brian had lost his mind, that he was "in outer space, or worse." (Brian particularly objected to that phrase, thinking I was trying to say he was drunk. I wasn't.)

Or, if Cohen is *not* representing me, but overtly making accusations against me on behalf of his law partner, then don't I deserve a lawyer to defend me, to object for me on the record?

Nonetheless, the judge has instructed me to speak only through my lawyer. I remain silent, and Cohen gets in even deeper.

"Billington is now refusing to cooperate or speak with his lawyer," Cohen continues.

("Objection!" I shout in my mind. "I've been pleading with Brian to see me, to talk to me, to get busy preparing for trial. He refuses, and ran off to Alexandria right after the court hearing five days ago!")

"Billington is demanding that Mr. Gettings take actions that are exactly opposite to Mr. Billington's actual interests. Not only on taking a jury trial, but in regard to who he should call as witnesses, how to cross-examine prosecution witnesses, and even on the opening. Why, Mr. Billington has even given Mr. Gettings a script for the opening statement, which is nothing but an organizational statement. All this has happened very recently, within the past week."

("Objection, Your Honor!" my mind shouts yet again. "This character is lying like mad, and *Gettings knows he's lying!* The agreement between us on witnesses and general strategy was settled before I hired him, and Gettings told you that here in this court, when you approved his taking over from Jim Clark. I've been sending him voluminous notes for months, on witnesses, on the opening, and other things, because he never comes to discuss these things with me. These are my ideas and my recollections, which he says I refuse to communicate to him.")

"I'll let Mr. Gettings fill in the facts now, Your Honor," concludes this stooge, and sits down.

Brian joins the stoning. "Back in your chambers, Judge, a few days ago, you asked me if I thought I was being set up. I said no then, but I've changed my mind. I can't prove it, and I'm not going to try. But I believe it was a set up—but *without Mr. Billington being a willful participant in it*. They were looking for something to erupt, some excuse. It happened over the jury issue, but it would have happened in any case. I guess they wanted to get press coverage, or some other supposed benefit."

Brian tells the court about the message from LaRouche, which suggested that Brian had made a mistake, probably without malice, and should be treated charitably.

"I don't *like* being treated with charity," says Brian. "It's creepy. It's not Billington instigating this thing. He's just the go-along, the tool, of him who declares charity."

("Well, well," I think, "the 'Get LaRouche Task Force' couldn't have said it more elegantly, Brian. You've now turned the whole organization into a devious, dictatorial cult out to destroy the judicial system, and perhaps the world, and LaRouche is the evil Don.")

But Harvey Cohen hasn't had his fill yet. He gets up again, replacing Brian. "Mr. Gettings has not expressed our concern as strongly as I think he should. The fact is, I'm worried for the *personal safety* of my partner!"

Harvey sits down. I stand up and tell the judge I'd like to respond now.

"Just a moment, Mr. Billington. If you're to be judged incompetent to stand trial, then all this will not be necessary. Before you or the Commonwealth respond, I want to determine the competency question."

Well, at least he plans on letting me speak, eventually—*or so I think.* Dr. Steven Hoge is called to the stand. I recognize him as the head of the three-person team which was prepared to give me the psychiatric exam. Dr. Hoge explains that Richard Bonnie, the director of the Institute (and our long-term opponent on drug legalization), was the first person contacted by the Commonwealth. It was Bonnie who assigned the team to do the examination. It had been a joint request from the Commonwealth and Mr. Gettings, he explains, and, besides reading the transcripts of the hearings thus far, they had held numerous discussions with both Mr. Russell and Mr. Gettings. He explains what happened when I arrived.

Mr. Russell asks: "Were you able to determine whether or not Mr. Billington was mentally competent to assist his lawyer at trial?"

"The question of his free will was not answered, since we were unable to examine him."

Brian got up. "Your Honor, I want to go beyond *privilege,* to *disclosure,* according to 19.2 169.1."

(What the hell is that?" I ask myself, jotting down the number.)

"This code allows me to break the attorney-client privilege in exactly this kind of situation," Gettings claims.

"Your Honor," I say out loud. "I clearly have no lawyer to represent me here. I'd like to be able to consult another lawyer, who is here in the courtroom, about what Mr. Gettings is trying to do."

I most honestly do not know what Gettings is up to, but I know that the confidentiality of attorney-client discussions is a basic protection of the law, and I can only imagine what whoppers Gettings will come up with if he's allowed to claim I told him things in confidence.

"No, Mr. Billington," snapped the judge, "I will not let you consult another lawyer. You have a lawyer, it's Mr. Gettings, and if you want to consult anyone, he's the one to consult." He turns to Gettings: "But, Mr. Gettings, I will not allow you to break the attorney-client privilege. So proceed carefully."

I've heard of lawyers *refusing* demands from prosecutors, and even from judges, to break the attorney-client privilege, but this is the first time I've ever heard of a lawyer, still representing his client, *requesting* to break the privilege!

Brian proceeds: "Mr. Hoge, let's take a hypothetical. Suppose Mr. Billington had told you that your Institute was actually run by the FBI and the Attorney General's office. Would that bring up the question of competency?"

(Well, I sure was right about Brian making up things I'd supposedly said. He's even making them up after the judge told him *not* to!)

"Yes," said Mr. Hoge, "that would make me suspect that if he's so unbalanced, that he may not be competent in other areas."

"And, in particular, not competent to assist his attorney at trial?"

"That's right," said the compliant doctor.

"And what would be your recommendations, Dr. Hoge?"

"If it were a question of his competence to aid in his defense, I'd recommend a further evaluation."

("Oh, oh, here it comes," I say to myself. I remember what Martha had told me—that Gettings said he wanted me committed to a state mental institution for at least a month of observation and treatment!)

Judge Weckstein steps in. "Dr. Hoge, Mr. Billington is being prosecuted by the Attorney General of the Commonwealth of Virginia. Assume that Mr. Billington obtained the 1987 Annual Report of your Institute, and found that the Institute gets grants from the Attorney General, that they work, quote, "in close partership," and in "collaborative activities" with the FBI Academy at Quantico. Would he be reading this correctly?"

(He's reading from my motion! Is he going to call Gettings bluff? Have I forced him to acknowledge what's really going on here?)

"Yes, Judge, those things are true," said Dr. Hoge uncomfortably.

"Then, would you still have competency concerns in that case, on objective grounds?"

"Well, Your Honor," said Dr. Hoge, squirming, "this is what ill people do. They see enemies everywhere. It raises my concern."

"But, beyond such hypotheticals," continued Judge Weckstein, "do you draw any conclusions from your actual meeting with Mr. Billington? Does declining to be interviewed cause you to draw such a conclusion?"

"Only in the negative," Dr. Hoge conceded. "There were no gross signs of mental illness."

Gettings panics. He jumps up. "But Dr. Hoge, let's get back to the hypothetical. Is there a basis for a further examination?"

"Yes," sighs Dr. Hoge.

"*Yes, yes,* there is!" shouts Gettings. The man has gone mad.

Hoge is dismissed, and Gettings addresses the court. "Your Honor, there is no alteration of my belief—Mr. Billington is clearly unable to assist me. It does not have to rise to the level of psychosis. My questions were adequate to interest Dr. Hoge in getting another evaluation. Let's get this done. There exists one way to make the determination once and for all. The way is there. We must take the next step."

(So the son-of-a-bitch wants to commit me to a mental institution. They'll probably strap me down and pump me full of drugs. God, what a sick man. You need help, Brian.)

Brian sits down, and I rise to speak. There is nothing I want to add in regard to the examination, but I certainly want to respond to the garbage from Cohen and Gettings, two of my three prosecutors. I also want to ask for John Flannery to step in to represent me.

But John Russell intervenes. "Your Honor, I think Mr. Billington should only be allowed to speak if he takes the stand and gets sworn in, and is subjected to my cross-examination."

"Your Honor," I quietly respond. "If I could have a lawyer to defend me, I would gladly take the stand. But without a lawyer, I'd be subjected to all three of these people accusing me of the most fantastic nonsense, and no one to object or protect my interests."

"You'll have to take the stand, Mr. Billington, if you wish to speak," said the judge. "I'll protect your interests."

(Oh, great! That makes me feel much better!) "That's well and good, Your Honor, but I don't have a lawyer. It's not the same." I feel like the world is crashing in on me. I want to testify, but taking the stand undefended, against all four of these guys might be suicidal. I gaze around the room. John Flannery catches my eye, draws his fingers across his throat and shakes his head, "no."

"Judge, you let Gettings have a lawyer. Let me have a lawyer." It's my last gasp.

"Mr. Billington, yea or nay?" I sit down, wondering where the State Mental Institution is.

But Weckstein apparently has something else in mind. "There is not one iota of evidence that Mr. Billington is not competent to stand trial, and to assist his lawyer," he says.

I sit up. I expected at least to be held in contempt of court—after all, I did refuse to obey a court order to take the examination. Is Judge Weckstein really coming around? Did I force his hand with my *pro se* motion? Will he let Flannery come in as well?

Russell jumps in, as if on cue. "Mr. Flannery has an unwaivable conflict, Your Honor. He represents Rochelle Ascher, and we plan to call Ascher as a witness."

That's an outrageous lie—there's not a chance in the world they'll call Shelley. But, again, it's obvious that things have been worked out ahead of time. Judge Weckstein gives a totally hypocritical lecture on why a lawyer must have a single-minded devotion to his client, and therefore Flannery is out, and Gettings is in!

"Mr. Billington, Mr. Gettings has done an outstanding job thus far. He's your lawyer, and he'll continue to be your lawyer. If you have differences on how to run the case, he decides."

Good God! This next month might be *worse* than being sent to the looney bin.

Trial as Farce

I won't detail the trial. It was largely a re-run of Alexandria, only without a lawyer for the defense. Gettings went through the motions on cross-examinations, but never challenged the government's theory of the case. He even told the judge on several occasions that "my head just isn't in it," and admitted in court that he simply hadn't done the necessary preparation. I continued to provide written background reports on various topics to help him, but he had little use for them. His attitude toward me turned downright mean.

A few days after the start of jury selection, I told Gettings during a session in court that I was filing another *pro se* motion in regard to my desire to testify. Gettings had still not spent a single minute talking to me about my testimony. He even said he was researching the possibility that he could *prevent* me from taking the stand under some obscure exception to the rule that a defendant makes that decision on his own. My motion, I told Gettings, would argue that, since my lawyer still maintained his belief that I was incompetent, and treated me with open hostility, that he could not represent my interests if I took the stand, as I wanted to do. Gettings asked how I was communicating with the rest of the legal staff, and I explained that we exchanged notes and material with the deputies at the main desk, and through Sandy Roberts, the paralegal on the Constitutional Defense Fund staff, who was maintaining contact with me.

That evening, Brian left for Alexandria for the weekend. Sandy came to visit, but was refused entrance. His right to visit had been lifted! Then I asked for a phone call, giving the guard John Flannery's phone number. This was also refused. I was told that henceforth I was *only permitted to call my official lawyer, Brian Gettings!* To top it off, I was no longer permitted to leave material for pick-up by my legal staff, nor could they leave material for me!

My contact with the outside world was to be confined to one man, Brian Gettings, who was hell bent on putting me away for the rest of my life, while doing as much damage as possible to my political movement. I was being strapped down through isolation.

By luck, the phone number I had given them for Brian Gettings was the apartment office he no longer occupied. But, I could reach the paralegals there. We managed to exchange papers during court appearances. After a week, and repeated protests, they relented and allowed Sandy to have legal visits again.

Gettings came to visit one afternoon after court. He brought Mark Thrash with him as a secretary, instructing him to take careful notes on the discussion. Gettings began by informing me, as if presenting "formal notification," that he would not call either

Lyn or Dennis. Ignoring the fact that this was an issue that went back to the first day we had discussed the case, he gave me a formal reason, with Thrash noting every word. "If either of them testifies, the Commonwealth will be allowed to question them about their prior convictions, for fraud, in regard to the same actions that you're being tried for."

"Brian, we discussed that back in March, when I hired you. That's nothing new."

He raised his voice. "Don't you get it? If they testify, the jury will learn that a Federal court convicted them of the same charges you're facing. Don't you get it?"

"Brian," I said quietly, "you knew that last March, and it didn't bother you."

He stood up. "Come on, Mike, you've been certified sane, and you still can't see the difference?"

"Brian, look. I've treated you with respect, in spite of hell. You could at least be civil. . . ."

He cut me off. "Let me get this straight. You can't understand that calling LaRouche and Small would harm your case?"

"As we've agreed since March, I don't think such a penalty is so great as to rule out having them testify—and neither did you."

"Let me get this down," he shouted, and scribbled furiously on a legal pad. "Here, sign this."

"Sign this?" I asked, stunned. "You want to use this in court against me? Are you making your case against me, Brian?"

"Well, maybe. I don't know if it will ever come to that," he lied. "Sign it."

His statement was incoherent, but I wrote my own note, saying what I'd already told him, and signed it.

Gettings also refused to subpoena a number of people whose testimony could have exposed the government campaign to destroy LaRouche, including ex-National Security Council officer Oliver North. When I insisted on calling both North and Barbara Newington (who had testified before the Congress in the Iran-Contra hearing that government official North had instructed her to stop supporting us), Gettings simply refused to call North, and sabotaged the subpoena to Newington, lying to me that it was too late.

He also refused to subpoena Boston FBI agent Richard Egan, whose testimony had completely shaken up the New York trial. Egan had been in court in Boston, during a post-trial hearing, when Judge Keeton directly ordered him to preserve all of the documents which had been produced to the grand jury—which included hundreds of cancelled checks proving we had paid certain debts to lenders. Agent Egan left the courtroom that day and proceeded to throw the documents into the garbage! When this was brought out in court in the New York trial, the jury—and the judge—were astonished. Gettings simply told me that it was too much trouble to call an FBI agent, and that his view (and his view must reign!) was that Egan's testimony would not help.

Gettings continued claiming he was looking for some legal basis to prevent me from testifying on my own behalf, until just a few days before I would have been called. Finally, he visited me one evening at the jail. When I sat down at the table, he literally threw a yellow legal pad down in front of me. "I can't stop you from testifying. You should write down everything you want to say. Have it ready for me tomorrow."

"That's it?" I asked.

"That's it," he responded.

We discussed a few other matters, but that was the sum total of the effort made by my lawyer to prepare me to testify, or to prepare for what would most likely be a grueling several days of cross-examination.

I had, until that point, held out some hope that I still had an outside chance to win the case if I were to testify, despite the malice from my lawyer. When I returned to my cell that evening, I felt totally discouraged. Gettings would not only throw me to the wolves on cross-examination, but he would not even prepare himself to be able to question me on direct examination in a way that could get the truth out. Gettings would do *nothing* to review the thousands of documents, or discuss with me the details of my relations with supporters, in order to prepare himself to counter the Commonwealth's claims. The Commonwealth could put on the record any number of outrageous lies during their cross, which would go unrefuted, and become part of the permanent record, both for my appeal and for the future trials of my co-defendants and for the piranhas in the press. Once again, I had to give up my burning desire to testify.

Only one courtroom episode is required to adequately convey the moral depravity of the prosecution, led by Assistant Attorney General John Russell. Their key witnesses were Mrs. Marie Fincham, the wonderful woman from Illinois I described earlier, and her daughter. Her daughter and her son-in-law, furious that their mother was supporting us, called in the FBI and Virginia State Police. Only after several grueling meetings with her family, and with prosecutors and police officers keeping her up for hours on end, subjecting her to treatment that can only be described as coercive manipulation, or, brainwashing, were they able to finally break her of her support, and convince her that we were somehow using her money for purposes other than what we had told her. Throughout the month that these meetings were taking place, Mrs. Fincham had told me over the phone, that she loved her children, but that they were acting as if "possessed." She told me that they refused to read our literature, which she had given to them, or to discuss the many issues involved in our work, but kept pressing her that everything we did was false, a front for taking her money. She and I had long discussions about the nature of the truth, and about the great scientists, artists, and poets of history who had stood up to the mob, to defend moral truth against popular opinion. At Christmas, I sent her a card with a Raphael Madonna, which we had discussed on the phone. On the card, I quoted from Keats, that the painting showed that "Truth is Beauty, Beauty Truth."

In the trial, Russell put the daughter on the stand, who cried and carried on about her mother being scammed. (Gettings didn't even bother to cross-examine her, even though I had written an extensive report for him!) Russell then put Mrs. Fincham on the stand. She was very frail, confused, and disoriented.

We later learned that Mrs. Fincham had developed Alzheimer's *in the past year*, although she was fine—even by her daughter's testimony—in 1985, when I had been talking with her. The prosecution failed to tell us of her having become senile, and, of course, Gettings never bothered to ask.

So how did Russell describe Mrs. Fincham in his closing argument to the jury? First, he wittingly lied that Mrs. Fincham was the same in 1985 as she had appeared on the stand: "The question is, did he have an intent to defraud? If that can even be a question, you can look for yourself. You heard Marie Fincham. You heard Marie Fincham just as Mike Billington heard Marie Fincham over the phone. Do you think he deceived Marie Fincham?"

Then, in a gesture which, to my mind, captures the entire cultural decay in America, as well as the depravity of the judicial system, Russell held up my Christmas card to Mrs. Fincham: "Do you want to know what kind of a man Mike Billington is? Look at how he manipulates people. Look at this one exhibit when you get into the jury room. It's a Christmas card he wrote to Mrs. Fincham. It says: 'This Raphael proves that truth and beauty are one.' That's the kind of person Michael Billington is. Michael Billington and his friends have to be taught what truth and justice are all about. You're the only people who can teach him that lesson. You can do that by finding him guilty of fraud on all nine counts. That's your duty."

A reference to Classical art and poetry, or an appeal to truth and beauty, can have no meaning to a pedant like John Russell. Unfortunately, the "average citizen" in a jury will follow the pedant, not the poet, and accept the charge that the poet is a fraud.

77 Years

"Before I announce my decision on the sentence," intoned Judge Weckstein, who by then seemed to me to be less like a judge and more like a comic actor performing in an 1890's melodrama, "I want to warn the defendant and his supporters in the courtroom against any emotional outbursts."

I suppressed a guffaw. There was no question in anyone's mind what his decision would be. The jury had deliberated for only a few hours in returning a guilty verdict on all nine counts, and assigned penalties of between six and ten years on each count, totalling 77 years. During their deliberations, the jury sent out a question to the judge as to whether the sentences would be served concurrently or consecutively. My "lawyer," Brian Gettings, had already gone home to Alexandria by that point, leaving me in the hands of his young "trainee" assistant Mark Thrash. Thrash had no idea what to say in response to the jury's question, and the judge chose to fudge the truth by telling the jury they could, if they wished, recommend either concurrent or consecutive sentences. The truth is, as the judge should have answered, that jury sentences are served consecutively, unless the judge wishes to reduce it.

And this judge was not about to reduce it. We had checked his record—he had never reduced a jury sentence. (That, of course, constitutes a breach of the intent of the jury sentencing statute, by eliminating the supposed safety valve for a runaway jury. Later, the Appeals Courts proved to be unconcerned about that fact.)

We learned, soon thereafter, that Judge Weckstein had other reasons to impose the full, barbarous sentence. During the next trial—that of my friend Richard Welsh—Judge Weckstein would be forced to reveal a series of personal letters exchanged soon after my trial between himself and the regional director of the ADL in Virginia, Ira Gissen. Writing on ADL letterhead, Gissen referred to their mutual friend, Murray Janus, the head of the Virginia ADL, and enclosed a package of hate literature on LaRouche, listing the titles in the text of his letter: "Nazis without Swastikas," "The LaRouche Cult's Fantasy World," and so forth. He added a postscript, that the ADL was lobbying the state government to appoint a Jewish judge to the Supreme Court of Virginia, "which you may find of special interest." The message was clear: keep up the good work in destroying these guys, and we'll make it worth your while.

Rather than bringing criminal charges against the ADL for attempting to bribe a sitting judge, Weckstein wrote a friendly letter back to Gissen returning the literature, explaining that he'd rather be able to claim that he'd not read any ADL literature on LaRouche. He added: "I'm enclosing, for your information and amusement, an additional publication which discusses both the ADL and me, which was being distributed in this area last week." The enclosure was a leaflet published by the Schiller Institute, called "The American Dope Lobby (ADL) and Judge Clifford R. Weckstein," which presented the story of Dope, Inc., the ADL, and Judge Weckstein's close relations with the ADL leadership in Virginia.

At my sentencing hearing, Judge Weckstein stopped short of endorsing the ADL slanders against us, but nonetheless praised the overtly political arguments put forward by the prosecutors. In calling for the judge to impose the entire 77 years, John Russell said, essentially, that "the LaRouche organization is still out there, still functioning. To stop them, we must make a terrible example of Mr. Billington!"

Perhaps they were unaware of what a "terrible example" a 77-year sentence would become, demonstrating to the entire world the tyranny of the judicial system in the United States.

The next day, Gail visited me at the jail. She was a visitor now, not a legal aide, so we spoke over a phone through a plexiglass screen. "Judge Bostetter threw out the involuntary bankruptcy," she told me. "He called it an 'improper use of the involuntary bankruptcy statute,' and he ruled that the government had brought the action against us in 'objective bad faith,' while the government was guilty of carrying out 'a constructive fraud on the court.' He even said that the government had failed to show that we were bankrupt, or even that we had established a pattern of non-payment of our debts!"

"In a normal world," I said, "all these cases would go out the window." We smiled at each other—this was anything but a normal world.

Soon after the trial, Brian Gettings developed throat cancer, and had a tracheotomy. He could talk only with a "computerized" sound, by placing a finger on the hole in his throat—which was his condition when we depositioned him during post-trial proceedings. He appeared otherwise healthy, but the loss of his voice meant the end of his career as a courtroom lawyer. It occurred to me that at least no one else would have to suffer through what I had suffered with Brian Gettings.

One of the most important claims in my appeal was the "ineffectiveness of counsel" regarding Gettings. But, before I was granted this hearing in Federal court, Gettings died. I was sorry to see him slip out before taking the stand, although we did succeed in getting him to expose himself on the record in the course of two long depositions. Lyn's response was most "LaRouchean": "Well, for the first time in his life, Brian will have to argue his case before a fair and impartial judge."

[17]

Prison Labor / Labor of Love

In December, I was shipped back to Allenwood. The officials there took one look at the 77-year sentence and said, "No way—you're not staying at this camp." I was put back in chains and carted off to a local county jail to await my further disposition. Thus began a six-month ordeal, known in prison lingo as "the bus treatment"—being shipped from place to place for no apparent reason, spending a few weeks in the "hole" (the jail within the prison, which stays on 24-hour lockdown) in each location. I finally ended up at the Raybrook, New York, Correctional Facility, near the Canadian border. But I must begin with Allenwood, during those few weeks preceding the Virginia trial before Judge Weckstein.

★ ★ ★

Allenwood Correctional Facility is sometimes called "Club Fed," one of the supposed glamour spots among the Federal prisons. This is foolish. There was no fence at Allenwood, as is the case at all the low-security camps, but if an inmate walks off, he's just as guilty of "escape," as if he'd climbed a wall. Only prisoners known to be unlikely to attempt escape were allowed in. There were fewer guards per inmate, making it cheaper to run, and anyone who caused any trouble was immediately shipped out. The myth of these places being "resorts" is absurd: The control and regulation of every aspect of life was actually more severe at Allenwood, than at several of the high-security prisons I would later occupy.

Allenwood was my first exposure to the use of prisons as a source of slave labor for private industry. Later, in the mid-1990's, private industry would move into the prisons in a big way, but back in 1989 this was a new phenomenon. The prison privatizers were moving very cautiously, hoping that the American people, and American labor unions, would not notice the devastating effect this would have on the nation and on the economy. The publicity put out by the Federal Prison Industries, called Unicor, said that only those prisoners who volunteered for the job were accepted. That was a lie. I was told straight-out that I must work at Unicor, even though I had explicitly informed them, in writing, that I did not approve of the private use of prison labor, and that I didn't want to "scab" on free labor. If I refused, I was told, I'd be punished, and probably removed from the compound, to a higher security facility.

I later published a series of articles for EIR on prison labor. I was particularly incensed when a group of Congressmen began harping on China's prison policy, which, they charged, produced goods for export using prison labor. I had neither reason nor desire to defend China's prison-labor policy, but I knew that the U.S. incarcerated a far higher percentage of its population than did the Chinese, that the U.S. also had political prisoners, and that American prisoners were also forced to work producing goods for the private market. It was pure hypocrisy for U.S. politicians to rail against China while sponsoring the same policies at home.

During my 18 months of liberty in 1991 and 1992, between serving my Federal and state time, I further investigated the question of U.S. exports of prison-made goods. The U.S. Congress was considering a bill to impose economic sanctions on China for exporting goods produced in prisons. I spoke to State Department and Bureau of Prisons spokesmen, who were contemptuous of my questions, claiming that it was ridiculous to compare American practice to that of the Chinese. However, I found the personnel at Unicor itself far more forthright and honest.

"We don't have anything to do with determining the final destination of the goods we produce," a Unicor official told me.

"They're government agencies, of some sort—once they buy it from us, they're free to do with it whatever they want."

I followed up on one prison product I found particularly interesting—electric cables used in fighter aircraft and in Patriot missiles! At the time of my investigation, immediately following the Gulf War, the U.S. was selling Patriot missiles all over the world. I traced the prison-made cables to the Redstone Arsenal in Huntsville, Alabama, where the missiles were stored before sale. The spokesman there assured me that they had absolutely no interest in whether the parts came from prison labor or not—they sold everything they could to the highest bidder. The hottest buyers recently, he told me, were Israel, Turkey, and Saudi Arabia!

So, while Virginia Congressman Frank Wolf—who happened to be *my Congressman*—was grandstanding in the House of Representatives, waving around a pair of socks produced in a Chinese prison (given to him during an official visit to the prison), claiming, without evidence, that these dangerous socks were destined to be exported to the U.S., a Federal prison in *Virginia*, at Petersburg, was producing parts for high-tech weapons for sale around the world!

This was not the end of my battle with Congressman Wolf and the hypocrites of the anti-China lobby. In the mid-1990's, when the development of strong ties between President Clinton and China's President Jiang Zemin became a potential axis of defense against the global economic collapse, the British escalated their efforts to destabilize China and to poison U.S.-China relations. One of their tools was the British intelligence operation known as Christian Solidarity International (CSI), run by Baroness Caroline Cox. CSI served as the cutting edge of British efforts to destroy those nations which refused to submit to IMF dictates, while also drawing the U.S. into their "New British Empire" campaigns, under the cover of "defending Christians against repression." The two nations targetted most intensely were Sudan and China. The leading member of CSI in the United States was none other than Congressman Frank Wolf, who acknowledged his role as an asset of this British intelligence outfit without a blush.

In 1997, Nancy Spannaus announced her candidacy for the U.S. Congress against Wolf. By that time, I had become quite familiar with the prison labor policy of the Commonwealth of Virginia under Conservative Revolution darling, Governor George Allen. Not only was Allen opening the prisons to private industry, selling prison labor products all over the world, but he even published glossy brochures describing this new, cheap labor force, taking these brochures with him on numerous junkets around the world. One brochure, entitled "Virginia Prisons: They're Open For Business," read, "There are no employee benefit packages to fund. No pensions, health insurance, vacations, or sick leave. And companies like the dependability of operating within the prison system. Workers report on time every day." On the cover was a picture of a prison guard tower and razor-wire fences, with the caption: "An ideal location your site selection committee may have overlooked." There appeared to be little change in Ole Virginie since the days of the slave auctions!

Congressman Wolf's legislation to sanction China was timed to disrupt the historic 1997 visit to the U.S. of President Jiang Zemin. I was incensed, and wrote a public denunciation, which we published in both *The New Federalist* and in our local Virginia paper, *EIR News for Loudoun County*. The article read in part: "Over the past several years, Congressman Frank Wolf has made himself the leading spokesman for the 'China bashers' in the U.S. Congress. He has compared today's China to Nazi Germany, accusing Beijing of running massive 'slave camps' and other horrible atrocities. He is lying.

"Over these same several years, I have been in prison, a victim of political persecution, ... In my seven years in prison, I have dedicated myself to an intensive comparative study of European and Chinese culture, science, philosophy, and art. I have published numerous essays, all available to the Congressman, on the historical efforts to build an ecumenical alliance between the Platonic/Christian currents born in the Golden Renaissance of Europe, and the Confucian currents which have guided each period of economic and cultural development in China over the past 3,000 years.

"The Congressman has apparently not read my writings on China, nor the extensive documentation published . . . by Lyndon and Helga LaRouche on the current burst of economic and cultural optimism in China, and their collaboration with nations across the Eurasian landmass in rebuilding the ancient Silk Road connecting East and West.

"The Congressman has chosen, instead, to obtain his information about China from the British. . . . Congressman Wolf has demanded that the U.S. *not* participate with China in the economic nation-building associated with the New Silk Road, but must instead punish China (and our own economy!) by imposing severe restrictions on trade relations between our nations."

After documenting some of Wolf's hypocritical complaints, I added: "The Congressman also visited prisoners in Beijing who had been incarcerated for their role in organizing political demonstrations. Such prisoners do exist in China—but Mr. Wolf has yet to visit the political prisoners *in his own district*. I encourage him to do so, as I would be most willing to provide him with much needed intelligence in regard to China policy. . . ."

That was in 1997. Back in 1989, my first experience with prison labor at Allenwood did not last long, as my Virginia trial began only six weeks after I arrived, and I was not allowed back in, with 77 years hanging over my head.

The Prisoner as Monk

After six months of living in solitary confinement, between the Roanoke County Jail and the "bus treatment," life at Raybrook Correctional Center in upstate New York was a great relief, and an opportunity to begin serious work. It was becoming clear that I would be spending a great deal of time in prison. Overturning the treachery of my Virginia trial in the appeals court was possible, but not likely. I therefore set my sights on long-term projects. At first, this meant an immersion in China studies, primarily historical, with a first reading of Confucius, Mencius, and the other classics of antiquity.

I soon realized that my life in prison was not totally unlike that of the monks of old in Europe, who withdrew from society in order to devote their entire mind and soul to study, research, analysis, and prayer. Many great contributions to human progress were achieved by such monks in Ireland, France, Germany, and across Europe. Like these monks, my life was austere, but I had enough food and exercise, and plenty of time to read and write. There was even a piano, which I played for about an hour each day. I did find my mind wandering, occasionally, to the famous wine cellars at those old monasteries—but this was, after all, prison!

I could not allow myself, even for a moment, to lose sight of my life's mission, or to get overly self-involved in the legal intricacies of my appeals. I had to do everything necessary to help my lawyers and the Constitutional Defense Fund staff—and I was not without hope that both the Federal and Virginia prosecutions could be overturned in the courts, no matter how corrupt. But, nonetheless, it was possible that I would spend the rest of my life in prison. If that were to be so, would I not have the same responsibility, nonetheless, to contribute whatever I could to mankind's future? Or was I somehow freed of the pressing urgency felt by any sensitive conscience, to bring to an end the horrors being imposed upon the world by the financial oligarchy? Was I, in fact, condemned to a life of mindless monotony, "doing time," as the saying goes, or did I retain my inalienable right to the *pursuit of happiness?*

I emerged from the nightmarish frame-up in Virginia with an impassioned strength of spirit, owing in part to the confidence in my own fortitude in the face of threats and bribes. The temptation to forgo truth in exchange for personal comfort, I recognized, is a chimera, since the apparent comforts come at the expense of moral compromises that injure the soul, and even leave the senses scarred. The constant search for immediate sensual gratification inevitably creates a very miserable person, and it certainly was not what Leibniz, nor the U.S. Declaration of Independence, meant by "the pursuit of happiness." I had not set out to be a martyr for the cause, but if that was what I must be, I was proud to assume the label. My real freedom was unfolding before me, as I launched into my own chosen form of "prison labor."

The immediate focus of my work on China was the issue of East-West collaboration throughout history. The two crucial junctures of such collaboration in modern times were, first, the era of the Jesuit missionaries in China during the 17th and 18th Centuries, and their correspondence with Leibniz and his circle in Europe; and, second, the period of Sun Yat-sen in the late 19th and early 20th Centuries, and his collaboration with the American System school in the United States.

LaRouche was himself spearheading the third historic drive for East-West collaboration. His first year in prison produced a further elaboration of his October 1988 proposals for vast development projects across Eastern Europe as a basis for reuniting East and West. He was renewing Leibniz's concept of a "Grand Design" uniting the entire Eurasian landmass through development and cultural collaboration.

I found, in the introduction to a journal called *Novissima Sinica*, published in 1697, an elegant statement by Leibniz of the vision which guided his work, and which I adopted as my own:

> I consider it a singular plan of the fates that human cultivation and refinement should today be concentrated, as it were, in the two extremes of our continent, in Europe and in China, which adorns the Orient as Europe does the opposite edge of the Earth. Perhaps Supreme Providence has ordained such an arrangement, so that, as the most cultivated and distant peoples stretch out their arms to each other, those in between may gradually be brought to a better way of life.

The potential for creating a new East-West Grand Design was dramatically enhanced in November of 1989, when the Berlin Wall crumbled before the eyes of a stunned and joyful world. Lyn's forecast of the collapse of the Soviet bloc, and the reuniting of Germany, had been borne out with precision. The chance for peace and development in a united Europe appeared within mankind's grasp, along with the end of the Cold War. Timing, however, was crucial. Lyn's proposals were now urgent, for only an immediate, collaborative effort between the nations of the East and West, to rebuild the shattered economies of Eastern Europe, could assure such peace, and prevent a recurrence of old ethnic and national conflicts. A new renaissance was demanded.

But not everyone shared this spirit of joyful renewal. Maggie Thatcher and the architects of a New British Empire unleashed a diatribe of vindictive propaganda against a united Germany, and hence against any new East-West development agreements. A "Fourth Reich" is being created, they screamed. German militarism will again threaten Europe, bringing back the "will to power," and the "natural" Nazi-like character of the German people. This was classic British geopolitics, a virtual replay of the process at the beginning of the 20th Century, when the British created the "Great War," for the same reasons—keeping East and West divided.

I was reading a book by Sun Yat-sen at that time, called *The Vital Problem of China,* written in 1917, which proved Dr. Sun to be the most insightful statesman of his age. He described the British intentions with uncanny foresight, precisely because he understood the *character of the British oligarchical world-view.* Germany, he said, was the only belligerent in the Great War dedicated to scientific and technological progress. "The alliance against Germany is the result of ten years of strenuous efforts on the part of England," wrote Dr. Sun, "of rallying the weaker countries to crush the strongest. . . . In order to maintain her own interests, England cannot allow any country on the European continent to grow too strong, and when any country grows too strong, she must get all the other countries to join her in overthrowing that country."

As to Britain's pretensions, claiming it was going to war against the Kaiser to defend weaker nations against a power-hungry Germany, Sun Yat-sen reminded his readers of British treatment of the weak and poor in India and China. "Every year England takes large quantities of foodstuffs for her own consumption from India, where in the last ten years 19 million people have died of starvation. It must not be imagined for a moment that India is suffering from underproduction. The fact is, that what India has produced for herself has been wrested away by England."

Dr. Sun continued: "Is it right for England to rob China of Hongkong and Burma, to force our people to buy and smoke opium, and to work out portions of Chinese territory as her sphere of influence?"

Sun Yat-sen wrote this book as a polemic against the British demand that China join the British side in the war against Germany. Sun's conclusion: "If one really wants to champion the cause of justice today, one should first declare war on England, France, and Russia, not Germany."

Sun also knew exactly how the British would treat their "friends" when they no longer needed them to help destroy their primary enemy: "When that country becomes too weak to be of any use to herself, she sacrifices it to please some other country." If China joined the war on the side of the British, Sun warned, the British would eventually treat China the way a silk farmer treats his silk worms: "After all the silk has been drawn from the cocoons, they are destroyed by fire or used as fish food."

This is exactly what happened to China at the Versailles Conference after the war. China, supposedly one of the "allies" in the war against Germany, was sliced up like a piece of salami, and parcelled out to the larger powers in "spheres of influence." The previously German-held areas were given to Japan!

I could see why this insightful book had been out of print for fifty years. It was even unavailable in Chinese—something we corrected in 1996, when we published a Chinese edition, to help our friends in China come to terms with contemporary British neo-colonialism.

With the fall of the Berlin Wall, the British again rushed to impose imperial divide-and-conquer policies and prevent the uniting of Eastern and Western Europe. As in 1914, a new war in the Balkans was instigated. Then, Maggie Thatcher and her obedient puppy dog, George Bush, launched the Iraq War in 1991. Even the 1992 Maastricht agreement, which established the euro as a European-wide currency, was essentially a British design to weaken Continental Europe.

Throughout 1989 and 1990, LaRouche polemicized vociferously from his prison cell against these British machinations, warning that, despite the apparent end of the Cold War, the world would move faster towards global chaos and war than before the fall of communism, if the West failed to act with reason and compassion at this critical juncture in history. The effect of his imprisonment was felt most severely in this regard, as national leaders, both East and West, grappled with the new political geometry—a geometry which LaRouche alone had forecast, and in which LaRouche had critical insights and ideas which were simply not available from anyone else.

Exoneration

With Lyn in prison, his wife Helga led a two-pronged mobilization of the organization. One was the thrust into Eastern Europe, open for the first time to our organizing. We greeted the throngs of visitors from the East as they poured across the open border, and sent organizing teams into the East bloc as it opened up—Poland, Czechoslovakia, Russia, Ukraine, everywhere meeting networks of new friends, and finding an extraordinary reception to Lyn's ideas.

The second prong of Helga's leadership was the drive to gain exoneration for Lyn, and all of us who had been prosecuted because of our association with him.

The exoneration fight addressed a crucial reality within the sovereign thought process of every citizen. If Americans did not confront, in their own minds, the fact that the political witch-hunt aimed at the destruction of the LaRouche movement was being carried out *only through the complicity of the citizenry*, then the American people would be unable to act to save their country. As Lyn's forecasts of the impending collapse of the world financial system were borne out, individuals had to be confronted with the fact that those who ran the brainwashing of the population in regard to LaRouche, were precisely the same individuals who were leading the world into economic and political Hell.

Similarly, around the world, even where LaRouche was not known, understanding the LaRouche Railroad was essential to understanding the United States. The fact is, the United States is special among nations. Its Constitution, and its three wars against Britain, established this nation as the unique, concrete expression of the nation-state, consciously and explicitly dedicated to the Renaissance principle that man is born in God's image, with the role of government to foster the creative, cognitive powers of each individual—implicitly including every human being on Earth.

Granted, there appear to be "two Americas" when you consider the many insanities carried out, domestically and internationally, in the name of the United States of America. But this "other America," is nothing but the continuing British subversion of America. Of course, the United States, its government and its people, are certainly not blameless for the evil that has been done in the name of American policy. But, to ascribe ultimate responsibility for such evil to America, is to be utterly blind to the truth. Unless the British policy direction is acknowledged, the world is condemned to be drawn into yet another holocaust in this century, or early in the next, again by the British, but this time on a far more massive scale.

For the people of Europe, Africa, Asia, and Ibero-America, understanding who LaRouche is, and why he is so hated by the oligarchy, is an essential precondition for understanding the nature of the British beast, and the necessity of winning the United States back to the American System, as the only hope for the future of civilization. The fight for the exoneration of LaRouche focusses attention on precisely the most important issues facing the human race: the battle between the American System and the British system; the interconnected battle for a revival of the Renaissance view of man; and the quest for beauty which that entails.

We published a number of pamphlets on the political war against LaRouche, in addition to the full-length book *Railroad!* There was a separate pamphlet reporting on my case, entitled "Treachery! The Soviet-Style Trial and 77-Year Sentence of Michael Billington," which circulated worldwide as part of our exoneration campaign.

Even though the U.S. Appeals Courts refused to review the voluminous evidence of government corruption submitted with our various appeals, the evidence was considered by numerous judicial bodies around the world, including the Human Rights Commission of the United Nations in Geneva, and parliamentary human rights commissions across Europe and Ibero-America. Helga led the fight, meeting with parliamentarians and national leaders on every continent, urging both exoneration and international support for the Productive Triangle proposals for Eurasian development.

Gail, who continued working with the Constitutional Defense Fund, also became one of the foremost organizational spokesmen for exoneration. She travelled to Paris, Mexico, New Delhi, and many places in-between, meeting with parliamentarians, jurists, human rights organizations, religious leaders, and the press. I have kept before me in my cell, next to my print of Rembrandt's "St. Paul in Captivity," a picture of Gail being interviewed in Paris, clearly speaking French (evident from the pucker of her lips). Such meetings and interviews were never simply "human rights" appeals, but in-depth briefings on the history of Lyn's political, scientific, and cultural work. Only such a global strategic briefing could capture the character of the political witch-hunt against us. Gail developed a presentation with slides, showing the mounting hue and cry against LaRouche in the press and from political enemies in the West and in the Soviet Union, in response to his several initiatives. Her meetings never failed to shock people into an internal confrontation with their preconceived ideas about how the United States works. The fact that her husband was serving a 77-year sentence, ostensibly for raising money for the campaigns, never failed to amaze, and usually convinced doubters that the trials were totally political in nature.

Gail became the U.S. representative of "Human Rights Defense Without Borders," established by Moscow City Council Member Victor Kuzin. Victor was one of many leaders of the nationalist movements in Russia and other Eastern European states who joined the Schiller Institute, and fought for Lyn's exoneration. There was a constant flow of foreign statesmen, scientists, economists and others, taking the long trip to Rochester, Minnesota, to visit the famous political prisoner LaRouche. Many of them also came to see me, which was a great honor, and a responsibility I took very seriously.

These were the days of "shock therapy" in Eastern Europe. The IMF, working in tandem with the British-sponsored megaspeculator George Soros, marched East with its demands for immediate, total deregulation and privatization of the decrepit Soviet industrial and financial system.

LaRouche issued scathing attacks on shock therapy, and the "Sachs maniac" from Harvard, Jeffrey Sachs, who was its public champion. The Soviet military-industrial complex represented one of the most valuable concentrations of scientific and technological expertise on Earth, LaRouche argued, which was desperately needed in the reconstruction of the world economy. Shutting it down, claiming that it was not profitable to foreign investors, was clinically insane.

Lyn liked to tell a joke about shock therapy: The communists used to tell their people that capitalists were just thieves; then, one day, they announced that they'd all become capitalists. And, sure enough, they were all thieves! In fact, organized crime took over much of the domestic economy, and the streets, in Moscow and across Russia, with the full faith and backing of the Western powers.

★ ★ ★

I finished my three-year Federal sentence in March 1991, with ten months off for "good time" (which is automatic if an inmate doesn't get into any trouble). On my final day, two Virginia State Police detectives greeted me at the Raybrook prison gate, chained me up, and flew me down to Virginia on a commercial aircraft. Being paraded through several airports in chains, with children gawking, frightened by the obviously "bad man," is a particularly disgusting experience. I ended up at the reception unit at Powhatan Correctional Center, called "The Farm" within the Virginia prison system.

My first day at Powhatan was a particularly memorable one. Arriving at Powhatan the same day was a man named Joe Giarratano, whom I knew, by reputation, as he also knew me. Joe was just arriving from death row, where he had been scheduled to die by electrocution the night before. Only a worldwide mobilization for clemency had convinced Virginia Governor Doug Wilder to commute Joe's death sentence at the last moment. Meeting Joe, on the day after his intended execution, was a deeply emotional experience.

Over the previous year, we had taken an increasingly active role in the effort to end the barbaric policy of judicial murder in the U.S. The ugliest side of the capital punishment frenzy was the public admission, by judges, politicians, and media-molded public opinion, that the sole purpose served by capital punishment was vengeance. The lust for blood must be satisfied, it was argued, in order to achieve something called "closure," a new psycho-babble term from the sociology workshops at Harvard to justify the sin of revenge, and the abandonment of justice. The Supreme Court not only approved of capital punishment, but ruled that procedural issues, such as filing appeals only within a legal time limit, were more important than the truth of guilt or innocence.

Joe Giarratano was intended to be one of the sacrificial victims. Joe had been a barely literate drug addict, who had no memory of the killings for which he had been convicted. There was no credible evidence of his guilt, other than a confession he had made while in a drugged state, which he later retracted. More important, Joe had, while on death row, educated himself on the law and on other matters, and had become a legal expert on the issues of the death penalty. He had personally saved several condemned men from death at the hands of the Commonwealth of Virginia, men who had been denied adequate legal counsel, and would never have been able to prove their innocence, nor expose the illegal measures used to obtain their convictions, without Joe's help. I was delighted to meet this life-saver.

Over the next 18 months, I became increasingly involved in the fight over capital punishment. I shared a lawyer with Giarratano, Gerald Zerkin, a Richmond attorney who represented numerous death row convicts on appeal, and who was a director of The Virginia Capital Resource Center, set up to provide assistance to capital murder defendants. Jerry, who got to know us through our work against judicial tyranny, became the head lawyer for my appeal, with my friend Barbara Boyd taking primary responsibility for research and preparation in coordination with Jerry.

My immediate legal concern at Powhatan was to get bail while I appealed my Virginia conviction. Unlike the Federal courts, which seldom grant appeal bonds, Virginia law grants this right to bail unless there is a danger of flight, or a danger to the community. Not surprisingly, Mary Sue Terry's office tried its best to deny me bail, arguing that I was a threat to society.

Nonetheless, after three weeks of wrangling, Judge Weckstein granted bail, but with extremely stringent conditions. I was permitted to work at EIR's Leesburg office, but not to enter any other office associated with the organization, anywhere in the world. This included the legal office, where my appeal was being prepared! I was not even allowed to raise money for my own legal defense, or for any other purpose whatsoever. I was forbidden to have any association with indicted members of the LaRouche movement—which meant walking around the office and not speaking to my numerous indicted associates.

But such foolishness did not lessen the joy of freedom, a joy shared by thousands of people around the world who had followed my fantastic judicial odyssey. The car ride home through the country with Gail, a steak on the grill with a glass of wine, seeing our four cats, and meeting the two monster dogs Gail had taken on in my absence (Newfoundlands, which look like small, black, shaggy bears)—the first few days of liberty were full of such delights.

18

Temporary Liberty

I stopped by the local barber shop the day after my release—not for a haircut, but to say hello to an old friend, Mr. Lassiter, the town barber. Mr. Lassiter was an institution of his own in Leesburg, having worked for many years at this crucial "intelligence listening post" in the community, while also being active in the Democratic Party. He was an African-American, with many stories to tell, always with passion and humor, about the battles with Jim Crow in this Southern town over the years, and was rightfully proud of his efforts in fighting for racial justice. During my first jail stint—the month in the Leesburg Hilton—I had been treated to one delightful surprise when Mr. Lassiter showed up to cut the inmates' hair, a job he had done for years. We talked for hours while he cut hair, although I was later reprimanded for signing up for a haircut when I didn't need one.

So, in 1991, I stopped to see my old friend as soon as I got out of prison. We slapped hands and chatted for awhile, and he told me he'd been meaning to tell me something. It seems that on Oct. 6, 1986, the day of the raid, a national reporter from one of the networks came into the barber shop with his camera crew, looking for spicy tidbits from local citizens on the "horrible LaRouchies."

"They asked me what I thought about you-all," Mr. Lassiter told me. "I told them, 'Let me tell you a story.' Well, the cameras started rolling, and the reporter looked like the bird who caught the canary. 'A while back, a stranger came to town, with a lot of people who followed him. They were all very dedicated, trying to do some good as they saw it. They thought they could change the world, and told anyone and everyone they could about their new ideas. But the powers that be didn't like that, and came and arrested him. And you know, a lot of the people, who wanted the authorities to know that they'd never do anything like that, gathered around and shouted, "Crucify him, crucify him." ' "

"Well, wouldn't you know, Mr. Billington, the reporter frowned and told the cameraman to turn off the camera, and they scooted right out of the shop. I watched the news that night, and it didn't surprise me in the least that they left me out!"

Mr. Lassiter reached over to the counter behind his barber chair and pulled out a card he'd been keeping right under his instrument box. It was a Christmas card I'd sent him my first year in prison—a Raphael Madonna and Child. Indeed, truth and beauty *are* one.

★ ★ ★

For the next eighteen months, while we waged a losing battle to get the Virginia Appeals Court and Virginia Supreme Court to overturn my conviction (they never even allowed an evidentiary hearing), I went to work in earnest on China. I helped Leni Rubinstein in New York on the publication of our Chinese newsletter, and met with many of our Chinese collaborators, whom Leni and others had organized over the previous two years. One particularly bright young man, Ray Wei, who had met us in Seattle, moved to New York and joined the organization. He had grown up in Sichuan Province, the son of a college professor. Like all students during the Cultural Revolution, his secondary school education had been suspended. With his entire family, he moved to the countryside for several years of farm labor. He was one of the first students to enroll in a university when they reopened in the late 1970's, and he came to the U.S. in 1987 to continue his education.

Ray was atypical among Chinese student and dissident networks, in that he was not only concerned about the crisis in China, but was intrigued by ideas, with a passion to learn everything. We developed a very close relationship, spending hours discussing politics and the history of China and the West. He eventually moved from New York to Leesburg with his new wife, Anna, a Pole, who shared Ray's intellectual enthusiasm, and who has been critical in building the Schiller Institute presence in Poland. When I later returned to prison, Ray remained a close friend and collaborator, by phone and through regular visits.

I toured the West Coast, meeting with our locals in Seattle, the Bay Area, and Los Angeles, and lecturing at forums organized on the regional university campuses. I presented a call to arms, posing Lyn's Eurasian development program, the New Silk Road, as the necessary centerpiece of the only global policy which could reverse the impending explosion of the speculative bubble economy. I compared this campaign to the two previous efforts to build such East-West collaboration: Leibniz and the Jesuit missionaries, in collaboration with the Kang Hsi Emperor at the turn of the 18th Century, whose program, had it been implemented, could have prevented the horrors of European colonialism in Asia; and, secondly, Sun Yat-sen in the early 1900's, whose American System program for Eurasia could have prevented the world wars of this bloody century.

My articles covering China in the EIR and *The New Federalist* were highly critical of the so-called "coastal cities" approach, which had been designed by China's President Zhao Ziyang. Zhao had the support of the "shock therapy" and "post-industrial society" crowd in the West. The Special Economic Zones along the coast were booming, and hot money was flowing in, but, as I warned, the economic base of this cheap-labor/export-industry approach, like the globalization process elsewhere, was a speculative bubble ready to burst. Nonetheless, China had one enormous advantage over the other developing nations subjected to globalization: By retaining strict currency controls, they could protect their economy, bubble and all, from a sudden attack from the speculators, as in fact happened worldwide in 1997.

Following the 1989 Tiananmen Square uprising, Zhao Ziyang was deposed, taking the blame for letting things get out of control. He was threatened with criminal charges which never materialized, but was heralded as a hero by the Democracy Movement and the Western media and NGO apparatus. I tried to counter this glorification of Zhao in an article called "The Real Crimes of Zhao Ziyang." His real crimes, I said, were not his support for democratic reforms, as charged by the government, but his sponsorship of the globalization process, the monetarist push to grant deregulated looting rights to Western speculators, which would eventually destroy China.

The prime example was the infamous George Soros. Zhao had personally arranged for Soros to set up his operations in China. While financing various "democracy" groups, Soros was also sponsoring the education of an elite group of young economists in British monetarist theory, based on the lie that there were only two types of economy: socialist state control of production, or total privatization and free trade; communism or free-trade capitalism. Having thus eliminated from consideration the American System of physical economy, Soros was churning out young Chinese hot-shots, the equivalent of America's yuppies, posing as "democracy advocates," while actually promoting a policy that amounted to a new colonialization of their country through "free trade."

Soros was thrown out of China after 1989, accused of being a foreign spy. Nonetheless, I ran into many of his creations among the Chinese exile community—in fact, the entire Democracy Movement in the West was placed under the financial wing of Soros and his "Human Rights Watch" operation, with help from the government-financed National Endowment for Democracy (NED). The NED, in addition to its work with the Ollie North drugs-for-guns gambit, also spawned thousands of NGO's across the globe as shock troops for the new "Brutish" Empire. Several of our friends among the various Chinese opposition groups confided to me that they had been explicitly warned by the NED that they must cut all ties to the Schiller Institute and must not print any of our articles in their publications, or else they would face an immediate and total cut-off of funding from the U.S. government.

Nevertheless, the Chinese EIR circulated widely, both in the West and in China and Taiwan. My own articles continued warning China of the dangers of globalization, but offered full support for the emerging shift towards large-scale infrastructure development in the interior, rather than pumping money into the free-trade zones along the coast. The decision to proceed with the massive Three Gorges Dam, which would save millions of lives from floods, while providing water for the arid north through a vast system of canals, characterized a strongly positive direction in Chinese policy. I emphasized the necessity of developing Eurasia as a whole, promoting the New Silk Road as an extension of Lyn's Productive Triangle program. Over the coming years, China would assume the leadership for this Grand Design, adopting the New Silk Road, under the name of the Eurasian Land-Bridge, as a central aspect of their national policy. Lyn and Helga were at the center of that process, including Helga's historic presence and presentation at the Beijing "International Symposium on Economic Development of the Regions Along the New Eurasian Continental Bridge," in May 1996.

'Dewey and Russell'

The most fun I had during that year of liberty was putting together a piece for EIR called "The British Role in the Creation of Maoism." I was intent on getting beyond the pabulum pumped out by Western scholars on the roots of the Cultural Revolution. They all totally ignored both the historic cultural conflict between the Confucian and Daoist world views within China, and all questions of Western influence, other than Marxist and related "Leftist" sources. I knew there was a wealth of long-buried historical evidence of British intrigue in China, waiting to be excavated. Finally free to do library research, I burrowed into the archives at the Library of Congress.

LaRouche had often referenced the influence of Bertrand Russell on the young founders of the Chinese Communist Party in the 1920's. Ray Wei told me that the words "Russell and Dewey," referring to Bertrand Russell and John Dewey, were still used as a single term in the Chinese language, synonymous with "Western influence" in China during the volatile era of the May 4th Movement—the years of social upheaval following the post-World War I British sellout of China. The Versailles Treaty totally confirmed Sun Yat-sen's warning, that China would be treated like "fish food" by its erstwhile British ally after the war, rather than being granted independence from the semi-colonial status that dated from the Opium Wars. Into the maelstrom of the May 4th ferment came Bertrand Russell and the American "pragmatist" John Dewey, both spending nearly two years in China during 1920 and 1921. That would be my starting point in search of the roots of the Cultural Revolution.

Soon after the Second Opium War in the late 1850's, the British chose a promising young opium addict, Yan Fu, to mold into their agent among Chinese intellectuals. Brought to London for training in British empiricism, social Darwinism, Malthusianism, and related racist dogma of the Enlightenment, Yen Fu became the translator of the "Western thinkers"—limited, of course, to the British Enlightenment pantheon. Huxley, Spencer, and Mill were soon being read across China, falsely presented as the ideological source of the West's wealth and power. Little or nothing of the Renaissance tradition in Europe was available to a young Chinese intellectual in the late 19th Century; neither were the works of Leibniz, nor the economic and philosophical writings of the American System.

Sun Yat-sen, like his contemporaries in the late 19th Century, read the Yan Fu translations, but he also learned of the cultural history of the American System and the Platonic/Christian tradition through his early education in Hawaii. Sun went to Hawaii to work with his older brother, and had the good fortune to meet up with the Damon family, leading members of the Lincoln-Carey circles from Philadelphia. He received a thorough education in the history of the American System and the continuing conflict with Britain. He also adopted Christianity as his religious faith. He returned to China with a revolutionary passion to save his homeland, which led to the republican revolution in 1911.

That revolution overthrew the Qing Dynasty and established a republic, but it failed to consolidate republican power. Still, at the time of the May 4th Movement, in 1919, the primary worry of the British colonial interests was Sun Yat-sen's threat to unite the country behind republican principles, with possible support from the United States. Top guns were required to combat Sun's influence, and Bertrand Russell and John Dewey fit the bill.

Russell's book, *The Problem of China,* written in 1922, provided me with precisely the evidence I had expected. After all, this was the same Bertrand Russell whose "masterpiece," *Principia*

Mathematica, was the subject of my very first serious philosophical inquiry, when I gleefully shared with Kurt Gödel his devastating exposure of the *Principia* as an absolute fraud. I was certain that Russell's view of China would be coherent with the worldview expressed in the *Principia*'s reduction of the human mind to a fixed, axiomatic structure—i.e., an empiricist British Lord looking for weaknesses in the Chinese mind, under the stress of a century of British drugs, gunships, and looting, in order to further the interests of the British Empire.

Virtually everything that Russell advocated in *The Problem of China*, would eventually be implemented during the Cultural Revolution 45 years later: the repudiation of Confucianism; the turning of father against son and son against father; rejection of all Classical learning and culture; violent opposition to traditional authority; glorification of the peasant (the classic British colonial "noble savage"); rejection of technology in favor of brute-force labor; and on and on.

Russell was a dedicated Aristotelian. He viewed Plato, and Christianity, as hopelessly idealistic for failing to understand the "simple truth" that men, being beasts, would "do as much harm as they dare, and as much good as they must."

Being an Aristotelian, Russell viewed science and reason as purely empirical and mechanical; but, as a *radical* Aristotelian, he feigned *to reject* the empirical and mechanical in favor of existentialist hedonism. Thus, while representing the highest levels of the British intelligence services, he could champion the "noble savage" against the culture of advanced industrial societies—especially those bloody Americans! He praised Chinese society, not for its Confucian tradition, but rather, as if the Chinese were nothing but Daoist nature worshippers: "Instinctive happiness, or joy of life, is one of the most important goods that we have lost through industrialization; its commonness in China is a strong reason for thinking well of Chinese civilization. . . . Progress and efficiency, for example, make no appeal to the Chinese, except to those who have come under Western influence. By valuing progress and efficiency, we have secured power and wealth; by ignoring them, the Chinese, until we brought disturbance, secured on the whole a peaceable existence and a life full of enjoyment."

Naturally, Russell lambasted Confucianism with the same venom found in his attacks on Christianity. His trip to China was arranged by the "Anti-Religion Society," one of the xenophobic predecessors to the Communist Party, with overt British support. The promiscuous Russell was particularly rabid about the Confucian virtue of filial piety, insisting that strong family ties in Chinese society be broken down. He would get his wish in the Cultural Revolution, when children would be coerced into "exposing" their parents, subjecting them to public torture or even death, for such crimes as reading Classical literature.

Russell's purpose was clear, and not even heavily disguised. Although the British officially supported the extremely weak government in Beijing, which actually oversaw a series of nearly autonomous regional warlords, they recognized that the Versailles sell-out could well provoke a revolutionary upsurge. Time-honored British colonial methods were activated to create a Jacobin, radical opposition, counter to Sun Yat-sen's republican movement. Such a radical opposition, while not always easily controlled, was far preferable, in British eyes, to an American System government under Sun Yat-sen and his allies.

Russell brought with him to China a first-hand, glowing account of Bolshevism from his recent stay in Russia, and in his classes he advocated Marxism for China (but not for Britain, of course). It was not communism he admired, but radical empiricism. Marxism was only a useful tool in the cause of Empire.

John Dewey complemented Russell's work. Dewey was the father of so-called "American pragmatism," and of de-schooling—the destruction of Classical education. Practical results, rather than the pursuit of truth, became the objective of education. "Learn through doing" substituted for the rigorous study of the great discoveries of science and the arts.

I expected, and found, that Dewey had launched a movement in China against Classical education, masquerading his de-schooling policies as "Western education." His ideas spawned a series of schools that substituted agricultural labor for school books, and sociological gobbledygook for the classics. The closing of the schools altogether during the Cultural Revolution, with students sent to the countryside to "learn from the peasants," was a direct application of Dewey's methods.

I was far more surprised, however, to find that Dewey, the much-proclaimed scholar from Columbia University, was an unabashed agent for the Morgan banking interests throughout the period of his stay in China! His entire trip was sponsored by the *New Republic* magazine, recently established by Michael Straight, the son of J.P. Morgan's senior partner. Dewey wrote a weekly column for the *New Republic* throughout his stay in China, while he openly promoted the policies of Morgan's official agent in China, Thomas Lamont, who worked directly with the British in controlling China's economy.

All in all, Russell and Dewey, while claiming to represent "Western learning," served to sabotage republican potentials, while creating an irrationalist tendency within the emerging Communist Party, which would occasionally come to the fore, as it did with a vengeance during the Cultural Revolution. This was "The British Role in the Creation of Maoism."

Bush and Ollie

My year of liberty was also an election year, with the Governor of Arkansas, Bill Clinton, winning the Democratic nomination. Lyn ran in the primaries from his prison cell, getting on the ballot in dozens of states, and making several national half-hour television broadcasts. Although the primary victory of a Democratic Southern governor tended to bring up the memory of the disastrous Presidency of Jimmy Carter, and although Clinton had all the problems of the baby-boomer generation, Lyn nevertheless emphasized Clinton's potential strengths, while identifying his weaknesses in a constructive and friendly fashion. In part, this was because Clinton did indeed show some intelligence. But even more importantly, it was because Lyn firmly believed the nation could not survive four more years of George Bush.

Anton Chaitkin and Webster Tarpley authored a book called *George Bush—The Unauthorized Biography*. Besides a detailed history of the leading role played by George's father in financing the rise to power of Adolf Hitler in the 1930's, the book also showed that young George, as a Congressman in the 1970's, had led a campaign to revive Nazi race science, promoting Harvard racist William Shockley on the floor of the U.S. Congress. And, of course, *The Unauthorized Biography* included all of our exclusive documentation of Bush's role as head of the secret government set up under E.O. 12333, including his direct responsibility for the Iran-Contra crimes, and the central role of drug trafficking in the Bush-run Contra scam.

We used the same truth-telling approach a few years later, when Col. Oliver North ran for the Senate in Virginia. Ollie was touted as the lynchpin for the 1994 "Conservative Revolution" takeover of the Congress. But despite the conservative sweep of the elections, he was defeated, entirely because of us. The Democrats, under incumbent Chuck Robb, were waging a totally weak-kneed, defensive campaign; meanwhile, Ollie was receiving massive media coverage, and the entire Pat Robertson machine was out in full swing for him. Sensing the urgency of defeating North, Nancy Spannaus founded the "Committee To Defeat that Son-of-a-Bush." Its first act was to issue a pamphlet entitled "Defeat Ollie North—That Son of a Bush," with a bumper sticker to go with it. The pamphlet exposed Ollie, who was parading around with Pat Robertson as a "family values" man, as one of the biggest drug dealers of modern times, going through the entire Bush/North secret government operation, and more. The pamphlet included a section by me, titled "Ollie North's Role in Putting Me in Prison, and Why He Should Take My Place." I reviewed the history of our War on Drugs, and North's work, with Henry Kissinger and George Bush, in supporting the drug trade, as well as the Barbara Newington story, and Ollie's illegal financial warfare against us.

We campaigned aggressively across the state, *especially* in the Pat Robertson strongholds, with two effects: We confronted Ollie with the truth, which popped his "family values" bubble, and forced him to admit to his fascist policies in service to the financial oligarchy—including especially his intention to eliminate Social Security. And, secondly, we kicked the Democrats into action—even Robb began to go after North's role in the drug trade. One of our members recorded a new version of the song, "Hello Dolly," substituting "Good-bye, Ollie," with all the dope on Ollie's dope business. People loved it, and radio stations picked it up all over the country.

When Ollie was defeated, Democratic Party officials in Virginia and nationally, acknowledged our responsibility, and expressed their appreciation—in private, of course!

March Against Death

My appeal was finally turned down in the Virginia Supreme Court in September 1992, 18 months after my release on bond. I had never expected the appeal to win at the state level—the fix was in too deep in Virginia. My one shot for justice in the courts would be at the Federal level, on Constitutional issues, which required filing a *habeas corpus* appeal, going through the Virginia courts again (another sure loser), and then, finally, reaching the Federal courts, where there was at least a glimmer of hope that the truth would prevail. However, I was not entitled to bond while filing a *habeas corpus* appeal. My lawyer arranged for me to turn myself in to Powhatan Correctional Center on Sept. 28, 1992.

By chance, that date had been scheduled as the beginning of a march from Richmond to Washington, D.C., against the death penalty. The march was organized by the Schiller Institute, with the Rev. Jim Bevel, one of Dr. Martin Luther King's lieutenants (and LaRouche's Vice Presidential running mate in the 1992 election), taking the lead, in collaboration with a number of church organizations, civil rights leaders, and others. It had been provoked by a campaign to legalize the death penalty in the nation's capital, and by a surge in executions around the country, with Virginia only slightly behind Texas as the leading killer. We had gathered all the statistics—that the death penalty does not deter, that many innocent people were on death row, that there was a severe bias due to race and poverty in the imposition of capital punishment, and other well-known facts, which, in a sane environment, would have ended this barbarous practice. However, we knew that no formal arguments would suffice to persuade people to use their common sense, to end judicial killing. It was necessary to directly address the shift in morality, in the underlying assumptions of the citizenry, away from the belief in the sanctity of life.

I know, from eight years in prison with hardened criminals, that every execution, far from deterring a criminal mind from committing murder, pumps up the blood lust, further convincing him that life is cheap, and that taking a life is a legitimate response to perceived offenses, real or imagined.

I was invited to stop on my way to prison at a site just outside Richmond, to address the marchers.

Then, unexpectedly, on the morning preceding my final day of liberty, I was presented with another opportunity to address the question of the death penalty. A few days previously, the government of Peru had succeeded in capturing Abimael Guzmán, the leader of the terrorist *Sendero Luminoso,* the Shining Path. Sendero was unquestionably the most psychopathic of the terrorist institutions on the planet, on a par with the Khmer Rouge of Pol Pot in Cambodia in the 1970's. It was common practice for *Sendero* to enter a village, select out the town leaders, teachers, nurses, and other officials and their families, butcher them before the gathered townspeople, and "enlist" the survivors into their armed forces, or as slaves on their coca plantations and cocaine factories.

It was recognized in Peru, and across Ibero-America, that we were in the forefront of the fight against narco-terrorism, and in exposing the ideological roots and political controls over the narco-terrorists headquartered in London and Paris. After Guzmán's capture, our Lima organization called a press conference to congratulate the government, and to emphasize the importance of this in the context of the unfolding world crisis. Members in Lima asked me to address the press conference by speaker phone.

My trial, as one of the LaRouche cases, and in light of my role in the fight against narco-terrorism, had been watched closely in Peru. It was known that the trial had particularly targetted my connection to the very famous book *Narcotráfico S.A.,* which had circulated widely in Peru, and even had been serialized in a leading newspaper. The Peruvians were extremely angry that the Bush Administration, rather than supporting President Fujimori's emergency measures to crush the narco-terrorists, had *denounced* him for abridging the "human rights" of the killers and drug dealers. Many Peruvians saw my case, and my outrageous sentence, as further evidence that the Bush Administration was, in fact, supporting narco-terrorism.

To our surprise, nearly the entire Peruvian press corps showed up, including even some of our worst enemies! Rather than the expected brief statement, and perhaps a few questions about my case, I was asked a series of extremely serious questions about the roots of narco-terrorism and the connection to the global financial crisis.

One of the most impassioned questions asked, was if I believed Guzmán should be put to death. I had not been briefed that this was a burning issue within the Peruvian government leadership. There were no provisions for the death penalty in Peru, except under certain conditions of active military conflict. Some leaders, including some of our friends, believed Guzmán should be treated under these military codes and put to death. Unaware of this, I responded: "Don't undermine your political and moral victory over these psychopaths, and their controllers in London, by treating life as cheaply as they do. He's been captured—put him on trial, expose his crimes, root out his sponsors at the highest levels, but don't participate in ritual murder." I told them about the march against the death penalty scheduled for the following day. I learned later that my answer had provoked some controversy—and that some of our own members had been, perhaps, less clear-sighted or firm on this question than I. I was glad to have had the opportunity to intervene.

On my final day, Gail and I, with another friend, drove down to Richmond, meeting the marchers at a rally site outside the city. The marchers had signs against the death penalty, including: "Tell Bloody Mary Sue To Put On Her Hood And Robe." Reverend Bevel made the point that Virginia Attorney General Mary Sue Terry had killed more defenseless black men than the Ku Klux Klan. There were also signs which read "Free Mike Billington." Speaking on a portable amplifier, I talked about Martin Luther King, Abraham Lincoln, and the Founding Fathers, as some of those who were there with the marchers in spirit, and that the fight against the death penalty went to the root of the moral decay of the nation. I reviewed the farce of my trial, and the outrageous sentence. I continued: "It is not just a sentence against me. It is a sentence against you, and each and every citizen in this nation, and around the world, who refuses to compromise. This sentence is a threat. The threat says that any of my associates, or anyone who may decide to become one of our associates, or anyone who fights against tyranny, is going to be threatened with the same treatment. The thinking is, that this will terrorize people into backing out. I was particularly targetted because I refused to accept a plea bargain. They told me that if I were to confess guilt to a crime I did not commit, if I would just say, 'Yes, I did it,' then they would relieve me of this prison sentence—any prison sentence at all. In other words, I was told that I could win my freedom, so-called, if I would lie before the court, before the nation, before the world, before God—lie, and say that this fight is a fraud.

"So, I refused to accept that form of freedom, which would have been, in fact, my submission to slavery, to tyranny, for the rest of my life. I chose instead to be truly free, despite the fact that these barbarians intend to keep me in captivity, possibly for the rest of my life. But my freedom will not be lost, my soul will not be sold to this kind of tyranny. That is not what the purpose of my life has been, that is not what I have done with my life, and it is not what I *will* do with it.

"I want to point out that this kind of plea bargain is offered to every one of you, to each citizen of our nation and the world, day after day, by the growing police-state apparatus, by this corrupt judicial system. Not only for those who are prosecuted, but for the average citizens, who are told that even though the world is decaying, even though your children are coming home doped up, even though they have adopted some new sex, even though your parents are suddenly thrown out of work, even though they are still killing our children, you should close your eyes, look the other way, and perhaps you can make it. Perhaps if you ignore what's happening to you and your children, or other people's children, or other nations' children, then they will let you get by. But if you don't agree to the plea bargain, you, too, will get 77 years, or get on the list for death row.

"I will be with you—not on the march *per se,* but I can assure you that I will be spending my years with all my heart and mind, contributing to this fight, and making sure we win, whether or not I get free myself. Each of us must make that contribution. Whatever the physical circumstances, what is called for at this moment in the world is to fight for the truth, no matter what the consequences to our personal well-being."

We left the marchers and drove off to "The Farm," Powhatan Correctional Center. Time was suspended for a moment, while

Gail and I shared a tearful last embrace, and I signalled the guards to let me in. "I'd like a room at the top, please, with a view," I said with a smile. "I think I may be enjoying your facilities for some time."

Later, a guard stopped by my cell. "Everyone's talking about you," he said. "Seventy-seven years, and he drives up, kisses his wife good-bye, and checks in. Amazing."

[19]

Discovery

Ironically, my next five months—spent crammed into the crumbling, red brick receiving unit at "The Farm," with several hundred other newly condemned prisoners—were to be the most intellectually explosive days of my life.

★ ★ ★

Conditions at the receiving unit were dreadful. Each cell block held about 50 men, confined in double cells along a ten-foot-wide hallway which served as a day room, with a TV blaring constantly. But I was as if in another world. I closed myself off in my cell, day and night, reading and writing. I slept in short stretches during the day, springing into action when the TV went off at 11:00 p.m. There were no desks in the cells, and only a bare light bulb over the sink, but my various cell mates were uncomplaining about my sitting up all night, on the single plastic chair, my feet propped up on the commode.

My task was to figure out the Renaissance—not the 15th-Century Golden Renaissance in Europe, but the Confucian Renaissance in the 11th- and 12th-Century Song Dynasty. Following Leibniz, my hypothesis was that China's vast population, the huge, efficiently run cities, and the rich cultural and scientific heritage—generally more advanced than that of Europe before the European Renaissance—proved that there was embedded in

China's philosophical traditions a knowledge of the most profound truths concerning man and nature. The Song Renaissance, which spurred a great leap in both art and science, and a burst in population growth, was the necessary starting point of my investigation.

I had read a great deal *about* the Song Dynasty, and the so-called Neo-Confucians centered around Chu Hsi (written "Zhu Xi" in the Pinyin system used today in China), but as I had learned by studying Western history, to depend upon the interpretations and distortions of the accepted authorities of modern scholarship, was to guarantee remaining ignorant. Only by reading the original works of the greatest thinkers, confronting in one's own mind the conflicts and potentials of the age, the actions and arguments of the oligarchy to suppress change, and the process of discovery in the minds of these scientists, artists, and statesmen, was it possible to *know* those discoveries.

I was armed for the battle. Before turning myself in, I had photocopied every available English translation of Chu Hsi and his many Song Dynasty predecessors and collaborators. I also had translations of Wang Yang Ming and his followers, who were also called "Neo-Confucians" during the Ming Dynasty, 400 years after Chu Hsi. Gail mailed this material to me in pieces, along with my Chinese language material.

I was faced with one severe constraint: my relative ignorance of the Chinese language. A dependence on translators is potentially just as misleading as reading textbooks. I obtained multiple translations whenever possible, and used my rudimentary Chinese to study the philological debates over crucial terms and passages. Ray Wei helped me as much as he could by phone, going over difficult passages in Chinese, and discussing the various interpretations.

Among Lyn's outpouring of political and philosophical writing in prison, were several studies known as the "Metaphor" series. These essays demonstrated the epistemological coherence of the creative process common to every discipline of thought: music, poetry, physical science, theology, philosophy, history, and physical economy. I drew heavily on these works as I probed the disparate elements of Song Renaissance thought, and the Song studies of the Confucian classics. I discovered that Chu Hsi (especially) used words in entirely new ways, applying new fundamental concepts to old terms, which he conveyed not by definitions, but through a series of metaphors which reached deep into the soul of the reader. I had found a new friend.

I was blessed with another valuable aid in my work. Will Wertz, my friend and co-defendant in the Federal trial, had spent much of his time in prison on an intensive study of Nicolaus of Cusa, including original translations of several of his works. We published a book of these translations, called *Toward A New Council of Florence: "On the Peace of Faith" and Other Works by Nicolaus of Cusa*, with an introductory essay by Will on Cusa's method. That book became my constant companion during those months of discovery, as I searched through the minds of Chinese statesmen and scholars of the 11th and 12th Centuries. Cusa's work in theology, science, and statecraft were a single, seamless tapestry which marked the contours of the unfolding Golden Renaissance. He had striven to create unity among men and nations, based not on the lowest common denominator of popular beliefs and customs, but on the highest level of man's common identity in the image of the living God, through the power of reason.

Although I had read several works of Cusa in the past, I had found them to be extremely difficult, and had achieved at best a superficial understanding. But, faced with the task of discovering the roots of China's civilization—knowing both that this was a crucial and urgent task for the crisis ahead, and that the textbook accounts would almost certainly be more of a hindrance than a guide—there was awakened in me a passionate desire to master the thought of Cusa, as also that of Chu Hsi. It was clear to me that they had faced very similar kinds of historical crises, within their otherwise very different cultural situations, and that both were reaching back to a Classical era of antiquity to find inspiration for the new discoveries required of mankind in their own lifetimes.

I took as a starting point a brilliant dialogue by Cusa, called "De Pace Fidei" ("On the Peace of Faith"). It is a dialogue between representatives of all the major faiths and cultures known to Cusa: Christian, Muslim, Jew, Buddhist, Persian, Indian, Chaldean, and others. Like Leibniz 250 years later, Cusa knew that the progress of civilization depended upon the increasing mastery of certain fundamental laws of man and nature, and that therefore, any culture which had provided for the successful sustenance and progress of some sub-set of the human family, must have embedded within it some expression of those truths. Since Cusa did not know Confucianism, he did not include it in the essay. I decided to extend the ecumenical effort of Nicolaus of Cusa to embrace the culture of China.

Ren and *Li*

Chu Hsi, like Confucius and Mencius, recognized *ren* as the guiding principle of the universe. The problem of translating *ren* into European languages was not simply a problem of translation, but a reflection of the enormous divergence of views within China on the meaning of *ren*. The term was used by Confucians throughout the ages, but also by Buddhists, and even Daoists, and it had come to mean many different things to different people. Just as Dr. Martin Luther King, in his letters from the Birmingham jail, drew a sharp distinction between *agapē* and lesser notions of love, and *eros*, so also did Chu Hsi, in his "Treatise on *Ren*," insist that *ren* cannot be viewed as simply "love," but as the *principle* of love, the *source* of love. Human love and compassion are the *effect of ren*, not its substance, he said. The closest he comes to defining the term is a beautiful metaphor: "The mind of Heaven to produce is *ren*. In man's endowment, he receives this mind from Heaven, and thus he can be productive." This clearly mirrors the Christian *capax dei*, that man is uniquely capable by his nature of participating in the unfolding of creation.

Chu Hsi not only renewed the teachings of Confucius and Mencius, but opened up entirely new areas of conceptual knowledge. The problem, as perceived by Chu Hsi in the 12th Century, was that China had experienced general stagnation for more than a millennium, with some brief exceptions, since the death of Mencius in 289 B.C.! During the Third Century B.C., one of the several states of China, the Qin, became the center of a fiercely anti-Confucian ideology known as Legalism, a combination of Sparta-like authority ruling over a slave society, mixed with the promotion of mystical Daoism for the pacification of the masses. When the Qin defeated its neighboring states in 221 B.C., creating a unified China under a single Emperor, the Confucian texts were burned, many Confucian scholars were buried alive, and the population was enslaved to work on grandiose projects such as the construction of the Great Wall. This tyrant Emperor, Qin Shi Huang, was the model ruler emulated by Mao and the Gang of Four during the Great Proletarian Cultural Revolution.

The Qin Dynasty collapsed on itself after only 15 years, giving way to the four centuries of the Han Dynasty. Confucianism was revived, but, Chu Hsi argued, it was not the true teachings of Confucius and Mencius, but a synthetic version of pseudo-Confucianism, mixed with Legalist and Daoist doctrine. In fact, the key, earlier "Confucian" followed by the Han Scholars was a man I came to call China's Aristotle: *Hsun Tze* (Xun Zi in Pinyin). Hsun Tze, who lived in the Third Century B.C., just after Mencius, declared himself a Confucian, but directly challenged several of the most crucial concepts in Confucianism. In fact, throughout history, every Chinese child has learned the arguments of the conflict between Hsun Tze and Mencius over the nature of man. Mencius, like Plato, viewed man as fundamentally good, born with the unique gift from Heaven of *ren* (Plato's *agapē*), which blessed each child with the potential for creative achievements, no matter what position he may have in society. Hsun Tze, however, like Aristotle, viewed man as naturally evil, willing to do anything to satisfy his bestial desires. The role of society, then, is to suppress man's natural desires, which are inherently evil. Hsun Tze, although claiming to be merely a separate track of Confucianism from Mencius, was the teacher of the founders of Legalism, who in turn, based their tyranny on the premises of Hsun Tze's world view. Man, as a beast, must be tamed through strict punishment and reward, by rulers whose right to rule is established entirely by force of arms.

The idea of "propriety" (sometimes called the "rites") in the works of Confucius and Mencius, referred to the proper ordering of society according to the *ren* of Heaven and Earth, allowing each individual to direct his or her life towards a positive connection to the universal. Hsun Tze, however, transformed propriety into strict rules of conduct—not natural law concepts such as the Golden Rule (which was prominent in Confucius' teachings), but detailed, ritualistic laws which, if broken, must provoke punishment by omnipotent rulers.

With the dominance of Hsun Tze's ideas during the Han Dynasty, Confucianism dissipated, while Daoism flourished and Buddhism was introduced from northern India. Buddhism and Daoism mixed to generate a hybrid called Ch'an, which we in the West call Zen today, from the Japanese. Chu Hsi saw his task, and that of the Song Dynasty, to free man from the illusions of Daoism and Buddhism, and, through education and a Confucian renaissance, to unleash the scientific and artistic powers of Chinese civilization.

One formidable task for Chu Hsi was to answer Daoist and Buddhist metaphysics. It was true that both Confucius and Mencius had only indirectly addressed most metaphysical questions, including those regarding the nature of the physical universe, matter and substance, and those regarding the nature of man's soul. Into that void, mystical conceptions from Daoism and Buddhism, such as reincarnation, or the denial of the soul in favor of an amorphous "unity of all things," became the basis of the proliferation of numerous irrational cults. Chu Hsi therefore took on the central metaphysical problems addressed by Daoism and Buddhism, answering them within the context of Confucian rationalism and *ren*. The most important of the concepts addressed in this way was *li*, often translated as *principle*. In fact, the philosophical worldview of Chu Hsi and his associates became known as the *School of Li*.

Leibniz, in his study of Chu Hsi, saw the idea of *li* as very similar to that of the Christian God, as the first principle. Leibniz's work on China came at the time of a raging battle within the Catholic Church known as the Rites Controversy, over whether or not Confucianism was compatible with Christian belief. This was not some an arcane theological debate amongst ivory tower philosophers. As Leibniz recognized, these Confucian concepts had been the key to the Chinese success in constructing an advanced scientific and cultural civilization, and the unique basis upon which the Grand Design for global development could be achieved.

As I worked through the writings of Chu Hsi and his associates, the hypothesis filled out, and took on a living, vibrant form of its own. Here, in Chu Hsi's notion of *li,* was the Idea of Plato, the Monad of Leibniz, but discovered in a different context. To

Chu Hsi, *li* was the true substance of the universe, while each and every created thing had its own particular *li*, its own principle, or Idea. To *know* something about anything, whether organic or inorganic, cognitive or non-cognitive, required discovering how it developed and how it changes in regard to everything else, and thus, how it reflects the universe as a whole. In that way, each individual participates in the universal *li*. This is, in its essence, the scientific method of Plato, and of every great scientist throughout history, which Leibniz called *analysis situs*.

Chu Hsi also recognized, like Cusa and Leibniz after him, that there is no human knowledge outside of the process of discovery within an individual human mind, and, in particular, a human mind which is impassioned by *ren*—the love of truth. This, in turn, gave further meaning to the works of Mencius, who had insisted that *ren* was the greatest of the four fundamental virtues (the others being righteousness, propriety, and knowledge), and subsumed the other three. Chu Hsi argued that man, through *ren*, and through Heaven's gift of reason, is uniquely capable of *perfecting* his *li*, to bring it increasingly more in accord with the universal *li* of Heaven.

To see how beautifully Chu Hsi's ideas confirm St. Paul's insight, that the truth is written in the hearts of all mankind, let me review here, as I did in my Powhatan prison cell, Nicolaus of Cusa's "On the Peace of Faith."

Cusa's scientific work, which laid the groundwork for the scientific advances of the Renaissance, was predicated on his development of St. Augustine's conception of the Trinity. Since he perceived the Trinity to be the highest expression of universal truth and of man's unique capacity to know the truth, he therefore set about to demonstrate that every sincere quest for truth, and therefore every true religion, would necessarily discover a "natural law" expression of the Trinity. For Cusa, the Trinity of God the Father, God the Son, and God the Holy Spirit, is embedded in the Creation itself in the form of three concepts: Unity, Equality, and Connection. The Trinity is therefore inherent in any form of knowledge of the One God.

To quote from my article, "Toward the Ecumenical Unity of East and West: The Renaissance of Confucian China and Christian

Europe,"* which first appeared in the Summer 1993 issue of *Fidelio* magazine:

"By *unity* is meant the One and the Many co-existing in God; that the One God is the cause of every thing singular, while every actual thing is singular in its essence precisely as it is a reflection of God's creation. This is God the Father. It should be clear that to the Neo-Confucians this is a description of Universal Principle (*li*), which is the One God, and which exists in each created thing as its nature.

"By *equality* is meant the unique capacity of man in his purest, God-given nature, in the living image of God, and through the intellect, to examine and discover the similitude of all things to the Creator. For Christians, God the Son represents perfect *equality* with God, while through the imitation of Christ, every man can be one with Him. For the Neo-Confucians, this describes man's 'innate luminous virtue,' the particular Principle (*li*) in each man, through which, if kept unobscured and nourished through the sincere *investigations of the principle in things*, can make it possible to walk in the Path of God (Dao).

"By *connection*, Cusa meant precisely that divine love which flows from the Unity of God, connecting Him directly with His creation through their Equality, or similitude, with God. This capacity to love is what defines man as being in the living image of God. To Christians, this is the Holy Spirit, St. Paul's *agapē*, which proceeds from the Father and from the Son. To Confucians, this is *ren*, the boundless love of Heaven and Earth."

Here, then, was the Confucian "Trinity," which lawfully, was the source of the greatest era of scientific, artistic, and demographic growth in Chinese history, just as the discoveries of Cusa unleashed the Golden Renaissance in Europe.

I was incredibly excited throughout those months at Powhatan, nearly oblivious to the unhappy people around me. As the picture unfolded before my mind's eye, I knew that I was breaking new ground of a crucial nature for the future, not because I had discovered some unknown historical fact, but because I had

* See Appendix I, p. 349.

applied a superior method—a method sadly lost over the past century—to the investigation. I also knew that I *knew* what Chu Hsi had discovered, although there was much I'd never read, and many parts I understood only incompletely. But, by reliving his discoveries, in the historical context of the universal history of that age, there was no question in my mind of what Chu Hsi was telling me. This was not mere opinion, even though nearly all the contemporary "China scholars" disagreed with me entirely!

My work provoked a healthy spirit of investigation of Chinese culture within the organization and among our networks. Most of my longer articles were translated into German, French, and Spanish, and a few into Chinese. In 1993, I wrote another *Fidelio* article, "The European Enlightenment and the Middle Kingdom," which compared the Enlightment in Europe to the Aristotelian Wang Yang Ming movement in China—both aimed at destroying their respective Platonic and Confucian Renaissance traditions. In 1994, I wrote "The Taoist (Daoist) Perversion of 20th-Century Science," which was published in *Fidelio* together with LaRouche's "How Bertrand Russell Became an Evil Man." I investigated the degeneracy in 20th-Century science following the 1927 Solvay Conference, when the Platonic school of science, led by Max Planck, Erwin Schrödinger, and others, was defeated by the radical Aristotelians, led by Danish physicist Niels Bohr. Bohr introduced a worldview of indeterminacy and non-intelligibility into microphysics, claiming that fundamental processes occurred without causality, but, at best, according to random probability statistics. This provoked Einstein to protest: "God doesn't play dice."

I discovered that Bohr, and even more so his associate Wolfgang Pauli, were committed Daoists, showing once again the coherence of epistemology, East and West! The Chinese were intrigued by my article about these connections. A semi-official journal in Beijing, which had previously published LaRouche's work on the development of China and Eurasia, translated and published the article. I had included in the piece my usual denunciation of the so-called "Three Religions"—the attempt to impose on all Chinese the acceptance of a syncretic amalgam of Confucianism, Buddhism, and Daoism as "Chinese thought." This (actually Daoist) conception, that everyone can believe everything at once, is not unique to China; it is precisely the same "moral relativism" peddled by the Enlightenment and by the post-1960's cultural morass today.

My attack provoked a virulent response from a leading scholar at the Beijing Library, who protested to the Chinese journal that Mr. Billington clearly knew nothing about China, or he would know that the Three Religions are accepted by everyone—which is not true, but his saying so proved my point. The scholar was even more upset by my denunciation of London's leading China scholar over the past 50 years, Joseph Needham. Needham, a close associate of Julian Huxley and Bertrand Russell, had throughout his career as a leading British intelligence operative, posed as a friend of China, even during the darkest days of the Cultural Revolution. He continued Russell's portrayal of "Western" science as limited to British empiricism, and claimed that Chinese science and culture had been retarded by the dominance of Confucianism, while praising the Daoists and alchemists as the true scientists! The Beijing Library scholar expressed outrage that I would speak badly of this great man. I was delighted to have provoked a healthy controversy.

Since the beginning of the reform under Deng Xiaoping, there has been a renewed interest and study in China of Confucius and the Confucian tradition. Hopefully, my work will contribute to that process. We need to build not only a physical Land-Bridge, but a cultural bridge, between a renewed Confucianism in China, and a renewed Classical culture in the West. In the words of our close friend, Beijing University professor Zhang Yushu: "A Renaissance will indeed begin; however, not the Renaissance of Chinese culture in the sense of China centrism, but a cultural and moral Renaissance for mankind, in which Europe and Asia alike contribute a great deal, and from which both cultural areas will equally profit."

[20]

'By Michael and Gail Billington'

While all the legal appeals were being prepared and presented, the real fight for our freedom was taking place outside of the courtrooms. Our organizing focussed on the necessity of overturning the Railroad, and exposing the crimes of the prosecutors, as prerequisite to achieving the economic and political tasks required to meet the world crisis. Privately, beginning in 1993, after President Clinton's inauguration, Helga and others organized thousands of letters from prominent citizens from every part of the world, to both the President and to the parole board, calling for Lyn to be given the earliest possible parole. His first eligibility for parole came in January 1994, after five years (one-third of his 15-year sentence) in prison. Although the letters remained confidential, they came from Presidents and parliamentarians, church leaders, military officials, labor leaders, civil rights leaders, and many others. The mobilization succeeded, and Lyn was granted first parole in 1994.

The impact of Lyn's freedom can not be overstated. Besides his direct input to the intelligence work, he also began regular visits (although partially restrained by his parole conditions) to Russia, Eastern Europe, and the Mideast. In Russia, especially, he addressed seminars organized by leading scientists and economists, and was made a fellow of the Moscow-based Universal Ecological Academy, a critical body of intellectuals formulating policy to save Russia from the collapse brought on by "Shock Therapy."

Several of these scientists and academicians developed strong ties to Lyn and Helga, and our influence in Russia spread rapidly. In 1998, when Russia finally declared a moratorium on its debt and took measures to reassert sovereignty from the IMF and Western speculators, a number of these leading nationalists were brought into government service. One of the most striking examples was Dmitri Lvov, the head of the economics branch of the Russian Academy of Sciences, who became a top advisor to the Prime Minister. The previous year, on the occasion of Lyn's 75th birthday, Academician Lvov had written in a Festschrift for Lyn: "Your school of physical economy is 'the ray of light in the kingdom of darkness' of monetarism. . . . I propose to consider your birthday to be the day of the rebirth of economic science, and to celebrate it in all countries."

★ ★ ★

In 1996, when I lost my *habeas corpus* hearing before Judge Williams (the decision described in the Preface), I had reached the end of the road in the appeals process, except for the unlikely possibility that the U.S. Supreme Court would hear the case. We submitted an appeal to the Supreme Court, arguing that Judge Williams's ruling that my political beliefs justified denying me my Constitutional rights, warranted reversal by the nation's highest court. Judge Rehnquist, not surprisingly, did not agree.

With the legal battles finished, Gail again picked up her old role as a Southeast Asia analyst for EIR.

Our intelligence work had been limited in Southeast Asia over the years of Lyn's incarceration, and Gail was now essentially on her own. She renewed her contacts in the Philippines from the 1980's, who had continued to follow EIR closely over the years. And, she recruited a collaborator—me.

The organization's work in China had expanded dramatically in 1995, as our New Silk Road proposals led to direct collaboration with leading circles within that country. Our European office committed more time to Chinese operational intelligence, relieving me of that aspect of my work. So, while I continued my Chinese historical and philosophical studies, I began to do background research and operational intelligence on the Southeast Asian nations, as Gail was establishing diplomatic contacts across the region. When asked to make a brief statement to an NCLC conference in 1998 concerning my work in prison, I explained that my wife had discovered a source of cheap prison labor, such that every time I called her she loaded me up with new assignments, so that I barely had time to stand for count!

The timing of our initiative in Southeast Asia was crucial. In the early 1990's, the globalization process was unleashed with a vengeance in the nations of ASEAN (Association of Southeast Asian Nations), and especially in Thailand, Malaysia, Indonesia, and the Philippines. Several governments were persuaded to set up offshore banking facilities, allowing foreign banks to speculate with virtually no regulation. Hot money poured in, but it was nearly all short term, flowing into real estate and stock market speculation, or cheap-labor industries, processing imported materials for re-export. There was a boom across the region, but it was a bubble ready to burst.

Until late 1994, the IMF had used Mexico as the model to be followed by all Third World countries. The IMF recipe went something like this: "Slash your budget, scrap all your infrastructure projects (major infrastructure projects were typically described as "boondoggles" run by corrupt "cronies" of the political leadership), privatize your state industries and banks, allow foreigners unrestricted take-over privileges—and you, too, can prosper, like Mexico!"

Then, in December 1994, the Mexican bubble burst. As the Mexican economy and living standards plummetted, the IMF quickly changed its tune. Now, the model was the "Tiger Economies" of Southeast Asia! Wherever we went, in Russia, Poland, Africa, South America, we were told that the international financial institutions were pushing the Asian Tiger model. Many of our friends were vulnerable to this fraud, since Asia appeared to be booming.

We warned that the Asian Tigers were about to head "down Mexico way." This was not entirely the responsibility of the ASEAN leaders, who had achieved extraordinary success in building up their economies in the years since winning their independence. In the 1990's, however, they had generally fallen prey to the lie that globalization was the only game in town.

I studied the history of the region, and Gail and I worked together on a series of EIR articles profiling the nation-building efforts in each country, and the IMF policies which undermined that effort. Most of the ASEAN leaders still had a living memory of 19th-Century colonialism, which ended only 30-40 years ago. In the case of Indonesia and Vietnam, liberation came only after bloody wars of independence. The articles by the Billington team showed our friendship and support for these nationalist governments, but bluntly criticized the monetarist "technocrats" within their ranks, and warned in the harshest terms that the "Asian Tiger model" was a dangerous fraud, a bubble ready to burst at any moment, which the financial oligarchy could *choose* to burst whenever it served its purposes.

No other economist or agency in the entire world, to my knowledge, concurred with LaRouche's prognosis of the "Asian miracle," but we insisted that Lyn's method and analysis would be borne out, sooner rather than later, as the globalization scam neared terminal implosion.

Our work became highly respected among the political leadership throughout Southeast Asia. Gail established close ties with both diplomats and other political layers, through meetings in Washington and in the course of several trips through the region. We presented the Land-Bridge proposal as the necessary centerpiece of a new world economic order, with Southeast Asia on the "Southern Route": from China, through Southeast Asia, India and Central Asia into Europe and Africa. Even the South China Sea, we argued, must be conceived of as an "Asian Lake," uniting the islands of Indonesia and the Philippines with the Asian mainland. These ideas were most welcome, and influenced the regional development policies which emerged from meetings among the Asian neighbors. Political leaderships deeply appreciated our exposure of the oligarchical roots of the rapidly proliferating environmentalist and human rights NGO's, which functioned as shock-troops for the IMF assault on their national sovereignty. However, they all steadfastly refused to accept our forecast of doom for the "Asian miracle."

Myanmar

The Billington team took on one of the most blatant cases of British attempts at "re-colonization"—that of Myanmar, previously known as Burma. As is well known, Burma was, and remains, the heart of the Golden Triangle, the source of much of the world's opium and heroin supply. The British, the UN, and the Bush boys at the National Endowment for Democracy (which Ollie North and his cocaine traffickers called "Project Democracy"), in collaboration with mega-speculator George Soros, mounted a massive international campaign to take control of Myanmar—a classic Dope, Inc. operation. Gail and I set about to stop it.

During and after World War II, Louis Mountbatten, the uncle of Prince Philip, was in charge of the campaign to recover the British colonies in Asia. His most formidable opponent was not Japan, but the U.S. under President Franklin Roosevelt, who was dedicated to ending European colonialism forever. FDR's vision for the post-war era did not survive his death in April 1945, but, nonetheless, the British knew that America's new strength in world affairs would not allow the maintenance of colonialism in the old form.*

Lord Mountbatten, therefore, orchestrated the bloody communal and religious riots in India, using traditional British methods of divide and conquer, to ensure that an independent India would be divided and weak.

Burma had been administered from British India throughout most of its century-long colonial history. The British had introduced opium production into the lush northern hill country, adding it to their Indian opium supplies for sale around the world. London did not want to lose control of this drug source, but it was no longer possible to run Dope, Inc. so openly. So, Mountbatten decided to grant Burma independence without a fight, but, meanwhile, the various ethnic and tribal groupings in the country, especially those in the Golden Triangle area, were cultivated by British intelligence to claim "independence" for their opium-

* In 1999, I wrote an article for EIR, drawing on my ten years of research on East and Southeast Asia, demonstrating that the "Cold War" was not primarily a war against communism, but a British-instigated cover for destroying the remaining influence of FDR and the American System, while reimposing a modified version of European colonialsim across the globe. Excerpts of this article appear in Appendix II, p. 393.

growing districts. The Burmese government was unable to gain significant control over the northern hills, and for the next 50 years the region remained virtually ungoverned—except by Dope, Inc.!

In the 1960's, Burma fell into a xenophobic seclusion known as the "Burmese way to socialism." A military dictatorship under General Ne Win broke almost all foreign ties, and Burma stagnated for about 25 years, while the rest of Southeast Asia moved forward. This was perfect for the British interests running the Golden Triangle. The flourishing drug production had little, if anything, to do with General Ne Win. British intelligence, the CIA, nationalist Chinese, communist insurgents backed by Beijing—nearly anyone willing to fight over drug routes—had a free hand in the region, with the indigenous tribes generally used as cannon fodder in ethnic armies or as opium farmers. The Burmese Army had almost no presence in the area whatsoever.

In the late 1980's, as a younger generation of military leaders came to the fore, Ne Win was forced to loosen the reins of power a bit, and to open up to the outside world. A combination of economic backwardness and pent-up frustration fueled mass demonstrations across the country in 1988, which turned extremely violent. The young turks in the military put down the riots, shoved Ne Win politely aside, changed the country's name to Myanmar, and set up a nationalist military junta (with the English-language acronym SLORC), committed to opening up the economy to modernization with foreign help, and to uniting the country through peace negotiations with the ethnic and tribal warlords, taking control over the northern hills for the first time in Burma's history.

The British were terrified that they might lose control of their precious drug supply, as well as their convenient leverage point on the Chinese border. They put their international human rights mafia into high gear, portraying SLORC as the world's worst tyrants and drug dealers. U.S. Drug Enforcement Administration (DEA) officials, on the other hand, reported that SLORC was dead serious about shutting down the world's biggest source of opium and heroin, and deserved U.S. support. Margaret Thatcher's faithful puppy dog, George Bush, ignored his own DEA, and withdrew U.S. support for Myanmar's anti-drug campaign!

Placed in charge of the NGO assault on Myanmar was none other than George Soros, the world's leading financial backer of drug legalization. He also financed Human Rights Watch, a group of NGO's used to undermine any Third World country which resisted IMF dictates, or was otherwise targetted for destabilization by the financial oligarchy.

Soros set up a group of new NGO's, centered around the "Burma Project," to run propaganda and finance insurgents. He worked closely with the Bush boys in the International Republican Institute (IRI), the Republican Party wing of Project Democracy, who openly bragged of their support for insurgents in the border regions.

The target was not just Myanmar, nor even just the drugs. Myanmar was a crucial crossroads for the southern route of the Land-Bridge, linking Southeast Asia with the Indian subcontinent, and as a bridge from China to the Indian Ocean. The British were particularly unhappy that ASEAN was planning to bring Myanmar into the association in 1997, along with Cambodia and Laos, which would complete the unification of the Southeast Asian nations.

An even more important target of the Myanmar destabilization was China. China had long since ended support for communist insurgency movements in Southeast Asia, and in the 1990's became a crucial source of support for Southeast Asian peace and development. Beijing's ties to Myanmar were particularly important, because the Golden Triangle, sitting on China's southern border, was the source of an exploding drug problem within China itself.

The NGO's running the destabilization of Myanmar were precisely the same networks which were targetting China. Soros, in particular, had it in for China, which had unceremoniously thrown him out of the country after 1989 (although they misidentified him as a "CIA agent," rather than the British agent that he is). The front person for the destabilization in Myanmar was Aung San Suu Kyi, the daughter of the leader of Burma's independence movement, Aung San. After her father was murdered by the British in 1947, Suu Kyi was taken to India and then to London, and educated by the elite of the British Foreign Office and Asian intelligence hands at Cambridge. She married a protégé of Hugh

Richardson, the old man of British intelligence in Tibet. After 40 years in England, Suu Kyi went back to Burma at the peak of the 1988 instability, and was transformed into the "hero of democracy," British-style.

Gail and I wrote articles in EIR on Myanmar, focussing on the British gameplan of insurgency against the central government. We were trying to reach an audience both in the ASEAN nations, who needed to persevere in their policy of "constructive engagement" with Myanmar, and in the Clinton Administration. Clinton was increasingly taking a sane and constructive approach towards China, recognizing to some degree that the U.S.-China relationship would be the crucial axis for future world development.

One afternoon in 1996, I was sitting in my cell, reading the State Department Foreign Broadcast Information Service (FBIS) reports from Myanmar. FBIS, which publishes leading news items from newspapers and radio broadcasts from around the world for use by the diplomatic corps and others, has generally followed the State Department standing rule that nothing is to be reported by or about Lyndon LaRouche, except slanders. I was shocked, therefore, when the FBIS for Southeast Asia that day included the following editorial taken from Myanmar's leading government newspaper, *The New Light of Myanmar:*

> An article titled "Myanmar and the Opium Trade" has been featured every day in this newspaper, and in "Myanma Alin" and "Kyemon" (Burmese-language papers) from November 22-24. The article is a reproduction of an article from the Oct. 25, 1996 issue of *Executive Intelligence Review* of the United States. The co-authors are Michael and Gail Billington. It is subtitled: "Will Dope, Inc. lose control of the Golden Triangle? A profile of the institutions trying to destabilize Myanmar."

I nearly fell off my chair. The *New Light of Myanmar* proceeded to report key parts of our article, focussing on the role of Bush. A follow-up article, also published in *The New Light of Myanmar*, again named our EIR piece and its translation into Burmese, adding: "For those who have not read it yet, please look up and read it. The article begins describing that it has long been George

Bush . . . and Lt. Col. North who introduced crack cocaine to America's inner cities."

I could just imagine the permanent bureaucracy at the State Department gagging as they read these reports. The fact that they chose to cover these articles in FBIS said a great deal about the changes going on in the Clinton Administration. Although Madeleine Albright and others in the administration continued to castigate Myanmar as a pariah, President Clinton made a firm decision to back up the ASEAN nations in their policy of "constructive engagement" with Myanmar, which facilitated a relatively smooth entry of Myanmar into ASEAN in 1997. We learned from a Philippines diplomat, that the Myanmar government occasionally mailed copies of our EIR articles to citizens of other ASEAN nations who showed interest in the fate of their nation. Later, a Myanmar diplomat told Gail that his country credits EIR with turning the tide against the British effort to isolate and destroy their nation.

Cambodia

Cambodia is another case where our intervention contributed to derailing a potentially disastrous British intelligence gambit. Although hard to believe, the British and their Project Democracy allies in the U.S. actually tried to resuscitate the genocidal Khmer Rouge, despite its well-known butchery of well over a million Cambodians in the late 1970's. Not only did the British promote these monsters, but they drew upon nearly the entire global "human rights" mafia to support them!

The British oligarchy was unhappy with the nationalist Cambodian Prime Minister Hun Sen. Hun Sen had come to power as an ally of the Vietnamese forces who overthrew the Khmer Rouge in 1979, and, after a UN-brokered election in 1993, shared power, as co-Prime Minister, with Prince Ranariddh, the son of King Sihanouk. Prince Ranariddh, who recognized that he was a sure loser in the upcoming elections, formed an alliance with a French-trained banker, Sam Rainsy, who was the darling of the IMF, the NGO's, and, in particular, the same International Republican Institute (IRI) which was running the Myanmar destabilization on behalf of the Bush machine. It must be noted, that it was this Bush machine which, in the 1980's—while the horrors of the

Khmer Rouge "killing fields" were being revealed and reviled throughout the world—nonetheless granted official U.S. recognition to the deposed Khmer Rouge, rather than recognize a Vietnamese-backed government in Phnom Penh!

Facing an almost certain loss in the upcoming election, the Prince and Sam Rainsy, and their foreign backers, turned to the Khmer Rouge. The Khmer Rouge itself had been reduced to a few thousand soldiers holding a small pocket of territory on the Thai border. Its support from China had been long since terminated, and their practice of finding refuge in Thailand was threatened by the growing unity of the ASEAN nations, and Cambodia's scheduled entry into the association in 1997. However, most of the old Khmer Rouge leadership—the infamous Pol Pot, theoretician Khieu Samphan, and "The Butcher" Ta Mok—were alive and well, and a continuing threat.

In an amazing display of chutzpah, Prince Ranariddh travelled to the Khmer Rouge headquarters and formulated an agreement with their second in command, Khieu Samphan, to join forces against Hun Sen! The British hand was revealed by the role played by the leading English-language magazine in British Hongkong, the *Far Eastern Economic Review* (*FEER*), owned by Dow Jones (i.e., the *Wall Street Journal* gang). An elaborate farce was set up, to be performed on international television. In June of 1997, a *FEER* reporter, with cameraman, was brought to Khmer Rouge headquarters, where no Western reporter had ever before been permitted, to observe a "trial" of "Brother No. 1" Pol Pot—not for the hideous crime of genocide during the Khmer Rouge reign, but for the killing of a factional opponent! Pol Pot, who was clearly dying anyway, was "condemned" to house arrest for life, and politely led back to his home. This was presented to the world as the purification of the Khmer Rouge, with all past evils credited to Pol Pot and Pol Pot alone. The rest of the Khmer Rouge leaders had supposedly undergone a miraculous conversion to "democracy"! Not only *FEER*, but the *Washington Post* and much of the Western press, played this fraud as if it were serious, trying to create a justification for Prince Ranariddh's signed agreement.

When Hun Sen responded by deploying the national army against the outlawed Khmer Rouge and their collaborators, Prince Ranariddh had left the country, and was being touted by the

NGO networks as an "oppressed democrat," and Rainsy was playing it safe in Paris or Bangkok. Gail and I went to work.

In a number of EIR articles, we published the full documentation of whose coup this really was. The Cambodian government had made available all the documents, including the signed agreement between Ranariddh and the Khmer Rouge's Khieu Samphan, but most other Western press covered it up! EIR published the damning documents, together with an historical account of Cambodia's holocaust:

• Henry Kissinger's decision to drop more than a half-million tons of bombs on rural Cambodia between 1969 and 1973, half of it in the last six months;

• How this mindless destruction transformed the Khmer Rouge from a nuisance into a huge, dedicated military force;

• How Kissinger and the U.S. then washed their hands of Cambodia in 1975, leaving the small nation at the mercy of the Khmer Rouge monster;

• How, when the Vietnamese joined with Cambodian opposition forces to crush the Khmer Rouge in 1979, the Western powers *continued official recognition of the Khmer Rouge regime,* even after the proof of their genocide had been disseminated worldwide.

This time around, however, we intended to prevent a replay of such treachery. Gail approached government agencies in the U.S. and Europe with documentation of the attempted Khmer Rouge revival, making it extremely difficult for either Ranariddh or Sam Rainsy to sell their "oppressed democrats" pitch, despite the hoopla from the "human rights" mafia.

When the attempt to revive the Khmer Rouge failed to garner international support and collapsed, Cambodian officials, like those in Myanmar, expressed their gratitude for the role we played in working to change the perception of their nation abroad, and especially in Washington. The war against British subversion was hardly over, but a significant battle had been won.

America's Uniqueness

One problem we ran into among Asian leaders, and Third World leaders generally, was the tendency to fall for the trap of identifying British policies as American policies. This is understandable, in one sense, since the U.S. has so often carried out British dictates

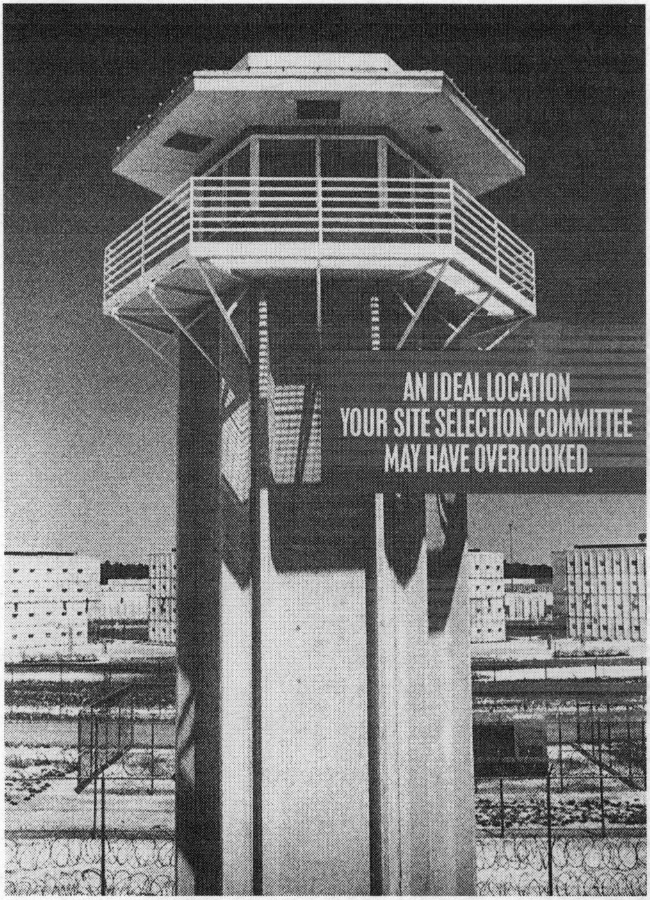

I first encountered the use of prison slave labor for private industry in 1989, at the Federal Correctional Facility in Allenwood, Pa. Private industry would move into prisons in a big way in the 1990's. This picture is from a promotional brochure issued by Virginia Correctional Enterprises.

Temporary liberty: Working on EIR's Chinese newsletter with Ray Wei.

EIRNS/Philip Ulanowsky

DEFEAT OLLIE NORTH,
THAT SON-OF-A-BUSH
Paid for by: Defeat that SON-OF-A-BUSH Committee - Not authorized by any candidate
3M National
Swift

EIRNS/Stuart Lewis

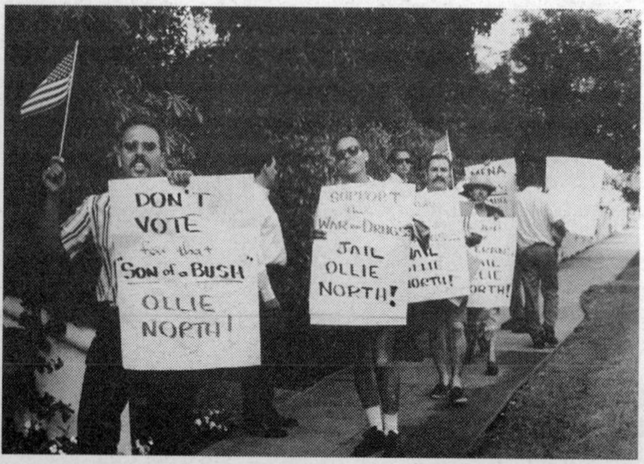

EIRNS/James Duree, Jr.

Ollie North was touted as the linchpin for the 1994 "Conservative Revolution" takeover of Congress, but our "Son-of-a-Bush" campaign threw a monkey-wrench into the plan.

Courtesy of Margaret Greenspan

Temporary liberty: Relaxing with Mom at Lake Erie, summer 1992 . . .

Courtesy of Margaret Greenspan

. . . and with Marg

Courtesy of Margaret Greenspan

. . . and with Gail.

EIRNS/Stuart Lewis

March Against Death, Richmond, Va., Sept. 28, 1992. Gail and I stopped on the way to turning myself in at Powhatan Correctional Center, to begin serving my 77-year sentence. Paul and Anita Gallagher are on the far left.

EIRNS/Susan Ulanowsky

"I talked about Martin Luther King, Abraham Lincoln, and the Founding Fathers, as some of those who were there with the marchers in spirit, and that the fight against the death penalty went to the root of the moral decay of the nation."

China's great philosophers Confucius (551-479 B.C.) (right) and Mencius (390-305 B.C.) (below). My intensive study of the coherence between Chinese philosophy and the Christian-Platonic tradition of the West, began on my return to prison in 1992. Ironically, those first months proved to be the most intellectually explosive of my life.

EIRNS/Rachel Douglas

Once released on parole in January 1994, Lyndon LaRouche was able to resume his global responsibilities as statesman and the world's leading economist. His travels brought him quickly to Russia, Eastern Europe, and the Middle East. Above, center: Leaving the Russian Institute of Africa with his wife Helga Zepp LaRouche, Moscow, April 1994. Below: Lecturing at the Russian Academy of Sciences.

EIRNS/Rachel Douglas

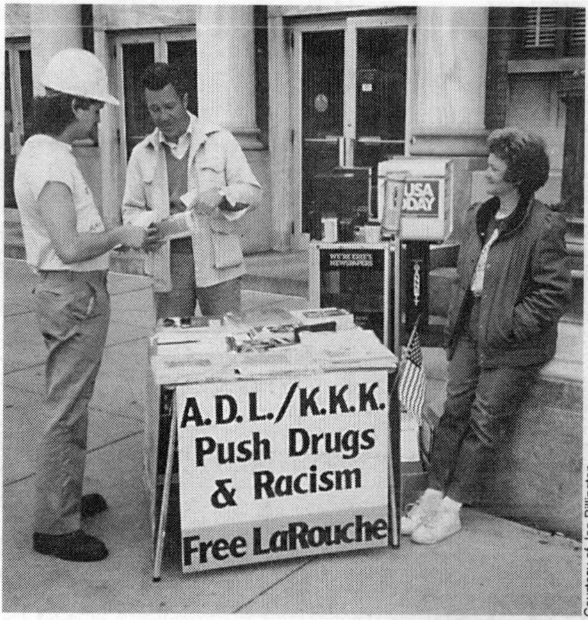

Courtesy of Joe Billington

My brother Joe and his wife Claudia organizing in Pittsburgh, Pa., early 1990's.

Courtesy of Michael Billington

With my friend and fellow inmate Evans Hopkins ("Hop"), Nottoway Correctional Facility, April 1996.

Prison visits, Nottoway Correctional Facility.

Courtesy of Joe Billington

The Billington family: Dan, Marg, Mike, Joe, Claudia, January 1995.

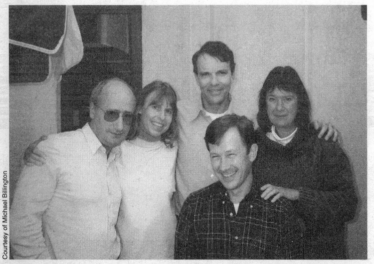

Courtesy of Michael Billington

Helga Zepp LaRouche (right), with friends Dino de Paoli, Renate Müller de Paoli, and Rick Magraw, November 1995.

Helga Zepp LaRouche visits China, Hebei Province, May 1996.

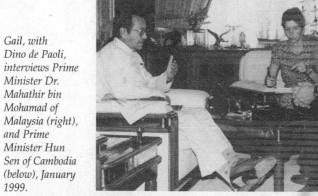

Gail, with Dino de Paoli, interviews Prime Minister Dr. Mahathir bin Mohamad of Malaysia (right), and Prime Minister Hun Sen of Cambodia (below), January 1999.

EIRNS/Stuart Lewis

"To understand the special nature of the United States, one need only visit the Lincoln Memorial in Washington, D.C., as I first did as a 12-year-old on a YMCA trip from Cleveland. . . . On the wall to the left is the Gettysburg Address, America's most beautiful poem. . . . Move to the right, and read Lincoln's Second Inaugural Address, from 1865, in which Lincoln grieves over the bloody destruction of the Civil War, wrought by two sides which pray to the same God for guidance and victory. He asks the most profound of all philosophical questions, the same as that addressed by Leibniz when he posited that God had created 'the best of all possible worlds.' . . . This is the unique character of America—founded as an international conspiracy for truth and justice, and chastened in blood to establish the principle of the equality of man."

over the past century. If it is difficult to get Americans to understand that the U.S. has repeatedly been used as London's patsy, and that our nation is destroying itself by following British doctrine, both economic and diplomatic, it is even *more* difficult to convince citizens of the developing nations of this same problem. After all, the U.S. is the most powerful nation on Earth, its economy dwarfs others in size, and it certainly claims to be carrying out policy in its own self-interest. But such a view is fatally flawed.

What's needed, is to grasp the extraordinary, unique quality of the American Republic—sometimes called "American exceptionalism." This does not mean that the U.S. has some divine right to rule, equivalent to the "White Man's Burden" heralded by British Empire apologists. To the contrary, it means that the United States, as an institution, is the repository of the best of European culture, science, and statescraft, as expressed in the Declaration of Independence and the Preamble to the Constitution. Our three wars against England were driven by that impulse. Abraham Lincoln and Henry Carey renewed that Renaissance tradition, when it was nearly extinguished by British subversion, and proceeded to carry the American System around the world.

To understand the special nature of the United States, one need only visit the Lincoln Memorial in Washington, D.C., as I first did as a 12-year-old on a YMCA trip from Cleveland. Stand for a while by each of the side walls to the right and to the left of the imposing, seated statue of President Lincoln. Read aloud the words inscribed in those walls. On the left is the Gettysburg Address, America's most beautiful poem. Hopefully, you will remember it by heart from your elementary school classes. Reflect upon Lincoln, as he in turn is reflecting upon our forefathers, and their founding of a nation "conceived in liberty, and dedicated to the proposition that all men are created equal," and of a "government of the people, for the people, and by the people." Move to the right, and read Lincoln's Second Inaugural Address, from 1865, in which Lincoln grieves over the bloody destruction of the Civil War, wrought by two sides which pray to the same God for guidance and for victory. He asks the most profound of all philosophical questions, the same as that addressed by Leibniz when he posited that God had created "the best of all possible worlds." Must we discern in this horrible war, asks Lincoln,

> any departure from those divine attributes which believers in a Living God always ascribe to Him? Fondly do we hope—fervently do we pray—that this mighty scourge of war may speedily pass away. Yet, if God wills that it continue, until all the wealth piled by the bondman's two hundred and fifty years of unrequited toil shall be sunk, and until every drop of blood drawn with the lash, shall be paid by another drawn with the sword, as was said three thousand years ago, so still it must be said "the judgments of the Lord, are true and righteous altogether." With malice toward none; with charity for all; with firmness in the right, as God gives us to see the right, let us strive to finish the work we are in . . . .

This is the unique character of America—founded as an international conspiracy for truth and justice, and chastened in blood to establish the principle of the equality of man.

Even when Lincoln and other nationalist Presidents were assassinated, and even under such Anglophile racists as Teddy Roosevelt and Woodrow Wilson, that tradition remained. It is the true self-interest of the United States, which made possible, for instance, the emergence of FDR, and America's ability to restore, under wartime conditions, its historic identity as a nation-builder, winning a just war and making some halting efforts toward building the post-war world with American technology. It is the spirit evoked by John F. Kennedy in creating the Peace Corps, which inspired me and other young Americans to pursue a higher purpose in our lives.

The near destruction of that tradition in the later 1960's cultural paradigm shift does not change America's essential nature. To angry leaders in Asia, Africa, or Ibero-America, who see the IMF destroying their nations, and perceive the U.S. as the power behind the IMF, Gail and I said, "No, it is America's historic enemy, Britain, and the British oligarchy's royal allies around the world, who are the problem. The 'Venetian party' of oligarchic finance, with its continuing war against the Renaissance, is the problem. A Third Worldist mentality, which leads you to strike out blindly against an undifferentiated Western world, is the problem.

"If you wish to save your nation, you must distinguish between the oligarchical British system and the American System, and contribute heart and soul to ending the rule of the oligarchy, now that the globalized IMF system has reached an existential crisis. Otherwise, your nation will not stand a chance.

"We are committed to bringing America back to its true character. Join us."

[21]

Virginia Prison Life

My life in Virginia's prisons took on a very rigorous order. The first year at Nottoway Correctional Center, one of the highest security prisons in Virginia, was rather difficult. The staff which evaluated me for placement at the Powhatan receiving unit, had recommended that I be sent to a low-security prison. But someone higher up wanted to give me the full treatment, so I got Nottoway. A good portion of its 1,100 inmates will never get out of prison. Very few are granted parole, even when they are eligible.

Surprisingly, I was to learn that many of these men, facing apparently hopeless futures, were more mature, and more serious about their lives, than the youngsters I later met at lower-security institutions, who often considered "doing time" as a badge of honor, a rite of passage toward making it big "on the street."

★ ★ ★

I was tested and threatened in various ways by other inmates over the first few months at Nottoway, but knowledge of my political identity soon spread, engendering curiosity and a certain respect. I sought out those who had an interest in political affairs, and arranged a free subscription to *The New Federalist* for anyone who seemed serious. The papers circulated widely on the compound, creating a kind of protective screen around me, as well as engendering a rather unique kind of political network.

The Muslims, both Sunni Muslims and the followers of Minister Farrakhan in the Nation of Islam, were by far the dominant organizations on the compound. (Seventy percent of the inmates were black, although only 17% of the Commonwealth of Virginia is black.) Soon after my arrival, I approached the head of the Nation of Islam, who was meeting with some of the Fruit of Islam security staff, in the rec yard. I introduced myself, and he smiled broadly at the reference to LaRouche, shook my hand, and asked if I'd join him on a walk around the yard. We walked slowly around the yard several times, followed at a short distance by his security detail. There was no question but that he was making an announcement to the prison population.

The leaders of both the Nation and the Sunni community were bright and serious, and were anxious to get our newspaper to their members. Both invited me to address their meetings occasionally.

There were many violent and irrational people in the compound, and nearly everyone was guilty of a violent crime, including even murderers for hire with multiple life sentences. Nonetheless, there were many intelligent people, especially among those who had been "down" for a long time, and had matured and educated themselves in prison.

It is standard to spend the first year in a regular cell block, with two people to each cell (although they were designed for one). The noise in my cell block was deafening, and serious work was nearly impossible. I succeeded in winning the librarian's approval to spend most of my time in the small prison library, where I managed to research and write my *Fidelio* article on Daoism and 20th-Century science. Friends in Leesburg xeroxed the books I needed and mailed them to me, a blessing for which I was most grateful.

Although life in the cell block was difficult, I had a good cell mate (a 330-pound, semi-literate Muslim weightlifter who was gentle as a lamb, with a heart of gold), and I had a Walkman radio and tape recorder, which helped to close out the chaos around me.

After a year, I was moved to an "honor building," with single cells which were locked only during the four daily counts. I established a night schedule, staying up until 5:00 a.m. and sleeping until lunch time. The six hours after 11:00 p.m. were totally silent, and I worked nightly in relative bliss at my make-shift desk. I often described to stunned visitors that I had finally discovered Earthly Paradise—only partially in jest!

I also met a true friend, and a recruit to Lyn's ideas, in Evans Hopkins, one of the inspirations for (and editors of) this book. Besides our hours of discussions, Hop and I also spent one night a week playing Scrabble, and several afternoons each week on the tennis court, where he taught me enough that I could give him a game. Hop had been a promising tennis star in his teens, with the same coach who had taught Arthur Ashe, before joining the Black Panther Party at age 17. He got caught up in crime when the Panthers fell apart.

Hop was an example of someone who had taken full advantage of the classes and special programs which were available to prisoners in the 1970's and 1980's. He had developed himself into an insightful and passionate observer of society, and an established writer on both prison-related issues and more general social matters. He published articles regularly in the *Washington Post* and elsewhere. The programs which did so much to help Hop and others of his generation in prison no longer existed, and we often grieved together over the thousands of young, mostly black, men, just like Hop 20 years ago, who were shoved into today's prison warehouses with ungodly sentences and no parole (parole was eliminated in Virginia in 1995), and no serious programs for rehabilitation or self-improvement. It was to these youth that Hop addressed his own book in progress, which he tentatively titled, "From Rage to Redemption." Hop won parole in 1997, after 17 years in prison, owing to the large number of prominent people in society who spoke out for his release—including even the prosecutor who had put him away! Things have not been easy for him on the outside, but he is continuing to contribute his special talents to saving this crazy world.

Gail visited me nearly every other week, visits which took on the character of battlefield strategy sessions as we tackled the Southeast Asia work. Visits from many others filled most of my weekends—both friends and associates from the organization, and many political friends from around the world. These, from Malaysia, Russia, Hungary, Mexico, China, and on and on, would almost always stop at some point in our meeting, look around at the crowded visiting room, and exclaim something like, "It is simply incredible that we are sitting here in such a place, joyfully discussing philosophy, history, and the ideas necessary for the survival of civilization, in the midst of such sadness and degradation. I wish everyone in the world could be here and see this!"

My family were among my staunchest supporters. Through regular calls and visits, Joe, Claudia, Margaret and Elliot became my eyes and ears in the organizing process in the field. Joe was particularly good at capturing the global significance of various developments with humor, designing polemics and slogans for field deployments. He also turned himself into a special resource for our phone organizers around the country, who would call on him to brief our contacts all over the country on the necessity of exoneration, drawing heavily on my continuing incarceration and the work that Gail and I were doing.

My mother grew stronger through the ordeal. Although it caused her great pain, the process of confronting the corrupt judicial system, and the mindless acceptance of that corruption by most of her friends, made her far more suspect of the liberal political establishment. At the age of 82, she took the plunge and mastered the use of these new-fangled machines called word processors, and assumed the monumental task of typing the handwritten manuscript of this book, because the prison had removed our typewriters.

My prison life took a turn after the five-month lockdown of 1996, described in the Foreword. I appreciated the single cell at Nottoway, but when the post-lockdown conditions turned into something approximating a concentration camp (no school, no programs, a two-hour limit per week of outdoor exercise, attack dogs escorting us to and from the chow hall), I requested a transfer. This was granted, and I was moved to the low-security prison in Staunton, Virginia. It had once been the state mental hospital, and, unlike the ugly, tree-less gray concrete of Nottoway, the Staunton compound was composed of red brick buildings, dogwoods, cherry trees, and huge lilac bushes, set among the rolling hills of the Shenandoah Valley. Seeing and smelling the blooming spring flowers for the first time in five years, was an unexpected delight. And, although we had to live in crowded dormitories, the televisions were set off in separate TV rooms, so that it was possible to concentrate in the day rooms. I also had the highly unusual benefit of a private office! I had taken a job as a tutor in the high school equivalency class and, since the school had not been designed for prisoners, there were a half-dozen cubby-hole offices for the tutors. I was able to pursue my own work in my office, while helping students who came in for individual help.

There was another unexpected benefit—my colleague and co-defendant Paul Gallagher was also transferred to Staunton, and I had the great pleasure of a Labor Committee collaborator and a dear friend. Paul and Anita, who were allowed only two five-minute phone calls each year, maintained their relationship through letters and through discussions with friends who could visit both of them. The loving and unpretentious way in which they dealt with the unnatural sacrifice forced upon them, is a testament to their strength of character.

Paul was involved in a project to revive the fight against Romanticism in English poetry, last waged by Percy Bysshe Shelley and John Keats, and to explore the use of metaphor by these two giants of the age of Schiller and Beethoven. One of his several articles in *Fidelio* appeared together with one I wrote on "The Deconstructionist Assault on China's Cultural Optimism," my last extensive study of the battle between Confucian humanism and Daoist ideology in Chinese history, with an analysis of the impact of that cultural tradition on recent developments in China, especially the 1989 Tiananmen tragedy.

Paul and I worked together on articles and research. Our most rewarding collaboration, however, was the creation of the extraordinary institution known as the Staunton Classical Chorus in the spring of 1998. With Paul's prodding, and with support from an assistant warden who loved classical music, we were given permission to form a chorus, meeting once every week, with the use of a piano. We signed up about 15 people, some of whom had singing experience, some of whom couldn't sing a lick, but wanted to learn. For the first time in six years, I had the chance to sing again, and to teach *bel canto* to a curious and dedicated group of men.

It was a totally diverse collection—Catholics, Protestants, Jews, Muslims, Mormons, and Seventh Day Adventists. We met in the chow hall, and soon our "no-no-no-no" arpeggio exercises were being echoed and mimicked throughout the compound. We worked hard on teaching the rudiments of producing a beautiful, full, vibrated tone, while learning some Renaissance canons, some spirituals, some Christmas carols, and the chorale from Bach's cantata *Wachet Auf*. One chorus member had been professionally trained, with a beautiful tenor voice, and several others could read music reasonably well. A smaller group of those with more experience began meeting a second time each week out in the rec yard.

It was quite a scene—eight convicts standing between the volleyball court and the basketball court, singing Mozart's "Ave Verum," and a Schubert setting of a Schiller poem, in Latin and in German, respectively, to the amazement of the prison population. The excitement and enthusiasm grew among the chorus members, as the depth and power of this music grew within them, and as our performance became adequate to convey that power.

After a few months, I introduced the "Prisoners' Chorus" from Beethoven's *Fidelio*—the scene in which Leonora has convinced the jailer to allow the prisoners to come out of their dungeon cells and into the fresh air, if only for a few moments. The filthy prisoners stagger forth, singing "*Oh, welche Lust*" ("O what joy"), to breathe the fresh air, and to allow the hope for freedom to well up from the depth of their souls—only to notice the guards' stern gaze, and slink back in fear, although treasuring that moment of hope. The music for this chorus is so exquisitely beautiful, that the members of the group were literally stunned, and their enthusiasm was transformed into passion.

One inmate, a long-haired, tattooed, "biker"-looking fellow, informed us that he had played classical violin before he got into gangs and drugs! With the help of the same friendly assistant warden, the prison purchased a violin for the use of the inmates. To our surprise, the young violinist was more than competent—he played with a fine touch, a true pitch, and clear phrasing. He became the "orchestra," with Paul on the piano, for the "Prisoners' Chorus" and several other pieces. We also took on Bach's "Jesu, Joy of Man's Desiring," which is essentially a violin solo with chorus accompaniment.

Adding some solo works of Handel, Beethoven, Bach, and Schubert, sung by myself and the other trained singer in the group, we scheduled a concert for December 1998.

Despite bureaucratic obstacles which almost scuttled the whole project, we managed to sing at three different church services around Christmas time, to the delight of the inmates and the total joy of the chorus members. At one point or another, each one of them approached me privately, to explain how much the chorus meant to him. These were emotions which were unfamiliar to many of these men, and even fewer had ever tried to articulate profound concepts from deep within their souls. Each, in his own way, expressed his pure wonder that such beautiful music existed, and that the discovery in themselves of the ability to participate in producing something truly beautiful, transcended their captivity—they had learned that freedom lies in the heart. As much as the music itself, these sentiments, from these men, are a memory to be treasured always.

★ ★ ★

Optimism

It is well known that hardship and unjust persecution can be turned to good benefit. Mencius said: "When Heaven is about to confer a great mission on any man, it first exercises his mind with suffering, and his sinews and bones with toil. It exposes his body to hunger, and subjects him to extreme poverty. It confounds his undertakings. By these methods, it stimulates his mind, hardens his nature, and improves his weaknesses." So, also Christ said: "Blessed are those who are persecuted for the sake of righteousness, for theirs is the Kingdom of Heaven."

I do, indeed, feel blessed—not as a "feeling-state" of pompous self-righteousness, but in that the adversity I've faced in these years of incarceration has served to stimulate my passion to seek the truth, to untangle mysteries, to explore the unknown, and to love beauty. Much of this I've learned from Lyndon LaRouche, and from those throughout history whom Lyn introduced to me. Others among my teachers I discovered on my own, searching through the 2,500-year-old works of Confucius and Mencius, or those of the 12th-Century Song Dynasty. I learned that to become a world-historical person does not entail acheiving a position, or fame, or even respect, except in the eyes of God. Quoting Mencius again: "I like life and I also like righteousness. If I cannot keep the two together, I will let life go, and choose righteousness. All men have that which they like more than life, and that which they dislike more than death. They are not only men of distinguished talents and virtue who have this mental nature. All men have it. What belongs to men of virtue is simply that they do not lose it."

I have been tested, but I, and all of us, will be far more severely tested in the difficult days and years ahead. It is my hope that I can live up to the standard set by Mencius.

The onset of the global financial breakdown crisis in October of 1997 brought with it a paradigm shift in the population in every part of the world, and most emphatically in the United States. Lyn was quick to observe and identify this shift, as the first generalized reaction against 30 years of the New Age, post-industrial, countercultural paradigm established by the 1960's baby boomers. The majority of the population has begun to recognize that the anti-growth ideology associated with "environmentalism" is unnatural, irrational, and dangerous. The pornographic political witch-hunt against President Clinton by the media not only disgusted the population, but has also forced many to question the police state apparatus within the Justice Department, and its associated private institutions. The steady erosion of living standards has made people question the myth of the "booming U.S. economy," and as the bubble bursts, all illusions will evaporate.

The character of these current changes has been shaped to a significant degree by our work over these many years. The emerging organized resistance to IMF policies, to the crimes of the Justice Department, to the world environmentalist hoax, and so forth, would not have been effective—or may not have happened at all—without Lyndon LaRouche and his association's efforts.

It is not the case, however, that the breakdown crisis will automatically bring people to our ideas. Such a crisis is also the breeding ground for fascism, for racial, religious, and ethnic hatreds to be exploited, in which individuals, in despair, turn inward, strike out at their neighbors, and lose their reason. We must use the ugly reality of the crisis as a wake-up call, but we must use beauty and truth as the tools of organizing. The crisis is an opportunity to achieve what should have been achieved long ago, and is thus a source of *optimism*—if the necessary leadership exists to awaken the creative passions of a soul-sick world.

In a 1998 videotape presentation, LaRouche posed that we are all, each and every one of us, born as angels, endowed with the miracle of creative reason. We must each find our mission, but no one lacks the potential and the means to contribute something of enduring value to the progress and general happiness of mankind. Mencius said something very similar two millennia ago: "Benevolence, righteousness, propriety, and reason are not infused into us from without. We are certainly furnished with them. A different view is simply owing to the lack of reflection. Hence it is said in regard to these qualities: 'Seek and you shall find them. Neglect and you shall lose them.' Men differ from one another in regard to them—it is because they cannot carry out fully their natural powers."

How do we bring such qualities forward in our fellow citizens, adequately enough to effect the transformation of civilization? We do not know precisely what tasks stand before us, but we must be prepared to act upon any critical crisis which might determine the fate of us all. I think often of Lyn's report of his own discovery, back in the early 1960's, after investigating the existing political institutions in American society, that if there were to be an organization dedicated to reversing the descent into a new Dark Age, and to initiating a new Renaissance, he would have to build it himself. This was not hubris, but a recognition of the failure of leadership in the 20th Century, and especially in the post-World War II era, coupled with a sense of moral responsibility to do everything within his power to achieve what he knew to be possible and necessary for mankind.

One must be willing to stand alone, even against the whole world if necessary, if truth is to be the only guide. The victory of the oligarchy depends on heteronomy, the willingness of the population to give up intellectual freedom and honesty in exchange for some notion of popular acceptance and approval. LaRouche refused such a deadly compromise, and inspired in me, and many others, a similar, ruthless pursuit of truth.

Oligarchs, of course, despise such people. To counter truth, Aristotelians throughout history have peddled the line that "there is no universal truth—truth is whatever you believe it to be." The purpose of the assault against LaRouche, as reflected in the attacks on me, in the courts and elsewhere, is to reinforce this moral relativism in the population: "LaRouche is clearly an extremist—he thinks he knows the truth." What is meant is, "He thinks there *is* truth, and we must not permit such dangerous thinking."

Truth-seeking makes me very happy. I have many worthy guides, whom I trust implicitly will not mislead me, even if they may sometimes err. I have this trust because I have come to know what they knew, and know their hearts and minds. I think first of Plato, of St. Paul, and of Confucius and Mencius, then Nicolaus of Cusa, Chu Hsi, Kepler, Leibniz, Beethoven, Schubert, Sun Yat-sen, Cantor, and, of course, LaRouche. Besides Lyn, they are all long deceased, but they are all watching me most closely, helping me, correcting me, and calling on me to continue their good work, to make their own lives, their own contributions, that much more meaningful. They can not be fooled; nor could I let them down.

Our time is very short, and there is much to do. There will be others after us, of course, but if we fail today, if a Dark Age brings havoc upon our world, we shall have betrayed our ancestors and our posterity—the as-yet unborn, who are counting on us to preserve and extend mankind's mastery over the universe, to prepare for their arrival. With both past and future civilizations thus depending upon each of us, while also inspiring our cognitive powers—what Lyn has called "living in the simultaneity of eternity"—we have the power to achieve our mission. I am most optimistic that we shall succeed.

[Afterword]

The Assault on the Asian Tigers

In the summer of 1997, the post-World War II world financial system entered its final deadly paroxysm. Although it appeared in the guise of an "Asian crisis," it was in fact the collapse of "globalization," and therefore, a crisis of the system as a whole. The collapse in Asia unfolded precisely as LaRouche had warned, and as Gail and I had documented it must. Not a single economist, anywhere in the world, had forecast the scope of the collapse, other than LaRouche. I still laugh today when I hear yet another pundit explain that "nobody could have known, and nobody predicted, the devastating collapse of the Asian miracle"—this often coming from leading experts who not only knew LaRouche, but had spent huge amounts of their time slandering or attempting to discredit him!

One result of the crash was a reappraisal by Asian leaders of LaRouche and **EIR.** When LaRouche's warnings were proven to be most painfully accurate, the region's leading economists and political officials put aside their previous pretensions about the "Asian miracle," and pulled out their EIR files for a thorough review.

About six months before the crisis exploded in July 1997, Gail had given a presentation at a national NCLC conference, titled

"On the British Plans to Bag the Southeast Asian 'Tigers.' " Together with me and Kathy Wolfe (who covered Korea and Japan), we prepared a package on the subject for EIR. Gail's presentation led with a photograph of the last great tiger hunt in Nepal, attended by Britain's Queen Elizabeth and Prince Philip. "Here's how the British like their tigers," Gail reported, and proceeded to demonstrate that the globalization process had undermined the region's nationalist ambitions for real development, while fattening them up (on hot money and speculation) for the kill.

At practically the same moment that Gail was presenting her conference speech, the financial slaughter in Asia was being quietly set in motion on the derivatives markets of Hongkong and Singapore. George Soros and his fellow speculators tested the waters in February 1997, with an attack on the Thai baht. Thailand was the most vulnerable, having graciously set up unregulated offshore banking facilities at the instigation of the international banks, and otherwise giving the speculators free rein. But Thailand was also a crucial *political* target to Soros and his controllers in London. It was both the geographical pivot for the Southern Route of the Land-Bridge, and had become the leading force for "constructive engagement" with China, Myanmar, and Cambodia. By June, the speculation against the baht became a mass slaughter.

In the deregulated markets of a "globalized" economy, the hedge funds could destroy entire nations with the punch of a few computer keys. And so they did. A subsequent investigation by the Thai government of the collapse of their currency and economy showed that absolutely nobody, including the head of the Bank of Thailand and the Minister of Finance, understood the consequences of the highly complex derivatives deals they had undertaken in a desperate attempt to save their economy, goaded on by imported yuppies running their new "exotic" futures markets. As was the case with Orange County, California, and dozens of other municipalities in the U.S. which were fleeced by slick Wall Street derivatives salesmen, the speculators simply stole them blind. In the case of Thailand, and subsequently all of Southeast Asia, the stealing meant the immediate impoverishment of millions of people, the collapse of 40 years of hard-won industrial development, and the threat of starvation and social chaos for absolutely no reason.

The assault on Thailand soon spread to Malaysia and Indonesia. At the same time, the huge South Korean economy was being torn to pieces by the same apparatus, and the "big potato" in Asia, Japan, was rushing headlong into a financial explosion. The IMF and the British/American/Commonwealth bankers were frantic to cover up the fact that the Asian financial explosion was a global, systemic problem. They filled the press with reports on the "local" problems in each country which supposedly caused the crisis locally—"cronyism" in Indonesia, too many "mega-projects" in Malaysia, and so on, even though they had been described as model economies only a few short months earlier!

But, the bankers' con-game didn't work as they had planned.

Malaysia's Prime Minister, Dr. Mahathir bin Mohamad, refused to passively submit to the rape of his nation. Taking the lead for all of Asia, and for the developing-sector nations generally, he denounced the speculators, and George Soros in particular, as no better than highway robbers, who were carrying out crimes that were only obscured by the unbelievable scope of their thievery and destruction. Nations such as ours, said Dr. Mahathir, which were one day praised as the best-managed economies in the developing sector, following every piece of advice provided by the international financial institutions, were, overnight, stripped of our life-blood by the very institutions we had trusted.

Even more important than Dr. Mahathir's attack on Soros, was his public admission that he had been wrong to believe in the good intentions of the IMF and the Western banks. "I believed," he said in several locations, "in a 'prosper thy neighbor' policy, that our growth and development was considered to be of mutual advantage to the advanced nations and their financial institutions. I did not believe those who told us that the Asian economies were being set up for looting, or that we would experience the disaster that hit Mexico in 1994. I was wrong."

There was no mistaking who it was who had given those warnings. In the summer of 1997, Gail received a call from an *Asian Wall Street Journal* journalist, an event about as likely as Henry Kissinger inviting LaRouche to tea. "What's the story on

EIR's relation to Malaysia?" he asked. He was particularly anxious to see our "report on George Soros," and asked for an interview with Lyn, which Gail arranged for him.

Dr. Mahathir was scheduled to be the keynote speaker at the annual international IMF conference, to be held in Hongkong the week of September 19, 1997. His invitation to give that speech demonstrates how much he had previously been viewed by the IMF as a hero of globalization. Now, however, the fire-breathing Prime Minister was feared to be preparing a stinging attack on the institution he was addressing!

On the opening day of the conference, the Asian edition of the *Wall Street Journal*—certain to be read by every participant at the IMF extravaganza in Hongkong—carried a front-page article entitled: "Malaysia's Mahathir Finds Strange Source For Soros Campaign—Asian Country's Media Tap U.S. Conspiracy Theorist Lyndon LaRouche, Jr." The article was co-authored by the editor who had spoken with Gail and Lyn. The standing order to never cover anything LaRouche actually said or did—only slanders allowed, please—was partially breached on this occasion, in an effort to discredit Dr. Mahathir by association with LaRouche.

The article described Dr. Mahathir's attacks on George Soros, and those of Malaysia's leading newspaper, the *New Straits Times*. "For readers of Mr. LaRouche's *Executive Intelligence Review*, [their] words would have rung a bell," said the *Journal*, and then quoted from the EIR Special Report, "The True Story of Soros the Golem." It did not use the normal obligatory label of "political extremist" for LaRouche, but only reported that "the U.S. political mainstream regards him as an extremist." "But," the article continued, "his theories receive a warmer reception in Malaysia, where the 60-page EIR report on Mr. Soros has been passed among Malaysian editors, intellectuals, and politicians. . . . A Malaysian embassy official in Washington says that the embassy has regularly dispatched EIR reports to Kuala Lumpur."

The crucial role of EIR in galvanizing resistance to the IMF and the speculators in Southeast Asia became even more explicit in September 1998, when Dr. Mahathir did the "unthinkable"—he broke with IMF free-trade dogma, imposing selective currency controls and shutting down speculation, exactly as LaRouche had recommended. Dr. Mahathir also did what every great leader must do in time of war—he fired the generals who had guided the economy into the arms of the enemy. He fired Anwar Ibrahim, his Deputy Prime Minister and Finance Minister, amid much hooting and howling from the press, the IMF, and their hireling NGO's.

Dr. Mahathir's defiance of the new colonialism, and the success of his currency controls and government-directed credit policies, rapidly became an inspiration and a rallying point for other Third World nations—with EIR serving as the agency spreading this offensive on every continent. China's Land-Bridge policy, identified everywhere with Lyndon and Helga LaRouche, increasingly brought Russia, China, and India together into a strategic alliance, while Dr. Mahathir's leadership brought Southeast Asia and much of the Third World to identify with this new "Survivors' Club," as Lyn called it, against the deepening world depression and the threat of war.

Then, in January 1999, Gail was invited to both Cambodia and Malaysia, where she interviewed Prime Ministers Hun Sen and Dr. Mahathir. Gail asked Dr. Mahathir what he thought about the call for Mr. LaRouche to be made an advisor to President Clinton. The Prime Minister responded: "This kind of contact must serve a useful purpose, and we would welcome that, certainly. Unfortunately, of course, the words are passed around that the EIR is a fascist grouping, which is trying to—this is told to me by some of your detractors, including my former deputy, who told me earlier that EIR is a fascist paper, so we shouldn't listen to it. So, that is the way of understanding any attempts on your part to try to promote the kind of ideas that EIR has always been focussed on."

This was a clear declaration by Dr. Mahathir to other leaders around the world: Don't be frightened or intimidated by lies and slanders about LaRouche—we must stand together with these ideas.

Lyn's message is being carefully studied and discussed around the world. Nothing less than a new Bretton Woods, a new monetary system, will suffice—eliminate the speculators by restoring fixed exchange rates, establish protective measures for national industries, replace the central banks with Hamiltonian national banks to establish credit for infrastructure and production, mobilize the world's nations for joint scientific research and Great Projects like the Land-Bridge, and, most important, foster, through policy and through cultural optimism, a revival of Classical forms of artistic creativity.

This is the moment for which we have prepared ourselves over these past 30 years—the moment which demands LaRouche's direction, as the necessary and unique basis for determining whether the 21st Century will be a new Dark Age, or a new Renaissance. It is a particularly difficult time to be locked up, away from the front lines.

[Appendix I]

Toward the Ecumenical Unity of East and West

The Renaissances of Confucian China and Christian Europe

I consider it a singular plan of the fates that human cultivation and refinement should today be concentrated, as it were, in the two extremes of our continent, in Europe and in China, which adorns the Orient as Europe does the opposite edge of the earth. Perhaps Supreme Providence has ordained such an arrangement, so that, as the most cultivated and distant peoples stretch out their arms to each other, those in between may gradually be brought to a better way of life.

G.W. Leibniz,
Novissima Sinica, 1697

In a world economy rapidly collapsing into the worst depression of modern history, the role of China, the world's largest nation, has become a crucial factor in determining the future of the world economy as a whole. The two dominant "systems" of the Twentieth Century—the Communist Soviet bloc and the "free enterprise" economies of the West—have followed one another into bankruptcy and social chaos. China, however, although still suffering from a relatively underdeveloped economic infra-

This essay first appeared in Fidelio, Summer 1993 (Vol. II, No. 2). It has been abridged and edited for inclusion in this volume by the author, who has incorporated material from his "The Deconstructionist Assault on China's Cultural Optimism" [Fidelio, Fall 1997 (Vol. VI, No. 3)].

structure and a low *per-capita* standard of living, is moving forward with a visible enthusiasm and technological optimism, finding its own way between the two proven failures of Marxism and Adam Smith's *laissez-faire* capitalism.

China is also reaching out to other nations, both its Asian neighbors and beyond, with proposals for cooperative development of huge dimensions, which could transform the region into an economic engine for world development in the next century. This fact alone explains the hysteria in some quarters—centered in such British Intelligence thinktanks as the I.I.S.S. (the International Institute of Strategic Studies) and their "Conservative Revolution" allies in the U.S. Congress—who are attempting to paint China as the new "enemy image" for the West. What most disturbs London is the cultural optimism emanating from China, which threatens to spread internationally, since culturally optimistic nations are less willing to submit passively to the dictates of the international financial institutions.

There are both positive and negatives impulses behind China's new optimism. From the negative side, the stark image of the ten years of hell known as the Great Proletarian Cultural Revolution, which tore China apart between 1966 and 1976, lives indelibly in the minds of the Chinese people. They compare that experience to the holocaust in Germany under Nazism, and are united behind the determination that such a devastation of China's people and their cultural identity shall never be allowed to recur.

The Cultural Revolution was a modern expression of the most infamous reign of terror in Chinese history, that of Emperor Ch'in Shi-huang (r. 221-206 B.C.). The Ch'in Empire was based on the principles of Legalism and Taoism, the sworn enemies of the moral teachings of the Confucian school established by Confucius (551-479 B.C.) and Mencius (372-289 B.C.). The radical Maoist leadership of the Cultural Revolution, known as the Gang of Four, revered Ch'in Shi-huang as China's greatest hero. Emperor Ch'in is most famous for burying the Confucian scholars alive and burning their classical texts, while imposing a vast forced-labor policy on a population stripped of education and culture. Most importantly, the Legalists and Taoists, like the Gang of Four, rejected the Confucian belief that man was fundamentally good, owing to the power of reason bestowed by the grace of Heaven.

Instead, they considered man to be a mere beast, devoid of any higher spiritual qualities, driven only by greed and the sensual pleasures.

There is an even more powerful *positive* impulse guiding the Chinese cultural and economic reconstruction. There is a renewed investigation into the vast span of Chinese history and culture, reviving a Confucian tradition which had been under attack throughout the Twentieth Century, and viciously suppressed during the hysteria of the Cultural Revolution. There is also a new dedication to defining a universal role for China, in shaping the future of mankind as a whole, after living in relative isolation from the Western world for much of its 4,500 years of recorded history.

Crucial to finding that universal role is the effort to revive, both in China and in the West, the sentiment expressed in the quotation of G.W. Leibniz at the head of this essay. Leibniz recognized the similarities between the Platonic-Christian worldview in the West and the Confucian worldview in China. Each of these moral traditions was enhanced by a great Renaissance during the first half of the current millennium, which renewed and strengthened its philosophical inheritance from antiquity. The purpose of this study is to demonstrate that the Chinese Renaissance of the Eleventh- and Twelfth-Century Sung Dynasty, associated with the Neo-Confucian school of Chu Hsi (A.D. 1130-1200), paralleled in all fundamental aspects the Christian Renaissance of Fifteenth-Century Europe. In particular, we will compare the extraordinary coherence between Chu Hsi's work and that of the central figure of the Christian Renaissance, Cardinal Nicolaus of Cusa (Cusanus) (1401-64). Reference to the works of a crucial predecessor of Cusanus, St. Thomas Aquinas (1225-74, more nearly a contemporary of Chu Hsi) will reinforce this comparison.

Cusanus dedicated himself to the effort to reconstitute the divided Christian Church upon the basis of the conception of man created *imago viva Dei*, in the living image of God, as expressed in the Christian Trinity. He set about proving this concept scientifically, historically, and philosophically, drawing on the works of Plato as well as the Church Fathers and St. Augustine. These efforts, which led to the brief unification of Christendom achieved at the 1437-39 Council of Florence, were the launching pad for the achievements of the Golden Renaissance in the arts and sciences.

Cusanus strove to establish world peace by forging an ecumenical agreement between Christendom and those whose belief in God was expressed through the other major religions of the world. His method was to demonstrate that the revealed truth of the Christian Trinity, the existence of the Triune God—God the Father, God the Son, and God the Holy Spirit—was also a scientific truth imbedded in the lawfulness of Creation, and that, therefore, every sincere seeker after truth would necessarily be brought to discover this natural law reflection of the Trinity. In *"De Pace Fidei"* ("On the Peace of Faith"), Cusanus uses this method to create an ecumenical dialogue between Christian, Moslem, Jew, Persian, Indian, Chaldean, Tatar, and others.

Cusanus was not familiar with Confucianism, however, let alone with Chu Hsi's Twelfth-Century contributions to Confucian knowledge. An included result of this study, therefore, will be to extend Cusanus' ecumenical approach to embrace China and Confucianism, demonstrating the coherence of the fundamental conceptions and worldview of Sung Renaissance Confucianism with the natural law expression of the Christian Trinity.

An Ecumenical 'Grand Design'

The greatest scientist and statesman of modern Europe, Gottfried Wilhelm Leibniz (1646-1716), did make extensive studies in Confucianism however, and of Chu Hsi in particular, through his correspondence with Jesuit missionaries in China. This collaboration represented the first, and perhaps only, serious effort by the West to discover the truths that made possible the development of the largest and oldest civilization in the world.

Following the Golden Renaissance, as part of the same process that led to the discovery and evangelization of the Americas, Christian missionaries from the Society of Jesus settled in China, studying and translating the Chinese classics, while preaching the Christian message and teaching the scientific discoveries of the Renaissance. They found in the ancient Chinese sages and the Sung Neo-Confucians, a deep understanding of natural law, and found nothing to conflict with the potential to adopt the Christian faith.

Back in Europe, Leibniz followed these developments with avid interest and hope. The existence in China of an ancient culture so in keeping with the truths of natural law discovered by Western civilization, were proof to Leibniz that the human mind must, through *reason*, naturally arrive at these truths—or, as he said, that these truths were "inscribed in our hearts" for all to read.

Father Matteo Ricci (1552-1610), the Jesuit priest who led the opening to China in 1581, had received intensive training in Rome in the scientific breakthroughs of the Renaissance, including the construction of astronomical and musical instruments. He believed that the leap in scientific progress in Renaissance Italy was inseparable from the parallel developments in Christian theology, but insisted that such scientific knowledge was not a "secret" of the West, but the patrimony of all mankind. He found the Chinese to be of a moral disposition to embrace Christianity, while also willing and anxious to enhance their rich scientific heritage with the scientific ideas and technologies that the Jesuits brought with them. Ricci concluded that if the Chinese would reject Buddhism and Taoism, and also reject polygamy and a few other relatively minor rites, they "could certainly become Christians, since the essence of their doctrine contains nothing contrary to the essence of the Catholic faith, nor would the Catholic faith hinder them in any way, but would indeed aid in that attainment of the quiet and peace of the republic which their books claim as their goal."

Leibniz, later, reflecting on the writings of the Jesuits and his own study of the classics, characterized Confucianism as follows:

> To offend Heaven is to act against reason; to ask pardon of Heaven is to reform oneself and to make a sincere return in work and deed in the submission one owes to this very law of reason. For me, I find this all quite excellent and quite in accord with natural theology. . . . Only by strained interpretation and interpolation could one find anything to criticize on this point. It is pure Christianity, insofar as it renews the natural law inscribed on our hearts, except for what revelation and grace add to it to improve our nature.

As will become clear in the course of this study, the historical conflict between Confucianism, on the one hand, and Legalism and Taoism, on the other, follows the same course as the conflict between Platonism and Aristotelianism in the West. And thus, just as the representatives of Renaissance Christian Platonism identified with the Confucian tradition when they encountered it in China, so too did the Western Aristotelians recognize in Legalism and Taoism a kindred spirit.

The nearly successful alliance of Christianity and Confucianism championed by Leibniz collapsed in the early eighteenth century. Within a century, the British imperial intrusion into China was unleashed, with opium and gunships jointly leading the assault to break the moral and political institutions of the faltering Ch'ing Dynasty. Immediately, the British empiricists launched cultural warfare against Confucianism, extolling Taoist mysticism and Legalist totalitarianism as the "essence" of Chinese culture.

British support for tyranny in China has been justified for centuries by the fraudulent argument that the Chinese have never believed in the freedom of the individual, individual civil and human rights, or other "Western" concepts, and thus the bloody suppression of any and all dissent, as carried out by dictators (Communist or otherwise), is justified by "Chinese" standards.

To the contrary, the dominant school of Confucianism for nearly a thousand years in China—the Sung Neo-Confucian school—proclaimed the role of the individual as the singular reflection of the love of the creator of Heaven and earth; an individual whose creative potential must be nourished and extended without bound in order to achieve both personal peace, in keeping with the Way of Heaven, and social progress, based on the expanding capacity of each individual to contribute to that process of development. This scientifically valid view of mankind is the necessary basis for ecumenical peace and global development. Accommodation to any other view will court disaster.

Part I. The Renaissance in Chinese Society

Following the collapse of the T'ang Dynasty in A.D. 907 and a period of general disunity, the Sung Dynasty emerged in 960. The T'ang era had seen the general collapse of the Confucian moral tradition and a broad degeneration of society and culture. The founders of the T'ang, and most of its Emperors, had been dedicated Taoists, but Buddhism also swept through the East during the Seventh to Tenth Centuries. The Taoists and Buddhists were occasionally in conflict (between A.D. 843 and 845, a fanatical Taoist Emperor totally suppressed Buddhism, closing thousands of shrines and defrocking the monks and nuns), but they generally merged into a syncretic amalgam, dragging most of the Confucian scholars into the soup.

There were some exceptions—notably Han Yü (968-824), who attempted to defend the teachings of Confucius and Mencius against both the irrationalist, animist mysticism of Taoism and against Buddhism, especially the pervasive influence of the Zen (Ch'an) Buddhist sect (Zen had developed in the East out of Mahayana Buddhism through contact with Taoism). He equally attacked those Confucianists who believed the three worldviews could coexist.

As the economy and society degenerated under the T'ang, Buddhist monastic communities became the centers of power for oligarchical families. Chinese law had long forbidden the rule of primogeniture, forcing a *division* of property and wealth between one's progeny, which hindered the development of powerful landed families, as well as the larger-than-life power of such "*fondi*" over several generations. However, the monastic communities were generally tax-exempt and were permitted to expand their property holdings indefinitely. Thus, families with oligarchical ambitions would establish their own Buddhist monasteries, and "contribute" extensive wealth and property to the monastic "community." These functioned much the same as the *fondi* in Europe—the monasteries ran businesses, owned vast agricultural lands, and even functioned as the primary source of credit, running pawn shops and loaning money at interest.

The Neo-Confucian school, often called the "Sung teaching" or the "Ch'eng/Chu school," emerged in the eleventh century as a direct counter to this pervasive corruption of government and society, which they blamed squarely on the "heterodox" teachings of Taoism and Zen Buddhism, and the capitulation of Confucianists to these heresies. Just as St. Thomas Aquinas (A.D. 1225-74) undertook the task of countering the destructive influence of Aristotelianism, which had increasingly corrupted Christian teachings in Europe, so the leading scholar of Neo-Confucianism, Chu Hsi (1130-1200), building especially on the work of four

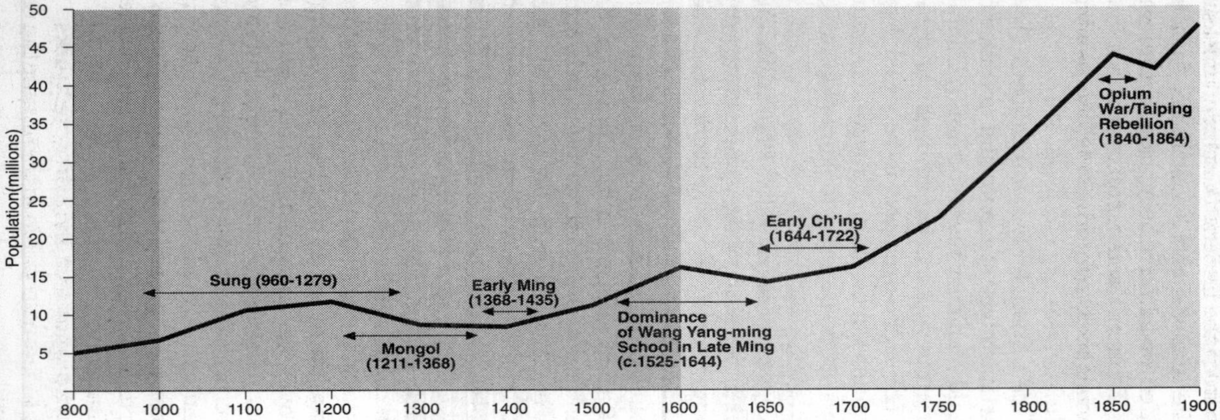

GRAPH I. *Rapid population growth accompanied the three major periods of influence of the Neo-Confucian (Sung) Renaissance worldview, while population collapse followed each recurrence of Taoist/Legalist rule. In addition to the Sung period proper, there were two major revivals of Chu Hsi's ideas as guides to the institutions of the Empire, each leading to a period of dramatic economic, scientific, and cultural advance: First, the early Ming Dynasty, following the devastation of the Mongol occupation in the thirteenth and fourteenth centuries; and second, the early Ch'ing Dynasty, following the collapse of the Ming in 1644 under the dominance of the school of Wang Yang-ming. British Empire "Legalist" policies, combined with their manipulated anti-Confucian Taiping Rebellion, resulted in another population collapse during the eighteenth century.*

Note changes in time scale at A.D. 1000 and 1600.

Source: Colin McEvedy and Richard Jones, *Atlas of World Population History.*

great scholar/statesmen from the Eleventh Century, unleashed a devastating attack on the immoral and scientifically fraudulent premises of Taoist and Zen Buddhist beliefs. Also, extending the comparison, just as St. Thomas, in the process of combatting Aristotelianism, had reached back to the ideas of Plato, as adopted and amended from a Christian standpoint by St. Augustine, and laid the foundation for the Christian Renaissance that followed, so, too, the Neo-Confucianists re-examined and advanced the teachings of Confucius and Mencius. The result was a Confucian Renaissance, a burst of cultural and scientific progress in the Eleventh and Twelfth Centuries, which was to be revived again in the early Fifteenth Century following the intervening Mongol occupation of China.

The Sung Economic Revolution

The Chinese discovery of woodblock printing in the tenth century led to a vast expansion of printed books in subsequent centuries. Not only were the Confucian classics printed and distributed, but also the works of the Neo-Confucians, by both government and private publishers. For the first time in history, scholars were able to reach the entire nation with their teaching. The other major category of printed books was scientific studies, covering agriculture, hydraulics, astronomy, and other areas of technological development. The Ch'eng/Chu dictum to "investigate the Principle in things to the utmost" led to an explosion of scientific and technological discoveries, with each discovery spread around the country rapidly through books and newspapers.

The agricultural revolution was the driving force for the expansion of the economy. Historian Mark Elvin has written: "It was the generalization over the country as a whole of the best Sung techniques, without a correspondingly large expansion of the area of farmland ... [by which] the foundation of China's enormous present population was laid." (Elvin) [*see* Bibliography for publication information] The potential population density exploded, as the following technological capacities were developed and implemented (*see* Graph I):

- **New hydraulic techniques and irrigation networks**;
- **New seed strains**, to increase yields and enhance the capability for double cropping;

- **Improved methods of soil preparation**, utilizing fertilizers and tools; and
- **Vast networks of roads and canals**, allowing broader marketing, and thus greater specialization of crops.

By the thirteenth century, "China had what was probably the most sophisticated agriculture in the world, India being the only conceivable rival." (Elvin)

Internal and foreign trade boomed. Shipbuilding became a major industry, producing thousands of inland and seagoing ships of a quality not seen in Europe for centuries. The mariner's compass, discovered in about 1119, led to the charting of the sea and advanced navigation techniques. A national customs service was established to regulate and tax trade, with over two thousand custom houses. Standardized coinage and the world's first system of paper currency were established in the early Eleventh Century. Federally issued notes, based on convertibility at any of several provincial Treasuries, facilitated safe and expanding internal trade.

Industries of a size not seen in Europe until the Eighteenth Century were developed. Iron works, using coke and other metallurgical discoveries, and silk factories with as many as five hundred looms, contributed to national growth and to rapid urbanization. By 1100, there were fifty-one prefectures which had over 100,000 households, far surpassing the cities of Europe.

Although there were many internal policy differences, the Sung leadership was generally the driving force behind the revolution in education and science. Books in all fields were prepared and published by the government, while great public works, public granaries, and infrastructure projects were undertaken at government expense. Chu Hsi was himself a significant figure in establishing these policies, both through his writings and through his various positions in government. His establishment of public granaries in the area under his jurisdiction, both to prepare for emergencies and to prevent speculation by "the propertied gentlemen who would stop selling grain in order to realized a profit" (*Further Reflection on Things at Hand*, 9:23), was adopted as national policy.

Chu Hsi's advice on infrastructure reveals an advanced sense of physical economy:

> Recruiting hungry people to build waterworks, and slightly increasing outside sums to be used for capital in beginning construction, is to protect against disaster and to create new prosperity, like killing two birds with one stone. . . . The cost would be minimal, but the advantages would last forever. (*Further Reflections*, 10:51)

Chu Hsi and the Conjunctural Crisis

Chu Hsi knew, however, that China had fallen into a severe, long-term breakdown crisis over the previous millennium, and that as important as the developments under the Sung were, the underlying problem had not been solved. He repeatedly warned that the rule of Universal Principle was lost among the people, and that a disaster (an "unnatural embankment") faced the nation:

> Today, the Principle of Tao is lost. Can we unflaggingly cultivate ourselves and restore it? This is why it is such an urgent matter. If we do not study, we will face an unnatural embankment. In normal times we could, perhaps, barely get by. But when we are faced with a critical matter, there will be only confusion. (*Further Reflections*, 2:35)

The works of his Eleventh-Century predecessors, in fact, had been subjected to severe attack. Cheng I had been banished in 1097, and his teachings prohibited. He was then pardoned in 1100, blacklisted in 1103, and pardoned again in 1106; but the ban on his teachings remained until 1155, when Chu Hsi revived them. In the interim, in 1126, the Juchin from Manchuria successfully invaded northern China, establishing the Chin Dynasty in the north, while the Sung were forced into the south.

Chu spent nine years in government office. He submitted numerous memorials on diverse subjects to several different Emperors, with varying effect. His proposals for specific government policies in water management, canal building, national food resources, and other areas were implemented regionally and in some cases nationally. He instituted the White Deer Grotto Academy as the center for his teaching, which became the pre-eminent intellectual center of his time, and the model for education in China, Korea, and Japan for centuries.

But his warnings made many uncomfortable. In his sixty-sixth year, he was dismissed from his last official position in the

Court, accused of teaching a "false theory" and of plotting to usurp the government. His leading pupil was exiled. It was in these last years that he devoted himself to completing his work on the Confucian text, the "Great Learning."

Part II. The Confucian and Christian Renaissances

The parallels between the Confucian and the Christian Renaissances are most obvious when both are viewed from the perspective of universal history. The converse is also true: without this demonstrably valid view of history, any attempts at comparison result in the wildest fantasies and concoctions. Such strained comparisons literally fill the scholarly texts on comparative philosophy. Chu Hsi, for example, has been compared often (and correctly) to St. Thomas Aquinas, but also to Alfred North Whitehead, G.W.F. Hegel, and Immanuel Kant, while even described by some as a polytheist. As we will see, such views belie a total failure to grasp the fundamental principles guiding Chu Hsi's thought.

Leibniz, in his 1716 *Natural Theology of the Chinese*, approached his analysis of Chinese philosophy by acknowledging that the highly cultured and learned civilization of the Chinese, and the relatively enormous population density, were proof that the Chinese had succeeded in mastering to a high degree the truths of natural law which govern the universe. He, therefore, in undertaking a study of the classic texts, *assumed the most positive interpretation possible* of the ideas presented, not out of a false sense of generosity or kindness to the Chinese, but in order to ferret out the truths which he knew must be contained within these writings, without, of course, ignoring disagreements on important secondary issues. Cusanus, although he was unfamiliar with Confucianism and thus did not address it directly in his writings, expressed the same principle in "On the Peace of Faith": "The divine commandments are very brief and are all well known and common in every nation, for the light that reveals them to us is created along with the rational soul." (Wertz, *Toward A New Council of Florence*)

Confucian *Jen* and St. Paul's *Agapē*

A crucial polemic of the Neo-Confucians revolved around the interpretation of the notion of *jen* (仁), a word usually translated as "humanity" or "benevolence," terms which do not adequately convey the meaning in Chinese. Confucius and Mencius defined *jen* as the highest of all virtues with which Heaven endows mankind, subsuming love and righteousness, propriety and wisdom. In the eleventh century, Ch'eng I, one of the greatest of Chu Hsi's predecessors, identified the fact that the interpretation of the term *jen*, over the centuries following the death of Mencius, had become synonymous with another term meaning "love." But since this term for "love" represented a human feeling, often ambiguously connected to notions of mere sensuality, it had become "an inferior and crude concept," in the words of one of Chu Hsi's students. (Ch'en Ch'un [1159-1223], cited in Hitoshi)

Even the greatest of the T'ang Dynasty Confucians, Han Yü, who extended the meaning of *jen* to be "universal love," still failed to comprehend the "loftier and nobler" concept intended by Confucius and Mencius, according to this Neo-Confucian school.

The failure to understand the deeper meaning of *jen* was blamed primarily on the acceptance, even by supposedly Confucian scholars, of the object fixation and irrationalism of the pervasive Zen and Taoist schools of thought. As shown below, Chu Hsi argued that these sects failed to recognize the divine spark of reason in man, man's capacity to participate in God's continuing creation of the universe, and they were thus reduced to a materialist view of the world, a God-less world in which man is impotent to rise above an animal state of sense perception.

The solution lay, said Chu Hsi in his "Treatise on *Jen*," in recognizing that *jen* is the "*principle* of love." Chu wrote:

> When one realizes that *jen* is the *source* of love, and that love can never exhaust *jen*, then one has gained a definite comprehension of *jen*. (Hitoshi)

Together with righteousness, propriety, and wisdom, *jen* is a virtue created by God for no "practical" purpose, but as a pure expression of his own boundless love. Human love and compassion are the *effect* of *jen*, not its substance. Confucius said that "spreading charity widely to save the multitudes" is not *jen*, although *jen* is the source of morality and of all moral deeds. Said Chu,

> It is not for the sake of anything that [*jen*] came into existence. . . . *Jen* is the principle of love and the way of life. Thus by living in *jen*, all four primary virtues will be covered. (Hitoshi)

Ch'eng I emphasized that *jen* is the "foundation of goodness," and as such can be considered as "universal impartiality" (Chu Hsi, *Reflections on Things at Hand,* 1:11), in the sense of God's impartial love for all creatures. Man's coherence with universal impartiality is guided by the Golden Rule, which is expressed by Confucius and Mencius in both positive and negative forms: "Do unto others as you would have them do unto you," and "Do not do anything to another which you would not have them do unto you." The principles of both charity and equity are subsumed in this notion of impartiality. Says Cheng I,

> Because of [man's] impartiality, there will be no distinction between himself and others. Therefore, a man of *jen* is a man of both altruism and love. Altruism is the application of *jen*, while love is its function. (*Reflections,* 2:52)

Chu Hsi identifies *jen* as the essence of creation itself:

> The mind of Heaven to produce things is *jen*. In man's endowment, he receives this mind from Heaven, and thus he can produce. Therefore, man's feeling of commiseration is also a principle of production. (*Reflections,* 1:42)

The divine spark of reason, which distinguishes man from beast, and provides man with the unique capacity to participate in God's continuing creation of the universe, is precisely this power of love, *jen*.

The effort to identify the more profound meaning of *jen* proves to be a process of discovery parallel to that of St. Paul in developing the concept of a higher form of love, or *agapē*. This higher notion of love, as distinguished from erotic love, was located in the love of God, the love of truth, and of mankind as a whole which must guide man if he is to find true meaning in his life.

One of the clearest expressions of the Neo-Confucian development of this concept came in the famous "Western Inscription" of Chang Tsai, also called "Correcting Obstinacy":

> Heaven is my father and Earth is my mother, and even such a small creature as I finds an intimate place in their midst. Therefore, that which fills the universe I regard as my body, and that which directs the universe I consider as my nature. All people are my brothers and sisters, and all things are my companions. . . . Respect the aged. . . . Show affection toward the orphans and the weak. . . . Even those who are tired, infirm, crippled or sick, those who have no brothers or children, wives or husbands, are all my brothers who are in distress and have no one to turn to. . . .
>
> To rejoice in Heaven with no anxiety, this is filial piety at its purest.
>
> He who disobeys [the principle of Heaven] violates virtue. He who destroys *jen* is a robber. He who promotes evil lacks [moral] capacity. But he who puts his moral nature into practice and brings his physical existence into complete fulfillment can match [Heaven]. One who knows the principle of transformation will skillfully carry forward the undertaking of Heaven, and one who penetrates spirit to the highest degree will skillfully carry out Heaven's will.
>
> Do nothing shameful in the recesses of your own house. . . . Preserve the mind and nourish the nature and thus serve them with untiring effort. . . .
>
> In life I follow and serve [Heaven]. In death I will be at peace. (*Reflections*, 2:89)

Several points are of special significance. First, the "Western Inscription" places the concept of *jen* as the guiding principle of God's creation, and defines man's nature as the same as "that which directs the universe." In Christian terms, this is to be "in the living image of God," *imago viva Dei*. It also addresses another related Christian concept, that man is created with the capacity to be like-unto-God, *capax Dei*, by acting in accord with His will. Here, Chang Tsai says that if man applies his true God-given moral nature in every aspect of his life, and subjects his physical nature to God's will, he can "match" God.

Secondly, the "Western Inscription" places a profoundly higher perspective on the meaning of filial piety—a fundamental Confucian virtue, but one often interpreted as merely a set of strict codes of conduct towards one's parents. Here, Chang Tsai holds Heaven to be the father and Earth to be the mother of man, in the sense of God creating man's physical body out of the substance of His material creation. Man exists in a dignified "intimate" place in the universe owing to his creation as a human being, a blessing he owes to God and to all of God's creatures who have gone before him, and in particular to his physical mother and father. In return for this endowment of life, man returns this love, to his parents, of course, but also to *all* mankind and to God himself. Thus, "to rejoice in Heaven with no anxiety—this is filial piety at its purest."

Lastly, while none of the Confucian nor the Neo-Confucian scholars explicitly taught the existence of everlasting life after death in the sense of the Christian Heaven, it is acknowledged that upon death, that part of man which came from Earth returns to Earth (dust to dust), while that part which came from Heaven returns to Heaven. The so-called ancestor worship of Confucianism is primarily a ritual of paying respect and love to the spirit of those departed souls. What was utterly *rejected* by Chu Hsi was the Buddhist notion of the transmigration of souls, and not the idea of an eternal soul. Therefore, the closing paragraphs of the "Western Inscription," like other similar expressions throughout Neo-Confucian teaching, which refer to attaining peace at death, can be interpreted as: "Follow God and serve Him, and you shall enter the Kingdom of Heaven."

Chu Hsi refers directly, although negatively, to the immortality of the soul in writing that if one fails to live according to the Way of God, "then one will live an empty life and die an empty death. . . ." (*Further Reflections,* 12:14)

Ch'eng I said that a virtuous man identifies a quality in himself which is more important than life itself, and implies that that quality is sustained in death when one's life is given for humanity:

> Some ancient sages sacrificed their lives. They must have truly understood that life is neither as important as righteousness nor as

> satisfactory as death. Therefore, they sacrificed their lives to fulfill humanity. (*Reflections*, 7:25)

Li: The School of Principle

The Neo-Confucian school is also known in Chinese as the "School of Principle." The primary new conceptual contributions to the Confucian body of knowledge by the Ch'eng/Chu School centered on the concept of *Li* (理), or Principle. Confucius did not use the term at all, while Mencius used it to mean "moral principle," but not as a fundamental concept in his teaching. Chu Hsi developed and used the concept in a manner analogous to Plato's concept of the eternal "Ideas." Leibniz noted that Chu's concept was similar to his own notion of the "monad." Lyndon LaRouche has developed his own notion of the "thought-object" as analogous to the historically specific concepts of Plato's Ideas and Leibniz's monads. The Neo-Confucian Principle (*Li*) is coherent with these various valid scientific discoveries concerning the fundamental lawfulness of the universe.

Chu Hsi defines Principle as follows:

> Universal Principle is indeed complete wholeness. However, we call it Principle in that it has a completely ordered pattern. . . . Universal Principle is simply a comprehensive term for the four virtues (*jen*, righteousness, propriety, and wisdom), and each of them is an individual enumeration for Universal Principle. (*Further Reflections*, 1:9)

Universal Principle is sometimes called the Great Ultimate, or the Ultimate of Non-being, or the Essence of Tao, where Tao means the Way or the Path. To Chu Hsi, these terms all refer to the one Creator God in the same sense as was understood by the fathers of Christianity and those who followed in the tradition of St. Augustine. (As these terms are used interchangeably by Chu and his school, we occasionally use the word God in place of them in these translations, although the works cited in the Bibliography do not do so.)

Leibniz, in his study of Neo-Confucianism, arrived at this same conclusion, while also equating Principle (*Li*) with Universal Reason:

> The first principle of the Chinese is called *Li*, that is, Reason, or the foundation of all nature, the most universal reason and substance; there is nothing greater nor better than *Li*. . . . [It] is not at all capable of divisibility as regards its being and is the principal basis of all the essences which are and which can exist in the world. But it is also the aggregation of the most perfect multiplicity because the Being of this principle contains the essences of things as they are in their germinal state. We say as much when we teach that the ideas, the primitive grounds, the prototypes of all essences are all in God. . . . The Chinese also attribute to the *Li* all manner of perfection . . . so perfect that there is nothing to add. One has said it all. Consequently, can we not say that the *Li* of the Chinese is the sovereign substance which we revere under the name of God? (Leibniz, *Discourse on the Natural Theology of the Chinese*, #4-9)

To Chu Hsi, God, the Universal Principle, is infinite, indivisible, and eternal. He is the creator of all that is, and preceded everything which was created. Most importantly, Chu developed the notion that Principle "is an all encompassing wholeness which contains everything, and which is contained in everything." (*Further Reflections*, 1:2) Principle is Unity, but "the myriad things partake of it as their reality. Hence, each of the myriad things possesses in it the Great Ultimate." (*Chu Tzu ch'üan-shu* [Collected Works of Chu Hsi], 49:8b-13a; hereafter CTCS. All translations from CTCS are from deBary, *Sources of Chinese Tradition*) The true essence of every individual thing in the universe is its Principle, which is given by God as its nature. In particular, the nature of man is Principle.

Leibniz, in his *Discourse on Metaphysics*, said, "It can indeed be said that every substance bears in some sort the character of God's infinite wisdom and omnipotence, and imitates Him as much as it is able to." Like Plato's Ideas, the individual Principle of any created thing is eternal, although the thing itself is, of course, not eternal. St. Augustine, drawing on Plato through the revelation of Christianity, said:

> Ideas are the primary forms or the permanent and immutable reasons of real things and they are not themselves formed; so they are, as a consequence, eternal and ever the same in themselves, and they

> are contained in the divine intelligence. (Wertz, *Toward a New Council of Florence*)

Cusanus extended this concept, saying that, "every created thing is, as it were, a finite infinite." It is finite, in that it is bounded by its material form, but it is infinite precisely as its nature reflects God's creation. The nature of every created thing (Chu Hsi's "Principle") is demonstrated by the fact of the coherent, self-developing order of the universe itself, or as Cusanus said: "The universe is ordered to its origin—through order the universe indeed shows itself as being from God—it is ordered to Him as to the Order of the order in everything." ("On the Not-Other," in Wertz)

This concept, that all created things reflect the lawfulness of the creation, and that this connection between all things and the Creator is the essence of each particular thing, is the necessary basis of any scientific knowledge, while also serving to refute any and all materialist views of the universe. To the Christian humanists, the empiricist tradition of Aristotle, which attempts to reduce the world to a mere collection of disconnected objects, and man's impotent observations (sense-perception) of those objects, was both false and an obstacle to the development of fruitful scientific knowledge of the universe.

In Plato's terms, true scientific knowledge comes from a process of hypothesis; when an existing state of knowledge is contradicted by newly discovered phenomena, an hypothesis based on this higher conception of the order of creation (Plato's Ideas) would provide the basis for advancing the state of knowledge as a whole, affecting the entire range of human knowledge, beyond the specific phenomena investigated. (*see* LaRouche, "The Science of Christian Economy" and "On the Subject of God")

Ch'i and *Imago Viva Dei*

Chu Hsi's understanding of science is in keeping with this Platonic method. The primary tenet of the Neo-Confucian teaching is that the nature of man, like the nature of all things, and of the universe as a whole, is Principle. Ch'eng I said: "Principle is one but its manifestations are many. . . . There is only one Principle. As applied to man, however, there is in each individual a particular Principle." (CTCS 49:1b)

God creates the universe through what Chu calls *Ch'i* (氣) or Material Force (*Ch'i* is also translated as "energy," "vital force," etc. Mencius used the term as that which "pervades and animates the body," subordinate to the will, and nourished by acting according to righteousness and reason. [*Mencius*, 2:12]) This Material Force, as developed by Chu, is not identical with Principle, but is created by it and cannot exist without it. Universal Principle, God, is infinite, incorporeal, and eternal. The Material Force, said Chu,

> refers to material objects, which are within the realm of corporeality; it is the instrument by which things are produced. . . . Before heaven and earth came into being, Principle was as it was. . . . As there is a certain Principle, there is the Material Force corresponding to it, and as this Material Force integrates in a particular instance, its Principle is also endowed in that instance (CTCS 49:5b, 6a, 8a)

The Material Force can be thought of as the lawfulness imbedded in nature, or, the non-linear geometry of the created universe. While the laws of creation are not the same as God, who precedes them, those laws are indistinguishable from God, and it is through these laws that the creation of all things takes place. All created things thus reflect these laws in their being, and God exists in them in this way. Inanimate objects, plants, and animals represent, in ascending order, this natural law, in that they reflect increasingly the self-generating principle of God, while only man has this natural law in such purity, through the power of reason, that he can reflect upon and perfect his powers of creativity and self-generation.

Leibniz also concluded that Chu Hsi's Material Force (*Ch'i*) functioned as the natural law created by God:

> Thus I believe that without doing violence to the ancient doctrine of the Chinese, one can say that the *Li* [Principle] has been brought by the perfection of its nature to choose, from several possibilities, the most appropriate; and that by this means it has produced the

> *Ch'i* [Material Force] with dispositions such that all the rest has come about by natural propensities. (Leibniz, #18)

This is a reference to Leibniz's concept that this world is "the best of all possible worlds," such that the laws governing the physical universe assure that the greatest good is achieved in the most efficient way possible: "we say that nature is wise; that she does all for an end and nothing in vain." (Leibniz, #8) Chu Hsi hinted at this by asserting: "Everything naturally has a way of being just right." (*Further Reflections*, 10:11)

In this light, it is important to note that Chu Hsi, like Cusanus and Leibniz, rejected any materialist idea that material objects were composed of some "fundamental particle," but, rather, saw in even the smallest being a dynamic existence in space-time. The laws of creation found in every created thing are intelligible to man, as Cusanus' Minimum/Maximum Principle or Leibniz's Principle of Least Action are examples. (*see* LaRouche, "On the Subject of Metaphor") Chu would have laughed at the modern-day search for the "ultimate particle," recognizing such efforts as a reflection of a Taoist view of the universe.

Leibniz saw in Chu Hsi's concept of the Material Force a reflection of his own notion of the continuum of space-time, and related it to his idea of the aether. Leibniz wrote:

> It seems that this *Ch'i* (Material Force), or this primitive air, truly corresponds to Matter, just as it corresponds to the instrument of the first principle which moves matter; just as an artisan moves his instrument, producing things. This *Ch'i* is called air, and for us could be called aether, because matter in its original form is completely fluid, without bonds or solidarity, without any interstices and without limits which could distinguish parts of it one from another. In sum, this *Ch'i* is the most subtle one can imagine.

Thus, to Leibniz, as to Chu Hsi, the Material Force (*Ch'i*) is the geometry of the universe, the non-linear ordering principle by which all things come into being, and the basis upon which all things interact with each other.

It is the Material Force in each created thing, its particular "geometry," which distinguishes the myriad of things from one another. In particular, although all things are equally created by God and reflect His perfection through their Principle, it is through the Material Force that God made man in His own image, just as the Bible identifies this fundamental truth for Judeo-Christian culture. Said Chu Hsi,

> From the point of view of Principle, all things have the same source, and, therefore, man and things cannot be distinguished as higher or lower creatures. From the point of view of Material Force, man receives it in its perfection and unimpeded, while things receive it partially and obstructed. Because of this, they are unequal, man being higher and things lower. (CTCS 42:27b-29c)

This, then, is the condition of each and every man at birth. Mencius had emphasized this fact, that Man is born Good, reflecting the Highest Good of God, and that this was the primary truth of mankind, without which nothing could be understood. Throughout Chinese history, those who wished to justify evil, those who wished to impose political tyranny, argued against Mencius on precisely this point. Like the Aristotelians in Western history, the Legalists in ancient China, based on Taoist ideology, argued that man was born as a mere beast, driven by greed and other animal instincts, who can be ruled only by enforcing a stratified, slave society, governed by punishment and reward. [*see* Billington, "The British Role in the Creation of Maoism," for a comparison of Legalism and modern British empiricism.] In particular, the Gang of Four, during the Cultural Revolution, totally rejected Mencius in favor of Legalism, going so far as to declare that "class enemies" of the Communist Party were, often by mere circumstances of birth, not human beings, and, therefore, not worthy of any basic human rights.

Chu Hsi extended Mencius' idea to a higher scientific level. It is this quality of perfected Material Force, or perfected potential, which makes man uniquely capable of both continuous expansion of his knowledge of the laws of the physical universe, and also of participating with God in the continuing creation of the universe, through the exercise of his "divine spark" of reason, the Principle (*Li*) endowed by Heaven.

In the Christian tradition, St. Thomas Aquinas and Nicolaus of Cusa distinguished between the intellect and lower levels of human thought, including mere linear, logical, inductive or deductive thinking, and the even lower level of sense-perception. The mind is always in danger of becoming entangled with the material, finite aspects of the things of this world, which are the objects of our senses, but by rising to the level of the intellect, which is that part of our mental powers which reflect the Creator, we can intuit the Absolute Infinite. This is because, as St. Thomas wrote,

> the intellect is a form not in matter, but either wholly separate from matter, as in the angelic substance, or at least an intellectual power, which is not the act of an organ, in the intellectual soul joined to a body. (*Summa Theologica*, Part I, Q. 7, Article 2)

Chu Hsi's notion of the mind is very similar to this. While the original nature of man is Principle, which comes from God, and man receives the Material Force "in its perfection," still, the mind is always in danger of responding to the appearance of material things rather than their essence, their Principle. In this way, the mind becomes "cloudy," dragged down by fixations on things in themselves, and the purity of the God-given original nature is obscured. Chu points out that man receives the Material Force in the clearest form, while animals receive it in a turbid state. "However," says Chu, "those whose Material Force is turbid are not far removed from animals." (CTCS 43:7a-b) Also:

> The essence of a person's original mind is also boundless. It is only that it is corralled by the selfishness of the thing, and stagnated by the paucity of knowledge. (*Further Reflections*, 1:56)

How does one overcome "selfishness" and "paucity of knowledge"? Chu insisted that true knowledge is not particular facts about particular things, but rather the knowledge of God, the Principle of the universe. Since the Principle of any created thing reflects the Universal Principle of the Creator, the investigation of the Principle of any particular thing will contribute to understanding the Principle of all other things, as well as the Universal

Principle itself. Also, by the fact that every created thing reflects God's creation, and that man's (unobscured) mind is based on that same Principle, man is uniquely capable of achieving an understanding of any particular thing or phenomena in the universe—i.e., the laws of the universe are intelligible to man.

Conversely, achieving such an understanding of the Principle of any particular thing improves one's knowledge of one's own nature, and thus increases one's ability to probe deeper into the Principle of other things and into one's own mind.

The following quotes illustrate the concept:

Chu Hsi:
When Heaven creates a thing, it gives each thing a truth. (*Further Reflections*, 1:66)

Chu Hsi:
There is not one thing in the universe, however great or small, or obscure or bright, that is without Principle. We cannot speak of inner and outer. If there is anything that cannot be reasoned out, then how could it mean Principle? (*Further Reflections*, 3:8)

Ch'eng I:
All things under Heaven can be understood through Principle. . . . Each thing necessarily has its manifestations of Principle. (Gardner)

Cheng Tsai:
By enlarging one's mind, one can enter into all things in the world. . . . The mind of ordinary people is limited to the narrowness of what is seen and heard. The sage, however, fully develops his nature and does not allow what is seen and heard to fetter his mind. Heaven is so vast there is nothing outside it. Therefore, the mind that leaves something outside it is not capable of uniting itself with the mind of Heaven. (*Reflections*, 2:83)

'Learning for Adults'

The message that man must pursue the scientific investigation of the ordering principles of things and phenomena in the physical universe, became a central theme of Chu Hsi's effort to save Chinese civilization. The Taoists taught that the laws of the universe were unknowable, that an irrational, mystical force governed Heaven and Earth, and that proper government required the suppression of knowledge in order to enforce order. The Buddhists rejected the physical world as unreal, teaching that enlightenment is found by suppressing thinking altogether, through quietism. To combat this, Chu Hsi chose a short passage from the ancient *Book of Rites*, which was probably written by Confucius. Called the "Great Learning," the passage consisted of only seven short paragraphs, plus commentary by a disciple of Confucius.

Through a new interpretation of two key passages in the "Great Learning," Chu turned it into a concrete starting point for the broad dissemination of his own fundamental epistemological contributions, using the words of Confucius himself. In fact, Chu Hsi even interpreted the title ("Great Learning") differently than had been generally accepted usage, taking the word for "Great" to mean "Adult": The title then is "Learning for the Adult." This contrasted with a common understanding that the classics were "learning for the sages." Chu Hsi's interpretation is in keeping with his life-long commitment to the establishment of universal education, both because such education is necessary for each individual to achieve true happiness through communion with the Creator, but also because the successful progress of the state depends on an enlightened population.

The first of the two passages from the "Great Learning" reinterpreted by Chu is in the first paragraph, which reads in Chu Hsi's interpretation:

> The way (Tao) of greater learning lies in *keeping one's inborn luminous virtue unobscured*, in renewing the people, and in coming to rest in perfect goodness. (Gardner)

Earlier scholars had interpreted the italicized phrase as "manifesting luminous virtue," with the intention that the sage or ruler must manifest outwardly a perfected virtue, which by example would inspire the people to virtue. Chu, instead, emphasized the "inborn" nature of the "luminous virtue," in keeping with his concept that the nature of man is the God-given Principle, which is one with *jen*, the highest virtue. This then applies to all men, not just the ruler. In addition, Chu changes "manifesting" to "keeping unobscured," which re-emphasizes the same point—that the nature of all mankind is good, but becomes obscured in the process of interacting with the physical universe. Chu says that although the God-given luminous virtue can become restrained or obscured by material things and human desires, "Never, however, does its original luminosity cease. Therefore, the student should look to the light that emanates from it and seek to keep it unobscured, thereby restoring its original conditions." (Gardner)

Chu Hsi retains the notion of teaching by example, as in the phrase: "renewing the people," which results from the love and charity *jen* of one who "keeps the inborn luminous virtue unobscured." But, again, this is something which each individual, not just the ruler, is capable of doing, and is called upon by Heaven to do.

The second section of the "Great Learning" (or "Learning for Adults") which Chu Hsi interpreted in a new way came in the famous passage which sequentially links proper government to the full development of the individual creative potential. In Chu Hsi's interpretation, this reads as follows:

> Those of antiquity who wished that all men throughout the empire keep their inborn luminous virtue unobscured put governing their states well first; wishing to govern their states well, they first established harmony in their households; wishing to establish harmony in their households, they first cultivated themselves; wishing to cultivate themselves, they first set their minds in the right; wishing to set their minds in the right, they first made their thoughts true; wishing to make their thoughts true, they first extended their knowledge to the utmost; the extension of knowledge lies in fully apprehending the principle in things.

Note that the last line is not part of the sequence, but is a general statement defining the extension or perfection of knowledge. This statement is, in the Chinese, ambiguous, and had been subject to drastically different interpretations historically. Chu's interpretation meant that the final source in the entire sequential process necessary for successful government was the scientific investigation of the Principle of all things and phenomena in society and in the physical universe by the individual.

This was a dramatic contribution to the interpretation of the classics, although Chu insisted that this was precisely the meaning understood by Confucius and Mencius. To justify his interpretation, Chu Hsi did something even more dramatic, making what could be called a *Promethean* intervention into history, past, present, and future. He argued that a chapter in the commentary by the disciple of Confucius, which discussed the meaning of this passage, had been lost and that he, Chu, had, in his own words, "Taken the liberty . . . of filling in the lacunae," and "made bold . . . to supplement it." This added chapter is an eloquent statement of Chu's understanding of the beautiful order of the creation:

> What is meant by "the extension of knowledge lies in fully apprehending the principle in things" is that, if we wish to extend our knowledge to the utmost, we must probe thoroughly the Principle in those things we encounter. It would seem that every man's intellect is possessed of the capacity for knowing and that everything in the world is possessed of Principle. But, to the extent that Principle is not yet thoroughly probed, man's knowledge is not yet fully realized. Hence, the first step of instruction in greater learning is to teach the student whenever he encounters anything at all in the world, to build upon what is already known to him about Principle and to probe still further, so that he seeks to reach the limit. After exerting himself in this way for a long time, he will one day become enlightened and thoroughly understand; then, the manifest and the hidden, the subtle and the obvious qualities of all things will all be known, and the mind, in its whole substance and vast operations, will be completely illuminated. This is called "fully apprehending the Principle in things." This is called "the completion of knowledge."

Note, first, that Chu Hsi rejects Aristotelian empiricism as a method of scientific exploration, demanding the investigation of the Principle of things, rather than mere observation of physical characteristics, and, second, that he identifies the necessity of the Platonic method of hypothesis—"to build upon what is already known to him about Principle"—in order to achieve true knowledge.

Chu Hsi is accused by his enemies with tampering with the Confucian classics and distorting their meaning. Serious study of those classics, however, confirms Chu's contention that the concepts he develops all come directly from Confucius and Mencius, or were coherent with the worldview taught by them. In fact, Chu Hsi himself carried out a comprehensive study of the classics, wrote extensive commentaries on all of them, and is even personally responsible for elevating the writings of Confucius and Mencius to become the central focus of all education and examinations in the Empire. Previously, it had been even earlier texts, which Confucius had studied (and helped to compile), that had functioned as the core of the scholarly curriculum. Chu chose two shorter sections from the *Book of Rites*—the "Great Learning" and the "Doctrine of the Mean"—which, together with the collected writings of Confucius and Mencius, were called the "Four Books." These texts, with commentaries by Chu Hsi, remained the core of the education and examination system into the twentieth century.

The Renaissance in the West

Chu Hsi's central concepts, discussed above, can be readily shown to be coherent with those which guided the Renaissance in the West. In Cusanus' "On Equality," he describes the universe and everything in it as "similitudes" of God, in the same sense that Chu sees the Principle of every created thing as coming directly from God and reflecting His creation. Then, as in Chu's central theme that "the extension of knowledge lies in fully apprehending the Principle in things," Cusanus says that the human intellectual soul sees the "knowable extrinsic through the consubstantial intrinsic. . . . The more it moves toward the other, in order to know it, the more it enters into itself." The shared concept here is that the laws of creative thought in the human mind are the same as the laws that govern the creation and development in the physical universe, and this fact uniquely defines man's capacity to know those laws, in an increasingly less-imperfect way.

In "On Beryllus," Cusanus restates this, in words similar to Chu Hsi's interpretation of the "Great Learning," which called on man to "keep one's inborn luminous virtue unobscured." Cusanus states that while God is absolutely infinite, and although the truth cannot be known in full by man, "but its similitude, which can be received to a greater or lesser degree, according to the disposition of the recipient, is communicable."

Cusanus said that man, by acting on his "similitude" with God, through exercise of the intellect, can become an "adoptive Son of God." Thus man is "relatively infinite," capable of comprehending the Absolute Infinite from within the finite, material body. (Aristotle, by contrast, argued that "the infinite considered as such is unknown.")

St. Thomas Aquinas had formulated these ideas in a manner which also reveals the parallel to Chu Hsi. In the *Summa Theologica*, St. Thomas said that man is capable of knowing God and the laws of the universe

> according to analogy, that is, according to proportion. . . . Thus, whatever is said of God and creatures is said *according to the relation of a creature to God as its principle and cause,* wherein all perfection of things pre-exist excellently. [emphasis added]

There is, furthermore, an explicit parallel between Chu Hsi's use of the concept of Material Force (*Ch'i*) as described above, and a concept introduced by Cusanus, "the potential-to-become." Cusanus distinguishes between the eternal, the perpetual, and the temporal. God, the eternal, is actual-potential. But every created thing which is actual in the universe had the potential-to-become, which was created by God. This "potential-to-become" is the perpetual process whereby all temporal things are created by God, in keeping with His law. According to Cusanus the potential-to-become is created out of nothing by God, who is the actual-potential. Therefore, the potential-to-become is created, but does not cease; rather it remains for all time and is perpetual, because it precedes everything that has become actual, which is temporal.

This is a scientific statement of Creation, of God creating the heaven and the earth out of nothing. Unlike the Aristotelian empiricist cults which dominate scientific thinking today, which describe a finite world with a fixed number of "fundamental particles" which is entropically "running down," Cusanus' notion describes the actual negentropic universe, undergoing perpetual creation through the potential-to-become, which was created by the actual-potential which is God.

Compare this to Chu Hsi's discussion of Principle (*Li*) and Material Force (*Ch'i*):

> God has no other business but to produce things. The Material Force of the origination revolves and circulates without a moment of rest, doing nothing but creating the myriad things. (CTCS 49:23b-24a)
>
> That which integrates to produce life and disintegrates to produce death is only Material Force. . . . Principle fundamentally does not exist nor cease to exist because of integration or disintegration. As there is a certain Principle, there is the Material Force corresponding to it, and as this Material Force integrates in a particular instance, its Principle is also endowed in that instance. (CTCS 49:8a)

This substantiates the view of Leibniz, discussed above, that Chu Hsi's Material Force (*Ch'i*) corresponded to his notion of the aether.

The Trinity

The coherence between the Neo-Confucian worldview of natural law as expressed in the concepts of *jen* and *Li*, and the fundamental concepts of Christian humanism, is most clearly seen insofar as these concepts are reflections of the ideas expressed by the Christian notion of the Trinity.

Cusanus argues that the revealed truth of the Trinity, the triune God, consisting of God the Father, God the Son, and God the Holy Spirit, always existed, even before the time of Christ, in the form of *Unity*, *Equality*, and *Connection*, and that the Trinity is thus inherent in any form of knowledge of the One God.

By *Unity* is meant the One and the Many co-existing in God; that the One God is the cause of everything singular, while every actual thing is singular in its essence precisely as it is a reflection of God's creation. This is God the Father. It should be clear that to the Neo-Confucians this is a description of Universal Principle, which is the One God, and which exists in each created thing as its nature.

By *Equality* is meant the unique capacity of man in his purest, God-given nature, in the living image of God, to approach equality with God, as a similitude of God, and through the intellect to examine and discover the similitude of all things to the Creator. For Christians, God the Son represents perfect *Equality* with God, while through the imitation of Christ every man can be one with Him. For the Neo-Confucians, this describes man's "inborn luminous virtue," the particular Principle (*Li*) in each man, manifested through the Material Force (*Ch'i*, or Cusanus' "potential-to-become"), and through which, if kept unobscured and nourished through the sincere investigation of the Principle in things, can make it possible to walk in the Path of God (Tao).

By *Connection*, Cusanus meant precisely that divine love which flows from the Unity of God, connecting Him directly with his creation, and which flows also from the creatures of his creation through their Equality, or similitude, with God. This capacity to love is what defines man as being in the living image of God. To Christians, this is the Holy Spirit, St. Paul's *agapē*, which proceeds from the Father and from the Son. To Confucians, this is *jen*, the boundless love of Heaven and Earth.

Thus, the three central concepts in Chu Hsi's Neo-Confucian worldview can be described as:

1. **Universal *Li*** (Principle), or the Great Ultimate, the origin of the universe;
2. ***Li*** (Principle), the nature of every created thing, imbedded in the process of creation through the instrument of the *Ch'i* (Material Force), the "geometry" or the lawful ordering principles of the created universe; and
3. ***jen***, divine love, the essence of the Creation.

These three concepts, to Chu Hsi, are One. They constitute an equivalence in natural theology with the Trinity of Christian Renaissance humanism.

This ecumenical vision came close to becoming a reality at the end of the Seventeenth Century, through the nearly successful evangelization of China by Jesuit missionaries working with Neo-Confucian scholars. The sabotage of that effort came primarily from Europe, from the Aristotelian faction whose reaction against the Golden Renaissance had fueled the Reformation, Counter-Reformation, and Enlightenment; it was assisted, however, by the existence in China of a movement against the Renaissance thought of Chu Hsi. But first, we must examine the faith of the Sung Neo-Confucians and their battle against Taoism and Zen Buddhism.

Part III. Countering Taoism and Zen Buddhism

Lao-tzu, the guru of Taoism, a semi-mythical contemporary of Confucius, said: "That which is looked at but not seen is said to be the invisible . . . and can never be fully understood by investigation." Man is immediately reduced to a grovelling beast, incapable of understanding anything beyond the mere appearance of things. Ruled out is any concept such as Plato's Ideas, or Chu Hsi's Principle. What Plato knew to be only the "shadows" of reality are to the Taoists, the limit of our intelligibility. The "Tao" of Taoism (the Way or the Path) is unintelligible by definition. The first sentence of Lao-tzu's writings states that anything that is capable of being expressed is not the true Tao.

By the time of the Neo-Confucians in Eleventh-Century Sung China, Taoism was pervasive, corrupting even the Confucian literati. The previous T'ang Dynasty had been founded and led almost entirely by confirmed Taoists, while Buddhism spread dramatically across China, developing a new "Chinese" form—Ch'an, or Zen as it became known later in Japan—through an interaction with Taoism. Although the two conflicted, the conflicts were more political than philosophical. When Buddhism was briefly banned by the Taoist regime between A.D. 843 and 845, the motivation is evident in the result: 4,600 Buddhist monasteries were abolished, while tens of millions of *mu* of land were confiscated!

As reported above, the Buddhist monasteries had become surrogates for would-be feudal lords, using the tax-exempt status and freedom from inheritance regulations to build up the equivalent of vast landed estates controlled by wealthy families.

Without attempting a thorough critique of either Taoism or Buddhism here, I will discuss the method and some of the content of the Neo-Confucian defense of the Confucian worldview against these "heterodox" teachings.

The Neo-Confucians recognized that the mystical and irrational aspects of the heterodox teachings were, in part, embraced by a population which was hungry for answers to questions of a cosmological and religious nature, especially as to the source of life and the disposition of the soul after death. These questions became even more urgent as the social and economic condition deteriorated throughout the T'ang Dynasty. Confucius and Mencius had not adequately answered these questions, although they were addressed implicitly in their writings. But the sweeping influence of Taoism and Zen, and the chaos and destruction they helped bring upon the Empire, necessitated a thorough confrontation and refutation if China were to survive. This was the self-defined task of the Ch'eng/Chu School.

Rather than simply rejecting the concepts proposed by the Taoist and Zen schools, Chu took them, one by one, refuted them, and reformulated the concept, within the Confucian worldview, as advanced by his own discoveries concerning the order of Creation. We will review this in regard to several concepts: the Tao (Way, Path) itself; the use of the ancient *Book of Changes (I Ching)*; "quiet-sitting" and emptiness of mind; and personal enlightenment.

The Tao

The Tao (the Way or Path) for Lao-tzu and the Taoists was mystical, totally beyond the comprehension or understanding of man, just as Aristotle argued that "the infinite considered as such is unknown," and thus finite man can never know the infinite God. Government, under such mystical conditions, where there is no intelligible higher standard of truth, can only avoid chaos through brute force suppression of knowledge and political freedom. Lao-tzu said: "The people become difficult to govern when they have too much worldly knowledge. Thus, if worldly knowledge governs a state, it becomes a state of outlaws." This was precisely the justification used by the Legalist Ch'in Dynasty to ban the study of history and the classics.

Chu Hsi agreed that God, or the Principle of the Tao, could not be named or expressed in words, but that did not mean man could not know God. He also agreed that worldly knowledge alone could not govern a nation without leading to chaos. Similarly, when the Buddhists argued that human desires were the source of evil in man, Chu did not entirely disagree. But he charged that the Taoists and Buddhists, rather than solving the problem of how to know God, or how to subject worldly knowledge to a higher moral order, or how to subject human desires to a higher moral purpose, instead simply adopted mysticism, empiricism, and asceticism, and denied the existence of such problems, or the possibility of any solutions.

Chu Hsi countered that the infinite God could be known by what He is not:

> God [Tao] alone has no opposite. (*Further Reflections*, 1:69)

> He [the Great Ultimate] is not spatially conditioned. He has neither corporeal form nor body. There is no spot where He can be placed. (CTCS 49:11a-b)

But man, graced with a nature which is the same Principle as the Universal Principle of God, and with an intellectual capacity capable of perfection, is uniquely capable of comprehending such an infinite being.

Chu's notion of "investigating the Principle of things to the utmost," contains an explicit understanding that there is a "negative" process involved in coming to know God. Chu says that in investigating the Principle of something:

> After we understand one layer, there is another layer under it, and after that another. . . . As we continue to try to understand, we shall reach the utmost. (*Reflections*, 3:9)

In the same place, Chu quotes Ch'eng I that this does not mean to investigate the Principle of all things in the world to the utmost, nor does it mean that Principle can be understood merely by investigating one particular Principle. Thus, man cannot know God in full, but through an ever-less-imperfect knowledge he can "face the Lord in Heaven all day." (Confucius)

The Book of Changes

The *Book of Changes (I Ching)* was one of the classics of the "Golden Age" preceding the time of Confucius. Confucius himself almost never referenced the book. It came to be identified primarily with the Taoists, who used it for divination, and it is still a favorite of occultists in both East and West today. The famous hexagrams were each assigned a meaning, and a text accompanying each provided moral teachings. Used as a Taoist fortune-telling book, the diviner throws a set of sticks like dice, to determine a specific hexagram. The accompanying text is taken as the answer to the problem at hand.

The Ch'eng/Chu school used the teachings from the *Book of Changes*, while cleverly exposing and ridiculing its fortune-telling aspects. One example will suffice to demonstrate the method of turning the book against the mysticism of the Taoists. When a specific hexagram, said Ch'eng I, "indicates that there will be good fortune, let the subject of divination re-examine himself as to whether his virtue is outstanding, lasting, and correct. If so, there will be no error."

Emptiness vs. Creativity

One of Chu Hsi's primary targets was the Zen Buddhist contention that to get to the original pureness of mind, all thoughts must be extinguished, all emotions and desires removed. Chu protested that this eliminates any notion of human creativity, and that this God-given creative power is the very nature of the mind. What they fail to understand, he said, is that the nature of the mind, like the mind of Heaven,

> is none other than the production of things; that if one interprets this mind any other way, one will invariably be drowned in emptiness and submerged in quietude, and will fail to attain the proper connection between substance and function, root and branch. (Sato)

Creativity and production are impossible without interaction with the physical universe, which the Buddhists considered unreal, illusionary. But Chu additionally warned against those who argued that Confucian teachings were best for ethical matters of society and government, while at the same time the Buddhists could be followed for their understanding of the transcendental realm of human consciousness. In a passage reminiscent of Plato's Allegory of the Cave, Chu said,

> The Buddhists are really in a dream world, seeing only shadows of mind and nature. They have never carefully looked at their genuine

mind and nature. Even if they are successful in preserving and nourishing, this is only the preservation and nourishment of the shadows they see. (*Further Reflections*, 13:15)

He quotes Ch'eng Hao:

> The Buddhists devote themselves only to penetration on the transcendental level, not to learning on the empirical level. This being the case, can their penetration on the transcendental level be right? Their two levels are basically disconnected. Whatever is separated is not the Way. (*Reflections*, 13:4)

Chu went further by emphasizing that although Confucian teachings on ethics were indeed completely opposed to those of Buddhism, the fundamental difference was metaphysical, not ethical:

> Those who refute Buddhism today rely upon the distinction between righteousness as the essence of the Confucian Way and self-interest as the essence of the Buddhist Way. . . . This distinction is rather secondary. . . . Buddhists take Emptiness as the essence of their metaphysical view. . . . Their metaphysical view is all wrong, consequently all other doctrines they maintain have to be equally wrong. . . . We Confucianists say all metaphysical Principles are real, while they say all Principles are empty.

Thus, to Chu, ideas are more real than the ephemeral, material substance of the objects of sense perception.

It is worth noting here that Aristotle was, in fact, a Zen Buddhist and a Taoist! Aristotle rejected Plato's concept of the Ideas, which is a rejection of Chu Hsi's parallel notion that the nature of each created thing is its particular Principle, which participates in the Universal Principle, God. In the *Metaphysics*, Aristotle says: "To say that the Ideas are patterns and that other things participate in them is to use empty words and poetic metaphors. . . ."

Aristotle's rejection of any nature or meaning in things and affairs other than what can be observed by the senses, is epistemologically equivalent to the Zen teaching that the material world is an illusion—that only the perception by the consciousness is real.

The ultimate goal of the Zen Buddhists was to find "peace" through contemplative enlightenment. Aristotle's view of "reason," his concept of the mind, and his view of the selfish aim of mental activity, are not far removed from the Zen Buddhists, as evidenced by this passage from his *Ethics*:

> The activity of reason, which is contemplative, seems both to be superior in serious worth and to aim at no end beyond itself, and to have its pleasure proper to itself . . . and the self-sufficiency, leisureliness, unweariedness (so far as this is possible for man), and all the other attributes to the supremely happy man are evidently those connected with this activity.

Chu did not denounce the concept of "emptying the mind," nor the value of meditation; rather, he redefined them. The process of investigation of the laws of the universe, of the "Principle of things and affairs," necessarily leads to the arousal of selfish desires and a fixation on "things " and "objects," rather than their Principles. This clouds up and obscures the "inborn luminous virtue," the creative process, creating a screen of habits and fixed notions through which reality, true Principle, is distorted. It is this screen, which Lyndon LaRouche has identified as the matrix of axiomatic assumptions through which one views the world, which Chu insists must be "emptied" from the mind. It must be emptied in full, not in part, since it functions as a whole to prevent the creative potential inherent in the mind from functioning. Said Chu: "Habit becomes one's second nature, causing one to get further and further from his nature." (*Reflections*, 1:14) Also:

> Modern scholars are unable to empty their minds and take a step back to slowly look over the teachings of sages and worthies in order to seek out their ideas. Instead, they directly take their own ideas and force them onto those [of the sages and worthies]. . . . (*Further Reflections*, 2:62)

Chu was most critical of self-described Confucian scholars who had adopted the various ideologies over the preceding millennium, and could not "empty their minds" of these prejudices to make a creative contribution. The Ch'eng/Chu School argued that the true Tao had been passed on by Confucius to his disciples, and then to Mencius, but with the death of Mencius in 289 B.C., the Way was lost. Significant efforts were made by individual scholars in the intervening years to rediscover the true teachings of the sages, according to Chu Hsi, but none were successful until the Ch'eng brothers. Errors and corrupting influences from Taoism and Buddhism, once introduced in a Confucian form, were passed on in an hereditary manner from teacher to student. As Lü Liu-liang, the brilliant follower of Chu Hsi in the seventeenth century, identified the problem: "Scholars' minds and hearts become like block-prints, and just as errors in the text of the block are reproduced in what is printed, they all repeat the same errors." (deBary, *Trouble With Confucianism*)

How can one "empty his mind" and at the same time "preserve the mind and investigate things"? Are these not contradictions? Said Chu,

> The Zen Buddhists see the mind as empty and possessing no Principle at all, while we see that although the mind is empty, it does possess all the 10,000 Principles completely within itself. (Fu) ("10,000" is used in Chinese to mean "countless" or "infinite.")

Here, Chu distinguishes between man's "human mind" and his "Heavenly mind." It is not that there are two minds. Rather, man's original nature comes from God, but as soon as man acts in the world, his free will subjects him to human desires, both good desires and selfish desires. If these desires are not governed by the "original mind"—i.e., by Principle—then they will become ensnared in evil. Chu said,

> At the moment that we perceive good and wish to do it, this is the first stirring of the appearance of our true mind. But once it does appear it is covered by the natural inclination for worldly things. We must personally and intensively investigate it. (*Further Reflections*, 5:16)

This "original mind," that of Principle, is what Cusanus distinguished as the "intellect," as opposed to mere linear reasoning or sense perception. Matters which appear as total contradictions to a mind "fettered by what is heard or what is seen" (CTCS 44:13a-b), such as the Aristotelian mind, limited to deductive or inductive reasoning, are no longer contradictory at the level of the creative intellect. Cusanus termed this the "coincidence of opposites" in the Divine Mind, where apparent contradictions are resolved in the absolute infinite (God) and in the relative infinite potential in the mind of man. The Neo-Confucians made the same point, calling God both the Great Ultimate or Universal Principle, in that He contains everything there is, but also the "Ultimate Non-Being," since He preceded Heaven and Earth. At the human level, man is both finite and infinite, his mind both "empty" and full of all Principles of nature.

Chu Hsi mocked any lesser concept of the mind, either the Taoist/Legalist argument that, in order to impose order on the ignorant masses, people must be treated like beasts, or the Zen Buddhist argument that the outside world should be rejected in favor of self-reflection and personal enlightenment. When many Taoists and Buddhists claimed to follow the Confucian tenet to "Hold the mind fast and preserve it," Chu Hsi responded:

> "Holding it fast" is another way of saying that we should not allow our conduct to fetter and destroy our innate mind which is characterized by *jen* and righteousness. It does not mean that we should sit in a rigid position to preserve the obviously idle consciousness and declare that "this is holding fast and preserving it." (CTCS 44:28a-29b)

Selfishness

When the Zen Buddhists prided themselves on repressing all selfish desires in their search for Nirvana, Chu made the obvious point that in reality they were totally selfish. To refuse responsibility for society as a whole is to condone or outrightly support the evil that exists in that society in order to selfishly find one's own peace through idle contemplation. "A person who has never spoken of doing good must first hate evil," said Chu. "Once they are able to hate evil, then they can do good." (*Further Reflections*, 5:24) Eliminating evil thoughts from one's personal life while refusing to act on the crisis in society is not even possible: "If our mind is unresponsive and stubbornly immovable, even though our mind is free of evil, still the refusal to move can only be an unjust principle." (*Further Reflections*, 5:35)

Similarly, professing a love of humanity, and even carrying out acts of charity, while at the same time refusing to fight evil, no matter what the personal consequences, will only lead to serious mistakes even in the intended acts of charity. Chang Tsai said,

> Because one hates inhumanity, he will never fail to realize it whenever he does anything wrong. But if one merely loves humanity but does not hate inhumanity, he will be acting without understanding and doing so habitually without examination. (*Reflections*, 5:35)

The ultimate selfishness of the Zen Buddhists, said Chu Hsi, is that they taught their students that they could become enlightened entirely on their own, without God. Students were told to concentrate their minds on places totally incomprehensible and unknowable, so that they will one day see by themselves and then get it. But this is simply case of claiming by oneself that he has it. (*Further Reflections*, 13:24)

Enlightenment

Chu Hsi did not deny the existence of a state which could be called "enlightenment," but, as the above quote demonstrates, he ridiculed the simplistic, cultist notion of "instant enlightenment," while motivating instead the long, arduous, but joyful process of study, political work, and scientific and artistic creativity to attain enlightenment and "face the Lord in Heaven all day." Chu spoke of students who came to him

> for the first time, always talking about this "sudden enlightenment," but afterwards, to the contrary, they were even more screwed up and out of whack. So it seems that what we call "sudden enlightenment" was at the time a slight comprehension, with a feeling of being completely pure and happy. But after a while, the feeling wore off. How can we ever depend on such a thing? (*Further Reflections*, 13:23)

Such Zen "enlightenment" came from drowning one's identity in an "all-is-one" soup which fails to distinguish between

God and the myriad things and ultimately rejects the existence of God the Creator, and man the creature of reason. Today's radical environmentalists would do well to consider Chu Hsi's rebuke to a Zen-influenced student who said, "Things share the same Material Force and form one body. Only when one is absolutely impartial and is without selfishness can one share their joy and sorrow without interruption." Chu responded,

> When have earth and trees been selfish? They are not concerned with other things. Man, however, fundamentally has this concern. That is how he can be absolutely impartial, without any selfishness, and can embrace all things without interruption. (*Reflections*, 14:19)

"Sudden enlightenment," said Chu, is in fact a rejection of everything real in the universe, and is the equivalent of embracing death as real, and life as an illusion. The Confucian "enlightenment," on the other hand, comes from an engagement in life in all its facets, and its attainment is not an end, but a new beginning. Said Chu,

> "Seeing into man's nature" is a Zen Buddhist expression; it means "seeing just once and for all." By contrast, the Confucians speak of "knowing man's nature"; after knowing the nature, the nature still requires a full nourishment until it is exerted to the utmost. (Fu)

True enlightenment, then, is not a sudden, mystical experience, but is the equivalent of the process described by Cusanus as rising to the level of the intellect, whereby man can become an "adoptive son of God," or, what the Confucians call a "sage."

Selected Bibliography

St. Augustine, "Eighty-three Different Questions," in *The Essential Augustine*, 2nd. ed., ed. by Vernon J. Bourke (Indianapolis: Hackett Publishing Company, 1947).

Billington, Michael O., "The British Role in the Creation of Maoism," Executive Intelligence Review, Vol. 19, No. 36, Sept. 11, 1992, p. 48.

Chan, Wing-tsit, ed., *Chu Hsi and Neo-Confucianism* (Honolulu: University of Hawaii Press, 1986).

Chan, Wing-tsit, ed., *A Source Book in Chinese Philosophy* (Princeton, N.J.: Princeton University Press, 1963).

Chang, Carsun, *The Development of Neo-Confucian Thought* (New York: Bookman Associates, 1957-62; reprinted Westport, Conn: Greenwood Press, 1977).

Chu Hsi, *Reflections on Things at Hand: The Neo-Confucian Anthology, compiled by Chu Hsi and Lu Tsu-ch'ien,* trans. by Wing-tsit Chan (New York: Columbia University Press, 1967).

——— *Further Reflections on Things at Hand: A Reader*, trans. by Allen Wittenborn (New York: University Press of America, 1991).

deBary, Wm. Theodore, ed. with Wing-tsit Chan and Lester Tan, *Sources of Chinese Tradition* (New York: Columbia University Press, 1960; 1964).

———, and Irene Bloom, ed., *Principle and Practicality: Essays in Neo-Confucianism and Practical Learning* (New York: Columbia University Press, 1979).

———, *The Trouble With Confucianism (The Tanner Lectures on Human Values)* (Cambridge, Mass.: Harvard University Press, 1991).

———, *Learning For One's Self: Essays on the Individual in Neo-Confucian Thought* (New York: Columbia University Press, 1991).

Dreyer, Edward L., *Early Ming China: A Political History, 1355-1435* Stanford: Stanford University Press, 1981).

Elvin, Mack, *The Pattern of the Chinese Past* (Stanford: Stanford University Press, 1973).

Fu, Charles Wei-hsun, "Chu Hsi on Buddhism," in Wing-tsit Chan, *Chu Hsi and New Confucianism, ibid*.

Gardner, Daniel K., *Chu Hsi and the Ta-Hsueh: Neo-Confucian Reflection on the Confucian Canon* (Cambridge, Mass.: Council on East Asian Studies, Harvard University; distributed by Harvard University Press, 1986).

LaRouche, Lyndon H., Jr., "The Science of Christian Economy," in *The Science of Christian Economy and Other Prison Writings* (Washington, D.C.: Schiller Institute, 1991).

———, *Cold Fusion: Challenge to U.S. Science Policy* (Washington, D.C.: Schiller Institute, 1992).

———, "On the Subject of Metaphor," *Fidelio*, Vol. I, No. 3, Fall 1992.

———, "On the Subject of God," *Fidelio*, Vol. II, No. 1, Spring 1993.

Legge, James, trans., *The Chinese Classics* (Hong Kong: c. 1861-72; reprinted Hong Kong University Press, 1960).

Leibniz, Gottfried Wilhelm, *Discourse on the National Theology of the*

Chinese, trans. by Henry Rosemont, Jr. and Daniel J. Cook, Monograph No. 4 of the Society for Asian and Comparative Philosophy (Honolulu: University Press of Hawaii, 1977).

Needham, Joseph, *Science and Civilization in China* (London: Cambridge University Press, 1954), Vol. II.

Rozman, Gilbert, ed., *The Confucian Heritage and its Modern Adaptation*, (Princeton: Princeton University Press, 1991).

Sato, Hitoshi, "Chu Hsi's 'Treatise on Jen,' " in Wing-tsit Chan, *Chu Hsi and Neo-Confucianism, ibid*.

Swanson, Bruce, *The Eighth Voyage of the Dragon: A History of China's Quest for Sea Power* (Annapolis: Naval Institute Press, 1982).

Tu Wei-ming, *Neo-Confucian Thought in Action: Wang Yang-ming's Youth, 1472-1509* (Berkeley: University of California Press, 1976).

Wertz, William F., Jr., "Why St. Thomas Aquinas Is Not an Aristotelian," *Fidelio*, Vol. II, No. 1, Spring 1993.

———, trans., *Toward a New Council of Florence: "On the Peace of Faith" and Other Works by Nicolaus of Cusa* (Washington, D.C.: Schiller Institute, 1993).

[Appendix II]

Britain's Cold War Against FDR's Grand Design: The East Asian Theater, 1943-63

II. Recolonization

Had the Truman administration not swung over to Winston Churchill's anti-American policies, the proper course of action for the post-World War II U.S.A. would have been to mobilize and expand the U.S. machine-tool-design sector as a whole, to supply the nations of Asia, Africa, and the Americas the high rates of development of infrastructure and technology needed to fulfill Roosevelt's vision of a post-war "American Century." Instead, we substantially collapsed the levels of production, rather than capitalizing the accumulated investment in war-production capacity as an active new industry for development of the world as a whole.

—*Lyndon H. LaRouche, Jr.*[19]

Immediately after the Japanese surrender, the British moved to occupy Burma, Singapore, Malaya, and Hong Kong, their former colonies, as well as Indonesia, Thailand, and South Vietnam. The shortage of troop transports, mostly American owned, caused some delay. While the Truman administration made some noises about not using U.S. materiel to reestablish

Excerpted from Executive Intelligence Review, Oct. 15, 1999 (Vol. 26, No. 41). Original numbering of footnotes has been retained.

colonialism, in fact it was U.S. ships and planes which transported the European colonial armies back to their former possessions.

The British vs. Sukarno

President Sukarno, the leader of the movement for national independence of the Dutch East Indies since the 1920s, issued a proclamation of independence for the United States of Indonesia on Aug. 17, 1945. The Dutch refused to recognize the Indonesian government, and declared Sukarno to be a Japanese collaborator who should be treated as an enemy.

Sukarno, in fact, was a collaborator. When the Japanese conquered the Dutch forces defending Indonesia in March 1942, the Japanese authorities immediately freed Sukarno from house arrest, where he had been confined for eight years by the Dutch. Sukarno and other nationalist leaders were told, that the Japanese came as liberators, with the eventual goal of an independent Indonesian state.

As early as 1929, Sukarno had forecast that Indonesian freedom would come only from a Pacific war, with Japan playing the central role in expelling the European empires. He, and others, accepted leadership positions within the Japanese occupation government, while maintaining contact with the underground opposition networks. While some aspects of the occupation were brutal and repressive (in particular, the impressed labor of hundreds of thousands of Indonesians in overseas work projects), Sukarno was given essentially free access to the population, both via radio and through direct travel throughout the archipelago. During the three-year Japanese occupation, Sukarno organized the Indonesian people into a united force, a nation, based on principles distilled from his study of the history of both Western and Eastern civilizations.

Sukarno had obtained a degree in engineering and architecture from the Bandung Technical School in 1926. His home in Bandung became the center of pro-independence ferment through the "General Study Group," that discussed history and politics. He published an article, entitled "Nationalism, Islam and Marxism," in the journal *Young Indonesia,* in 1926, which was to characterize his entire life's dedication to a unity of principle between these three apparently disparate paths of political and social organization. He was critical of the Marxist rejection of religion, but he distinguished between "historical materialism" and "philosophical materialism," defending the former against the latter, and he insisted that Marxism need not be anti-religious. The common goal of nationhood, and a dedication to universal principles, provided the basis for unity.

The character of Indonesia, with 17,000 islands, and multiple ethnic, linguistic, and religious divisions within the population, convinced Sukarno that the concept of "self-determination" could easily be used *against* the struggle for national independence, as a tool of colonial control, by dividing a nation against itself. He insisted that nationalism must embrace the nation as a whole, while providing each citizen with the means to participate in both national and international affairs.

In March 1945, the Japanese occupation government, aware that the war was lost, established a committee for independence in Indonesia (and implemented similar measures in other Southeast Asian nations). On June 1, Sukarno spoke to the committee, presenting a concept he called Panca Sila (Five Principles), which were to become the constitutional principles of the Republic of Indonesia, and are still to this day. As presented in that speech, the Panca Sila are:

1. Nationalism—"one National State . . . one Indonesian soil from the tip of Sumatra to the tip of Irian."

2. Internationalism—but "not cosmopolitanism, which does not recognize nationalism. . . . Internationalism cannot flower if it is not rooted in the soil of Nationalism."

3. Representative government—"the principle of consent, of consultations."

4. Social justice—"in the field of economy, too, we must create equality, and the best common prosperity."

5. Belief in God—"Free Indonesia with faith in God the Almighty," with full freedom for all religions.

Sukarno was a great admirer of Abraham Lincoln, and also of Dr. Sun Yat-sen, the founder of republican China, who was himself a follower of Lincoln. Like Dr. Sun's Three Principles of the People, which Sun had accredited to Lincoln's concept of "government of the people, by the people, and for the people," so also, Panca Sila contained these three notions of nationalism, representative government, and social justice, with the additional points of internationalism and belief in God.

Sukarno then compressed the five principles into three. Like Friedrich Schiller, he insisted that one must be simultaneously a patriot of one's nation and a citizen of the world, and therefore united nationalism and internationalism into a single principle. Also, since democracy without social justice "is not democracy at all," he combined representative government and social justice. The resulting three principles, in turn, were combined into one, which Sukarno called "mutual cooperation."

Sukarno and the Panca Sila inspired nationalists throughout Southeast Asia over the coming decades of struggle against colonialism. In Malaya, especially, a nation of very similar racial and cultural roots, Sukarno and his associates were viewed as heroes. The Committee for Independence in Indonesia even voted, in 1945, in favor of including Malaya and the British colonies in northern Borneo as part of a united Indonesia, an idea that was to be revived in the 1960s.

The British arrived in October 1945. Sukarno agreed to their presence, but only to oversee the release of European prisoners held by the Japanese. Within two weeks of the prisoners' release, however, the British broke the agreement, militarily seized the city of Surabaya, and launched bitter and bloody fighting against nationalist forces. Mountbatten, as usual, deployed almost entirely Indian, not British, troops against the nationalists, along with air strikes. He later ordered the capital, Jakarta (then called Batavia), and most of Western Java, to be cleared of nationalist forces, but again ordered the British officer in charge to use Indian troops, since he did not want British wives "widowed at this time so long after the war."[20]

This paved the way for the arrival of the Dutch in November, on U.S. ships. While the U.S. population was revolted by reports of the brutal recolonization in Indonesia (and elsewhere), the Truman administration continued quiet but explicit support for the Dutch. For public consumption, Truman struck a hypocritical pose reminiscent of the Northern Abolitionists during the American Civil War, who decried the horror of slavery, but led the opposition to Lincoln's war effort, arguing that the North should be free of slavery, but should let the South go its own way!

Without lifting a finger to prevent re-colonization, Truman ordered an end to all U.S. participation in Mountbatten's SEAC. This "Pontius Pilate"-like act was only the beginning of Truman's complicity in British tyranny.

The Dutch were brutal in reasserting power. They only reluctantly agreed to even talk with Sukarno's government, and refused to consider discussions about independence, because of the "manifest incompetence of the Indonesians to rule themselves," as they told the British.[21]

The British performed the role of "soft cop" after the arrival of the Dutch forces, telling the Dutch to compromise with the nationalists, while telling Sukarno to settle for less than independence. The most interesting aspect of the British role in Indonesia, was the plan put forward by Mountbatten's political adviser, Sir Esler Dening, for the Balkanization of the country. If the attempt to get the Dutch and the nationalists to agree on a (colonial) policy failed, argued Dening, the British should divide the country between western and eastern Java, mineral-rich Sumatra, and the outer islands in the east, with the Dutch taking over western Java. He proposed this to Mountbatten as a means of assuring that the United States would not intervene to mediate. This plan, we shall see, in nearly the same form, was to be implemented ten years later under British and American covert direction, in order to subvert both Sukarno's rule and the emerging movement of the non-aligned nations.

Burma and Thailand

At one point, the British advised the Dutch to deal with Sukarno the same way the British had dealt with Burma's nationalist leader, Aung San. This could be interpreted in various ways. Although Mountbatten negotiated Burma's independence with Aung San, the British also arranged for Aung San's assassination soon before the scheduled date for independence. Perhaps not coincidentally, the assassination of Aung San took place on the day before the "First Dutch Police Action" in Indonesia in July 1947, the first of two rounds of full-scale war against the nationalists.

Burma was not a major source of mineral wealth—its importance was more geopolitical. The mountain country in the north, bordering Thailand, Laos, China, and India, was a desolate but strategic pivot point in Asia which was under nobody's control. Sparsely populated by various hill tribes, it was the site of some of Britain's richest opium production. In 1946, Mountbatten decided to grant Burma full independence while retaining covert control of the hill-tribe country. Aung San, a nationalist leader who, like Sukarno, had worked with the Japanese occupation forces (he and his "30 comrades" had been trained militarily and politically during the 1930s in Japan), was the only figure who could conceivably have united the country. With his assassination, the country predictably fell into civil war immediately following independence. The hill country became a staging ground for British and U.S. covert operations in the region for the next fifty years, and a primary source of drugs for London's Dope, Inc.

Although the British policy toward India's independence is not a subject of this report, it must be noted that Lord Mountbatten, following his de facto partition and instigation of civil war in Burma, proceeded to oversee the British-mandated partition of India into India and Pakistan, assuring instability and bloody communal warfare for many years to come.

Mountbatten tried to portray himself as the friend of nationalism, both for his role in decolonizing Burma and India, and as a vocal critic of the Dutch and the French for their heavy-handed treatment of nationalist forces in their colonies. But, in fact, Mountbatten's crucial role for the Empire was in recognizing that the existing form of nineteenth-century European colonialism could not survive in a world forever changed by the U.S. role in World War II, and the threat of a U.S.-led world economic order based on technologically driven collaboration among sovereign nation-states. To preserve the reality of the British Empire in a new form required granting independence, but only after fostering multiple points of division. The "weak China" policy was applied universally. . . .

Vietnam

The disaster of America's involvement in Vietnam, Cambodia, and Laos in the 1960s and 1970s will remain a black page in the history of the twentieth century. To understand how the incompetent accountant's mentality of Robert "Body Count" McNamara, and the genocidal fantasies of London's asset Henry Kissinger, guided America through that nightmare, we must look at London's launching of thirty years of colonial warfare in 1945, using French and American forces to carry out their policy.

As referenced above, the British were particularly concerned that Roosevelt would take a stand in Vietnam against the restoration of colonialism. FDR told Secretary of State Cordell Hull in 1943 that "France had the country—thirty million inhabitants—for nearly a hundred years, and the people are worse off than they were at the beginning."[23] Just before his death, Roosevelt consented that perhaps France could itself run the Trusteeship for Indochina, but only if eventual independence were the stated goal.

Despite FDR's death, London had another problem in Vietnam—the OSS. The China-based OSS had been in close contact with Ho Chi Minh and his Vietminh forces. Unlike many nationalist leaders across Southeast Asia who collaborated with Japan's "liberators" from European colonialism, Ho gave his full backing to the Allies, in the expectation that they would defeat the Japanese and grant independence to Vietnam. This was in spite of the fact that the Soviet Union was at the time in an alliance with Hitler (the Hitler-Stalin Pact) and had instructed communists worldwide not to oppose the Axis powers. Ho would not obey.

Ho Chi Minh had joined the communist movement in 1920 in Paris, and spent several years in Moscow. But, he would later insist that "it was patriotism and not communism that originally inspired me."[24] He also served as interpreter to Mikhail Borodin in China in 1924, when Borodin was Soviet adviser to the coalition between the Chinese Nationalist Party and the Communist Party at Whompoa Military Academy, where Chiang Kai-shek and Zhou Enlai worked closely together under Sun Yat-sen's direction. Ho returned to Vietnam in 1941 after thirty years abroad, to lead the Vietnam Independence League—the Vietminh—with Pham Van Dong and Vo Nguyen Giap.

Ho Chi Minh was much respected by the American OSS officers who trained and supplied his forces for operations against the Japanese and the Vichy French regime which was collaborating with the Japanese. In fact, OSS officers saved Ho's life with malaria medicine dropped into his jungle base.

Ho had long admired the spirit of the American Revolution, and had hopes that America would live up to the Atlantic Charter. He saw the American tutelage in the Philippines, with the peaceful granting of independence and national sovereignty, as a demonstration of American sincerity and goodwill. Even earlier, as a young man of 29 in 1919, Ho had prepared a charter on behalf of Vietnam to present to President Wilson at the Versailles Conference following World War I, but he was snubbed by Wilson. Ho spoke fluent English (and about a dozen other languages), and had spent a year living in the United States during World War I.

OSS officer Archimedes L.A. Patti became a friend and confidant of Ho Chi Minh during the war. After the Japanese surrender, Patti accompanied Ho and the Vietminh into Hanoi, where they assumed power. Patti even helped Ho draft the Vietnamese Declaration of Independence, delivered by Ho on Sept. 2, 1945, in Hanoi Square, quoting directly from the U.S. Declaration of Independence on the inalienable rights of man. Ho sent a letter to President Truman through Patti, and several subsequent appeals asking the United States to intervene and to accord Vietnam "the same status as the Philippines," with a period of tutelage leading to independence. He appealed to the Atlantic Charter, the UN Charter, and even to Truman's own words of support for national self-determination. The Truman administration refused to even answer the letters.

The only concession regarding Southeast Asia that Truman had demanded of the British at Potsdam was that the Chinese be allowed to accept the Japanese surrender in the northern half of Vietnam. Chiang Kai-shek's forces arrived and performed their duty, but, unlike the British in the South, the Chinese made no effort to replace Ho Chi Minh's Vietminh government.

In the South, British troops arrived in September 1945 (on U.S. C-47s) and immediately declared martial law, closed the Vietnamese newspapers, and released 1,400 French Vichy troops who had been interned by the Japanese when they turned against their Vichy collaborators in March 1945. These French Vichy troops went on a rampage, expelling the Vietminh committees which had assumed power, and generally looting the city of Saigon. The Vietnamese called a general strike which paralyzed the city, and general warfare broke out.

The OSS team in Saigon, headed by Lt. Col. Peter Dewey, clashed directly with the British commanding officer, Maj. Gen. Douglas Gracey, over his outrageous colonial policies and tactics. Gracey accused Dewey of collaborating with the enemy (i.e., the Vietnamese nationalists). This was particularly disingenuous since Gracey was collaborating with the real enemy—the Japanese troops and their Vichy allies—to suppress the native population!

Gracey threw OSS officer Dewey out of the country. The night before his scheduled departure, one of Dewey's officers was attacked and injured. The French blamed it on certain Vietnamese nationalists, and Dewey went to meet with them. For reasons that have never been explained, Dewey was ambushed and killed—the first of nearly 60,000 American deaths in Vietnam over the next 30 years.

The British were determined to get out quickly, leaving the chaos they had provoked in the hands of the French. A request to use U.S. ships to bring in the French Army met with no objections from Washington.

IV. Spirit of Bandung

The most important factor in the process leading to the 1955 Conference of Asian and African Nations was the fact that, in several cases, the colonial powers were simply defeated, militarily, despite their vastly superior technology. The Republic of Indonesia's victory against the Dutch in 1949 showed that nationalist military forces, with republican leadership, could defeat a European occupation army. India's Prime Minister Jawaharlal Nehru had sponsored two Asian conferences, one in 1947 and another in 1949, aimed at forging Asian unity against colonialism, with the defense of Indonesia a primary focus. Indonesia's victory gave hope to colonial nations throughout the world. By 1953, it was clear to all but the blind, that the French in Vietnam were soon to face the same fate as the Dutch in Indonesia.

There were also serious changes taking place in all three of the nations which had been the pillars of FDR's Grand Design—the Soviet Union, China, and the United States. General Eisenhower was inaugurated as President in January 1953, Joseph Stalin died in March of that same year, and in China, Zhou Enlai's approach, toward "peaceful coexistence" with the West, was winning out over the advocates of sponsoring violent revolutions abroad.

Eisenhower had certain positive instincts in favor of technology-driven global development, as reflected in his "Atoms for Peace" policy to spread nuclear energy capacity worldwide to fuel industrialization. His military experience served him well in resisting British pressures aimed at drawing the United States into reckless and potentially disastrous military adventures. However, Eisenhower also had John Foster Dulles, and his brother CIA chief Allen Dulles, running his foreign policy.

Truman had appointed John Foster Dulles as Ambassador-at-Large in 1950, despite the fact that Dulles had been Roosevelt's sworn enemy. Dulles spearheaded the diplomatic side of Truman's McCarthyite Cold War—including the refusal to recognize the People's Republic of China. As the primary powerbrokers in the Republican Party, the Dulles brothers chose to sponsor Eisenhower's candidacy (over that of General MacArthur or Robert Taft), believing Eisenhower would be a weak President, and thus maximizing their own influence. The Dulles brothers ran the State Department and CIA as arms of London's Cold War strategy, while undermining the occasional positive impulses emerging from the President.

Stalin's death in 1953 led to proposals for an easing of tensions from the new Soviet leaders, proposals which were welcomed by Eisenhower. Détente was seriously discussed, including even a joint U.S./U.S.S.R. development program for China. John Foster Dulles was violently opposed to such ideas. He also tried to sabotage the armistice in Korea, by placing impossible demands on the Chinese. Eisenhower reined in his Secretary of State, at least in regard to Korea, in order to carry out his campaign pledge to end the war.

Dulles was extremely unhappy that the Chinese were even "allowed" to participate in the Korean armistice talks. In 1954, when the French were searching for a way out of Vietnam, Dulles reacted even more vehemently against the proposal for a conference in Geneva on Vietnam with China's participation. But he was again overridden by Eisenhower, and the 1954 Geneva talks proceeded.

Despite Dulles's efforts to isolate the Chinese at the Geneva Conference—including his ostentatious refusal to accept Zhou Enlai's outstretched hand—Zhou nonetheless established contacts within the U.S. delegation to the conference. As a result, the United States and China set up a process for regular formal (if unofficial) meetings in Geneva, beginning in August 1955 and lasting into the Kennedy administration. Zhou Enlai's personal leadership role within China was crucial in the move toward establishing normal relations with the West.

The Soviet-sponsored North Korean invasion of South Korea had occurred only months after the 1949 revolution in China. China's subsequent massive involvement in the Korean war, beginning in October 1950, cost the country dearly in lives and resources, aggravating the already massive task of reconstruction facing the new government. The ongoing wars in Korea and Vietnam served to promote the interests of the more radical voices within China, such as those who had denounced Nehru, Sukarno, and Burma's U Nu as puppets of imperialism. With the Korean armistice in 1953, Zhou Enlai's approach, advocating peaceful coexistence with China's neighbors and the Western powers, rose in influence within China, such that by 1956 Zhou was Premier, Foreign Minister, and the second-ranking member of the hierarchy after Mao Zedong.

In April 1954, just before the Geneva Conference on Vietnam, Zhou initiated bilateral agreements with India and with Burma which established the first expression of the Five Principles of Peaceful Coexistence. The Five Principles declared mutual respect for sovereignty, territorial integrity, equality, and non-interference in internal affairs. This initiative by Zhou, Nehru, and U Nu, would become a central concept motivating the Spirit of Bandung.

The day before the opening of the Geneva Conference, the Vietnamese Army under General Giap overran the French position at Dien Bien Phu. Dulles's position—his "brinkmanship"—was essentially defaulted on the field of battle. Zhou Enlai, rather than gloating, used his influence to persuade Ho Chi Minh to accept a compromise, allowing a continued French presence in South Vietnam pending a national election within 24 months. Zhou believed that any more militant stance would push the United States toward the Dulles policy, and U.S. forces would simply move in to replace the French. He hoped that a temporary peace based on a divided Vietnam and neutrality in Cambodia and Laos, as was established at Geneva, would allow time for broader agreements on regional and international development, even though the Vietnam settlement itself was full of loopholes and uncertainties, and wasn't even signed by most of the participants. The stage was set for Bandung.

The original idea for an Asian-African meeting came from Indonesian Prime Minister Ali Sastroamidjojo at a meeting of the Colombo group, comprising India, Pakistan, Ceylon, Burma, and Indonesia—an alliance of formerly colonized nations. The proposed conference was to be the first time that nations of the Third World had met together, without the Western powers present. Sukarno described it in his opening speech as "the first international conference of colored peoples in the history of mankind."[29]

The unifying principles were anti-colonialism and the commitment to peace and development in nations which had won their independence. But the most crucial strategic issue in the minds of the conference initiators was the threat of a U.S.-China war. The initial statement calling for the conference to be held in Bandung in April 1955, included a reference to "the desire of the five sponsors to lay a firmer foundation for China's peaceful relations with the rest of the world, not only with the West, but equally with themselves and other areas of Southeast Asia peripheral to China."

George Kahin, an American scholar who attended Bandung and interviewed many of the leading participants, said that the conference initiators were concerned both with war avoidance, especially in regard to U.S.-China relations, and the curtailment of Chinese and Vietnamese military and political sponsorship of subversive activities in Southeast Asia. This was hardly a "pro-communist China" grouping, but, as Nehru told his Congress Party after the 1954 China-India agreement on the Five Principles of Peaceful Coexistence, China should have a chance to prove itself.

The twenty-nine nations from Asia, the Arab world, and Black Africa who attended the conference had many serious differences, especially in regard to alliances with either the West or with the Soviet bloc, which threatened to disrupt their unity of purpose. These conflicts resulted in an extraordinary process of constructive dialogue and diplomacy, with Zhou Enlai, the head of China's delegation, exerting exceptional leadership. But before examining that dialogue, a review of the opening speech by President Sukarno, the host, will demonstrate the level of consciousness of the world historic nature of the undertaking by the participants themselves.

Sukarno, speaking in the city where he had been introduced to the struggle against colonialism, called on the nations of Asia and Africa to take world leadership to project reason and moral strength into a world of chaos:

> Great chasms yawn between nations and groups of nations. Our unhappy world is torn and tortured, and the peoples of all countries walk in fear lest, through no fault of their own, the dogs of war are unchained once again. . . . The nations of Asia and Africa cannot, even if they wish to, avoid their part in finding solutions to these problems. . . . We have heavy responsibilities to ourselves, and to the world, and to the yet unborn generations.
>
> The peoples of Asia and Africa wield little physical power. . . . What can we do? We can do much! We can inject the voice of reason into world affairs. We can mobilize all the spiritual, all the moral, all the political strength of Asia and Africa on the side of peace. Yes, we! We the peoples of Asia and Africa, 1.4 billion strong, far more than half the human population of the world, we can mobilize what I have called the Moral Violence of Nations in favor of peace.

He referenced Franklin Delano Roosevelt, without needing to speak his name: "We are living in a world of fear. . . . Perhaps this fear is a greater danger than the danger itself."

Sukarno's tribute to the American Revolution was a stirring call to arms:

> Today is a famous anniversary in that battle [against colonialism]. On the 18th of April, 1775, just 180 years ago, Paul Revere rode at midnight through the New England countryside, warning of the approach of the British troops and of the opening of the American War of Independence, the first successful anti-colonialist war in history. About this midnight ride the poet Longfellow wrote:

> A cry of defiance and not of fear,
> A voice in the darkness, a knock at the door,
> And a word that shall echo for evermore. . . .
>
> It shall echo forevermore. That battle which began 180 years ago is not yet completely won.

He identified neo-colonialism at its roots—the free trade dogma of the British colonial system:

> Colonialism has also its modern dress, in the form of economic control, intellectual control, actual physical control by a small but alien community within a nation. . . . It behooves us to take particular care to ensure that the principle which is usually called the "live and let live principle"—mark, I do not say the principle of laisser-faire, laisser-passer, of Liberalism, which is obsolete—is first of all applied by us most completely within our own Asian and African frontiers.

As with Roosevelt, Sukarno knew that China's Republican hero Sun Yat-sen would be recognized by his words alone:

> Bear in mind the words of one of Asia's greatest sons: To speak is easy. To act is hard. To understand is hardest. Once one understands, action is easy.

Sukarno concluded with an appeal to the liberation of the human spirit, applying his Panca Sila to the universal family of mankind:

> The highest purpose of man is the liberation of man from his bonds of fear, his bonds of human degradation, his bonds of poverty—the liberation of man from the physical, spiritual and intellectual bonds which have for too long stunted the development of humanity's majority. And let us remember, Sisters and Brothers, that for the sake of all that, we Asians and Africans must be united.

Although Bandung is generally considered to be the beginning of what came to be called the Non-Aligned Movement, the question of non-alignment was actually the most contentious issue at the conference. Prime Minister Nehru was the most passionate advocate of non-alignment, arguing that picking sides in the Cold War would prevent economic development and inevitably lead to World War III: "If all the world were to be divided up between these two big power blocs . . . the inevitable result would be war. Therefore, every step that takes place in reducing that area in the world which may be called the unaligned area is a dangerous step and leads to war."

Contrary to most Soviet historical accounts of Nehru's position at Bandung, he did not single out the Western military blocs as the only problem. NATO, said Nehru, "is one of the most powerful protectors of colonialism." But he believed that it was equally true that the "Cominform"—the bloc of communist nations formed in 1947—"cannot in the nature of things fit in with peaceful coexistence." Nehru told the Bandung delegates: "I belong to neither [bloc], and I propose to belong to neither whatever happens in the world. . . . India has stood alone without any aid against a mighty empire, the British Empire, and we propose to face all consequences. . . .

"Are we, the countries of Asia and Africa, devoid of any positive position except being pro-communist or anti-communist? . . . It is most degrading and humiliating to any self-respecting people or nation. It is an intolerable thought to me that the great countries of Asia and Africa should come out of bondage into freedom only to degrade themselves or humiliate themselves in this way."

The resistance to non-alignment came primarily from the Asian members of the Southeast Asia Treaty Organization (SEATO). SEATO was put together by the British and John Foster Dulles immediately after the Geneva agreement on Vietnam, as an anti-communist bloc. It served to place the United States in a direct military alliance with the colonial powers in Asia, Britain and France, along with the Commonwealth countries Australia and New Zealand. The only Asian members were Thailand, Pakistan, and the Philippines.

The opposition to non-alignment by these three Asian nations was not, however, merely paying obeisance to their Western allies. Several smaller nations argued that India was a huge nation, with the capacity to defend itself against powerful enemies, but that smaller nations could not afford the luxury of non-alignment in the Cold War environment of the 1950s. Thailand, in particular, was legitimately concerned about Chinese support for communist insurgency movements in the country and on its borders. Prince Sihanouk of Cambodia had similar concerns. Prince Wan Waithayakon, representing Thailand, told the conference that the Vietminh forces had militarily occupied portions of Laos in 1953 and 1954, and were only a few miles from the Thai border. They could not be disregarded as a threat, said the Prince, of either subversion or even direct aggression. He protested the fact that Pridi Bhanomyong, the former Prime Minister and Free Thai leader, was in exile in China, and was reported to be organizing Chinese of Thai ethnicity for subversion against the government of Thailand.

Connected to the fear of Chinese-sponsored subversion across Southeast Asia was the question of the Chinese diaspora. Millions of ethnic Chinese lived throughout the region, and, although a minority, they played a disproportionally significant role in the business activities in each country. Under the Chinese Nationalist government, both on the mainland before 1949, and later in Taiwan, the overseas Chinese were recognized as citizens of China, regardless of their place of birth. This issue of "dual citizenship" posed a serious dilemma to Southeast Asia's national leaders, who sometimes questioned the patriotism of the Chinese minority. The possibility that that minority might support communist insurgency, supported by the government in Beijing, was not paranoid or racist speculation. Forming a military alliance with the Western powers, it was argued, was the only defense available to small nations against such dangers from China or from "world communism."

At Bandung, Zhou Enlai did not try to deny that such concerns were legitimate. His critical contribution to the conference was the pursuit of solutions to such problems based on the common interests of all nations—including the Western powers. He appealed directly to participants to "facilitate the settlement of disputes between the U.S. and China by peaceful means," and insisted, "We have no bamboo curtain." He said that China's "struggle against colonialism lasted more than 100 years," and he pledged that China would not do anything for the expansion of communist activities outside its territory. He quoted Confucius, who said, "Do not do unto others what you yourself do not desire."

Zhou met privately with Prince Sihanouk and Prince Wan, as well as the delegates from Pakistan, the Philippines, and Laos, assuring them that China was anxious to reach agreements based on the Five Principles of Peaceful Coexistence. He invited Prince Wan to visit China, and to inspect the newly established Thai ethnic autonomous region of Sipsongpanna in Yunnan Province, to confirm that there were no subversive activities or intentions.

He announced that China was prepared to solve the dual nationality problem, which he described as "something left behind by Old China." Agreements were set in motion such that ethnic Chinese born in Southeast Asia would choose one or another nationality. (Such a choice was also complicated by the pretense of "two Chinas," because the UN still followed the U.S. policy of recognizing the Nationalist government in Taiwan as the legitimate representative of all China.)

Historian Kahin's appraisal at the conclusion of the Bandung Conference was that Zhou Enlai "had done much to convince previously skeptical delegates that Nehru's thesis was plausible, and that peaceful coexistence with Communist China might be possible after all."

A Moment of Hope

President Eisenhower sent a message of greeting to the Asian-African Conference. He also called a Four-Power summit in Geneva, with the British, the French, and the Soviet Union, held in July 1955. However, in the days preceding the summit, Eisenhower gave his approval to a Dulles brothers' scheme to deploy secret U-2 surveillance missions over the Soviet Union—a blatant breach of territorial integrity. Then, before those spy missions had begun, and very much to the surprise of his Secretary of State, Eisenhower proposed to the Soviets in Geneva an "Open Skies" policy, allowing surveillance flights by both sides as a measure of mutual assurance against war preparations. The offer was refused by Premier Nikita Khrushchev, much to the relief of the Dulles brothers.

President Eisenhower spoke of the "Spirit of Geneva" and the potential for détente, although John Foster Dulles adopted the habit of appearing before the press the day following one of Ike's various proposals for peaceful relations, "explaining" what the President had meant in Cold War terminology.

Still, some concrete steps were taken toward reviving America's nation-building approach to foreign policy in Asia. In February 1956, a team of American engineers from the Bureau of Reclamation met with representatives of Vietnam, Laos, Cambodia, and Thailand to begin a survey of the Mekong River basin. With the Tennessee Valley Authority as a model, the United States signed a joint development agreement with Laos, Thailand, and Cambodia in 1957.

The United States had not yet adopted the British policy of "technological apartheid" so common today, whereby technology is denied to Third World nations due to its supposed "dual use" for military purposes. In Burma, for instance, the United States provided a nuclear library as part of "Atoms for Peace" to that neutral nation, even while the Soviets were providing technological assistance.

To John Foster Dulles, on the other hand, the idea of neutrality "has increasingly become an obsolete conception, and except under very exceptional circumstances, it is an immoral and shortsighted conception." As we shall see, Dulles soon set to work with his British allies to eliminate those guilty of such "immoral" neutrality. . . .

To understand how U.S. foreign policy under John Foster Dulles had become subservient to the British colonial world-view, we need only review the instructions which Dulles imparted to the newly appointed U.S. Ambassador to Indonesia, Hugh S. Cumming, Jr., in September 1953.

Recall the fierce conflict during World War II between Franklin Roosevelt's policy of a strong, united China versus Winston Churchill's policy of a weak, divided China. Dulles's orders in regard to Indonesia, as recorded by Cumming, were as follows:

"Don't tie yourself irrevocably to a policy of preserving the unity of Indonesia. . . . The territorial integrity of China became a shibboleth. We finally got a territorially integrated China—for whose benefit? The Communists. . . . In between a territorially united Indonesia which is leaning and progressing towards Communism, and a break-up of that country into racial and geographic units, I would prefer the latter as furnishing a fulcrum in which the U.S. could work later to help them eliminate Communism in one place or another, and then in the end, if they so wish, arrive back again at a united Indonesia."[34] . . .

VI. Kennedy and the Non-Aligned Movement

John F. Kennedy entered the White House in 1961 in the midst of several ongoing explosions detonated by the Cold Warriors, and when several other time bombs ticked away on a short fuse. The ill-conceived Bay of Pigs adventure in Cuba was in the final planning stages, and there were extensive U.S. covert operations both in Africa and in Asia in defense of European colonial interests.

In the Congo, which had been granted independence from Belgium in 1960, British and Belgian mineral cartels had sponsored the separation of the mineral-rich Katanga Province by a subservient warlord, Moise Tshombe. Only weeks after Kennedy's inauguration, nationalist leader Patrice Lumumba was murdered while being held captive by Tshombe's forces. The CIA had been deeply involved in plotting Lumumba's assassination. In Laos, a "dirty war" run by CIA operatives was backing an army which was fighting not only the communist Pathet Lao, but also the neutralist government. And, of course, there was Vietnam.

Kennedy, as a Senator in the 1950s, had distinguished himself as an enemy of colonialism, while equally outspoken on the subjects of Soviet- or Chinese-sponsored subversion and terrorism. Kennedy had spoken forcefully, in 1951, against support for the "desperate effort of a French regime to hang on to the remnants of Empire in Indochina."[40] A 1957 speech in defense of Algeria's right to independence was roundly denounced in London and Paris, but won the admiration of nationalists everywhere. As his friend and adviser Theodore Sorenson put it, Kennedy "considered communist aggression and subversion as intolerable, but not communism itself."[41] Kennedy told Khrushchev: "What your government believes is its own business; what it does in the world is the world's business."[42]

Just after his inauguration, Kennedy wrote: "Where nature makes natural allies of all, we can demonstrate that beneficial relations are possible even with those with whom we most deeply disagree—and this must someday be the basis of world peace and world law."[43] Such a view of alliances between sovereign nation-states was despised by proponents of world government, of either the old colonial variety or the new surrogate colonialism run by financial institutions and raw materials cartels.

Soon after the April 1961 Bay of Pigs invasion, the same advisers who had persuaded Kennedy to approve that strategic blunder, were telling him to send U.S. military forces into Laos to stop the dominoes. JFK refused, although he would not abandon the country to a Pathet Lao takeover backed by foreign powers. He pushed instead for a neutralist government, which required negotiating with the Chinese and the North Vietnamese. He was encouraged on this latter course by his meeting in April 1961 with Gen. Douglas MacArthur, who strongly advised him against any new ground war in Asia. This advice was later backed up by another General with some experience in Southeast Asian affairs, Charles de Gaulle.

Despite the considerable tensions between the United States and France under De Gaulle, the General and the young U.S. President established a strong rapport. "I could not have more confidence in any man," said Kennedy, describing De Gaulle as a "wise counselor for the future."[44] As to his advisers, who often seemed to be clones of the Dulles brothers, Kennedy quipped: "Thank God the Bay of Pigs happened when it did. Otherwise, we'd be in Laos by now—and that would be a hundred times worse."[45]

The Non-Aligned Movement

The Non-Aligned Movement (NAM) was founded in Belgrade, Yugoslavia, in September 1961, eight months after Kennedy took office. The criteria for membership included support for national independence and liberation struggles in the colonial world, peaceful coexistence between sovereign nations, and no participation in multilateral military alliances, including NATO, SEATO, the Central Treaty Organization, and the Warsaw Pact. As a result, only 16 of the 29 participating nations at the Bandung Conference were qualified to join NAM. From Asia, only Indonesia, Cambodia, Burma, and India were founding members. Neither China nor the Soviet Union were invited, although communist Yugoslavia was a member and the host of the founding conference.

The primary organizers of NAM were Nehru, Nasser, President Tito of Yugoslavia, Kwame Nkrumah of Ghana, and Sukarno. Cuba was the only Ibero-American member, but others joined in 1962. They viewed their enemy as the Cold War itself, which was serving to maintain colonialism in both old and new forms while preventing the economic and social development of the Third World.

NAM was inspired by the Spirit of Bandung, but, as with world affairs generally, the hope of 1955 had been subjected to intense Cold War pressures. Even before the Bandung Conference, the Communist parties of Asia had formed an Asian Solidarity Committee, which expanded into the Afro-Asian People's Solidarity Organization, including Nasser and other African leaders, after the Suez crisis. It was not an alliance of nations, but of parties, and was not exactly counter to the Spirit of Bandung, but was clearly driven by the Soviets and the Chinese, combining Nasserist anti-colonialism and communist anti-imperialism. The organization grew through the early 1960s, but disintegrated along with the new phase of the Sino-Soviet split, after 1965.

Within NAM, there were intense debates over the role of the U.S.S.R. and China. NAM leaders generally welcomed the East bloc's support for armed liberation wars against colonialism, but not their effort to dominate the political and economic policies of the liberation movements themselves, nor their support for communist subversion within independent nations.

Another debate within the NAM centered on economic policy: Should they demand a New International Economic Order based on the transfer of technology to the developing nations, or should all offers of assistance or investment from the North be treated as neo-colonial subterfuge aimed at domination?

This latter view was given a theoretical cover, known as "developmentalism," associated with Raúl Prebish, an Argentine economist who headed the UN Economic Commission for Latin America. Prebish had an extensive resume as a British asset—he had negotiated a treaty between England and Argentina in the 1930s, which tied Argentina to debt payments during the depression, even while other Latin American countries declared debt moratoria. Then, in the 1950s, after the overthrow of nationalist Juan Peron, he collaborated with the Bank of England to scrap Argentina's National Bank, in favor of a British-style Central Bank. His "Developmentalism Theory" rejected the development of heavy industry in the Third World in favor of light industries producing consumer goods as "import-substitution," thus saving foreign reserves—to assure payment of the foreign debt.

Prebish's developmentalism locked the Third World into relative backwardness, while imposing an artificial economic model on the development process which considered the industrial nations as themselves "dependent" upon exploitation of the Third World, due supposedly to the nature of capitalist development. This obscured the distinction between British free-trade economics and the Hamiltonian, American System policies for nation-building.[46]

A more radical version, called "Dependency Theory," was promoted by certain Marxists, by the British and the French at their training centers for colonial assets in London and Paris, and at European-run institutions in the Third World, such as Dar es Salaam University in Tanzania. Dar es Salaam University peddled "autonomous socialist development" through "self-sufficiency" and "self-reliance." These often violently anti-West and anti-technology ideologies served the colonial powers by undermining those nationalist forces dedicated to the form of a New International Economic Order which is based on technological progress and industrialization. In their most extreme forms, mixed with the rhetoric of the Cultural Revolution, these ideologies produced such horrors as Cambodia's Khmer Rouge and Peru's Shining Path.

However, the core of NAM member nations were dedicated to the New International Economic Order, based on peace between East and West as well as North and South, and global collaboration to industrialize the sovereign nations in the South. John F. Kennedy believed such collaboration was both possible and necessary.

Kennedy ridiculed Dulles's formulation of neutrality as "immoral." He argued that neutralism had been "part of our history for over 100 years," and that it was "inevitable" among the emerging free nations. He wrote: "Our view of the world crisis is that countries are entitled to national sovereignty and independence. . . . That is the purpose of our aid. . . . That is a different matter from suggesting that, in order to be entitled to our assistance . . . they must agree with us, because quite obviously these people are newly independent, they want to run their own affairs, and would rather not accept assistance if we have that kind of string attached."[47]

Kennedy was worried about communism, but insisted that "those who make peaceful revolution impossible will make violent revolution inevitable." In words reminiscent of Sukarno's opening speech at Bandung, Kennedy said: "The great battleground for the defense and expansion of freedom today is the whole southern half of the globe—Asia, Latin America, Africa and the Middle East—the lands of the rising peoples. Their revolution is the greatest in human history. They seek an end to injustice, tyranny and exploitation. More than an end, they seek a beginning."[48]

Motivating Kennedy's promotion of numerous programs for Third World development (including The Alliance for Progress, The Peace Corps, Food for Peace, Atoms for Peace, and U Thant's UN Development Decade) was an understanding that this new revolution was both the spark and the fuel for global peace and development. He told the Democratic Convention, in his nomination acceptance speech: "More energy is released by the awakening of these new nations than by the fission of the atom itself."[49]

Kennedy versus Pugwash

The demise of JFK's vision for the world, marked by his assassination in November 1963, and the subsequent horror across (especially) Southeast Asia, can be usefully understood as the result of a showdown between Kennedy and the Pugwash movement.

Pugwash, founded in 1958 by British intelligence networks launched by Bertrand Russell and H.G. Wells, was an alliance of scientists and political representatives from both the U.S.S.R. and the West, committed to the British utopian policy of world government. The keynote speech at the founding conference was given by the U.S.-based physicist Leo Szilard. Szilard had become a protégé of H.G. Wells while a student at Oxford, and his Pugwash speech presented Wells's version of nuclear terror as a basis for establishing world government. The policy became known as Mutually Assured Destruction (MAD).

The Russell-Szilard Pugwash doctrine, which became U.S. policy under SALT I and the 1972 ABM treaties, was set forth in lurid detail in what came to be known as Szilard's "Dr. Strangelove" address, delivered at the Quebec Second Pugwash Conference of 1958. This "Dr. Strangelove" dogma was supported by Wall Street's John J. McCloy and McCloy's agents, such as McCloy's New York Council on Foreign Relations subordinates McGeorge Bundy and Henry A. Kissinger. This MAD doctrine called upon the two superpowers to amass enough nuclear firepower, targetted against each other, to assure mutual annihilation in the case of full-scale war—supposedly assuring that such a global holocaust would never occur.

Regional wars, including the use of tactical nuclear weapons, would let off steam while keeping up the environment of terror, so that all nations would relinquish their sovereignty to a world government in order to avoid destruction. The underlying thesis, however, was that in the thermonuclear age, the constant upgrading of military and industrial technology was no longer necessary for security purposes, since MAD eliminated the possibility of global war.

Thus, the sponsors and dupes of MAD assumed, the New Age, post-industrial-society paradigm-shift would end the American System of scientific and technological progress. The Orwellian New Age of post-industrial, world-government utopianism, could be safely ushered in by its London creators.

The Cuban missile crisis in the fall of 1962 set the New Age process toward world government in motion. With Pugwash creator Bertrand Russell providing guidance and support to Pugwash supporter Nikita Khrushchev along the way, the world was brought to the brink yet again—but this time, far closer to the physical and psychological environment of the American population.

Lyndon LaRouche has vividly described the effect of the Cuban Missile Crisis on the baby-boomer generation in the United States, and the subsequent flight into the fantasy world of the counter-culture of the 1960s and 1970s.[50]

Simultaneous to the Cuban Missile Crisis, the 1962 border war between China and India destroyed the potential for Indian-Chinese collaboration. The history of this dispute was rooted in British imperial policy. Both Nehru and Zhou Enlai, who had argued against the invasion within China, saw their dream of Indian-Chinese collaboration and peace evaporate, along with the remnants of the Spirit of Bandung.

Nehru appealed to Moscow for assistance, but, despite the escalating Sino-Soviet split, Khrushchev, preoccupied with the Cuban events, and apparently unwilling to risk a second front against China, said no. The three pillars of FDR's Grand Design were now at each others throats.

Nehru then turned to the United States, and Kennedy immediately took India's side, offering public support for India's position and substantial supplies of military equipment. Kennedy harshly criticized the Chinese as being "in the Stalinist phase, believing in class war and the use of force."[51] In fact, in the mid-1960s, China descended into chaos and political hysteria during the bloody Cultural Revolution, while the name of "Maoism" was used worldwide by fanatical, terrorist sects, usually created and controlled by London.[52] . . .

Vietnam, Again

The Spirit of Manila and the Spirit of Bandung were essentially dead. However, Pugwash and the MAD doctrine required more tension—surrogate warfare between the superpowers, sustaining global tension through a controlled conflict stopping short of full-scale strategic confrontation. The British and their Pugwash-connected allies in the United States, including the circles around National Security Adviser McGeorge Bundy and Undersecretary of State Averell Harriman within the Kennedy administration, geared up for their desired bloodbath, with Vietnam the convenient target.

President Kennedy, however, had not gone along with the drive for war in Laos, and opposed another war in Asia. He agreed to the expansion of the number of U.S. advisers in Vietnam, including Special Forces, to train the South Vietnamese Army, but he refused to deploy ground troops or provide large-scale

U.S. air cover. Nonetheless, under the direction of Harriman, Bundy, and Secretary of Defense Robert Strange McNamara, the war was being transformed into a British colonial-style "population war," including McNamara's infamous accounting tool, the "body count," to measure the war's progress.

Harriman protégé Roger Hilsman, head of the Far Eastern Bureau at the State Department, and Bundy's aide Michael Forrestal, during several trips together to Vietnam, allied themselves with British Colonial Office official Robert K.G. Thompson, who had designed the Strategic Hamlet program in Malaya. Hilsman and Forrestal lavished praise on Thompson and his Strategic Hamlet strategy, and persuaded Kennedy to go along. Hilsman's own glowing description of the model strategic hamlet could just as easily be describing a U.S. prison: ". . . consolidate the inhabitants into a compact, defensible unit which could be surrounded by a moat and barbed wire. . . . In some cases whole villages would have to be moved, as had happened in Malaya. . . . Plastic identity cards had to be issued, curfews established, and forces trained to set up checkpoints and ambushes during curfew hours. An iron grid of security had to be established to control the movement of both goods and people, of rice and recruits."[55] Areas outside these concentration camps became free-fire zones, where anything that moved was a fair target, while defoliants were used to destroy crops and forests which might serve as protection for the Vietcong. By the end of 1962, fifty-five hundred strategic hamlets were completed or under construction.

Kennedy was not unaware of the pending disaster of this misguided policy. His friend and economic adviser, John Kenneth Galbraith, on his way to assume his post as Ambassador to India, stopped for an inspection tour of Vietnam at Kennedy's request. His report back warned the President that the United States was becoming wedded to certain failure, that a political settlement with Ho Chi Minh was essential, that India's Nehru could help in that regard, and that in any case the strategic hamlets and the use of defoliants must end immediately.[56] Several others conveyed similar messages, and Kennedy took them seriously.

Kennedy decided to disengage from Vietnam. But he did much more—he began to move directly against the entire Pugwash agenda of world government, balance of terror, and post-industrial society, much to the discomfort of McGeorge Bundy and his fellow Cold War strategists. As opposed to the arguments from both "left" and "right" that the age of Mutually Assured Destruction no longer required rapid technological development, Kennedy insisted that peace were possible only through strength, both militarily and economically. His most dramatic presentation of this rejection of Pugwash was planned for Nov. 23, 1963, in Dallas, Texas. Kennedy's prepared text for that speech ridiculed the post-industrial society advocates, who "assume that words will suffice without weapons, that vituperation is as good as victory and that peace is a sign of weakness. . . . But we can hope that fewer people will listen to nonsense. . . . If we are strong, our strength will speak for itself."[57] Kennedy insisted that such strength must include improvements in both nuclear and conventional forces, expansion of space exploration, education for all Americans, and a technologically developing economy. He concluded: "That strength will never be used in pursuit of aggressive ambitions—it will always be used in pursuit of peace." That speech, of course, was never delivered.

Earlier in the year, Kennedy had announced a pullout of U.S. advisers from Vietnam, beginning with 1,000 immediately, to be completed by 1965.

Among those who were considering an end to the war based on an agreement with Ho Chi Minh and a neutralist government were the leaders of the South Vietnamese government itself. Ngo Dinh Diem, the nationalist President, his brother Ngo Dinh Nhu, and several of the leading generals, were negotiating with the North in order to achieve a peace agreement. Hilsman complained bitterly that there were "repeated intelligence reports that Nhu had some notion . . . that he could negotiate an end to the war and that he had been attempting to set up a secret channel of communication with Hanoi."[58]

French President de Gaulle, while maintaining his personal contact with President Kennedy, established diplomatic liaison between Diem and Ho Chi Minh through a Polish diplomat, Mieczyslaw Maneli, who visited both Hanoi and Saigon regularly as part of the Geneva agreements from 1954. The last message from the North Vietnamese before Diem and Nhu were murdered was their agreement to work toward a peaceful settlement, and a pledge that the North would defend Diem in the case of a clash with the United States.[59]

Harriman's man Hilsman, meanwhile, told Secretary of State Dean Rusk that if the Diem regime negotiated with Hanoi, the United States should "move promptly with a coup," and should bomb the North if they sent troops to defend President Diem.[60]

Despite serious reservations from Kennedy, and even more so from his brother Robert, the Harriman-Bundy faction in the administration pushed events toward full-scale war, including the elimination of anyone who stood in their way. U.S. Ambassador to Vietnam Frederick E. Nolting and CIA station chief John Richardson were dumped for being too close to Vietnamese President Diem. Kennedy's choice to replace Ambassador Nolting was Edmund Gullion, who had been ambassador to the Congo during the period that Kennedy and U Thant had crushed the insurrection run by the mineral cartels in Katanga Province. Harriman and Bundy rejected Gullion, demanding that a "strongman" be appointed "whose character and reputation," as Hilsman put it, "would permit him to dominate the representatives of all other departments and agencies."[61]

Their man was Republican Henry Cabot Lodge. Harriman's intent was for Lodge to run a coup against the Diem government in order to prevent any neutralist peace agreement. Kennedy reluctantly consented to Lodge's appointment, believing it necessary for bipartisan support for his Vietnam policy, but he continued refusing to endorse a coup.

The events of August 1963, leading to the coup on Nov. 1, as described by Hilsman and others who were involved, were aimed not only against the Diem government, but against President Kennedy's policies as well. As Lodge was travelling to Saigon to begin his mission, Harriman, Bundy, and Hilsman drafted a directive on Vietnam policy, threatening to cut U.S. aid to Vietnam if Diem did not accept certain demands, including firing his brother, Nhu. The Diem government's heavy-handed suppression of protests organized by Buddhist monks was cited as the primary grievance, but this was for public consumption. The architects of the coup admitted that their actual concern was Diem and Nhu's overtures for peace with Ho Chi Minh.

The directive on Vietnam was prepared behind Kennedy's back, during a weekend while the President was in Massachusetts and other cabinet members were out of town. Kennedy was read only parts of the directive over the phone, and was led to believe, falsely, that all the other cabinet members had read and approved it. Hilsman then leaked the content of the directive to UPI, including "background" implications that there would be a coup if Diem failed to follow orders. This UPI report was then played on Voice of America in Vietnam just as Lodge was arriving as Harriman's "strongman."

Kennedy strongly reprimanded Harriman and Hilsman when he learned what had happened, and the cabinet meeting broke into a brawl over Harriman's insistence on Diem's overthrow.[62] Almost immediately, however, Lodge began sending back reports that a coup by certain Vietnamese generals was inevitable, unstoppable, and that the United States would be breaching Vietnam's sovereignty by trying to prevent it.

Lodge, meanwhile, was both plotting with the military to carry out the coup, and directly supporting the ongoing Buddhist protests against Diem. The Buddhist faction running the protests, which included gruesome self-immolations broadcast on television around the world, were both anti-communist and anti-Diem. Lodge, as his first act as ambassador, before even visiting President Diem, visited the Buddhist leaders of the anti-government protests, and invited them to take refuge in the U.S. Embassy, which became the command center for the continuing protests.

Madame Nhu, the wife of Ngo Dinh Nhu, stated publicly in regard to Lodge: "They have sent us a pro-consul." Hilsman, reflecting his complete adaptation to the British colonial worldview, reported proudly: "She was right!"[63]

Except for an initial meeting with Diem, Ambassador Lodge refused to visit the President, insisting that Diem must come crawling to him. Within six weeks, Diem and Nhu were murdered. Three weeks after that, Kennedy was dead, killed by the same British intelligence apparatus which carried out multiple attempts on the life of President Charles de Gaulle.[64]

With Kennedy eliminated, the Pugwash committee within the administration took charge, with President Lyndon Johnson's acquiescence. While the Vietnam debacle unfolded, China descended into the nightmare of the Cultural Revolution, Indonesia burst into bloody hysteria, America's 1960s counter-culture waged war against the nation's historic commitment to progress, and the world economy began its slide into post-industrial decay.

It is often heard today that the United States won the Cold War when the Soviet Union dissolved in 1992. This misconception is based on a false premise, of British design, concerning the nature of the Cold War itself. The fact is, the Cold War was lost in the 1960s. The United States, Europe, the Soviet Union, China, and the entire Third World were the losers. Among sovereign nation-states, there were no winners.

In April 1999, Cambodia was formally inducted into ASEAN, completing the unification of the ten Southeast Asian nations for the first time in history. This peace is closely connected to the emerging strategic and economic alliance between Russia, China, and India, encompassing the majority of the world's population. President Clinton has committed his administration to strengthening U.S. relations with these nations of Eurasia, but, as in the Kennedy administration, he is surrounded by proponents of world government who are promoting regional wars to destroy any impulse toward rebuilding the FDR Grand Design, or the Spirit of Bandung. The strengthening unity of the Asian nations in the face of global depression must, this time, be the engine for international peace and development rather than the cauldron of war.

Notes

19. Lyndon H. LaRouche, Jr., "Where Franklin Roosevelt Was Interrupted," *Executive Intelligence Review*, July 17, 1998.

20. Peter Dennis, *Troubled Days of Peace—Mountbatten and the Southeast Asia Command 1945-46* (New York: St. Martin's Press, 1987).

21. Rolf Tanner, *A Strong Showing—Britain's Struggle for Power and Influence in Southeast Asia 1942-1950* (Stuttgart: Franz Steiner Verlag, 1994).

23. Barbara Tuchman, *The March of Folly; From Troy to Vietnam* (New York: Ballantine Books, 1984).

24. Stanley Karnow, *Vietnam—A History* (Harmondsworth, Middlesex, England: Penguin, 1983).

29. All the following quotes from the Asian-African Conference are from: George M.T. Kahin, *The Asian-African Conference; Southeast Asia Progress* (Ithaca: Cornell University, 1955).

34. Audrey R. and George M.T. Kahin, *Subversion as Foreign Policy: The Secret Eisenhower and Dulles Debacle in Indonesia* (New York: New Press, 1994).

40. Roger Hilsman, *To Move a Nation: The Politics of Foreign Policy in the Administration of John F. Kennedy* (New York: Doubleday, 1967).

41. Theodore C. Sorenson, *Kennedy* (New York: Konecky & Konecky, 1965).

42. *Ibid.*

43. *Op. cit.*, Hilsman.

44. *Op. cit.*, Sorenson.

45. *Ibid.*

46. Lyndon H. LaRouche, Jr., *Operation Juárez, EIR Special Report*, Aug. 2, 1982.

47. *Op. cit.*, Sorenson.

48. *Ibid.*

49. *Op. cit.*, Hilsman.

50. Lyndon H. LaRouche, Jr., "How Bertrand Russell Became an Evil Man," *Fidelio*, Fall 1994.

51. *Op. cit.*, Sorenson.

52. See, e.g., "British Under Attack for Harboring Global Terrorism," *Executive Intelligence Review*, Jan. 2, 1998.

55. *Op. cit.*, Hilsman.

56. *Op. cit.*, Tuchman.

57. Theodore C. Sorensen, ed., *Let the Word Go Forth*, the speeches, statements, and writings of John F. Kennedy, 1947-63 (New York: Delacorte Press, 1988).

58. *Op. cit.*, Hilsman.

59. *Op. cit.*, Karnow.

60. *Ibid.*

61. *Op. cit.*, Hilsman.

62. *Op. cit.*, Karnow.

63. *Op. cit.*, Hilsman.

64. See, "Why the British Kill American Presidents," *New Federalist* pamphlet, December 1994.

Sponsors

The publisher would like to thank the following people, whose generosity in contributing to the effort to free Michael Billington has made publication of this book possible.

Donald Adams
Anna Ahlers
Ashmead and Janice Ali
Carmen Alexander
Helen Allem
Lores Allemon
Terry E. and Sandra Allen
Gerald A. Allison
Carl Anderson
Edward A. Anderson
Mark Carlton Anderson
Paul C. Anderson
Letitia Angelone
Frank Artiss
William J. Ashton
Dr. Edward K. Atkinson
William Hungerford Atwell
John Bailey
Wayne Baker
John J. Barrett
Cavell Bean
Normand Belanger
Sid Benson
David Bernard
Thomas Bethel
Jennie and Charles Biehler
Dan Billington
Ruth O. Billington
John Bigelow
Duilio Bini
Criselida Boaz
Patrick Boggins
Violet S. Boles
Jane E. Booth
Virginia Booth
Glen Borders
Verda Bostrom
Virginia Bostick
Frank Bostwick
Joan Bowser
George Boyd
Emma Brackin
Helen Breneman
Georgia Brink
Thelma Brown
Vivian Browner
Patrick Buckley
Anne Buffinga-Sidnam
Neil Burgstaler
David P. Burleson
Michael Burnette
Herman J. Byrd
Helen Campbell
DeEtta G. Carey
Clara Carpentier
P.J. Carter
John W. Cartwright
Paul Cavanagh

Raphael Cervera
Glenford Charles
Mary Cheek
Eva Cheesman
Huiling Chen
David and Lydia Cherry
Erma Christiansen
Beatrice Clark
Don and Judy Clark
Willie Mae Clayton
Georgia Cobb
Virginia Cobb
Clara H. Cohrs
William Collignon
Richard Stevens Condon
Mari Lynn Conley
Adrian J. Conrad
Dorothy C. Conrad
Cecil and Joan Conry
Hal Cooper, Jr.
Margaret Copenhaver
Lucie May Covey
Douglas T. Crawford
Juanda Crawford
Albert Cristiani
Santon Curti
Walter Dallas
Ronald D'Angelo
Dickson Dangers
Andrew Davis
Fred S. Davis
David Davisson
Max Dean
Molly Defremery
Rick Delano
Sharon Del Principe
Julie Devlieg
Adele Diaz
Michael DiMarco
Thomas A. Dinnocenzo
Laura Ditsch
Charles S. Dodd
David J. Dodge
Harold L. Domerude
Joseph G. Donohoo
Rod Dotson, M.D.
Art Dunn
Floyd Dunn
Iris Dye
Dennis Dymszo
Norris Echternacht
June Eby
Col. Gerald B. Edwards (ret.)
Isabel Ehrman
William Einzig
Karl Ek
Cherrie Elder
Dorothy Elliott
Gerald Eschen
Wilma Eyster
Muriel Fairchild
Catherine Ferguson
Hugh Field
Gerald A. Fillman
Irene Findlay
Georgia Flanagan
Elliott Florin
Della C. Folendorf
Rich Forbes
Ronald C. Force
Bernice Fountain
Bill Franchuk
Daniel L. Frederick
Norma Fredrickson
Paul D. Frelich
Darrell C. Friddle
Mary Frueholz
Hugh Gallagher

Julia Gerland
Paul Gerrish
Arthur Gessert
George Gessler
Todd Gilchrist
Helen Ginsburg
Howard J. Giske
Mike Glynn
In memory of Miriam Goodman
Gary T. Gool
Marie Gorden
Peter Grabber
Ila Grambling
David Greenspan
Betty J. Gregory
Herbert Griffith
John B. Grohl
Gerard Guay
L. Elizabeth Gulick
Valere Hache
Geneva Hall
Jeremiah Hallaren
Ann C. Hanse
Howland Hanson
Edgar Harder
Robin Hardmon
Marjorie D. Harnest
Marjorie Harris
Lou Ann Harrison
Ethelbert W. Haskins
Martin Hauser
Yvonne D. Henk
Alice Hill
Charles J. Hill
Phyllis Hill
Clovis Hinton
Richard L. Hitchcock
George Hollis
R.R. Holman
George and Marilyn Holter
Staman Hook
Charlotte Hopfstock
Leslie E. Horner
William H. Horning
Marian Hosler
Mildred Houser
F.B. Hover
Paul P. Hryniewicz
Celia Thaxter Hubbard
Perdita Humphreys
Lucetta A. Hunt
Mabel Hunter
Leo Huntting
W. Morris Hutcherson
Donovan G. Hyde
Winifred W. Ingram
Doris Jackson
Eric Charles Jansen
Will Jewett
Alicia F. Jimenez
Evangelyn Johnson
Rev. A. James Johnson
Wayne Johnson
Doris Johnston
Evelyn Johnston
Virgil Jordon
Edward Joshie
Ella Mae Joy
William Kaeser
Patti Karkalits Karr
William & Carol Keane
Charles Kearns
Adrian Keefe
Frances Kellum
Chris Kelly
In memory of John T. Kemper

Emily and Ted Kennedy
Dave Ketchum
Jimmy and Martha Kibbe
Michael D. and Deborah Kiggans
Gustav Kirchmann
Eugene Klymyshyn
Harry Knights
In memory of Michael Kohanow, Jr.
Mike Kostic
Michael L. Krishart
Martin W. Kron
Garrett and Madge Kruger
Wesley Kujawski
Gregg LaCava
Tom Lacey
Lloyd T. Lamb
Alfred and Laura Lang
Conrad Laperle
Robert E. Lauten
Jean-Philippe Lebleu
Rodney Leeb
Russell and Angelika Lemieux
John Lesick
Charles Lieberman
Robert Lincoln
Elizabeth Lindberg
David R. Lopez
Douglas J. Lougheed
Kerry L. Lowry
Robert M. Lucas
E. Luther
Mildred Lynch
Richard MacIntyre
John Maltby
Theodore Maravelias
Luigi Marietti, Sr.
Thelma Marland
Dr. Dorothy Marsh
Roger M. Martin
In memory of Ray M. Martino
Jean Maurice Masse
Marilyn Matthews
Brett Mayette
Michael Mazes
Paul McCartney
Margaret McDermott
Jack McDonald
Loretta D. McGann
Clark McLain
Bernadette McMahon
Richard D. McMeekin
Lucile B. Melcher
Aileen Mercurio
Allison W. Merriam, Jr.
Dale Merrick
Edith Messina
James T. Michaelson
Maria Elena and Bruce Milton
Louise Mitchell
Merrill Mitchell
Carmen Molina
Geraldine Moore
Julia Moore
Kevin Morgus
Laura Morland
William Moule
D.S. Moyer
Ray Lynn Mull
Alexander K. Murphy
Helen Murray
James P. Murray
Joseph F. Napierala
James J. Navis, Sr,

Amet Newland
Edna I. Newmeyer
Martha F. Nichols
Yoichi Nishimoto
Lawrence J. Nixon
Norma Norvell
Ned and Judith Nuerge
Roy R. O'Hern
Thomas P. O'Leary
Arthur E. O'Neal
Brian O'Neill
Jeanne Oles
Fred Ordone
Elizabeth and E. Allan Orem
Lucinda Ortiz
Sigurd Overgaard
Florence Palmer
Athena Pappajion
Dave Penner
Adeline G. Perdew
Lucille Perry
William E. Perry
A. Viola Peterson
Roger Petitpas
Edmund Pfennig
Angelas Philolias
Keith Phinney
Richard Pierson
John Pillars
Marjorie Pipitt
Yvonne Pitcairn
Lavon Platis
Robert Poczulp
Bonita Potts
Mary Pratt
Robert K. Prince
Robert Purvis
Elizabeth K. Putnam
Lloyd Quick
Robert Radcliffe
Edna Ragsdale
Bob Rapp
Dominique Reca
R. Reddy
Elsie L. Reed
Olala Reinheimer
Lois M. Ringquist
Salvatore Rizzo
Alice J. Robb
Sue Roberts
Timothy Robinson
John Fiske Robson
Daniel Roche
Julian Rojas
Robert Roseburg
Franz Rosenberg
Martin A. Rowland
Herman A. Rudolph
Melvin H. Ruff
Luther Rutledge
James M. Ryan
Robert Rykbost
Susie Salayko
Steve Salem
Albert J. Sambuco
Rev. Shellie Sampson
Gordon M. Samuelson
John Sauber
Ralph Saul
Joseph J. Scavullo
John P. Schafer
Evelyn R. Schlosser
Marlene A. Schooler
Anna Schow
Ronald S. Schraeder
Herbert A. Schulz
Donald Schwarzkopf
David Schweitzer

William Seet
Eugene & Lee Shannon
Seamour & Gerte Shavin
Audrey Sheehan
Don Sheffield
Marshall Shepard
Vern Shipley
Thomas Lee Simpson
Brenda Slater
Olive N. Slater
Frank J. Smentowski
Donald R. Smith
Frances B. Smith
Conner Soules
Michael W. Sperry
Velma Stark
Claudine Steiner
Fred A. Steiner
Aldona Stephenson
Leo Stewart
Walter Stiess
James R. Straub
Maryann Sullivan
Norma Sutton
Gerda Talesnik
Marlene Tarigo
Roberta Tidland
Arthur Tiedtke
Paul A. Tiedtke
Danny Tipton
Nancy Tooke
Charles Torres
Rita Thouin
Peter Umana
Karl Untch
Richard Van Bergen
Robert Van Hee
Leo Van Velzen
Polly Vaughan
Rao Veeramachaneni
Jose Velasquez
Lois & Larry Vigil
Frances Viviani
Edward J. Vnuk
John Vulcanoff
James Wagner
Timothy Gene Wagner
Robert L. Wanner
Helen G. Warriner
Fred W. Weiler
Ty Weiler
Ralph Wendorff
John R. Wheeler
Alice Wickey
Dorothy Wida
Peggy Wienholz
Lera E. Wilhite
Murlene Wilkes
Harold Willey
J. Carolyn Williams
Mary Williams
Bill D. Willibey
Ruth N. Willis
Velna Willoughby
Brian Wilson
Frank Wilson
James Winey
Norv Wunderlich
Francis and Alexia Yaklin
Will Yaussy
Ella Mae Zimmerman
Kevin L. Zondervan